INDIAN GODS AND KINGS

INDIAN GODS AND KINGS

THE STORY OF A LIVING PAST

By

EMMA HAWKRIDGE

GYAN

Published by

GYAN

Gyan Publishing House
5, Ansari Road
Daryaganj, New Delhi-110002
Phone: 011-47034999, 9811692060
E-mail: books@gyanbooks.com

Distribution Network
gyanbooks.com
India, USA, Canada, UK, Australia, France

ISBN : 978-81-212-6671-0 (PB)
First Published, 1887

2nd Impression 2022

Printed at: Gyan Press, Delhi.

INDIAN GODS AND KINGS
Author: EMMA HAWKRIDGE

SEATED BUDDHA AT SARNATH

EMMA HAWKRIDGE

INDIAN GODS AND KINGS

THE STORY OF A LIVING PAST

With Illustrations

1935

Intention

THIS book is meant for the intelligent but uninformed reader who wishes to begin to know India. It is an attempt to bring together simply and compactly some of the material available in scholarly studies of many periods and phases. The selection from such wealth must be personal — the answer to one's own questions — a starting-point.

It means to suggest the past still alive in the present of India as a basis for understanding today. The method will be to tie some detail which the traveller may see — whether a living custom or remaining architecture or art — to a causal story from the past.

The stories are strung on the thread of time for the reader at home in an armchair. But for the traveller who is in India, looking at the temples of her gods and the palaces of her kings, the tales are indexed by place so that they may interpret the scene of their action.

India cannot be put between the covers of a volume. This book may give some sense of the beauty which is there and the drama which has been. It will not attempt to present modern social problems, but suggest in what they root. It will not reach to present political questions, but draw a few strokes of the intricate background to them.

Picture

TO IMAGINE India, forget traffic and sharp noise and staccato living. India, away from cities, is a land of silence and slowness and spreading spaces. The sky is a compelling presence, enormous lapis-lazuli, with the man-killing sun a focus never to be ignored, which forces life to its terms. Below that sky, teeming India has stretches of empty brown earth, seeming bare of humanity until at a trifle, people spring up like prairie dogs from nowhere. Riding over endless dusty lands of northern India, one tries to analyze the charm of the country, which is potent and never to be lost. A still twilight turns the horizon to slow, ample gold, and mystifies the fields. By day the sun lives in colours that women and men know how to wear; it clarifies the silks of flame, apricot, turquoise, lemon, and lavender of a group in Karachi, strolling to their tryst under a banyan tree; it burns in the smouldering reds and oranges of women in Agra and Jaipur with triangular swishing skirts and clashing silver anklets; and enriches the dusky wines and grape purples tucked between the legs of the women of the Deccan. The farther south, the hotter the land and sky, the more powerful the colours grow — until at Travancore, in the very south, they fuse to white again.

Perhaps the visual charm of India comes from grace of movement — low-caste women in the fields in their wisps of red, supplely bending, all of a motion, to the ground; or women who walk like slow-passing friezes, carrying on their heads loads of copper jars or trays of dung cakes, as proudly as dancers. Perhaps it is all the slow rhythm of highroads, bordered by dusty nim or pipal trees, or by banyans that drip fringes of parallel roots to the ground, making a green twilight of shade. The passers-by may include a foolish camel, intensified in artlessness by a rider who sits side-saddle over the hump, and carelessly smokes a hookah; a procession of camels carrying the wares of nomads; endless, humpbacked bullocks with drivers squatted upon their wooden yokes, and carts with solid wheels; or a water buffalo, horns akimbo, ambling muddily in from a rice field. A Maharajah's elephant hung with silver bells disputes the right of way in a Rajput state with a peacock, or with the velvet-hung bullock carts hiding and probably stifling high-caste ladies.

Contents

Illustrations

Picture

To imagine India, forget traffic and sharp noise and staccato living. India, away from cities, is a land of silence and slowness and spreading spaces. The sky is a compelling presence, enormous lapis-lazuli, with the man-killing sun a focus never to be ignored, which forces life to its terms. Below that sky, teeming India has stretches of empty brown earth, seeming bare of humanity until at a trifle, people spring up like prairie dogs from nowhere. Riding over endless dusty lands of northern India, one tries to analyze the charm of the country, which is potent and never to be lost. A still twilight turns the horizon to slow, ample gold, and mystifies the fields. By day the sun lives in colours that women and men know how to wear; it clarifies the silks of flame, apricot, turquoise, lemon, and lavender of a group in Karachi, strolling to their tryst under a banyan tree; it burns in the smouldering reds and oranges of women in Agra and Jaipur with triangular swishing skirts and clashing silver anklets; and enriches the dusky wines and grape purples tucked between the legs of the women of the Deccan. The farther south, the hotter the land and sky, the more powerful the colours grow — until at Travancore, in the very south, they fuse to white again.

Perhaps the visual charm of India comes from grace of movement — low-caste women in the fields in their wisps of red, supplely bending, all of a motion, to the ground; or women who walk like slow-passing friezes, carrying on their heads loads of copper jars or trays of dung cakes, as proudly as dancers. Perhaps it is all the slow rhythm of highroads, bordered by dusty nim or pipal trees, or by banyans that drip fringes of parallel roots to the ground, making a green twilight of shade. The passers-by may include a foolish camel, intensified in artlessness by a rider who sits side-saddle over the hump, and carelessly smokes a hookah; a procession of camels carrying the wares of nomads; endless, humpbacked bullocks with drivers squatted upon their wooden yokes, and carts with solid wheels; or a water buffalo, horns akimbo, ambling muddily in from a rice field. A Maharajah's elephant hung with silver bells disputes the right of way in a Rajput state with a peacock, or with the velvet-hung bullock carts hiding and probably stifling high-caste ladies.

Endless and endearing variety of beauty, or incongruity, or terror fascinates the eye — a man wearing a brocaded coat but no trousers who rides a bullock with horns painted green; a washerman striding a calf with fat bundles of laundry all over its back; a Kashmiri Brahman meditating beside a pool full of sacred flapping fishes; crocodiles that are watchdogs for a crumbling palace; bazaars with their angling merchants, monkeys leaping from station roofs, scurvy starving dogs, ribby cows, the red stain of spat-out betel, men's thin brown legs, babies' uncovered heads wobbling in the sun... the marble mosques, the god-covered temples, the tranced worshippers....

The land is as dramatic and varied as the people. Himalayan peaks in the north hold the perpetual snowline above seventeen thousand feet, and grow lush jungles on their lower slopes; a northwestern desert glares like a copper mirror; the tangled Vindhya hills cut the north of the triangle of India from the south — from the thin-aired plateau of the Deccan and the steamy palm groves of the southern coasts whose inlets and harbours sparkle like spilled sacks of jewels. Heat lies over most of India, as definite a medium as water to live in, creating a different race that must adapt itself to it, opening pores, deepening passions, bringing stimulation, lassitude, weariness.

Sky, space, colour, slow motion and bewildering variety, and the ever-present sense of centuries emanating from the soil. Centuries have strewn cities of amazing beauty like driftwood over the land — to be treasured in any other country, but here so numerous that they lie in wastes forgotten by all but archæologists. India, the *cul-de-sac* into which tribes and nations poured from the northwest before history began, is as varied as the leaves of her own jungles. India of the mass of Hindus lives scrupulously by the metaphors of long-dead poets — and faced with the machine age, believes it unimportant compared to a bath in the Ganges.

The American traveller to India steps through the Looking-Glass. His own education, rooted in Greece and the Mediterranean, flowering from Europe and England, has plumply ignored the other circle of the world — the right-hand map of the two map hemispheres. But the eastern face of the earth, having lived its tumultuous centuries, holds heaping riches of story of which he knows nothing. As to India, perhaps he inherits a Kashmir shawl or a bit of Delhi-carved ivory from some travelled ancestor. He has heard of Buddha, of widows jumping onto funeral pyres. Lately he has read 'Mother India' or gone to a lecture on Gandhi, according to his inclination. But unless he is unusually a student, when he lands in India and sees the first carved rock story of gods and heroes standing in some jungle, the first dead temple, the scattered walls of the first desolate city, or the wild precious delicacy of the first Indian painting he has noticed, he is at a loss. The symbols are different. The past of India is a strange language, of which these syllables are meaningless jargon.

Yet they haunt and tease, the strange buildings and carvings, the cities of kings and tombs of little princesses, the temples wilder than the most fascinating nightmare, and domes more stately than one's best imagination. Who built them, and why, and how did those people live and think who were impelled to create such art?

They lived and thought most variously. In India, one man thought, and another man acted. The thinker need not act, for the outer world was an illusion to be escaped. The man of action need not think, for his conduct was minutely prescribed for him by ancient tradition. This cleavage, almost of two different worlds, makes a cleavage in the history of India sharper than in other lands. The inner history of thought and custom that still rules India today separates from the outer history of kings and conquerors who left their traces in stone, but little trace on the ways of the people.

Of the outer story of India, from ancient times until the eleventh century, there is too little known. Hindu chroniclers mixed gorgeous imagination generously with their fact. Their early kings go past like a procession of phantoms, but their gods live and are real. Actual deeds were lost, but the happenings of thought were treasured in memory and manuscript. Until the Mohammedans came with their literal historians, the outer story of India is scattered and fragmentary. It is deduced by scholars from buried coins, from allusions in poetry, from inscriptions on carvings, or from traveller's chance tales, but not from Indian historical manuscripts, for these do not exist. What little has been recovered of early fact is so bare to the bone — lists of kings without flesh to them, of dynasties that fell and boundaries that shifted — that one's best-intentioned interest or memory fails. So any possible ampler moments, small islands of certainty in the sea of surmise, give more of a suggestion of life in ancient times than a complete list of dynasties and states — a moment here and a moment there from the past, where the names have ripened into a semblance of character, where the deeds take on importance or a fulness of light falls upon some richly civilized or peaceful period. Because these periods are unrelated, usually cut off, one from another, by turbulent ages of meaningless battles, there is little logical sequence except the thread of time to give a sense of continuity in India.

And in later days there is too much record of too many places, unfocussed to a centre. After the stiff-necked sons of Allah came conquering in the eleventh century and refused to be digested (making the wide, persistent schism between Hindus and Mohammedans — strange origin of the neat signs in railway stations

'Water for Hindus' — 'Water for Mohammedans'); after the Mohammedans brought their battle-loving historians, they told so many happenings in so many states, all vivid, picturesque, and about equally important, that to follow is to be breathless. The choice again must be random.

If the outer history of India, the stories of kings and conquerors and queens, is to have meaning, it must be understood by the background of thought and custom — the same that still moulds the lives of the brightly dressed, ambling people today.

For the past in India is never entirely past. The people follow ancient ways far more closely than we. Perhaps that is why one has a strange feeling there of coming back to ancestors. One sinks into the deep feather bed of the past with a certain comfort in the experience. The centuries are all there. The country treasures everything, discards nothing. Odds and ends of habit that have lost all meaning or use are held equally precious with some great verity. Old age accumulates and discards unwillingly.

Primitive magic is not dead, nor demons and earth goddesses. The many-armed gods live on in the credulity and affection of most Hindus. Although a stream of thought may clear to a deep religious philosophy for some minds, the many backwaters hold the silt of ancient belief, like a great swamp of unchanging waters spread over the land. One can plunge to a deep past in the folkways of primitive people, one can visit nearer centuries, like those of mediæval Europe, in some courtly Indian state, then reach the present day in the islands of the intelligentsia — though even the intellectuals must be interpreted from their background of India, not from the West.

Of all this background, Hinduism seems the strangest, the most alien and mysterious to the mind of the Westerner. For single-minded Mohammedans slashing in the name of Allah are simpler for the sons of Puritans and Crusaders to understand. Parsees, eminently practical, do not seem too different. But the introspecting, many-guised Hindus with their castes are sheer wonderland people, moulded and moved by alien reasons. It is Hinduism chiefly that gives the dark fascination, the awe and fear, the enlightenment, annoyed contempt, or the sentimental rhapsodies that a Westerner may feel on first contact. But it is incredible, he says — and knows he has stepped through the Looking-Glass.

India does not simplify, and to tell some details rather than others does violence to the truth. The thought is too rich to clear, the acts cannot be chosen in just proportion. But somewhere one must begin. And as a person plucks a lily-pad to see how deep the water is, one may touch things that lie on the surface of Indian life, and pull up the long, long stem.

PART I
THE WAY OF GODS

I. *The Beginnings of Hinduism*

HINDUISM TODAY

WORSHIP — worship. People are walking the roads of India on their way to worship. They are walking to a temple to break a coconut shell before the god's lingam, walking to a river to plunge into sacred waters and wash away rebirths; travelling by ox-cart, by train, to temples that rise like cactus shapes. A man is measuring his length on a red road, moving like an inchworm toward his god to do penance; women carrying baskets of marigolds that will make the unescapable wreath for pilgrims, slip into the depth of shade under a sacred banyan, whose trunk is daubed with the vermilion trident of a god, and faced by his fat little stone bull. Pilgrims are spending treasured rupees to worship a shabby calf, pouring Ganges water on its hoofs, holding its tail while mantras are mumbled. Brahmans, naked to the waist, wearing a sacred thread over an oiled shoulder, are blowing conch-shells inside the forbidden temple to awaken the god. A goat's head has been severed for Kali, the Mother Goddess, and devotees prostrate themselves on the spot where the blood has flowed. Fakirs are sitting on the ground, dressed in the ashes of their sacred fire, and the pious come to take the dust from their feet. Women are circumambulating a banyan tree, turning around, bowing flat to the ground, and crying out for a boon, and in their brass bowls they have rice and plantain and milk to offer to the carved images of snakes set up under the tree.

Random details like these on the bewildering surface of Hindu custom go back to the ways of people who lived in India centuries before Christ, building the habits of India today.

In the West, the cults of savage ancestors break through the crust of the present in trivial superstitions'and servants' magic, in Maypole dances and details of Christmas and Easter festivals — and in much madness. They live more flamboyantly in India. Bright-coloured acts, based on no present reason, which strike down to the depth of our common inheritance, are strong and clutching as the roots of the fabled universe tree.

The centuries hang suspended in Hinduism. Many races poured

into ancient India, and all races stayed. Those with ability to grow reached their stature. Those incapable of change stayed at their early levels. The religious system now called Hinduism grew from all their gifts, from the habits of primitive aboriginals, from the ways of worship of industrious dark Dravidians, and from the imagination of invading Aryans who created the Vedic philosophy — from the clash or fusion of all together. The religion engulfed later races who flung with bows and spears over the passes to conquer India. Any tribe which acknowledged Hinduism, or a phase of it, was incorporated loosely or tightly into the huge, tolerant, living organism which encircled alien things like an amœba, and made them a source of nourishment.

The Hindu religion today cannot be defined even so clearly as many-branched Christianity, or Buddhism with its sea-changes. A Hindu need follow no prophet nor saviour, no god nor pantheon of gods, no creed, no one philosophy, no pope, no archbishop. A man is considered a Hindu if he is born into a recognized caste and does not openly break its particular laws. The small unit is rigid and the large system loose — a great stream, carrying entities of custom as separate as fish.

Of the three hundred and fifty million Indians today, nearly two hundred and forty million are Hindus.

A cultured Hindu may interpret the religious system as a desire to worship God, rising from the most primitive form to the most spiritual. The passion for worship is strong and universal. But since the overwhelming mass of people are very simple and ignorant they adore most varied immediate objects.

Stones, trees, and animals begin — an unshaped stone set on end as the village worshipping place; the tulsi bush enshrined in family courtyards and tended as part of religious ritual; the sacred pipal trees daubed with vermilion or wound with string and circumambulated; the mangoes that in some places may not be cut; even the devil-harbouring cactus hedges; the carving of snakes standing on their tails and offered food, or the living snakes to whom part of the compound of homes of the Nair caste is sacred.

Sun and ocean, river and mountain, are holy.

More humanized conceptions are of village mother goddesses, sometimes demonesses, who bring diseases, or who spare in return for sacrifice; local gods concerned with harvest, and the many stone shapes that symbolize sex organs. Ghosts and ghosts — malicious little bhuts who bring mischief to hapless men and women — linger around the villages. More manlike gods, sometimes still half animal, so closely are they tied to their past, have quarrels with their wives, and many passionate interludes.

The worship becomes subtler in devotion to one of these incarnations of ultimate God; love of Vishnu or Siva, expressed ardently and humanly. Or it becomes an attempt to find the universal God that is one's own soul, to withdraw from sensuous existence and thought entirely, to break the imagined chain of incarnations and unite with the Infinite.

All these ways of worship, seldom sharply separate, often strangely blended, are part of Hinduism today. Individual Hindus are sharply contrasted: the Brahman who chants Sanskrit hymns to the low-caste man forbidden to hear the sacred syllables; the priest who valets a god image with literal precision to the outcaste Hindu who would defile even the temple's courtyard; the sceptical university man weaned from pious routine to the orthodox father of a high-caste family who follows an elaborately specified daily ritual from dawn to bedtime, praying and purifications and the five sacrifices to gods, ancestors, ghosts, Brahmans, and men, as ordered by his sect. The women of his household — on a lower level — may not touch the household gods, but are left the more ancient forms, adoring an ammonite stone sacred to Vishnu, tending his sacred tulsi plant. The ascetic who shuns food and woman contrasts with the sensualist who loves both, and with the 'left-hand' Sakti sect, who worship women with literal orgies. Hinduism includes them all, not as neurotic individual variations, but as followers of permissible worship.

To look for the reason for some of the stranger-seeming habits of the religion today, one must consider the races who began to build living India millennia or centuries before Christ.

ABORIGINES

The first of these people, though the least important, were living in the late stone age, and keep that pattern of life. One or two tribes have legends of upstart iron smelters who offended the nostrils of their god by the thick smoke of furnaces — a conservative scorn worthy of solid Neolithic families.

About eight million people in India are followers of primitive tribal religions, outside the shifting border of Hinduism. Of these, some three million speak dialects called Munda, which no other races in India can understand, but which is more like some of the languages in Burma or in such far places as Easter Island, Madagascar, and parts of New Zealand. This strange speech may be the certificate of India's first inhabitants.

Such primitive tribes of differing physique and habit live centred on the plateau and rolling hills of Chota Nagpur in Bihar, and spreading into Bengal and adjoining lands — usually muscular, sinewy men of darkest skin, with flat noses, low foreheads, and thick lips, sturdy and jolly, fond of hunting and wild tribal dancing and harvest orgies. Some are so primitive that they live by twisting creepers into ropes for barter or snaring monkeys for food. Their farming may be the earliest known — burning over a patch of jungle, and then dropping seeds into the ashes between stumps.

Their history no one knows — they themselves are their only history. Perhaps some of them shared in the life of the ancient cities of the northwest — but if so they lost that civilization. Or perhaps they lived in the east of India, driven to wild hills where they kept their tenacious habits untouched.

Today, various outside influences are melting these tenacities. Some have mingled with superior tribes and been lifted from their wild identity. A few have been converted to Christianity and given up their sacred groves, their potent stones. Some, finding valley settlements and learning a little about rice cultivation, take on a Brahman priest and a detail of Hindu worship, and are accepted far down in the scale of Hinduism as peasant, labourer, or robber caste.

Although counted outside of Hinduism, an osmosis goes on, carrying up into its tolerance their old persistent worship. Their influence on the whole is negligible, but they keep a pattern of certain ancestral ways of mankind that resemble the more developed customs of Hindus — and throw light on many puzzling habits.

Totemism is their system, sometimes fragmentary now. A totemistic tribe feels a mystic unity with some animal, vegetable, or thing, which it reveres as sacred and considers its ancestor, and receiver of souls after death. The tribe takes its name from the ancestor totem and is forbidden — and fears — to destroy it.

A clan honouring a tiger considers it more dreadful to kill a tiger than to murder a man. One Indian clan whose totem was rice had some difficulty in holding it sacred, since rice was also its main diet. So it compromised by making it tabu to eat the scum from the top of the rice-pot. Although the life of the totem is preserved, there is, classically, a yearly festival at which the totem animal is killed and its flesh eaten as a sacrament by the members of the tribe, in the belief that this sacrifice gives new life to the fields, to the year, to the tribe. There is a recollection of this in the spring wild-boar hunt of the Rajputs, in the wild boar's head of old Christmas dinners. All the worship of animals and trees and stones, that penetrate in disguise into many religions and live on in fairy stories, is believed by one school of thought to go back to such totemism.

Totemistic people have strong tabus — things which 'are not done' because they are, *per se*, *ex cathedra*, potent and dangerous. The tabu is not the wisdom of experience, for poison berries may not be tabu, while a king's glance may. Human blood, newborn children, women in childbirth, food offered by strangers, and corpses inspire it. The tabu is a barrier effective as a charge of electricity.

Tabus especially affect marriage. Since all people of the same totem believe that they have a common ancestor, to marry within that group would be incestuous. Rigid laws force men to take wives from outside a given totem division, although inside a larger encircling class. They cannot usually take food from another tribe. The Kols, who have a stiff frame to their lives, cannot eat, marry, or have sexual relations with outsiders. They are even wary of their own tribesmen who have moved to another place, and will not eat or marry with the exiles.

It was a totemistic belief that souls went wandering after death, and that the dead neighbours might reappear in some animal or other shape.

Though scorned by Hinduism, such clans preserve an older pattern of touch-nots and eat-nots and marry-nots, that suggest comparison with Hindu caste regulations, defined and explained by an elaborate later reasoning literature. For the rest, the aborigines are as inconsequential as squirrels, except that they represent to the Government another kink in the tangle of minorities — people with ability to do nothing but continue their own, museum-specimen existence, keep the ancient design for living that has strange tracings in present India, and help make her story, from far times, continuous.

Dravidians

Settlers before 2000 B.C.

A greater race in India, the Dravidians, carry down to today cults that were practised in the first cities of the world in India — in the age of stone, copper, and bronze.

The dark-faced man whom one sees in Tanjore or Madura, with his long sleek hair hanging down his back, his skirt dipped in red at the border, his broad nose and mournful eyes, has the blood of Dravidians who were rich and fecund on the steamy soil, masters of India before 2000 B.C.

Now, although they have mixed some with aboriginal races, and with later races who came to India, they live in purest type and predominant numbers in the southern half of the triangle of the map — the last geographical stronghold below the Vindhya hills, which alien conquerors seldom reached. There they speak their different languages — Tamil, Telegu, Kanarese, Malayalam; and there, since the Middle Ages, they have left great temples, incredible as a tropical jungle, that rise in truncated towers, carved over every foot with gods and demons and lovers. In those middle ages they bred spiritual leaders, writers of a rich Tamil literature, sculptors who could turn the outcropping rocks at Mamallapuram into stately story books — as well as mute, unnumbered primitive people. Literature, architecture, and saints were the contribution of their mediæval years. From distant times they preserve strange cults.

The lingam of Siva, a stone cylinder symbolizing the penis, is worshipped all over India today wherever Hinduism prevails or is tucked into the nook of a Moslem state. In shrines and temples, little and big, it stands, guarded by the bull of Siva, wreathed with marigolds or jasmine, or cooled with water and bel leaves by the faithful. In a dark southern temple a bell rings and a priest places rice on the image, which a little calf strolls up to lap away. Simple worshippers, bringing their offerings, make routine reverence, or pray to it for sons. Mystical interpretations are made by the few, leaving the many to be literal since they must. All over India today the stone lingams stand, or are being set up, relic of the once widespread human habit of fertility worship.

Less regarded and less frequent are the stone images of the female yoni, though one still may see a row of them in some Hindu temples. But the Mother Goddess, whom they personified, the goddess worshipped in other lands as Ishtar or Isis or Aphrodite, was a favourite for Dravidians. Simple village people turn their goddesses into demons — they have the seven sisters who bring cholera and smallpox and such diseases, and must be propitiated often by gruesome sacrifice. To more cultivated Hindus, the mother goddess is a wife of Siva in one of her many aspects.

The present worship of the symbols of sex is an extreme conservatism, apparently carried down by the Dravidians, along with other cults and cultures, from cities that flourished in the Indus Valley more than five thousand years ago.

About two hundred miles by rail from Karachi, seen from the air like an earthworm's burrowing in the glaring sand, not far from the lazy swinging arc of the Indus River that brought it life and death, rise the exact walls of one of the first cities built on earth, that traded with Ur of the Chaldees and had a similar glory.

Mohenjo-Daro was buried under the desert sand and bristling bush until a few years ago when an enthusiast, digging in the Buddhist stupa above it, held in the palm of his hand a small carved seal, and recognized it as the sort used at Ur. Cities seven deep were excavated, the upper cities built upon those below, until well curbs stand up like chimneys. Below the lowest city, the water level was reached, beneath which even older walls can be seen. The city lived between 3500 to 2700 B.C. when the Indus River swung round again and flooded or choked it with silt, and it was abandoned.

Methodical people built the city, strong in habit, able to plan a broad straight avenue running due north to south, and for centuries to keep its direction and the line of its houses accurate. Their artists could magnificently design and carve their seals. Their greater families had wells, and bathrooms — sloping floors draining through a hole in the wall, like the bathrooms of India today. The city maintained drains in the street, covered conduits of precise bricks, connecting in the great avenue with an underground pit which scavengers could clean. After seeing modern Indian villages or cities like Lahore, one can grow lyrical over the drainage of Mohenjo-Daro which India itself never improved, and which Europe did not equal until about the nineteenth century.

If later India did not change the drains, neither did she abandon what appear to have been the religious cults of the city, the worship of mother goddesses, and many lingam and yoni stones. The marvellously carved animals on the seals, the trees, the snakes, were perhaps the totems under whose protection property could be placed. A little carved god was found, sitting in yoga position, identified as Siva's prototype by his accompanying bull.

The women's jewels, the headbands of thin hammered gold, the nose discs and necklaces of jade and gold; the copper tools, the clay toys and games — were all found in the city apparently deserted about 2750 B.C.

What races built Mohenjo-Daro no one is yet certain, nor what became of their genius. It was one of those ages which spread a high level of intelligence to many lands, from Thessaly and Egypt to Honan in China, from Mesopotamia and Persia to Baluchistan and India. Apparently this city's population was the mixture usual in port and river towns. Among the races may have lived the ancestors of the present Dravidians.

But where the Dravidians came from no one knows. They may have been invaders from the northwest, advancing on the desired plains, for in a little pocket in the Baluchistan hills is left an island of Dravidian speech. The first certain light comes about two thousand years before Christ, when they were the undisputed masters of India, building rich towns of brick, and using iron as well as copper and silver and gold. They had strong castles and forts, and they were ample traders, in due time sending cargoes of apes and ivory and peacocks to Tyre, and bargaining with Egyptians and Phœnicians on their palmy Malabar coast.

In their settled prosperity of agriculture they worshipped the earth as their central deity — the good nourishing earth, source of food and life. To ensure the earth mother's fertility they worshipped sex, for, by immemorial magic, human mating was supposed to generate good crops. This was the earliest form of farm relief. One representative of earth to them was the snake, crawling from under ground. In time snakes became half human, kings and queens called Naga, believed to be the ancestors of certain tribes and founders of dynasties — one still sees carvings of Naga kings, coils and scales below the waist, and human form above, often crowned by a hood of seven cobra heads. Outside a cave at Ajanta the Naga king and queen have become wistful, almost human beings, who seem listening to some far music.

As matriarchy and polyandry were once widespread among the Dravidians (and now left in vestiges, as among the Nair caste who inherit through the mother), the Dravidian female deities outranked the male. Their goddesses were as comparatively large and devouring as the female spider with insignificant mate. Later it came to be thought that the female half of the god was the fighting unit. He was passive, she his energy — an idea much elaborated in later philosophy. Its elementary form is the worship of village 'mothers' and demonesses who bring disease and pestilence, and in aspects of the goddess Kali, most beloved and feared, as later stories tell.

Thirty-five hundred or more years ago these people, busy about their farming and building and their accepted worships, probably thought their solid cities were theirs for all time. But at the northwest corner of the upside-down triangle of India, there was a break in the mountain wall. Those ranges of peaks protected the warm, fertile plains of India from the tribesmen on the bleaker Asian highlands. The weak place in the wall of mountains was to become a menace.

Down upon the Dravidians farming in the north came sudden surprising attacks from ruddy tribes driving chariots with that newly mastered animal, the horse. They were fierce and stalwart men hardened on the bracing tablelands of Central Asia, whose relatives were turning west into Europe to be our ancestors, but who themselves — Aryans of the Vedic days — chose the eastern course down into India, the beginning of a long adventure.

Aryans of the Vedic Age

From 2000 to about 550 B.C.

What is left of the invading Aryans? Mounds near Delhi may be their epic battlefields, and the cyclopean walls of Rajagriha may be left from the last Vedic days. Today few can claim pure Aryan blood, but the nearest type seems to be among the proud Brahman pundits of Kashmir, and certain fair castes of the Punjab with aquiline noses and coin-pure features, or delicate faces of the Nambudri Brahmans of Travancore.

But a magnificent literature lives from their time, and Hindu culture roots in their imagination. The four Vedas, collections of prayers and incantations to their gods, are the earliest Indian literature. Although today only a few learned men may read these Sanskrit songs, Hinduism accepts their sanctity, and recent modern reformers had as their slogan, 'Back to the Vedas.' High-caste Hindus still say daily prayers from the Vedas, and they are used in the ritual of birth and wedding and death. The later literature that sprang from them has shaped all Hindu thought, and seeped down to the merest peasant. Intangible things, thoughts, but more powerful than castles.

Details of custom are more tangible. India goes on pilgrimage as her Vedic forefathers did. The third-class railways of India, jammed to the windows with travellers to shrines and holy places, may credit some of their fares to the Aryan impetus. The fakir by the temple covers his body with grey ash from his sacred fire of cow dung. Fire was an Aryan divinity.

Here is a holy river at dawn, when the bathers shiver on the stone steps that the river laps or stand waist-deep in the stream. The light on pearly clouds is unreal. Tall and noble buildings crowd the portion of the bank that is sacred, with an upward pressure that confined space gives, whether from cost of ground in Manhattan or sacredness of ground on the Ganges. Women bathe and change their wet clothing deftly and modestly; men stand in the river, holding a nostril for the breathing rites; sputtering, blinking brown babies are being ducked under the water by the braceleted arms of their mothers. People are at all stages of bathing, sipping, mouth-rinsing, and scooping up water in brass jars above the burning ghats, where the cinders of the dead float downstream. In tranced passion they pray themselves out of sin, out of life.

'The waters bless us, all that rise in desert lands and marshy pools. Bless us, waters brought in jars; bless us, the water of the rains.' That prayer from Vedic hymns is said by a Brahman of one sect. Another Brahman, bathing, may be purifying himself from the pollution of the daily acts of life by repeating, 'Whatever of sin is found in me — whatever evil I have wrought — if I have lied or falsely sworn... waters, remove it from me.'

The waters were goddesses to the Aryans, who could cleanse from defilement and moral guilt, and give long life and immortality. They were the gay young wives of Fire, whose union meant fertility. All over India today, at little sacred springs, at paved oblong tanks and holy rivers, tense-eyed women are bathing and praying for a son to save their souls; and scrupulous, conforming men are washing away figurative defilement. The idea that waters bless and wash away guilt is widespread over the earth, and the Aryans shared it.

The gorgeous sun that they worshipped has lost favour, except in disguise. He is still the ancestor of the Rajput princes of Udaipur, and even of certain humbler castes. And high-caste Hindus should daily make oblation, emptying a spoonful of water toward the sun, for every drop of a Brahman's oblations washes away a thousand of the sun's enemies. Brahmans must daily recite the Gayatri, or prayer from the Rig-Veda to the sun, so sacred that no low-caste person, or woman, must hear it. 'May we receive the glorious brightness of this, the generator, the God who shall prosper our works.' A strict Brahman should repeat this three hundred and twenty-four times a day. If he fails, he has committed as great a sin as killing a cow.

Why is it a sin to kill a cow? That leads to another custom, whose origin may vault back to totemism, or may partly derive from Vedic economy. Down the steps, at the worship of the river Jumna at Brindaban, while the priest is chanting and bells are ringing excitedly, a cow wanders through the throng of worshippers, as though up the aisle of a church. At the Benares burning ghats, a heifer picks her way through cinders and mud down to the thin, cotton-wrapped corpse, and, unhindered, eats the marigold wreath from its neck. The cow is so sacred that her five essences, milk, butter, ghee, urine, and dung, mixed together, form a food eaten to purify a Hindu from terrible defilement. Yet the ownerless, starving cows who cannot be killed make a practical problem. Over the sparse pastures of India barren scrub cattle are wandering, using up food, cows long since separated from their function of milk-giving, starving and pathetic as animals, but turned into religious symbols.

Go back through the ages to nomad Aryans, whose lives depended upon their cattle.

Singing men came down from the mountains into India more than fifteen centuries before Christ — Aryans who pushed a way over the hard Afghanistan peaks. They drove cows and goats before them through the devious mountain passes to the widespread level of northern India, in wave after wave of migration.

They performed spells to make Nature obey them — to bring rainclouds and crops — and their chants were vital to the life of a tribe. If a change was made in a syllable or a gesture, it lost its power to compel the storm. Those learned ones who could invent or remember the magic formulæ to manage lightning and defy the plague seemed to the tribesmen their chief defenders. Awe-stricken men on an uncompromising earth leaned on the mysterious power of their priests.

The Aryans were imaginative and sensitive, and their minds were growing. They knew the barrier mountains of India, over whose bleak folds they had driven their flocks. They knew the

Himalayan snow in the blue air — the high, cloudlike line of white that followed their plains. They knew the fertilizing and flooding rivers, the dawn colours, and the sun that took three strides through the sky. To all of these they gave consciousness, or divinity. But mainly they worshipped the sky, as the darker Dravidians did the earth.

And the sky of northern India suggests their mood still: the blue cup of air fitted over the circle of the plain; the sun, strong enough to kill; the silent yellow twilights following the great blue day; calm, arid winter; then the mounting heat, sinister, and the violent onset of the rains. Translate northern Indian nature into gods, and follow the path of the imaginative Aryans.

They were a lusty people wearing clothing of skins or sheep's wool and preening themselves, men and women alike, with gold anklets and bracelets, necklaces and earrings. They were joyful, warlike, and healthy, of simple and partly savage habits, with samples of various human vices. When they travelled, they piled their belongings on oxen and bulls and goats; and dogs and sheep followed the procession. They loved to race horses, and gathered with shouting gusto to see them hurtling past over the bumpy ground. They drank and diced and gambled as heartily as their far kinsmen of Norse sagas, rewarded their bards lavishly, and listened to their musicians playing drums and flutes.

The women were rather free and rather moral. They were normally under the protection of father, brother, or husband, and failing that strong arm might necessarily be a prey to any man, but in general they led a sturdy, unrestricted life, brought a good price from an inferior bridegroom, or were offered with a dowry to a superior one. They were not married as children.

The cow, which was life-giving to a wandering people, became their coin, their unit of value and exchange. A cow standard was perhaps safer than a gold standard. To an unimaginative people, she would remain a useful milk-giver of sluggish habit. The Aryans in Vedic days did not consider her too sacred to kill and eat. But their poetical minds began to make metaphors. They held her in wistful esteem, their second mother, the fountain of nourishment. They imagined her the symbol of earth and fruitfulness.

They had the social life of pioneers. The most highly respected might work with his hands. The man who made wooden chariots was well regarded, and the metal-worker who melted his ore in an oven, using the wing of a bird as fan to the flame. Although classified into priests, warrior-kings, and common people, the aristocracy of a slave-owning society had not yet come.

But these homogeneous Aryan tribes, each under a petty chief or king, in his chariot with the tribal priest beside him, advanced on an India already well peopled. They came down fresh from their mountains, and their chief and joyous business was warfare, and cattle raids a pleasing prowess. They considered civilized cities meaningless or distasteful, and the strange dark-skinned inhabitants like monkeys or demons — people without noses, they said, for their own noses were shapely.

Terrifying with horses they charged down on this dark-skinned race who were hard to conquer — 'bull-jawed' — and 'having impregnable castles and forts of iron.' Though few in number, the Aryans spread their lordship from the mountains of Afghanistan and Kashmir over the plains of the Punjab, and perhaps as far east as the Jumna River. They did not get so far as the India of rice and tigers, and the elephant was still fabulous to them — 'the creature with the hand.'

They lived as masters, and felt distaste for the defeated Dravidians, 'enemies, slaves, abject tribes devoid of sense,' who worshipped disgustingly, and the wrong gods. Although they inevitably mingled, they met the colour problem as most races do, by considering their own fair skins superior and trying to keep that inheritance pure. They used the word Varna, meaning colour, to describe the four classifications which they finally made of society. The three highest were the priests (Brahmans), warriors (Kshatriyas), and commoners (Vaisyas). These they kept for themselves, as 'twice-born' (reborn in ceremonies of the Vedas). Below the twice-born, they let the Dravidians form the lowest Varna called Sudra and, to hold them, had to admit their religious customs. Below the Sudras, the dirty savage tribes were left in outer darkness.

In other lands, warlike tribes have come conquering down from mountains and left little trace. But these Aryans, people of genius, had a power to think that outleaped the simplicity of their lives. Their hymns and spells were held in the memory of priests for perhaps a thousand years before they were written down, to become the fountain-head of Hindu religion and civilization today. There is a joyousness, a freshness and certainty to the early hymns, unlike the later troubled, despairing, ecstatic, or quibbling thought of the race after it had lived long centuries in the hot valley of the Ganges.

Though their lives were simple, their imagination was strong as a Himalayan waterfall. Their literature performs the amazing feat of recording the development of men's thoughts, from primitive magic, and the personifying of sky and rivers, to the conception of one spirit, permeating the universe, and the individual's identity with that spirit.

Their literature began with the four Vedas, collections of hymns and chants and spells. The earliest, the Rig-Veda, brings the gods into being with the two parents, Sky and Earth, whose mating produces all things. The Sky, Dyaus, is the father god, the 'bull who bellows downward' or a 'black steed decked with pearls.' Sky-and-Earth, invoked together, are 'far extending, unaging, yielding milk, ghee, honey in abundance. The one is a prolific bull, the other a variegated cow, and both are rich in seed.'

The sun has many names and is worshipped under many aspects. As Mitra he is the rising sun, as Varuna the setting sun, as Vishnu the one who takes three strides through the sky. As Surya he is vaguely personified. His rays become hands and tongue, and he drives yellow horses.

Auspicious are the yellow horses of Surya, bright, swift, worthy of praises.
Bowing they mount to the back of the sky; round heaven and earth they go quickly.
Endlessly his yellow horses now bring clear brightness, now darkness.

The gods of morning are two handsome young men who yoke chariots to ride across the sky at the moment that dawn, the goddess Ushas is born. As the gods are more definitely personified, they become warriors or priests, wearing clothes like men and driving celestial chariots, after the model of man's. They eat the favourite food of men, which Fire, the god Agni, carries up to them at the sacrifice; or they swoop down in their chariots and take the food from the altar. They drink the immortal Soma juice, which becomes a divinity itself, and whose very grinding-stones are gods.

Indra, the thunder or storm god, who kills the demon of drought and darkness, who slays his father to steal the soma nectar, is the most anthropomorphic — a rather rowdy god. With his big strong arms and beautiful lips, when he has drunk heartily of soma juice, he moves his jawbones with pleasure and shakes his fair beard. The gods are honest gods. They are bright and strong and mainly benevolent, and can be persuaded by offerings to befriend and help a man.

The hymns to them are often very beautiful. MacDonell gives a few translations in 'India's Past.' This, from the Rig-Veda to the dawn, already has a touch of sadness, of looking before and after.

Again and again newly born though ancient,
Decking her beauty with the self-same colours,
The goddess wastes away the life of mortals
Like wealth diminished by a skilful player.
Gone are the mortals who in former ages
Beheld the flushing of an earlier morning.
We living men now look upon her shining; —
Those will be born who shall hereafter see her.

Although the gods are benevolent and bright, the Indian northern climate suggests other things: a still, level sunshine for months of flat time, late autumn and early winter, gracious days of intensely coloured sky and cooling night. Then the slow mounting of heat into unbearable power in the spring — smothering heat that makes men walk softly, and move as little as possible, limp and drenched by sweating. It becomes sinister, working up to the summer storms. Then, sudden and melodramatic, the black clouds of the monsoon advance, a wall of rains coming forward with lightnings, beating up the earth, a force to dismay armies. Nature is not gentle, nor has she easy transitions in India. It seems too near the electric source of things, too untempered. Destruction is implicit.

Rudra is a minor sky god in the Vedic hymns, little invoked and who has in him the germ of malevolence. Here come Rudra's sons, the storms:

> They gleam with armlets as the Heavens are decked with stars;
> Like cloud-born lightnings shine the torrents of their rain.

And

> The Maruts spread the mist abroad
> And make the mountains rock and reel,
> When with the winds they speed along....
>
> Before you, fierce ones, even woods bow down in fear,
> The earth herself, the very mountains tremble.

And this is the god Parjanya, the raincloud:

> Like charioteer, his horses lashing with a whip,
> The god makes manifest his messengers of rain.
> From far away the roaring lion sounds,
> What time Parjanya veils the firmament with rain.
> The winds blow forth; to earth the quivering lightnings fall.
> The plants shoot up; with moisture streams the realm of light.
> For all the world abundant nourishment is born,
> When by Parjanya Earth is fertilized with seed.

The songs of storms suggest that cruelty and destruction have a place in the cycle of life. The storm god Rudra, little invoked in the stalwart Aryan days, becomes the great Hindu Siva, god both of destruction and creation. The sinister power of Nature in India had its effect in the facing of death and cruelty as half the dual nature of the creator.

A few hymns look forward to a coming belief. The sky god Varuna finds a spiritual significance that suggests the psalm 'Whither shall I flee from thy presence?' This is from the Arthava-Veda, in Max Müller's edition.

> And all this earth King Varuna possesses,
> His the remotest ends of yon broad Heaven;
> And both the seas in Varuna lie hidden,
> But yet the smallest water-drop contains him.
> Although I climbed the highest Heaven, fleeing,
> I should not there escape the monarch's power.

And the 'Creation Hymn,' from the Rig-Veda, has been called the 'earliest specimen of Aryan philosophic thought.'

> Nor Aught nor Naught existed; yon bright sky
> Was not, nor Heaven's broad roof outstretched above.
> What covered all? What sheltered? What concealed?
> Was it the water's fathomless abyss?
> There was not death — yet there was nought immortal,
> There was no confine betwixt day and night;
> The only One breathed breathless by itself,
> Other than It there nothing since has been.

And after describing the bursting of the seed of creation, the poet asks:

> Who knows the secret? Who proclaimed it here,
> Whence, whence this manifold creation sprang?
> The Gods themselves came later into being...

From the ancient Vedic pantheon, some of the sky gods will survive — Indra as a thunder god on his elephant, little more than a decorative guardian in sculpture; Brahma with only two temples in India; but Vishnu, a sun god who takes three strides of morning, noon, and night, will be the great protecting and preserving god Vishnu of nine incarnations. And Rudra, the storm — mingled with a Dravidian fertility god — will become Siva, the strange destructive, creative god, most powerful in India. The rest of the gods will die or lose prestige, and live on only as local divinities or godlings, perhaps, however, with untold influence on the daily lives of simple people.

The fourth Veda, the Arthava-Veda, of older origin, is mainly of magic spells and incantations; man's attempt to compel Nature to his will, the beginning of science. The Arthava-Veda founded the Indian system of medicine. How piteously futile the potent metaphor was, one may gather from this cough remedy. One should shoot an arrow, with this incantation:

> Just as the arrow, sharpened well,
> Swift to the distance flies away,
> So even thou, oh, cough, fly forth
> Along the broad expanse of earth.

The joyous force of Aryan youth spent itself. Life in the later centuries of Vedic time grew more complex and literature reflected that. As Aryan tribes advanced and conquered slaves and serfs from other races, they were less likely to work with their hands or consider it respectable. The priests and warriors first became hereditary. Then the commoners, the Vaisyas, split into many divisions of occupation and kin, and began to regard these divisions as absolute. The Vaisya had little to boast of. He was sinking in the social scale toward the Sudra's level, defined in sacred books as 'tributary to another, to be lived on by another, and to be oppressed at will.'

Women — their clothes dyed in saffron — were also sinking a little. They could not inherit or own anything. Whatever they earned from their own work went to father or husband. Usually a man had only one wife, but the habit of having many began with kings and was spreading to nobles. In the patriarchal families a son was coming to be considered a 'light of highest Heaven,' while a daughter was a 'source of misery.'

Religion was growing more elaborate. Attached to the Vedas are books called Brahmanas, the first Indian prose, still clumsy and abstruse, that show the beginning of castes, and the growth of ritual. A priest had to serve a long apprenticeship to a teacher for whom he worked and begged. The sacrifices grew so detailed and amazing that sometimes it took seventeen priests to make the proper offering of rice and milk to the god. The building of an altar might be a portentous affair with a mystic symbolism — an analogy to the construction of the earth. Sacrifices of animals might take from twelve days to a year to perform properly. And dark details were mentioned of human sacrifice.

The power of the Brahmans increased, for, if the will of the gods and the influence of lucky days and stars dominated human lives, the men who could influence all that must be powerful as deities themselves. An unlearned priest who made a sacrifice with the wrong gesture, or sang a chant with the wrong intonation, would have no effect. A malicious priest might purposely damage his patron by slipping in a false syllable. But priests who sang and sacrificed correctly could stop the sun in his course for the sake of man. Individually a Brahman might be a learned philosopher or ignorant, he might be austere or sensual, might temper the despotism of his king with wisdom or scheme for his own ends. But an inheriting group that was held in such awe made for social rigidity.

Beside the dead weight of priestly tradition, the blind alley of all thought, another literature was growing, ignoring ritual, trying to think; throwing the clutter of ceremony aside, trying to find the true nature of this world in which the Aryan found himself. The Upanishads, books of philosophy attached to the Brahmanas, which in turn are attached to the Vedas, began some time before Buddha to puzzle about the reason of existence.

Ritual meant little to these thinkers of the Upanishads, and sacrifice less. They were concerned with a man's soul, Atman, and the World Soul, Brahman. They conceived of Brahman, the cosmic spirit, as an immortal thinker and knower, an Eternal 'in which space is woven, and which is interwoven in it.' For the first time on earth, man conceived of the absolute. With that conception came the idea, fundamental in Vedanta philosophy of later India, influencing European philosophers and startlingly corroborated by modern science, that the material world is an illusion.

Only the soul was reality to those early philosophers. The Aryans had long believed, in common with totemistic forbears and with European kin, in a soul which at death of the body flew out like a bird from a cage to a new life. Gradually it seemed logical that this soul would find an endless chain of new incarnations in man, god, insect, animal.

To find a reason for the different fates, they evolved the idea of *Karma*, the retribution or result of past deeds on the next incarnation. Whatsoever man sows in a past life, that shall he reap in the next. By the sixth century before Christ this idea had been written.

The relentless thought was to pile a terrible burden upon the spirit. There seemed no reason to try to avert calamity, if misery or joy were determined before birth. In time the weight of fear grew heavier. However many good deeds one might pile to one's credit, a single mistake or hasty speech would send one slipping to the bottom of the heap, to be reborn as an outcaste, a cripple, an unpleasing animal, a woman. Retribution was so pitiless that a good man might earn a hundred thousand years as a god, only to be reborn as a dumb man because he once told a scandal.

But an escape could come from the bodily prisons through correct knowledge. This the Upanishads tried to find.

Some seem very difficult and full of dross to our uninitiate minds; sheer nonsense in fact

> Then he said to them all: 'You eat your food, knowing that Vaisvanara Self as if it were many. But he who worships the Vaisvanara Self as a span long, and as identical with himself, he eats food in all worlds, in all beings, in all Selfs.'
>
> Of that Vaisvanara Self the head is Sutegas [having good light], the eye Visvarupa [multiform], the breath Prithagvartman [having various courses], the trunk Bahula [full], the bladder Rayi [wealth], the feet the earth, the chest the altar, the hairs the grass on the altar, the heart the Garhapatya fire, the mind the Anvaharya fire, the mouth the Ahavaniya fire.

But the depth of a passage of this sort is more easily grasped:

> 'These rivers, my son, run, the eastern toward the east, the western toward the west. They go from sea to sea.' [Up to the clouds and down as rain.] 'They become indeed sea. And as those rivers, when they are in the sea, do not know, I am this or that river,
>
> 'In the same manner, my son, all these creatures, when they have come back from the True, know not that they have come back from the True. Whatever these creatures are here, whether a lion, or a wolf, or a boar, or a worm, or a midge, or a gnat, or a mosquito, that they become again and again.

'That which is that subtile essence, in all that exists has its self. It is the True. It is the Self, and thou, O Svetaketu, art it.'

'Please, sir, inform me more,' said the son.

'Be it so, my child,' the father replied...

Indian philosophy was born. In a brief verse like this it could give the kernel of its thought:

This, my Atman [soul], in my inmost heart is smaller than a grain of rice...
This, my Atman, in my inmost heart is greater than the earth, greater than the sky, greater than the Heavens, greater than all spheres...
This, my Atman, in my inmost heart is the Brahman (God).
With him, when I depart out of this life, shall I be united.

2. *The Lawgivers of the Hindus*

THESE were the races in India when the Aryan priests began the codes of Hindu law: the Neolithic savage; the dark, industrious Dravidian; the imaginative, cowherding Aryan. Later races were to come, of Scythian and Turkish and Mongolian origin. But the earliest lawgivers already saw sharply differing types.

The Brahman priests, who were the only learned men, wrote rules for conduct in magic, religion, and social life, for nearly a thousand years. Beginning possibly about 600 B.C., they compiled meticulous laws, which they attributed to divine sages, and which grew to have the heavy weight of sanctity.

Laws crystallized mainly before A.D. 400 might seem remote from today's situation. But the holy codes, called Shastras, still rule, or deeply influence, Hindu society from bottom to top, with less or more rigidity. Since the purpose of Hindu life is worship, religion keeps secular matters under its control. Therefore, to change a law for a social or even sanitary improvement often violates some interpretation of the Shastras, and offends the priesthood and the conservative majority. By the principle of religious toleration in India, the courts of the land respect the religious law for Hindus and Mohammedans — and the sacred customs of any tribe. This does not mean that some legislative reforms have not gone against them — legalizing widow remarriage, and forbidding the marriage of girls under fourteen. But it is like walking uphill in deep snow to pass laws and enforce them against the will of the ancient lawgivers. Their burden upon the people is not trivial. The marriages of little girls, the shaming of widows, the dirt and sepsis of childbirth, have had, in these codes, strange origin, without cruel intent, but of terrible effect. The vast, cumbersome, gradually growing, hair-splitting system of caste was codified first in these law books.

Caste still makes Hindu society so profoundly different from Western — so silently, deeply different, that so-called modern influences slide off like rain from rocks. To discuss it with a travelled and educated Hindu may be to feel that it is melting like ice in spring. But to see India even superficially is to believe that the melting is more like a spring thaw at the snout of a glacier — encouraging, but not immediately so.

Hindu society is still like a jigsaw puzzle, seeming to make one picture, but dropping to pieces at a touch. Each man is born, dines, marries, and dies within the barriers of his caste, which combines the sanctity of church, the solidarity of a fraternal order, the practical help of a mutual benefit society, the snobbishness of any given social set, and the firmness of a family. Such a group has its place in an evolving society. But with modern ways, it puts up sharp and stilted barriers between men of the same religion and nation. The foreigner in India is forever alien, since Indians are themselves so estranged. Each man's first devotion is to his own caste.

The caste rules vary greatly, the strictness usually increasing with the social rating. But in general their great concern is marriage and food.

Today a litter on the shoulders of four men is tossing a young bridegroom in Kangra Valley, his face veiled in tinsel, to his wedding ceremonies. Skyrockets and drums elsewhere announce that a richer bridegroom cometh. And in a princely state he lolls in a Rolls-Royce, preceded by elephants whose tusks bear candelabra and vases of flowers, by camels with mounted guns, by horses with golden anklets. Humble or princely, Hindu marriages have one rocklike certainty in common. The wish of the boy and girl is not decisive. The marriage is arranged and bridegroom chosen by the precise law of caste.

Eating and drinking might seem spontaneous things, especially for the underfed. But a tattered Hindu starveling looks hungrily at a lavish picnic luncheon and refuses to take any because he would be polluted by food from a Christian or Mohammedan. Even some untouchables will not eat with men of similar or kindred caste. In one college dormitory for outcastes, the lowborn boys split into two groups who objected to dining together. In some universities, all the caste Hindus will share kitchen and food, refusing only to eat with Moslems. But in a particularly pious city and university, each caste of students insisted upon different kitchens. A distracted master, having only one room left, suggested that two Brahman boys of the same subcaste might cook together. But they refused, because these subcastes now lived in different places. A chalk line was drawn across the kitchen, and each boy then cooked contentedly on his own side. That bears out the old proverb, 'Three Kanaujia Brahmans need thirteen kitchens.'

Except a few emancipated, or the lowest of the unclean, Hindus do not eat with outsiders for fear of pollution. That great theory governs their restrictions and tabus — the idea that souls are incarnated in bodies of varying degrees of purity according to Karma, the place won in former lives, and that this purity can be smirched by various defiling contacts. An orthodox Hindu is busy avoiding such things as food cooked by improper people, water defiled by outcaste or alien, the touch of a woman who is bearing a child. One result is the misery and sepsis and death of mothers considered so polluting that only an unclean place, unclean rags, and the dirty and ignorant hags of an unclean caste may surround the birth. The purity which a good Hindu struggles to maintain has nothing to do with cleanliness or virtue. It is a mystic purity, the result of Karma, the position earned in the eternal scheme of things by former lives.

This eternal hierarchy of Karma is represented on earth by the relative position of castes, theoretically as vertical as a ladder. Democracy is absurd to the caste system, which petrifies the inequalities of men and holds the relative positions rigid. A somewhat democratic government may allow a low-caste man to rise to an important position. A somewhat industrial city may allow him to become very wealthy. Conquering ancestors may even have put him upon a throne — but he remains inferior. A Brahman may be a chauffeur or cook or follow some other menial work so long as it is not forbidden by sacred law. But he remains pure and an aristocrat. A story is told of a Hindu government official, hurrying in to an appointment with the Viceroy, who stopped to bow to take the dust from the feet of the Brahman doorkeeper. Wealth or worldly place has nothing to do with caste status, only mystic purity achieved in former lives. No man may climb in this lifetime higher. He must accept his place and duty, whether a sweeper of filth or a holy Brahman.

Practically speaking, there are instances of castes or subcastes, as groups, raising their relative status in the holy scheme by acquiring a little land and wealth, and bribing some disreputable Brahman to invent a mythical ancestor. That is unusual, and takes time. It is far easier to lose caste, and go hurtling down to the bottom of exile.

Race, tribe, language, occupation, and religious sect may divide one caste from another; yet groups having some or all in common may be also separate. Although likely to have hereditary work and skill, one caste may follow several occupations, or one occupation spread over several castes. The divisions seem without rhyme or reason, but a man inevitably marries within the limits of his caste, the largest of which may offer about fifteen million families from which to choose a bride, the smallest, about fifteen.

The ancient and needless miseries of caste a few enlightened Hindus are working to improve. One might expect painful customs to go at a breath of criticism, but fear habit and religion hold the ignorant. So few people in India can read and write in any language that the spread of ideas is slow. And a thin alien idea fights anæmically with a tough herd habit. Consider the courage that it takes for even a bold Western woman to wear a skirt of different length from the fashion, and one can realize how even an educated Hindu woman hesitates to defy opinion and rule. When one considers how unhappy a Western man is in dinner clothes before a certain hour, one can realize that a Hindu, who may slide over caste rules in strange countries, does not transgress in conservative places where 'it isn't done.' Add to convention the force of religious sanctity...

Modern life insists upon some compromise with convenience. Railroads, factories, cities, and universities, boy scout clubs and little bluebird girls' clubs are dissolving agents. But they influence only a few. Seventy-five per cent of the people of India live in villages, and the villages may be so remote that they are not touched by road, only by path.

To change conservative opinion in India means to change the opinion of ignorant village women — and the way to their education is thick with obstacles. They could only be taught by women teachers, and only respect those of good caste. Heretofore the tradition has been that teachers were the dregs, as nurses were in the days of Sairey Gamp. Women of good caste have to overcome great prejudice and difficulties to venture into forsaken little jungle villages. They must have a chaperon. A married woman could seldom teach unless the husband did also. And there are practically no spinsters in India. And widows have an aura of shame and are sometimes considered bad omens. So it goes round and round in circles.

Caste bursts into politics. The question of communal representation, meant by the English to give fair representation to non-Brahmans, stirs the caste Hindu. Gandhi fasted to force agreement between the Brahman and non-Brahman groups. He wants also to free untouchables of their pollution. But he does not want to do away with caste entirely: he would go back to the four great Varna of Vedic days. Other learned Hindus believe in keeping caste entirely sacred. Certain reformers see its grave ills, but feel that to remove society from its containers would be like taking the shell from a shellfish, that it has had a definite function in holding civilization firm. A few would clear out caste completely. These have to stop the merry-go-round of cause and effect.

How did this system solidify to such permanence that reformers from within and cutthroat conquerors from without hardly made it quiver? There have been Hindu reformers in many centuries who defied the system, and declared that all men were equal — and their followers were engulfed as subcastes of Hindus again. There have been plenty of Moslem conquerors who offered a casteless religion at the sharp edge of the sword — in fact, tied people in sacks and dropped them midstream when they refused it. There have been persuading, hospital-bringing, school-teaching Christian missionaries. But the firm jelly of caste hardly shivers. The age of machines is the latest solvent, but still no one knows the answer.

Perhaps there is an emanation from the soil of India that affects everyone.

Not only Hindus in India separate. The Mohammedans, all equal under Allah, tend to stratify. Converted Christians keep the rudiments of caste. The English, accurately numbered according to rank, stay neatly within their proper groups, and the visiting foreigner cleaves to his kind. Even the chauffeur on the front seat realizes his state and has a menial to open the radiator cap; while the menial, in turn, finds a lesser menial to fetch water from the brook. It is in the soil.

Caste, the enigma to the alien, begins to be understood when one imagines two things — the India at which the lawgivers were looking, and the sacredness which their view acquired.

The Brahman priests, more than two thousand years ago, were brilliantly imaginative. They observed people in various stages of tribal development, and they imagined the reasons, and working from both fact and fancy, made laws into which they fitted everyone.

The geographical and racial and economic facts which these priests saw in specimen places in India were not unlike conditions in many countries and many stages of social advance. There are resemblances to phases and times in Egypt, Greece, Rome, Jerusalem and mediæval Europe. But from similar phases or details, no other country developed a rigid and lasting caste system. The inner causes of religious imagination of the priests and people of India were the unique factors.

To begin with the causes of fact — the life as the Brahmans saw it several centuries before Christ.

They knew the life of villages, groups of huts inside a stockade, with rice-fields and patches of grain near-by, and the village grove beyond which the herdsman tended their cattle. Beyond that was the 'great wood' — uncleared jungle that spread wide and threatened the venturer with dangers of beasts, brigands, or spirits; beyond that the thousands of miles of unknown, mysterious India where the next-door kingdom was strange. Threading through the forests were trails for caravans, working their way to river or sea, piloted by a professional land steersman who guided by stars in the cool of night across deserts.

The land, even on the plains, must be so broken by the dense forests, and by rivers that had no bridges, that even people of similar stock would get isolated in pockets, and develop their local ways and prejudices, and look at their former tribesmen askance when they met. Recognized customs of one part of the country were not good usage elsewhere. In the south, one ate with one's wife, elsewhere forbidden. In the north, one might deal in arms, drink rum, and sell animals with teeth in upper and lower jaws — practices that other places might consider sin.

One village tended to develop an art or craft. There were villages of woodwrights, and villages of ironsmiths, and villages of potters. And as towns grew, the trades would localize in certain streets, the quarter of the ivory workers, the dyers, or the weavers. Many of the trades became hereditary, and the tradesman took the name of the craft — as Smith and Smithson. There were instances of villages of Brahmans, and there was a robber village up in the hills. The trades developed a certain number of guilds, with their headmen. And some trades, such as hunting, fishing, butchering, tanning, dancing, acting, snake-charming, and music, came to be considered undesirable socially. The localization and inheritance of trades tended to the origin of the occupational caste, which theoretically follows the craft of ancestors. But the same phase of industry in Europe made only trade guilds, which were not exclusively hereditary, since they allowed their members to marry beyond the group or admitted skilled outsiders. Trade guilds were not castes.

Occupations were only one origin. Tribes were another. There are many customs, usual in tribal development in all parts of the world, which were carried over into caste. This is the time to remember the aborigines and their totems and tabus. Though even a widespread and detailed study today might show only fragments and isolated survivals from totemism, and though no one can make the exact link in ancient days between a totem clan and a caste, there are suggestive resemblances: in marriage laws, the insistence upon marriage outside a certain circle; and in various curious usages about food.

Things tabu to savages, which categorically must not be touched, might be considered dangerous either because too unclean or too holy — a newborn child, or the water in which a holy person had washed. Kings might be tabu because powerful, or scavengers because unclean. A polluted thing pollutes the person who touches it. The lawgivers looking out upon the tribes of India would notice the prevailing customs that they saw, even though they offered their own explanation.

Another system which the lawgivers saw was the worship of ancestors. The dead spirits needed feeding. They might wander restlessly, they might cause sickness if not fed. In time it was believed they had power to help their descendants. The service to them was very important, for if not meticulously carried out, the ancestors might fall from Heaven, and the whole family be destroyed. Because of ancestor worship, the patriarchal type of family grew strong. The father was the priest, and he in turn must beget a son to carry on the rites to save himself and them.

If the tribes who touched, as they shifted and moved over India, had been fairly alike, they would probably have mingled gradually. But the invading Aryan race was sharply different from the aborigines. The range in mental ability must have been enormous. A cultivated Brahman, able to memorize most of his ancestral literature and to compose more in meticulous verse, the graceful adviser of kings, would have little in common with a tufty-haired savage who smelled of rotten meat and smoke and sweat and who could not get beyond his stone age. The Brahman, seeing this, visualized society as a ladder, and naturally he put himself at the top and worked out a scheme of society which placed every man in a different position. It might be done quite rationally according to man's innate ability and function as a specialist. But not having psychological tests available, the Brahman was forced to do it by his intuition and by metaphor.

He had that important source of pride — colour of the skin. Light-skinned conquerors usually hold themselves — or at least their women — aloof from the dark men. But the fair invaders were likely to capture the enemy women in raids and find charm in the brown skins. Conquerors took wives from the conquered, but would not let their daughters take husbands; from the feeling that a man might marry below him, but a woman should marry above.

The offspring of mixed marriages were accepted by neither black nor white, but formed their own social group, like the present Anglo-Indians in India, or the mulattoes in America. Each later race that invaded India added a pure stock and a supply of half-breeds to the Indian mixture. Men proud of their race made rather terrified rules to maintain its purity.

In other countries different races, religions, and trade guilds blended in time into a single political unity, a nation, in which people mixed fairly freely, with only the barriers of snobbishness and taste. But in India the nation never formed or won loyalty. Each sharply separate group hugged its own as a matter of religious safety, rooted in its particular past.

What setting fluid held these self-sustaining units apart for two thousand years? What stabilized the mass of priestly law? How did it happen that the kings of India, in spite of strutting and striding, chariots and umbrellas and war elephants, had no voice in Hindu lawmaking and little effect on the social life of the country, while priests prescribed the simplest detail of life to the greatest?

One reason was the early weakness of kings, compared to the

enormous thing which was India — the rivalry and jealousy of tribes and chieftains, so busy defending themselves or going out to carve up a neighbour that warfare could be their only function. Kings had to be fighters and punishers, and the classifying mind of India held them to their rôle. The masses were ignorant and unconcerned. As kingdoms grew larger, a sudden collapse of dynasty might leave a wide area in chaos. Then the future of the humble people was all question marks, and the only solidity lay in the teachings of the Brahmans, who were not at the mercy of the outcome of battles. The personal laws of the Hindus, bound up with caste, took no account of the limits of all the states into which India was from time to time resplitting. The good Hindu gave his allegiance primarily to the caste laws defined by the priests, secondarily to the king. The result was that in spite of an incoherent and unstable political rule in India, the social government was steady.

Priestly lawgiving is a stage which many societies have discarded. But in India today it is a strong influence on the lives of two hundred million Hindus. Does the great heat make the effort of change too intolerable, or the long centuries of acceptance? The very fact that India was brilliant so much earlier than other present nations, precocious in the days of miracles and marvels, may have made the habit of credulity strong, before the cold blasts of scepticism blew. A superior and brilliant effort of an early civilization to govern its ways lasted as a firm container.

One reason for the persistence of priestly law was the belief in India that this life is only a trivial link in the long, long chain of existences; this earth only an illusion — Maya — a capricious, shifting covering over the real. Earthly laws cannot compete with the laws of eternity. Value lies only in escape from the illusion of human life, to unity with the inner truth, sometimes called God.

So the priests, as guides in the labyrinthian ways to such reality, had the prestige of eternity on their side. It took imagination to ignore the present and focus on the ultimate, but the Indian mind could do it. It may also have taken a profound unhappiness, a dread of life pressing in about one, a wish to escape. However it was, if the world was a mere featherweight, an unfortunate dribble of illusion, the comings and goings of kings would be chancey and immaterial compared to the laws of the Brahmans. The priests knew by magic, by ritual, by all the reservoirs of tradition and philosophy, how to benefit a man's soul in its lengthy journey through reincarnations.

That their methods mingle hokus-pokus with brilliant intuition does not matter. Magic was time-honoured, mythology was branching and flowering, the birth-rate of the gods was high. All came under the regulation of the Brahmans. Their authority went back to the Vedas. To accept the authority of the Vedas was to be a Hindu.

Kings could not alter the absolute, unchangeable laws of these codes. Their duty was to maintain them, to punish lapses, and prevent that unthinkable thing, mixture of castes. Kings themselves — even the gods — had to obey. The masses were held docile by the threat of twenty-one hells, or rebirth in the womb of lower animals or barbarians.

The legal literature began about 600 B.C. with the Sutras, handbooks of priestly rites and sacrifice. Later these local books included recipes for household magic, the villager's guide to the gods and spirits about his door, and the careful definition of what food to offer, and where, to such beings as Rudra, the Earth, Space, Love, and Wrath, and how to avert the dog-demon of epilepsy, and what rites to perform from conception to burial. Later than the Sutras, the Dharma-shastras (laws of duty) broadened the scope. Of these books of duty, the most famous is the great code of Manu, written somewhere probably between the second century B.C. and the second century A.D. Manu included the religious ceremonies for each stage of life, the daily duties, the magic and metaphysics, along with a body of real legal matter, the actual trial-and-error laws of trade, and punishments for crime, all fitted into the early rudimentary system of caste. After Manu, other law books clarified and developed his teachings. But the later writers were too reverent to be original or rebellious. As Manu stood, in the main, Hinduism has stood.

It has stood, rooted in poetry — the two great metaphors at the basis of Manu's law, the theory of the four Varnas, and the theory of purity and pollution.

The Varna theory is one of the neatest rationalizations of racial pride — like the recent 'white man's burden.' It was so parallel to reason that it was easy to maintain. This is the way Manu puts the theory of the Varnas:

> He, the resplendent, assigned separate duties to those who sprang from the mouth, arms, thighs and feet [of God].
>
> 1. To Brahmans — teaching and studying Veda, sacrificing for themselves and others, giving and accepting laws.
> 2. To Kshatriya [warriors and kings] — to protect people, bestow gifts, offer sacrifice, study Veda, abstain from sensual pleasure.
> 3. To Vaisya — to tend cattle, bestow gifts, offer sacrifices, study Veda, trade, lend money, cultivate land.
> 4. One occupation only the Lord prescribed to the Sudras — to serve meekly even these other three castes.

Although this mighty idea of the four Varnas never seems to have fitted exactly the fissures of society, it might just as well have, for people believed it. The real unit, however, was much smaller —

the 'jati' or what is now called caste and subcaste. There were only about fifty such in the time of Manu, but everybody believed himself descended either from a head or feet or thighs, and thought well or ill of himself according to the physiology of his origin.

Since the body was scaled as pure or impure, beginning pollutedly at the feet and working up to purity toward the head, a man who thought he came from the feet would have a desperate inferiority complex, stultifying to energy. A man born to serve meekly would not consider himself concerned in the state. A Magna Carta would not thrust up in due season. The theories help to explain the historical reality: that in India a despot, benevolent or otherwise, yielded only to another despot, or chaos.

The Varna idea assumed that every human being, not merely in India, had his special rank in the system. Hindus took it for granted that everyone in the world belonged to their religion, that it was the only one, and eternal. When foreigners came into India, the Hindus gave them their rating. They thought the Greeks, keen fighters and a ruling race, must be Kshatriyas. But, since Greeks ignored the ceremonies for the twice-born, their fathers must have married Sudra women, and thus mixed their caste and lost standing. When any strange tribe was willing to take on Hindu religion and rite, it was admitted as a new caste, a half or a third up the ladder, according to its quality. Of course the savage tribes, and people whose habits or trades were considered filthy, were left as outcaste and untouchable. Foreigners who did not adopt Hindu rites were called Mlechchas — barbarians — and had the status of outcaste, the position held, to the orthodox mind, by English and Americans today.

According to its place in the scale, each person, and even each animal and thing, was believed to have an unchangeable duty, called *dharma.* Even minerals had their dharma. That of gold was yellowness and brightness; that of stone, was weight. The dharma of a tiger was fierceness. A tiger was quite within his rights and functions when he pounced on cattle and men. But the dharma of man was to abstain from injuring creatures, to be truthful, not to steal, to be pure. That was the general human law. Besides that, each person had his particular dharma according to sex, age, and caste; as king or subject; and if twice-born, as student, family man, or forest recluse. The dharma differed for girl, wife or widow. Each family group had its own. The caste had its laws, usually administered by their own council. The whole evolution of life was visualized in the caste system, from minerals to man — a magnificent conception, except that it was arbitrary and stiff as glass.

In criminal law, the punishments grew more severe for the lower orders. When a king told a witness to speak the truth, he was advised to assume that honesty varied with caste. To a Brahman he should say, 'Speak.' To a Kshatriya, 'Speak the truth.' To a Vaisya, 'Speak the truth by your kine and gold'; but to a Sudra, 'Speak the truth or you will be held guilty of every crime.' A Kshatriya only paid fifty coins for defaming a Brahman, whereas a Vaisya paid one hundred and fifty, and a Sudra was beaten. But a Brahman could say what he pleased about a knight, and pay only fifty coins, and twenty-five for a commoner, and twelve for a servant.

It distinctly paid to be a Brahman. He had immunity from the death penalty, though he committed all possible crimes; whereas a man of low caste who merely insulted a twice-born could have his tongue cut out. And if he swore, in the usual way of the East, 'mentioning the names and birth of a twice-born with contumely,' an iron nail ten inches long could be thrust down his throat. The pretensions of the Brahmans ran so high that Manu makes this statement: 'The Brahman is born to fulfil dharma... whatever exists in the world is the property of the Brahman... he is entitled to all... he eats but his own food, wears but his own apparel. Other mortals subsist through the benevolence of Brahmans. Let a Brahman be ignorant or learned, still he is a great deity.' To a Brahman, it is said, the three worlds and the gods owe their existence, for without the sacrifices of the Brahmans, the demons might get power to overthrow the gods.

The second enormous religious theory that held all castes to their predestined places — a not uncommon sort of theory in tribal development — was the idea of purity and pollution. Everything in the world was classified as either pure or impure. The holiness scale was applied to places, things and animals as well as to people. Castes were ranked according to the difficulty of their laws of purity; for oh, how easily it could be soiled.

Pure castes were as delicate as new white linen, and the impure people and places and things as smudging as soft-coal smoke. Fortunately there was a third class of substances or agencies which were considered purifying, so that after the smirching the pure man could be recleaned by bathing in the sacred rivers, by control of the mind, by performing the rites, and by reading the Vedas.

Purity had no relation to goodness or morality, any more than to actual cleanliness. It was poetry, a figure of speech, tabu. The most meticulous man became impure after a death in the family, by the touch of a Sudra on his food, by travel into an outlying country. 'He sins in his feet who visits the Kalingas.'

Hunger and sex were carefully regulated by endless purity laws which grew stricter and more varied with time. To this day, castes are considered good in proportion to the arduousness of keeping their own laws of food and marriage.

Food, as a carrier of pollution, scales their difficulty. Just as milk, on the way from cow to consumer, may be touched by germs that grow and multiply out of all reason, so any pure food, by Brahmanical ideas, could get a mental or theoretical pollution, as injurious to the soul as diphtheria to the body. To show how hair-splitting the idea grew, consider the present evaluations. If caste A is polluted by food cooked by caste B, but caste B can eat food cooked by caste A, caste A is superior. The test of a clean caste in Bengal, for example, and elsewhere, is whether a Brahman will accept water from that caste.

If the Brahman will accept food cooked in oil, the caste is better still, and if he will go so far as to accept food cooked in water, that caste is very clean indeed. The practical difficulties of living today by such rules are enormous, and if followed without exception and without the fortunate devices of atonement and purification, would limit a man of good caste to a small circle of human contact. By their own momentum such laws have increased in meticulousness through the years. The purity rules are more detailed and limiting now than in the time of Manu. But they must make some compromise and readjustment to the present anachronistic day.

The impure castes have also their downward scale of smudginess. Untouchables have definite varying spheres of dirty influence. The sort of substance a man can pollute determines his offensiveness. He is not quite so potent if he defiles only water as if he can affect an earthen vessel or the still harder brass bowl. He is worse if he can harm the courtyard of a temple. In recent years there has been the curious and rather terrible anomaly — an organized group of outcastes, following strike methods, 'picketing' a Hindu temple, in order to be allowed inside: feeling the tragedy of denial of the rites to save their souls, but denying the validity of the same laws which made them outcaste. The orthodox Hindu group put up barbed wire to keep them out, so that the temple would not be ruined past all but very expensive repurifying.

The metaphorically filthiest people are those with ability to pollute a whole town if they live in it, and who therefore are compelled to live outside the limits. In the south there was the problem of access to wells for such people. They could not get water from the wells of the pure castes, and British administration had to see that they were in some way served. That line, between unclean and clean, also complicates the gargantuan problem of education for the masses; separate schools for girls, for boys, and then for clean and unclean.

In the time of Manu the rules about marriage and touching and eating were neither so elaborate nor so rigid, but the sturdy beginnings were there. People of different jati then were not obliged to eat apart, but the rules given for a Brahman's selection of food show the purity idea in its fertile minutiæ. Imagine having to consider all these things:

'A Kandala, a village pig, a cock, a dog... must not look at Brahmanas while they eat... nor a lame man, a one-eyed man, or a man lacking a limb.' A Brahman recluse must not eat food given by the 'intoxicated, angry, sick... that in which hair or insects are found ... nor that at which the slayer of a learned Brahman has looked... nor food a bird has pecked nor a cow smelt... nor food given by a thief, a carpenter, a usurer, a miser, a hermaphrodite, an unchaste woman or a hypocrite... a physician, a hunter, a cruel man... nor by a female with no male relatives, nor by an enemy, nor by the lord of the town, nor by outcastes, nor that on which someone has sneezed... nor by an actor, a tailor, an ungrateful man, a blacksmith, a trainer of hunting dogs... a washerman, a dyer, a man whose wife has a paramour'... (Excuse me, sir, but before I accept this food — has your wife a paramour?)... 'Or one who is ruled by his women. The food of a king impairs his vigor... the food of a Sudra his excellence in learning... the food of a physician is vile as pus.' If a man eats food given him by a doctor, he must then fast three days to purify himself.

It was a constant, steady task for the twice-born man to keep himself pure, for the daily acts of life polluted him. 'A householder has five slaughter-houses — hearth, grinding-stone, the broom, the pestle and mortar, the water vessel — by using which he is bound' (with the fetters of sin). To atone for his daily sins, the sages prescribed for him the five daily sacrifices. Every day he should worship the sages by the recitation of the Vedas, the gods by burnt oblations, the spirits of the dead by funeral sacrifices with food, water, milk, roots, and fruits, mankind by gifts of food to Brahmans, and the Bhuts by a bali offering, a bit of food thrown at a designated spot. The religious, expiating rites for a Brahman took him practically all his time. In a modern manual for a certain Brahman sect, the editor remarks that formerly it was considered enough for a man to devote an hour and a half a day to earning the family living. The rest of the time he went through his religious routine. Now a Brahman must often work five or six hours earning a living, and make mental substitutes for the noontime bath, and other compromises. But the ancient ideal is still held up for those who can follow it. 'He who performs these is not tainted,' says Manu. But 'He who does not feed these five — gods, guests, dependents, manes and himself — lives not, though he breathes.'

From conception to burial, a series of careful ceremonies marked and still marks the path of the twice-born through life. Before the navel string was cut, a newborn boy should be fed with honey and butter and gold. Each little event of childhood, first steps, first eating of rice, first walking out, first shaving of the head, had its religious ritual. The most important was that of initiation into caste on reaching manhood. There was a definite period within which this must be done. If a man were not given the sacrament within the properly appointed time, he lost caste — was dropped out into the abyss, perhaps alighting in some dubious caste far down the scale, certainly being ostracized by his own. His right to caste meant his right to marriage, to dining and convivial life, possibly to trade, and even to such silly but necessary things as the services of the caste washerman and barber. (Shaving and the paring of toe nails take on a significance, and social prestige. If a caste barber will pare the toe nails, that caste is better than one with a barber who does not.) In any event, exile from the caste was a mental St. Helena. 'With such,' says Manu, 'let no Brahman, even in time of distress, form connection.'

Man's life was divided into periods. As a youth he must be a student of the Vedas. The number of years he studied depended on his Varna. Then, as a householder, his duty was to beget sons and offer the daily sacrifices. Finally, when his hair was white and his skin wrinkled, he should take to the forest as recluse (with or without his wife) and fix his mind on the attainment of final liberation. 'Worlds, brilliant in radiance become his position if he gives promise of safety to all created beings. He must not desire to die, not desire to live — patiently bear hard words, insult no one, bless when he is cursed, delight in what refers to the soul, sit in postures prescribed by Yoga, abstain from sensual enjoyments.... His hair, beard and nails being clipped, carrying an alms bowl and a staff, he must continually wander about, controlling himself....'

The daily rules of ritual were inconvenient, perhaps, but seldom tragic. They gave a rhythm of habit to the days, and freed a man from planning and decisions. Unless they lessened initiative, they were without deforming effect on the race. But when the purity idea in all its extravagance and distance from reality became a factor in marriage (even if only one of the factors), it had in it the promise of misery for untold little terrified Indian girls and the undersized babies they produced, a promise of weakening the human muscles of the country, skimping the force of the minds.

The hyperbolic Brahmanical idea of purity was that, marriage being an eternal thing, a woman must never love another man but her husband. If before her marriage she had wafted the faintest affection, the vaguest day-dreams toward another man than the selected husband, she was not theoretically pure. Therefore, it was wise to marry her before her imagination wandered, or, as Manu put it, before she was old enough to wear clothes. In the extreme interpretation of the 'ahimsa' doctrine — that one must hurt nothing living, not even a twig — the idea came that it was as bad as abortion not to give a girl a chance to bear a child at the earliest possible time. Manu suggests these ages as proper: for a bridegroom of thirty, a wife of twelve years; for a bridegroom of twenty-four, a wife of eight. The epics give an earlier age. Sita was supposed to have married Rama at six.

Snobbishness comes into the matter somewhere. Since it was considered degrading for a family to wait until its daughters were mature before marrying them off, each farseeing family went about the business early. Frequently the supply of bridegrooms in the subcaste within which a girl might marry was so limited that, as in Western countries parents enter their children on the lists of a school in infancy, prudent Hindus entered the baby girls for matrimony.

Manu's laws of intermarriage were not so strict as today's. But a most important rule of Manu, which came down from tribal days and came up to the present in certain castes, especially in Bengal, is the law that a woman must marry her superior. Such a marriage is 'with the hair'—it rubs the fur the right way. The marriage of a woman to an inferior man is 'against the hair,' and the children of such marriages are socially penalized. The ancient conquering man took the captured woman, but would not give his daughter to the defeated. The modern connection is in the Bengal castes, the notorious instance being the Kulin Brahmans, where the supply of bridegrooms from a superior sept of the caste was so limited that the sought-after men married a whole series of wives at once, and haughtily accepted a fat sum of money for each.

Imagine parents, whose desire for sons has only brought on a number of daughters, who absolutely must marry these daughters into one certain limited group of men that happens to be too few for all the eligible girls—parents with no means to compete in dowries—what are they to do? They are helpless. An impossibility is absolutely decreed for them. In this *impasse*, the one solution seemed to many pious families to kill the extra girl babies. Baby girls have been killed in many parts of the world where patriarchal families prevailed. The custom from ancient times had its instances in India in the last century—maybe there are weirs and hedges now that could tell a tale of desperation.

The strong reason for forcing immature girls into child-bearing was, and is, the religious belief, widespread among patriarchal, simple people and terrible in its insistence, that only a son can save the soul of his father and ancestors by performing the proper ceremonies. The man without a son is doomed. The ancestors will drop from Heaven and the whole family will be ruined. Woman is only important, to Manu and to most of India still, as the mother of sons who can in turn become the priests of the family. As a girl, as a barren wife, as a widow, she is a total loss—the fruit of sins in a past life, her own punishment.

Savage tabus fastened themselves upon her. She became unclean and defiling when pregnant and in childbirth, and the terrible present habit of allowing only filthy outcastes to tend the birth of children has such ancestry. Babies die and women suffer in India today, and reformers are powerless to help. Blood was tabu to savages.

Manu's laws about women were contradictory. They were all classed with Sudras — excluded from hearing the Vedas. They were allowed no initiative. 'Nothing must be done independently by woman,' said Manu, 'not even in her own house. In childhood, she is subject to her father, in youth to her husband, at his death, to her sons. A woman must never be independent.'

A few pleasant things were said in the law codes. Sometimes woman was praised as equal to the father in honour. In one place it was ruled that in default of sons, she might inherit her husband's property. Women were not yet forced to live in purdah, hidden from sight. Although there is mention of some high-caste 'guarded women,' Manu thought there was not much use in it. However, within the home he prescribed virtues that probably had their influence in making Indian women the loving and devoted creatures they are today. In fact, to an outsider, the half measures that have been meted out to women, the denial, seems to have made them better specimens than their lavishly indulged lords. Manu told them always to be 'cheerful, clever in household affairs, careful in cleaning utensils, and economical in expenditure.' And on festivals and holidays men should honour them with ornaments, clothes, and food, though that had an ulterior motive. 'If a wife is not radiant with beauty, she will not attract her husband... no children will be born.'

A wife bore all the burden of marriage companionship. 'If she desires to dwell after death with her husband, she must never displease him, whether dead or alive...' she must abjectly obey him. 'Though destitute of virtue and seeking pleasure [elsewhere] or devoid of good qualities, a husband must be constantly worshipped as a god by a faithful wife.' But she had not equal liberties: 'a virtuous wife who remains chaste reaches Heaven, though she have no son. But if a woman has children by another man, she brings disgrace on herself, and loses her place in Heaven.' 'By violating her duty toward her husband, she enters the womb of a jackal, and is tormented by the punishment of her sin.' The poor jackals howling in the cold, skulking about camps, slovenly creatures of the night, are simply the souls of undutiful wives.

Her husband could divorce her if she had no children, or only daughters. He could even slay her for unfaithfulness. But she must be faithful to him even as a widow. 'Nor is a second husband anywhere prescribed for virtuous women.' Widows were not absolutely forbidden to remarry then. The practice of suttee, on her husband's funeral pyre, was not advocated. That primitive custom was temporarily in abeyance, and gained power later through the ideal of pure devotion. But widows probably lived miserably as objects of scorn, as they do now. For if family and friends believed that her guilt in a former life killed her husband, why should they not punish?

Woman was also the temptress. The idea of sex susceptibility in one passage is so exaggerated that it seems easily the soil for the later unhealthy seclusion of half the population. Even without the invading Mohammedans, with their own curtained wives and their violent attacks, women seem doomed to distortion. Manu says: 'It is the nature of women to seduce men in this world. For that reason the wise are never unguarded in the company of females. For women are able to lead astray not only a fool, but even a learned man, to make him a slave of desire and anger. One should not sit in a lonely place with one's mother, sister or daughter, for the senses are powerful, and master even a learned man.' The tropics were powerful over the senses. Women could not escape. Even the gods had to emphasize passion. Purdah might be foreseen.

The idea of woman's purity helped hold the caste system firm. Marriages were made for girls so early that romantic love was not given its head. So long as sober elders, thinking only of the family souls and social prestige, married off passive children, they could easily keep marriages within caste and the laws of their small group as sacred and definite solidities.

In the course of time, castes did not combine, but split to more and more minute divisions. Today the process goes on. Part of a caste grows prosperous and educated, and gradually eases away from the inferior members, and defines laws of eating and marriage that separate them as a new subcaste.

Even when a Hindu reformer tries to free his followers from the system, the story is that he simply succeeds in creating another caste. There were the Lingayats, founded in the twelfth century by a rebel who declared that all men were created equal and tried to abolish Hindu purity rules. His boldness succeeded merely in separating his followers into a caste called *Lingayats.* And at a recent census their representatives petitioned the Government of India against the 'most offensive and mischievous order' of the census takers, who had lumped them under one caste instead of under their superior and inferior subcastes. In 1901, the million and a half Lingayats had seventy-one subcastes, as mutually exclusive as Brahman subcastes. India does not like reforms.

But the final setting fluid, the fire that hardened the soft clay, so that things which gradually crumbled in other lands remain firm in India, so that her society instead of fusing chemically remained a mechanically divided thing, was the idea of Karma — the retribution or justice which is pursuing each individual through his centuries or eons of incarnations, meticulous effect from causes in other lives. Man's place in this life is the exact sum total of his acts in former incarnations. It is not a thing which he can improve in this existence. But he can waste his slippery attainments by polluting himself.

The certainty that the only way to improve future lives is to obey exactly the laws of the Brahmans holds caste steady. The certainty that his past acts have determined his present fate makes a man accept the lot to which he is born, though it be that of a sweeper of refuse and a human drainpipe — he thinks he cannot and should not attempt a finer life. He can refrain from defiling his betters. And his betters can refrain from being polluted. That is the great thing to be hoped.

3. *Buddha, the Dissenter from Hinduism*

563 B.C. — 483 B.C.

A THINKER arose who stands isolated. He derived from those Brahman schools of philosophers who were thinking boldly and freely in the sixth century B.C. He was born before the great lawgivers. But he was to their thought a heretic and a rebel.

The contemplating Buddha figure, so tiny, carved from brass, that he can be held in the hand; so enormous and enduring, carved from grey rock, that he outlives the temple to house him; tall wooden Buddhas overlaid thick with gold leaf; Buddha in porcelain, Buddha jewelled, the Buddha figure throughout the Orient from India, Burma, Ceylon, Java, Siam, China, Japan, epitomizes the East to the Westerner. Yet so dimly does the story live, to the usual traveller, that he may think, vaguely, that Buddha never walked the earth except in elaborate myth, or that Buddha is the Eastern name for God.

In India his religion has long since faded away. Near Darjeeling a few prayer flags may flutter at the four corners of some Buddhist shrine; or an old man from Tibet may walk through the Sunday market swinging a prayer wheel intently, bringing his depraved version of Buddhism over the Chinese border. At Sarnath, near the remains of a monastery, a solitary woman pilgrim is bumping her head before his image. But not until one reaches Ceylon or Burma do the yellow robes of the Buddhist monks become predominant or important, or the teachings of Gautama Buddha have vitality.

Yet the carvings are left in India from the days when his worship was dominant and powerful, when monks hacked caves in the living rocks of hills for monasteries. The innermost figure of the cave was Buddha, guarded by four giant stone watchmen. At Ajanta, early Ellora, Karli, and Bagh, the deep caves hold all that the monks found precious, focussed in that silent form. Over the lintels the sculptor may carve gay little inconsequential gods and lovers, mingled with wreaths and flowers — but the austere Buddha dominates all.

The face varies with the locality and the racial type. Yet nearly always it has strength, and a great sweetness like a bloom from inner power. The sculptor often suggests the perfect balance of the long-held pose, the breath expanding the back of the figure. The face is seldom stereotyped into insignificance. One may sit in the long upper hall of the three-storied cave at Ellora, with its rows of haloed Buddhas under trees or umbrellas, or before the great Gupta Buddha in the Sarnath Museum, and feel rebuked. Anything less than the best in an individual, these calm faces seem to reject.

Most Buddha figures in India are the work of monks, made first in the Greek-influenced northwest from about 100 B.C. and over a wider area until A.D. 600 or 700. Before that time, he was expressed only by symbols — carved footprints, stupas, the royal umbrella, the wheel, and the sacred bo-tree. After those centuries his worship was crowded from India.

His sayings were carried in memory for more than two hundred years after his death, when the Emperor Asoka convoked a council of Buddhist monks, who wrote, in the Pali language, their oral traditions. They conceived of a man relentlessly thinking, greatly pitying, who took humanity's troubles upon him, and found a wisdom for living. But even this earliest record was so embedded in marvel and myth that scholars still work to separate history from symbolic legend. Later Sanskrit writings grew more and more marvellous, elaborating ancient traditions of a Great King, and a Wise Man (Arhat) of many incarnations, and fusing many symbols of sun-worship around the Buddha, turned into god. Some scholars claim that Buddha was only a re-embodiment of a sun myth, while others think that the great man arose and myths that were in the air clustered about him, like mists to a mountain. This is his story.

Gautama Buddha was like Christ in gentleness and loving-kindness, but there was striking difference between their earthly lives. Buddha was not bred to barest poverty and scorn. He was a young aristocrat, son of the ruler of an upstanding country, a bejewelled young lordling, an athlete, a lover. Starting from opposite worldly experience, Christ and Buddha meet at the same centre — a fine misprizing of all material things and high valuation of the spirit of man.

Siddartha, the future Buddha, was born possibly about 563 B.C., of the family Gautama and the clan of Sakyas, in the city Kappilavasthu, about one hundred and fifty miles northwest of Benares. His father, of the Kshatriya caste, was chief of the Sakyas. India then was grouping into larger states. But among the despotic kingdoms there were fifteen small republics. The land of the Sakyas was one, and Siddartha's father its elected Rajah. He sat in the mote hall of the clan assembly, under a roof supported by carved pillars, open to green air and winds, and presided over the gathering of his people. So much may be historic; then the legends begin.

His father had been childless for many years. To be without a son meant that one's immortal soul was adrift. So when his wife, who was forty-five years old, was about to give birth to a child, the event made an easy nucleus for wonder stories. She was walking toward her father's house and stopped to rest, standing with one hand on a tree in the Lumbini Gardens, when the wonderful child was born. Presumably a lotus did not spring up at each step that he took, but that was one way that people felt about him. Siddartha's mother lived only briefly, leaving the child to the care of her sister.

If beauty plays a part in determining thought, Siddartha had his share of its influence. The land of the Sakyas included part of the present Nepal, in the lower slopes of the Himalayas. The foothills were thick folds of jungly peaks, rich with rainfall, where the tree ferns grow tall as palms, and heavy vines drip down from the matted forests and great leaves are pendant. The air grows keen toward the hills. Far up in the sky, above any conceivable base to the earth, hangs the line of the snow peaks, as inaccessible as clouds — a noble landscape on a scale for giants.

Legend tells that a wise man prophesied that Siddartha would be surpassingly great: if he stayed at home, as universal earthly monarch; or, if he led a houseless life, as fully enlightened Buddha. And his father, the warrior chief, preferred to have him a conqueror who would annex many neighbouring states. To that end, he tried to bind him to the world. He married him to a delicious little princess, and gave him a harem of the loveliest girls of the tribe. At each apparent uneasiness of his heir, who seemed given to brooding, he devised a new allurement of music and delight. Siddartha was the most sheltered child of story.

> I was tenderly cared for, monks, supremely so, infinitely so. At my father's home lotus pools were made for me; in one place for blue lotus flowers, in one place for white lotus flowers, and in one place for red lotus flowers, blossoming for my sake. And, monks, I used only unguents from Benares. Of Benares fabric were my three robes. Day and night a white umbrella was held over me, so that I might not be troubled by cold, heat, dust, chaff, or dew. I dwelt in three palaces, monks; in one for cold, in one for summer, and in one for the rainy season. When in the palace for the rainy season, surrounded during the four months by female musicians, I did not go down from the palace.

But luxury could not dull the spark of his mind. He began to ponder the oppressing sadness of old age. One day, pious legend continues, when Siddartha rode forth from his palace in his chariot, the royal umbrella held over his head, through lanes of rich houses and streets that were supposed to be cleared, by his father's orders, of unpleasing sights, he saw a beggar, a grovelling creature in rags, whose bones stuck through his skin. Siddartha went home, shocked by his first sight of poverty.

Still another day he rode forth, and this time, among crowds of holiday people, he saw a man wasted by a horrible disease. For the first time he knew that there existed in the world deforming sickness.

On the third riding-forth he saw, for the first time, a corpse.

Poverty, pain, and death. These he saw were to be reckoned with in life.

On the fourth riding-forth he saw an ascetic at his contemplation, and believed that here was a strength to conquer the miseries of the world.

Siddartha was acutely sensitive to want and suffering. There was no lack in his life, but he was haunted by the misery that men must endure. Somewhere there must be an answer; one must find the door through that wall of terror. Old age and pain and death. He felt he must give his life to find some way for mankind.

Siddartha's home was flashing with dancing girls and the prettiest little beauties of the country, clinking anklets over the floor. Music was played to him, and highly flavoured foods were served obsequiously. But his mind was tormented with pity and puzzle, and would not leave the riddle of pain. He stayed away from the sports and contests that were befitting a chief's son. Only once, stung by reproof, did he show that he could draw the heaviest bow and aim the truest. That done, he returned to his problem. He felt he must give his life to find some path for mankind. Around him it was very satisfying. The snows of the Himalayas cooled the air of his gardens. His lovely young wife bore his first child — a son. At that point, his own happiness was too full; it could chain him to a sensuous life so firmly that he would never leave its plenty; he would sink into deep content without finding the answer for the pain of mankind.

While the palace was silent at night and the dancing women sprawled in the abandon of sleep, he went to the chamber where his wife lay with the newborn child — and did not dare take him in his arms for good-bye. He rode away into the forest where the jackals were wailing and tigers padded. His groom begged to go with him, to be his disciple. But Siddartha sent him home to explain his absence. Meeting a poor huntsman, he exchanged clothes with him, giving away his finery and jewels, and taking his sword to cut off his long princely hair. He set out afoot through the night forest.

Maya followed him — the spirit of temptation waiting for a chink in his strength.

Siddartha walked for days and nights, and finally came southward into a valley in Maghada, surrounded by five hills, where hermits in caves meditated and discussed their philosophies. Two of the hermits, sitting cryptic and serene, accepted him as disciple, to study Hindu philosophy, to find the answer to pain and sorrow. At this point his story begins to tie to real places and people.

The hermits taught Siddartha the causal chain of reincarnation.

All these varied shapes and sizes into which one may be born and suffer grief were unreal, a mirage of life, yet endless. But a man might practise certain rites and austerities or attain a certain kind of knowledge, and thereby break the chain of incarnations, destroy his wandering shadow identities, and reunite himself to the True, the Great Soul, the fertile underlying Spirit.

The longing to escape life on this earth came to the hill-bred Aryan after he had lived centuries in the oppressing heat of the Ganges Valley. Some thought of the mastered Dravidians may have subdued him. At any rate, melancholy hung, widespread, over Siddartha's India.

Priests lighting altar fires with endless, prescribed gestures, and chants and animal sacrifices; philosophers trying to find the nature of reality; forest ascetics, starving themselves, torturing their bodies to find truth—all these were in India when Siddartha Gautama, the future Buddha, studied with the hermits in the Vindhya hills.

He was still unsatisfied when he had studied all the hermits could offer. He had not, however, tried asceticism. This powerful magic tenet of certain Brahmans was that self-denial and torture of the body could force the gods to yield their gifts. Severe and constant penance could act as a lever to pry up the world. Siddartha tried to see what could be gained by the much-vaunted method. He withdrew into a jungle near Bodh-Gaya. By this time he himself had acquired so much learning and sanctity that he had five followers. With them he began the most rigid penance. He fasted until he wasted to a shadow and his bones ribbed harshly through his torso. Trying to get near illumination, he held his thought silent, and he controlled his faint body by the strength of his will.

Such extremities of self-inflicted pain can bring the multitudes gaping. The young athlete and prince surpassed other men in the length and awfulness of his control. His fame 'spread like the sound of a great bell hung in the canopy of the skies.'

But denial of body did not bring the mental clarity he sought. The longer he fasted, the less he could find any solution for the riddle of human suffering. Nor could he think of one certainty in the universe upon which to build. And until he found one fixed and certain base, all superstructure was useless. His body grew weaker and more wasted, and he began to realize that he might only succeed in killing himself, without discovering his truth.

When he one day staggered and fell, this fear was sharpened. If his body died, of what use was it as an instrument for thinking? He was not, apparently, at all tempted, by the admiration which he had aroused, to keep his prestige as ascetic. He began to take food.

At this sign of yielding to the flesh, his disciples left him as a man. He had only his inner, self-determined search for truth to support him. He went to Benares, already the home of the philosophers, and here, too, all men believed that the way to mental clarity lay through the suppression of the body and denial of all its wants.

Gautama, now that he had found austerities valueless, saw very temptingly the good of the rich life he had given up. Now that evil Maya saw his chance. Temptation that had been waiting for a chink in Siddartha's resolution found it and came in. The old Buddhist monks personified this as the onset of Maya with his hordes of evil warriors and his troupe of honeyed women (the evil and the good things of life, by each of which he should be unmoved). When Maya attacked Gautama, monks wrote, a thousand meteors fell and clouds and darkness piled up the sky. Rivers flowed back toward their sources and mountain peaks fell crumbling to earth.

Nearly broken by his opposing thoughts, Gautama wandered to a river where a kind-hearted village girl brought him a bowl of warm, nourishing food. He sat under a bo-tree to think again. Suddenly, all the conflict of his mind was resolved: a great mild light seemed to shine over everything. The solution was clear, infinitely simple. The conquest of sorrow, he saw, depended upon no outward help. It depended upon oneself. Simple enough — but a starting-point that could not be denied. The control of one's own emotions and conduct offered salvation regardless of the World Soul, regardless of gods great or small or the tribes of demons. Selflessness and love toward others could defeat sorrow. This was his certainty, his great enlightenment.

But now he felt loneliness. Who would believe so simple a solution, in place of wild and dramatic austerities or charms and spells and mysterious propitiation of gods? He went to the deer park near Benares, where Sarnath now raises crumbling ruins, and there in the grove of the gentle, protected deer, he found his haughty five ex-disciples, who would have none of him. They could not refuse to let him sit with them, as he was of Kshatriya caste. But they felt that nothing worth listening to could come from such a renegade.

There to his haughty, doubting disciples, Buddha 'turned the wheel of the law.' The phrase has travelled all over Buddhist lands and become the subject of endless scrolls of painting. It meant to set rolling the chariot wheel of truth and righteousness to make empire over the world. This ancient figure of speech, the Buddhist wheel used as symbol in pious carvings, goes back in imagery to the sun's chariot wheel across the skies.

Siddartha Gautama, now become Buddha, sat before his five disciples, his face lighted to calm joy. The deer came up and nibbled at the shoulders of the silent men, as he preached his first sermon.

This is the gist of the sermon, upon which all later teachings were based:

> There are two extremes, monks, which he who has given up the world ought to avoid: a life given to pleasures and lusts... is degrading, sensual, vulgar, ignoble, and profitless... a life given to mortifications is painful, ignoble, and profitless. The middle path leads to insight, wisdom, calm, knowledge, supreme enlightenment, and Nirvana.

And he expounded the 'Four Noble Truths.' This was his logic in reasoning toward a means of conquering sorrow:

Birth causes growth, growth causes decay, and decay causes death. Birth has in it all the seeds of suffering.

The reason that men suffer from this decay and diminishing of life is that they care too greedily. The keener the zest in the pleasures of sense, which old age will inevitably weaken and destroy, the keener the suffering from their loss. Therefore, man must get above joy and sorrow, hope and fear, the suspense of the gambler whose stake is the pleasure of life. He must reach a calm above those waves; he must conquer his own insistent ego with his demands.

Buddha believed that by following an 'eightfold path' a man released himself from devastating passions: right belief, right feelings, right speech, right actions, right means of livelihood, right endeavour, right memory, and right meditation. And since the word 'right' may need interpreting from those distant times to ours, a very early Buddhist scripture may suggest the gentle spirit behind it: 'The Buddhist should have knowledge and purity, courtesy, uprightness, peace, and universal love, far-reaching, great, beyond measure.'

If a world could follow that!

In the cool of the evening in the deer park, Buddha the enlightened one converted his five strayed disciples. A pleasant legend tells that later he went to his home, and his forgiving wife and his small son came to hear him preach, and were converted to the doctrine of the excellent way of self-culture and self-control.

For forty-five years Buddha walked from village to village in the valley of the Ganges publishing the good news, gathering small but sincere bands of followers, and establishing his orders of monks — the first monasteries of history — to perpetuate his principles. He lived peacefully and benignly, and died peacefully and benignly in his eightieth year, surrounded by loving and nearly worshipping disciples.

Many prevalent ideas of the period, which were not Buddha's primary thesis, grew and luxuriated over his simple doctrine of self-control until they very nearly choked it. Although he did not believe in souls, he continued the doctrine of Karma — the effect on the present of past causes. Without any reincarnated souls, Karma could only continue by way of desires. A dying man, still thick with passion for this world, by the flare of his greed lights that torch in a newborn life. The sequence is only ended when an enlightened, passionless wisdom cuts the links of that particular chain. Nirvana is not extinction of life, but extinction of egoistic craving.

Buddha was rather contemptuous of doctrines of future life, and advised his followers not to dabble in metaphysics, but try to get as near to wisdom and goodness as possible in this world. 'Trouble not yourself about the gods and curiosity and desire about future existence. Search only after the fruit of the noble path of self-culture and self-control.'

How well his followers could hold to this simplicity, one may see later.

THE BUDDHA JATAKA

The austere and mild images of Buddha portray the great philosopher, renouncing desire, and thinking of eternal truth.

But simple people must bring thought to their own terms. Many non-Buddhist and anti-Buddhist legends were swept into the orbit of the enlightened teacher, and the tales are illustrated by lively little stories in stone, scattered throughout India, in museums in Peshawar, Muttra, Lahore, Calcutta, Madras, or standing outdoors on walls of early Buddhist buildings like Sanchi. They may seem perfectly meaningless to the unaccustomed eye — the small slabs of carving in high relief, crowded with little figures of animals and men and women, bobbing, bending — the episodes of the story side by side, often rather entangled and hard to search out.

These Jataka — or stories — are the art of the people: mostly much earlier than the Buddha figures made by scholarly monks. Whether they are the grey stone of the Greek-influenced Ghandara school of the northwest, or the red sandstone from the city of Barhut in the second or third century, or the lovely, later enwreathed figures carved by another race in Amaravati, they express a spirit akin to that of the carvings in choir stalls of European cathedrals, pious and devout, but very human and village-like, humorous, tender, a Gothic mood of bringing infinity down to earth and one's own village.

The Buddha stories, full of childlike marvels, are gentle and mostly unalarming, filled with sweetness and naïveté. The stories look before and after, with elaboration and wonder.

According to these tales, and the fatal thought that was choking essential Buddhism, the Gautama was only one of many Buddhas, many wise men who had attained arhatship, past and to come. He himself had also had some five hundred and fifty different births as bird or beast, king, sannyasin, tree god, preacher, scholar, monkey, goose; and in each stage he was an outstandingly noble example of his species.

As king of the monkeys near Benares, he and his whole tribe fed on a mighty mango tree. The king of Benares, with evil intent, sent his foresters to surround the tree and capture them. The isolated tree offered no escape. But the future Buddha made his body a bridge, and all his subjects ran across him to safety.

Again, Buddha was a golden stag, who magnanimously saved a drowning man by carrying him on his back across a river. The ungrateful man told the episode at court, and the royal command was sent out to capture so beautiful a beast. But when he was brought, bound in a cart, before the king and queen, he preached so eloquently and mildly to them that they were converted and gave orders that no more deer should be hunted.

At another time he was an elephant, six-tusked, the wise king of his kind. Unfortunately, one of his wives had a jealous disposition, and his mild magnanimity gave no security against that. One day, when he was shaking the boughs of a tree to drop food for his wives, it chanced that all the tender shoots and flowers and pollen dust fell to one wife, while the jealous one, as unluckily so often happens, got nothing but red ants and dead twigs. The slighted queen was so furious that she starved herself to death — which might have been rather a good thing, except for the power of the dying wish. As she died, she desired to be reborn as a beautiful queen of Benares. No sooner had that happened than she sent out her huntsmen to pursue the still living elephant husband. The huntsman hid in a pit, as one carving neatly shows, and shot his poisoned arrow up at the elephant's stomach. The sweet and forgiving animal, dying, laid himself down so that the hunter could more easily cut off his six tusks. The huntsman took them to the queen — who then died of a broken heart.

The future Buddha progressed into human form. Once he was born as a devout youth who wanted to make offering to the then present Buddha, but had no flowers. Disconsolate, he happened to meet a girl carrying six lotus buds. He asked her for five of the flowers, and she bargained that, if she gave him the lotuses, in all future births she should be his wife. The young man agreed hastily and ran to greet the Buddha. He threw the flowers into the air above the Arhat's head, and they stayed miraculously there, forming a halo. He let his long hair form a mat for the Buddha to walk on. The Dipankara Buddha was touched, and prophesied that in time the young man also would attain to enlightenment and become a Buddha. So, in his life as Siddartha Gautama, the maiden who sold him lotus flowers is Yasodhara, his lovely bride.

There is an interlude in which Buddha is born as a god, and in a serene heaven of worshippers he meditates on four things — the time, the continent, the country, and the family in which he will be born for the last time, to attain perfect enlightenment, to become at last a Buddha, and so escape the cycles of rebirth.

The place and the family are chosen, and then comes the dream of his mother, a favourite and much-repeated carving: A small elephant, proportionately as large as a rabbit, is hurtling down through space, aimed at the sleeping form of the little queen, who dreams on, with her maid crouched below her and the torch burning beside her, while the elephant comes down in his halo. So much the stone can tell. The story goes on that the queen called the palace Brahmans to interpret the dream. They told her that she would bear a son having the thirty-two marks of a great man, and that if he stayed at home he would become a powerful, universal king; but if he shaved his hair and beard, and, putting on orange robes, left home and renounced the world, he would become a perfectly enlightened Buddha.

Such a child needed a miraculous birth, which is a favourite of sculpture. The inevitable tree worship creeps in, disguised. His mother is always standing beside a Sal tree; she grasps the bough with one hand, while the wonderful child issues from her right side. The god Indra stands ready to receive him on a golden cloth, and Brahma is also patronizing the scene.

On the day that Buddha was born, all nature put forth. Five hundred princes of the Sakyas were born, of whom Nanda, the beloved disciple, was the first. Five hundred maidens were born, Yasodhara, his wife, the foremost. Five hundred servants, Chandaka, his groom, the foremost; and five hundred horses, Kanthaka, his horse, the foremost. A carving shows a stable scene with a serene mare being fed from a bowl, the little foal beneath her, which is to live to such ripe old age, while the groom's wife nurses the infant groom of the infant Buddha's newborn horse.

The groom and the horse, both so faithful, are touching subjects. When Gautama rides from the city, the Yaksas hold up each of the horse's hoofs through the air, so that he will not awaken the guards. At parting, the horse kneels at his master's feet and waters them with his burning tears.

The temptation by Maya is another favourite carving. Extremely ugly warriors come up to attack the future Buddha.

Maya, who is tempting him as the Devil tempted Christ, is supposed to be offering him great worldly power. He leads the onset of ugly warriors and beautiful women to try to force Gautama from his seat of meditation. But the Bodhisattva drops one hand to Earth, to ask her to testify to his right, earned in former lives, to his position. The Earth upholds him, and evil Maya is vanquished. The Bodhisattva becomes the perfectly enlightened Buddha.

There are many carved stories of miracles: Buddha subduing poisonous snakes into his begging-bowl; calming a raging elephant, rather smaller than himself, by a stroke on the forehead. An animated tale is that of the little white dog who barked. Buddha was calling on a man named Suka, who was not at home, and whose little dog set up an outrageous barking. Buddha remonstrated with the dog, and told him that he had been reborn thus because he had been too rich in a former life. The dog was ashamed and crept into a corner. When Suka returned, Buddha told him that the dog was his own father, and advised asking him where he had buried the treasure hoarded in his former life. At that the dog crawled under the couch and began to dig in the earthen floor, and underneath, the treasure was found.

The stories, pointing morals and illustrating virtue, often show clearly the prevalent valuation of thought above things. Buddha and his monks were mendicants, going their rounds at a certain hour with begging-bowls, and depending upon the offerings of the pious. As Buddha walked past two children at play on the roadside, still such babies as to be naked, tumbling in the dust and building houses from it, one of the children scooped up a generous handful of his dust and ran up and put it into Buddha's bowl. Buddha was so touched by the child's generosity that he prophesied the boy would become a mighty Buddhist monarch in some future life. In truth he turned out to be — in a later life — the Emperor Asoka.

4. *Yoga, a Logical Extreme*

YOGA to the foreign mind connotes Indian mystery and the wildest of her extremes. Is the ascetic performing yoga when he lies on a bed of spikes, or holds up an arm to wither away, or stares at the sun until blind, or swings face downward over flames? Such painful endurance may truly be part of yoga, though it is not a necessary exaggeration, and though self-torture may be used by worshippers in other religions. The strange negative strength is partly a vestige of magic to force the gods to give the enduring man limitless power, magic that anciently terrified the king of the gods and melted his throne; but it is far from being the central purpose of yoga.

Occult power is also popularly thought of as yoga. News still travels mysteriously in India, as though it passed from mind to mind. Hypnotism has been long known to India. And as for levitation, the classic old works on yoga declare that by practice a man came into 'a balanced state of lightness like cotton fibre,' as preliminary to walking on air. First he became fine textured enough to step on water. Then he needed only a spider's thread. After much practice on such waving filaments, he tried a simple moonbeam. And when he learned to walk lightly and securely on a moonbeam, he might try the unsupporting air. One visualizes yogins walking off on moonbeams into the big night of India — where moonbeams seem quite strong enough to walk on; hearing their friends think across continents; or sitting, central and solitary, seeing past and future spread out before them like a map, containing all geography within themselves.

But such supernatural powers — clairvoyance, clairaudience, levitation, and other wonders — are only by-products of yoga, flowers by the wayside, not the goal and purpose. He who makes them the end may put them to evil uses. The true yogin is strictly forbidden to seek these powers as an end, and anciently he was told that it was a sin to be punished with a hell from which there was no release.

Yoga is a philosophy, and a stern and relentless one. The word yoga means yoke — to yoke or harness the wild horses of the senses, or to join the individual to the All. The logic of it wings up, springs from the earth of daily fact into air, and pedestrians can only watch it gradually vanish, carrying the practising yogin.

Yoga intends not merely to expound a theory, but to practise it to the extreme of its conclusion. And the method of knowing, of realizing or *doing* this theory, is by a series of exercises that only years of single-minded effort can master. It is a philosophy plus a technique believed to give intuitive realization — as if one did not merely study Kant or Bergson, but bore pain, sat, breathed, and gave up thought in order to perceive their truth.

Yet, though the exercises are believed to be the means of realizing the philosophy, it is probable that the exercises came first and the reason for them later. The priestly statue found at Mohenjo-Daro has gazed for five thousand years at a point between his brows, as yoga recommends, and a small carving of a god has sat in a yoga posture. Sanskrit literature of about 700 B.C. tells of the habit of fixing the mind on one object, to stop the movement of sense and mind, and to achieve miraculous powers. The Upanishads describe such posture and breath control as a method of salvation. No wonder that with such length of heritage the exercises of yoga seem natural to Indians, though only marvellous to others.

Yoga as a system of philosophy was classically written much later, possibly as late as the fourth or fifth century A.D.; no one is certain and some think it much earlier. Patanjali achieved the clarity and brilliance of order which is authentic for the system. His ideas were drawn from great accepted Indian thoughts, and branched away to their difference.

All Indian philosophies, except Buddhism and one early school of scoffing cynics who denied everything, believed in the soul as ultimate reality, living through past and future. In the brilliant centuries before Christ, yoga was one of the six philosophies which branched out from this common belief: that the supreme soul through successive ages functioned through forms of gods and people and things. All agreed that this temporary union of soul to body produced misery, for body-and-soul acts, and thereby produces consequences; and to accomplish the long coglike interaction of such results, or Karma, Heaven and Hell do not give time enough. Souls sticky with former deeds must be cleansed through innumerable bodies of god or demon, plant or person or stone, like a rusty needle through emery. This rationalization of the old totemistic idea, that souls wander after death into new shapes, has had common acceptance in Indian religion from that day to this. The system of Karma — and also of yoga built upon it — is logical, in the main, if one accepts the premise.

Later European thought did not accept the premise of a pure utterly wise soul within each person. From this watershed of belief the two halves of the world differed in practice. The West sought philosophy mainly as a means to a fuller life. The East considered a good life only valuable as a preparation for understanding philosophy.

The yoga system did not agree with the Vedanta that God is the only reality. It followed more nearly the Sankhya which saw Creator and creation as separate realities, like a dancer and his audience. Yoga believed that matter — which is real — and mind-stuff — which is also real though changeful and sorrowing — enmesh the unchanging soul.

The great clarity of the central soul, its absolute wisdom and firmness, can be reached only by husking the sheaths of thought and feeling. This is done by a series of exercises, at first physical and then mental, which slough off the wrappings of sensuous experience and tightly clinging thought, and finally reveal the soul in its bare majesty, capable of intuitively knowing everything in the universe, one with inexhaustible Energy.

To reach this clear self within, this ultimate value, one must actually destroy the mind. A modern philosopher, Dasgupta, compares the soul to a white light in a coloured dome, and explains that the only way to restore the purity of the white light is to smash the dome. 'The only way in which the spirit can be made to realize, in its own non-conceptual way, its own lonely light, is by breaking the mind to pieces.'

That is the terrifying, logical conclusion to the premise of a perfect soul within, buried in equally real, painful sheaths of thought.

The technique of clearing the path to this soul, step by step, was long and arduous, sometimes, especially in later and modern fluctuations, reaching the most trivial absurdities. But the original logic, however dogmatic and breath-taking, has a majesty. The classic steps of the system, as Patanjali outlined them tersely, are these: All is pain, but escape is possible through 'insight sevenfold advancing in stages to the highest.'

There were eight methods to yoga. Five were indirect — the abstentions, observances, postures, regulations of the breath, and withdrawal of the senses; and three were direct — fixed attention, contemplation, and concentration.

A man first prepared his morals negatively, by abstentions from injury, from acceptance of gifts, from theft, from incontinence. Abstention from injury, Patanjali said, 'begets a suspension of enmity even from enemies whose hostility is everlasting like the snake and buffalo.' These, in the presence of a good yogin, 'conform themselves to his mind-stuff and renounce altogether their hostility.'

Secondly one practised the positive virtues, the 'observances.' These included cleanliness and contentment, study and devotion. Such human virtues do not seem logically necessary to a person who is withdrawing from human life, but were explained as calming and preparing for further understanding. Self-castigation was also included in the list of observances, although not stressed. It offered the rich field of torture to those who were so inclined, for it was described as the bearing of heat and cold, of standing and sitting, of mortifications and fasts; and was supposed to give perfection of the body and some magic powers such as hearing and seeing at a distance. The followers of Alexander the Great saw ascetics at their endurance. The Buddha jataka tell of naked holy men who swung in the air like bats. And the Mahabharata praised a sage who decided to live in the water — at the confluence of the Ganges and Jumna — sometimes like a log, sometimes standing, until his limbs were covered with river grass and snails, and, all one green slime, he was pulled into a fisherman's net. His spiritual descendants today at the same place swing upside down over fires or bury themselves to the neck in earth. Misery has a way of being considered a virtue in itself. But Buddha, whose followers were so agile and extreme in self-castigation, rated it as nonsense.

The third preparation for yoga was the posture of the body, and many different kinds might be taken, such as the lotus posture, the hero posture, the mystic diagram (with the left foot between the right shin and thigh, and the right foot between the left shin and thigh — the familiar posture of Buddha figures). Another, called the bedstead, was described as lying down with arms stretched around the knees. Others were called the seated curlew, or seated elephant. However remarkable the position or name, its aim was relaxation and a state of balance. When all effort to maintain it ceased, the posture had been achieved — a thing 'stable and easy.' It was supposed to give ability to endure heat and cold.

The next aid was the regulation of the breath, and by this, amazing powers came. The yogin circulated his breath through one nostril, or both. He learned gradually to hold it for hours or days, and even for months and years, and in this suspended animation his heart did not beat. With his tongue turned back toward his tonsils, he sat apparently lifeless. The final ideal was complete suspension of breath. But he was supposed to accomplish positive results through breathing. He gained control of the involuntary muscles which regulate the bladder, heart, stomach, and excretory organs. He could sit in a tub and take water into the intestines by expelling air and thus forcing in water — 'thus washing his stomach and bladder' as often as he chose! But this exercise was still a mere preliminary to quiet bodily disturbances, passions, and antipathies.

The fifth step was called withdrawal of the senses, and the reasoning was this: Matter has reality, and the mind also has reality. The mind-stuff acts as a binder, fastening the unchanging inner Self to shifting outer things. To cut this cord, the method is 'to confine the span of attention to one object.' This was called 'meditation,' which did not mean thinking, but its opposite, closing the focus of the mind like a lens until only one object was in sight. The beginner might choose a crude object like a polo ball; but he learned in time to fix the mind on a subtler thing, until ultimately he could think of God alone. By the intensity of the focus on one object, all other things were excluded, grew fainter and non-existent.

The yogin for his last three steps achieved 'fixed attention,' binding the mind-stuff to a place, be it the navel or the tip of the nose, it did not matter; then by 'contemplation' focussing his single idea upon that place. When those two had been mastered, he reached his final stage called 'concentration,' when, 'as it were, emptied of itself, the consciousness shines forth as the intended object and nothing more'; a fusion of the thinker, the thought, and the object thought of. The ultimate end of yoga was achieved in the separation of Self from feeling or reasoning, the suppression of all desire, and the elimination of personality.

The road up to these three achievements had its rewards in supernatural powers. The 'constraints' in yoga brought forth a violent and vast release of what was constrained. Some resemblance is haunting there. The American Indians, when they wanted the corn to be fertile, stayed away from their wives before planting. One sort of restraint brought forth another sort of plenty.

There is sometimes a connection that sounds logical by the way of magic, in what the yogin restrained and the power he gained, but at other times it is hard to see how the fantastic connections are made. As a result of constraint upon his powers, the yogin gained 'powers like those of an elephant.' From holding the idea of an object steady and unmoving, he gained knowledge of its past and future — of all pasts and futures, the knowledge of his own births and of his latter end. As a result of constraint upon the sun — whatever that may be — the yogin gained the knowledge of the arrangement of stars. By practising restraint upon friendliness, he won greater powers of friendliness. As a result of constraint upon the outer form of the body there came a 'disjunction of light and eye' and the indiscernibility of the yogin's body. As a result of constraint upon body and air, he came into the balanced state of lightness when he walked upon air at will. He knew the cosmic spaces. He could penetrate the body of others.

The sensations experienced by the yogin have been compared by a modern psychologist to the ecstasies induced by drugs in some savage religious ceremonies, which gave the devotee a sense of omniscience and omnipotence. Patanjali does not recommend the use of drugs, but alludes to them: 'Perfections proceed from birth or from drugs or from spells or from self-castigation or from concentration'; and the comparison between the sensations produced by drugs or by yoga exercises is interesting. The ancient commentary says that 'agelessness and deathlessness and other perfections may be had by the use of an elixir of life.' The stages of the process of emptying the mind gave the yogin a sense of unlimited power, the pleasure of fancy unchecked by reason and flying to the skies. Physical pain grew less or, when the trance was profound, went completely; and the pains of thwarted ambition or emotion vanished. The yogin felt instead a delight, such as the Christian mystics felt in their communion with God. The pleasure of love in the world, or content in Paradise, are not to be compared to the sixteenth part of the pleasure of the 'dwindled craving.' The yogin might well feel himself capable of vast and divine power, regardless of what usual human limits he actually exceeded. All these miraculous powers were not really important to his final goal of annihilation of the personality.

The magic mastery over space and time is perhaps an earlier idea that lasted on into the later reasoning. The eastern mind turned inward, discarding life and its stuff, while the western mind turned outward to study life and its stuff. The east found clairaudience and a path upon moonbeams. The west found radio and airplane. Sometimes saints and scientists touch fingertips.

Finally in the culmination of concentration the yogin attained complete Isolation with the intuitive knowledge of all things and all times, an inclusive whole without sequence. Karma was dissolved, and the need of rebirth ended. The liberated Self, grounded in itself, the clear soul was free to live eternally at peace.

A passer-by, seeing a yogin near his final stages, might not be impressed by the outward appearance of the emaciated ascetic, with matted hair and dazed eyes, too weak to commit either good or evil, shrunken to a caricature of himself. What the final trance is like inwardly, no one can describe very definitely, because of course no one comes back from it. Dasgupta says that in the last stage of yoga intuition, all truths concerning the nature of the true self or the mind and the material world become clear, and as a result of this, and also as a result of the gradual weakening of the constitution of the mind, the latter ceases to live and work and is dissociated from the spirit or self. Then the spirit shines forth in lonely splendour. 'The highest and ultimate revelation of truth is therefore not only non-conceptual and non-rational, but also non-intuitional and non-feeling. It is a self-shining which is unique.'

A steep path.

Very few held unswervingly to this climb. Many were content to go a short way up the mountain and pick such flowers as they could, or find devious new paths. In the early centuries after Christ, the Buddhist and Jains and Hindus borrowed freely from yoga and there was much interplay of ideas between them all.

Yoga branched into several paths and its enlargements grew meticulously wonderful. Raja-yoga followed Patanjali's ultimate goal. Mantra-yoga was the form followed by Siva's worshippers. Bhakti-yoga was the devotion and love of God and self-surrender. Karma-yoga, the secret of work and duty — which was however to help the individual, not the world. Hatha-yoga, most practised in parlours by wide-eyed Westerners, was the yoga of health through control of the breath and involuntary muscles. The fragmentary details that linger in the memory of quack lecturers concern the breathing-in of 'psychic prana,' and sublimating the sex force by rousing the serpent Kundalini from its triangle at the base of the spine to the pineal gland.

The present meanderings are many and wonderful. A quotation from a manual on 'First Elements of Yoga,' written in 1897, gives rules which Alice in Wonderland would have rejected. A man who did not wish to leave the world entirely might make yoga his avocation. He should practise before sunrise, before leaving bed, by feeling from which nostril the breath was coming, and he should then take his first step with the foot on the same side as his breath. One can only think that most of the devotees must have had colds in their noses. If the breath came from the right nostril, he should take three, five, or seven steps with the right foot; if from the left nostril, two, four, or six steps with the left foot. He should sit for a half-hour in the Sidhasan posture, described thus: 'the yoni or anus should be pressed by one of the heels and the other placed upon the lingam or penis; and with eyes fixed upon the eyebrows the student should concentrate and collect his senses.' Then, after a bath, in a silk garment if possible, to protect against evil influences, he should meditate.

Most fearful and wonderful physiology and neurology is described, and convenient recipes are given at the end for curing bad odours, destroying unwanted hair, strengthening the memory, or curing diabetes — as well as ways of telling by the shape the breath forms on a mirror which element of the eight that make the world is in circulation.

It seems amazing nonsense — to spend one's days planning which nostril the breath could come from by the dark of the moon. But a human being must pass the time one way or another. The muddled trivialities are perhaps no sillier than some other avocations, though a foolish mind could grow immeasurably more foolish by practising them.

But the enormous structure of the severe old yoga philosophy stands as appalling as a pyramid, as strange as the lion god. The actual physical control it has taught has not been thoroughly studied by science and separated from its magic and illusions and rigmarole; but every now and again a blinding resemblance flashes, which men today work to understand — the control of involuntary muscles, the release of sex energy in sublimation. As for the deathlike trance, is it a self-induced insanity, or a great ancestral magic, or has it discovered something? Only one wiser than I can tell.

5. *The Gods of the Hindus*

'THE gods themselves came later into being.' The amazing Hindu pantheon of gods did not arise until many centuries after Buddha and the six schools of philosophers sat in their groves and caves and worked out their logic. Thought in the sixth century before Christ was strong and forceful. But the mediæval stories of gods in the Puranas, wild and rambling and ramifying, seem born of weaker minds.

Yet in India one steps into the thick of that still living mythology, into a land peopled by breathing gods. Greece let Zeus and Aphrodite die, and the Northlands have forsaken Baldur. But India still tends her Krishna and Siva, Hanuman and Lakshmi. For the essence of a god is that he needs worship. Missing that, he fades.

The gods of the Hindus today need their own census-taker, for their traditional number mounts to three hundred and thirty million. Each god or godling, however humble and unknown to the outer world, is important as demon or protector to some villager and arbiter of his life and luck, sickness or ruin. The gods who have risen to personification later than the obscure village deities have shape and personality and story. They are never so clear as Greek gods, but they can be carved and their legends told.

They grow as familiar even to a foreigner as old friends—Ganesh, with his elephant head and fat belly; and Lakshmi, goddess of prosperity, with two elephants pouring water over her, each protecting the gateway to merchant's shop or Rajah's palace. On cliff or temple Vishnu is sleeping on his seven-headed serpent; or he has become a wild boar, or the child Krishna stealing butter-balls. Siva and Parvati are human lovers; or Parvati is turned into terrible black Kali, and Siva is dancing wildly with many arms and the lust to kill; or Nandi, the plump bull, faces Siva's lingam.

The little images are alive. Wreaths of fading marigold or jasmine, smears of red paint or sacred rancid butter, even the drainway smelling of sacrificial blood, all testify to their reality and the idea that they must still be nourished. In the kitchen, the sacred place in a high-caste home, the special household gods have their alcove, and the father daily bathes the images and rubs them with sandal paste, waves burning camphor and sounds a small gong, repeats a mantra and offers them food. In a certain temple in Orissa the worship grows absurdly elaborate; the god is awakened by bells, has his teeth cleaned with a big stick, is dressed and offered breakfast, and goes through the day like a princeling until his bedstead is brought in at night. The anthropomorphic needs are taken seriously. A Maharajah may set aside a sum of rupees each month for feeding the palace images. The architect of a Hindu temple in a British college for princes recently made specifications for an electric fan to cool the temple god.

The sophisticate will tell you that the humblest peasant knows that these gods are mere creations of illusion, or pathways of approach to the Eternal One, interceding helpers like the Catholic saints. The Supreme Being present in each is really the object of offerings. No country loves abstraction so well as India. But no country more swiftly turns all abstractions concrete and makes ideas material. The simple-minded masses need the little god figures to dress and undress, to fan and feed; a wonderful ceremonial playing at dolls, which has the great advantage of being a magic means to get the good things of life — sons or riches — and to frighten away disease.

The gods carved today are decadent as art and do not inspire awe. But they were terrible or beautiful in the sculpture of the early middle ages. On the outcropping cliffs at Mamallapuram, in the caves of Ellora and Elephanta, the gods become figures of power. In such places one can glimpse the metamorphosis; an abstract idea or gleam of philosophy turns into a poetic metaphor, and then the figure of speech proceeds to have its portrait carved.

The Cave of Elephanta near Bombay is a good introduction to the powerful gods. Sail across the hill-encircled harbour, climb up a steep path to the shadowed cave, and come upon the big grey stone forms at the rear, standing in damp silence. Here are Siva and Parvati as wistful human beings; and Siva and Parvati in their terrible aspects; and Siva as half male, half female. But the most striking portrayal is the conception of God as trinity, the three-faced head of Brahma, the creator of the passion which called the world into being, Vishnu, the merciful preserver, and Siva, the wrath that destroys. Though interpretations blur away from this simplicity, the stone embodies the brooding spirit of creation with more than one aspect — with destruction included in the benevolence.

What are the stories behind these figures, and is there a system or order to them? They have been growing for centuries, dividing, subdividing, spreading, budding, in the moist warmth of Indian imagination. A richer, less-trammelled invention it would be hard to find. Most of the stories of little gods have never found their way into writing.

But the literature which evokes the great gods begins with the Vedic hymns, and continues in the Mahabharata and the popular Puranas to elaborate. It is the Puranas, meaning ancient, which are the great storehouses and basis of popular Hindu mythology now. The teacher comes to a Hindu householder today to read and expound from some Purana. There are eighteen bulky volumes, written probably from about the seventh century until the seventeenth. A Purana includes myth and kingly legend, and is supposed to deal with five subjects: the creation of the universe, its destruction and re-creation at the close of each æon, the genealogy of gods and patriarchs, the reigns of the sages, and the dynasty of the sun and moon races. Some Puranas are devoted to Siva, some to Vishnu, and some to the Female Principle. The devotees of each follow each. One of these volumes is written for the low-born and for women, who are, sacredly speaking, lumped together. Altogether they are massive and amazing mixtures of brilliance and naïveté, of poetry, philosophy, folklore, imagination, and rigmarole — of most of the contradictions of India.

To attempt to be clear and simple about the gods in the Puranas is to end mad. Sectarian quarrels confuse the personalities of gods. But this may serve as a few planks over the marsh of approach:

Briefly, the one eternal, indestructible reality, or God, is called Brahman, the neuter essence of the universe. 'Brahman,' explains Monier-Williams, 'when it passes into actual manifested existence is called Brahma; when it develops itself in the world is called Vishnu; and when it again dissolves itself into simple being is called Siva.' All the lesser gods are also mere manifestations of the Eternal. To tell a few stories may suggest the compass and contradictions of Indian mythology.

The Hindu genesis, the beginning of all life, is described in the Vishnu Purana thus: 'The indescribable One produced waters, and placed his seed in them.' The seed became a golden egg, brilliant as the sun, and in the egg he was born as Brahman, the progenitor of the world. As he slept or woke, the universe slept or woke. Each of his days and nights was an æon, as long as a thousand great ages, and each great age was as long as four million, three hundred and twenty thousand mortal years. The great ages were divided into four deteriorating periods, like the golden, silver, bronze, and iron age of the Greeks; but the Indian ages were named from the numbers on dice. In the first age men lived to be four hundred years old and accomplished all their aims and were happy and free from ills. Unluckily, we are living now in the fourth, the evil, 'dark-bodied' Kali age.

Now, without being too rigid or consistent, imagine the ineffable Brahman divided into his three aspects, popularly summarized: Brahma as creator, Vishnu as preserver, and Siva as destroyer, each with his legends.

In story and sculpture each god is married to one or more wives, and each rides an animal called his vehicle. Brahma did not appeal much to the people. Sometimes he is called arrogant. His wife Sarasvati (a Vedic river) is the goddess of music and literature and speech, a marriage of creation to expression. To show how swiftly conceptions blur from sublimity into childishness, one Puranic story tells that Sarasvati is the daughter of Brahma, sprung from his body. He fell in love with her and she tried to hide behind him, at which he developed four heads to find her and make love. To punish him, the gods refused him worship, and he has only two temples now in India. He is represented as having four heads and four arms, and often he is a tiny figure sitting on a lotus which emerges from the navel of the sleeping Vishnu. The conception of him is never very clear. He does not dramatize so well as the others.

But Vishnu, holding a shell, a lotus, a discus and a mace — Vishnu of the nine incarnations, descendant of the Vedic sun god — what a deity he is for the tropics! Saviour of the earth, he loops down in one amazing form after another. He is married to Lakshmi, goddess of wealth and beauty. He rides a fabulous man-headed bird called Garuda. And his last incarnation is still to come. Some day, in the most troublous times, Vishnu will reappear to save the earth.

The stories of Vishnu are the richest. His nine incarnations in animal or human form may have totemistic origin, or may be interpreted as a metaphor of life evolving from its lower forms. In each incarnation he still represents the whole power behind the universe.

The Vishnu Purana tells his adventures. He took the form of a fish to save mankind when the earth was overwhelmed by floods. He preserved a king named Manu, very Noah-like, with the seed of all existing things in the ark. The ark had to be tied to the horns of the Vishnu-fish, so great serpents came to act as ropes. The enormous fish pulled the ark safely over the floods. Inside the boat, meanwhile, conversation was intellectual, and included such topics as creation, the kingly dynasties, and duties of a householder, and the legends of Siva and of Vishnu himself.

Another incarnation was in the form of a tortoise, which acted as a pivot to hold up the mountain when the gods churned the ocean.

The story of the churning of the ocean is rich in variety, and much loved, and carved excitedly in stone as far away as the forests of Angkor. The three worlds had lost their vigour, plants withered and men grew lax. As man's sacrifices to the gods diminished, the underfed gods grew so weak that the demons dared attack. Now the cause of all this wilting lassitude had been the merest whim of Siva, fragmentarily incarnate in a haughty Brahman holy man, who offered a garland to Indra on his elephant. The elephant was unfortunately 'dim with inebriety' and flung the wreath to the ground. The Brahman, like most ascetics, was 'prone to wrath,' and cried: 'I am not of a compassionate heart, nor is forgiveness congenial to my nature.... I will not forgive, whatever humility thou mayest assume.' Indra was powerless, and the worlds at the holy Brahman's curse began to wilt.

Despairingly the gods turned for help to Brahma, and he turned to Vishnu, who was living suburbanly on the north shore of the Sea of Milk. Since the story is written by Vishnu's followers, it makes Brahma speak humbly to Vishnu for a page or two as follows: Thou, 'the unperceived, indivisible Narayana, the smallest of the smallest, the largest of the largest elements, in whom are all things, from whom are all things... whose faculty to create the universe abides in but a part of the ten millionth part... that nature which the yogis, after incessant effort, effacing both moral merit and demerit, hold to be contemplated in the mystical syllable Om... Vishnu, one only god — the triple energy is the same with Brahma, Vishnu, and Siva.'

This invocation put Vishnu into a favourable mood, so he promised to restore the strength of the world. He ordered the gods and demons to throw medicinal herbs into the Sea of Milk, and then to take Mount Mandura as a churning-stick and the serpent Vasuki for the rope, and commanded the gods and demons together to churn the ocean for ambrosia.

As they threw in the herbs, the Sea of Milk grew radiant as the thin and shining clouds of autumn. The gods stood by the tail of the serpent and put the demons at the head. This was strategy, as the demons were scorched by the flames from the serpent's head, while the vapours which formed were driven toward his tail as clouds and refreshed the gods.

Vishnu, or Hari, took the form of a tortoise and acted as a pivot for the mountain. At the same time, in another aspect, he helped the gods to pull the serpent and sat on top of the mountain to hold it steady.

The churning had excellent results. The Sea of Milk brought forth first a cow, the fountain of milk and curds worshipped by the divinities, and 'beheld by them... with minds disturbed, and eyes glistening with delight'; then a goddess of wine, her eyes rolling with intoxication; a fragrant tree, perfuming the world with blossoms; the apsarasas, nymphs of Heaven; the cool-rayed moon; a bitter poison, of which the gods took possession; the cup of amrita (the nectar of immortality); and finally, the goddess Sri, or Lakshmi, the goddess of prosperity, radiant with beauty. The world received her with delight. The gods sang, the nymphs danced, the holy rivers came to bathe her, the elephants of the skies poured down their waters from vases of pure gold for her ablutions. And the very Sea of Milk in person presented her with a wreath of never-fading flowers. This seems almost the limit of personification. When the goddess was bathed and adorned, she flung herself upon the breast of Vishnu, and has since been his wife.

The demons nearly foiled the miracle by trying to drink from the cup of amrita, and live forever. But Vishnu quickly changed himself into a lovely woman and lured the demons away until the gods had time to drink the ambrosia. Furious at the trick, the demons charged back. But the gods had tasted nectar and become immortal, and easily scattered the devils. The sun shone with a new splendour. The three worlds were happy. Lakshmi, or Sri, was incarnated always with Vishnu, as his most beloved.

This legend of the churning of the Sea of Milk is most popular. Was it a great nature myth, of clouds and storms? Gods and demons, good and evil, struggle all over the world. In this story the imagination is bubbling and overflowing. Nothing has limits and form. Everything yields to the temptation of endless new invention. Anything can be personified — even a Sea of Milk — and anything can acquire, given time, an allegorical meaning. To show how subtle the learned interpretations of myth may be, the Sea of Milk is elsewhere explained as ascetic penance, and ambrosia as the final liberation of the soul.

Vishnu as a wild boar, in the Varahar incarnation, lifted the earth upon his tusks. At that time the universe was fluid, and he stood looking at it wondering how to develop it, when he noticed a lotus leaf, and thought, perspicaciously, 'There is something on which this rests.' He assumed the tusker's form, and diving down, found the Earth below and raised her to the surface. In carving this story, Indian artists usually made the Earth a small woman's figure, and gave Vishnu a boar's head on a giant's body.

Incarnated as Narsingh, half man, half lion, and hence not to be classified in the animal kingdom, he killed a dreadful demon who had won a promise from some devout but short-sighted Brahman that neither man nor beast could kill him.

As a dwarf, he practised another trick to save. A terrible person, King Bali, had conquered the three worlds and was besieging Indra's Heaven. The desperate gods had to flee disguised as animals. Vishnu incarnated himself as a dwarf, and going to King Bali asked a boon, namely, all the land he could step over in three strides. Bali thought that was a trifle, and readily agreed. At which Vishnu rose to his full proportions, and placed one foot on earth and one on heaven, and walked over all the regions — the Vedic sun god with his three strides through the sky.

Rama with an axe — or Parasu Rama — cleared the earth of the Kshatriya caste, who were getting very arrogant and trying to rule the Brahmans. This strange story was a device of the Brahmans to intimidate the warrior caste when they threatened to rebel.

The seventh and eighth incarnations were as Krishna and Rama. The ninth was as Gautama Buddha, a device by which Buddhism was blended into Hinduism. The tenth incarnation is still to come. Mrs. Besant thought it could be managed with her Krishnamurti, until he decided he could not qualify. When and where Vishnu will really be incarnated next to save the world is still a mystery, but it is almost time he came.

The incarnation as Krishna is the most popular among simple people, and is especially loved in the neighbourhood of Muttra. Krishna, the child of cowherds, the practical joker, the defending fighter and the incredibly amorous man, was probably originally a tribal hero who worked his way up into divinity. He is very lusty and alive. Simple people can take him to their hearts as one of themselves, not too demanding. The lewd can find him a comrade. Mystics interpret him as God, and explain all the passionate wives of cowherds who left their husbands for Krishna as the soul's ecstatic need to find God.

Nothing is rigid in Hinduism. All minds may play upon all stories. The rôles of the gods are inextricably confused. This is the Vishnu-Puranic version of the Krishna legends.

The earth was again oppressed by giant demons and begged Vishnu for help. Although the demons were really only one aspect of himself, nevertheless Vishnu had to employ definite strategy to outwit and kill them. The greatest demon was Kansa. He was chariot-driver to a king and his beautiful bride, when a mighty voice from Heaven told him that their eighth child would destroy him. The demon was about to kill the queen, but the king pleaded for her life, promising to give up each child as it was born.

Thereupon Vishnu arranged that the first six children were only incarnate demons anyhow. To make the seventh and eighth child, he plucked two hairs from himself, one black, one white. The black hair was to be born as Krishna, and the white as his brother Balarana.

To save Krishna at birth, Vishnu appealed to his wife, or Female Energy. She had to be born of a cowherd, while he was born in the palace as Krishna. The two babies were to be secretly exchanged. Why Vishnu could not have killed the demon in his own incarnation is hard to explain, but it makes a better story as it is, and may use episodes from the life of the tribal hero Krishna.

Vishnu's wife is here made to seem like Siva's wife. She is called 'the goddess Yoganidra, the great illusory energy of Vishnu, by whom, as utter ignorance, the whole world is beguiled.' A fascinating conception — the creator's female half produces the illusion which is the world, from which illusion men must escape to reach the creator again.

When the queen was pregnant with Vishnu's incarnation, Krishna, she had celestial radiance, and the gods themselves worshipped her. They called her the goddess of speech, the energy of the creator of the universe, the parent of the Vedas. 'Thou art sacrifice, whence all fruit proceeds; thou art the wood, whose attrition engenders fire. Thou art the parent of the gods; thou art the mother of their foes.... Thou art contentment, whence resignation is derived; thou art intelligence, the mother of knowledge; thou art patience, the parent of fortitude; thou art the Heavens, and thy children are the stars.'

'The lotus petals of the universe expanded.' On the day of Krishna's birth, 'the quarters of the horizon were irradiate with joy, as if moonlight was diffused over the whole earth. The virtuous experienced new delight, the strong winds were hushed, and the rivers glided tranquilly.' The child was born with a complexion of lotus leaves. He had four arms, and a mystic sign on his breast. The child spoke to his mother and said, 'Princess, in former times I was prayed to by thee and adored in the hope of progeny. Thy prayers have been granted, for I am born thy son.' So saying, he was silent.

While the guards at the gates at Muttra were charmed and heavy rain fell, the two babies were exchanged. The rivers stilled for Krishna's coming, and the many-headed serpent Sesha spread out his hoods to protect Krishna from the rain. The baby was placed in the bed of Yasoda, the cowherd's wife, who was delighted with the newborn boy, black as lotus leaves.

The girl child which Yasoda had borne was placed beside the queen. The demon Kansa called to kill the infant and started to dash it against a stone. But the newborn child rose to the sky, expanded into a gigantic shape with eight arms, each wildly waving a weapon, taunted Kansa, and vanished. It does not seem sensible not to have killed Kansa with all those arms and weapons — but that again would spoil the story.

Kansa called together all the demons to war against gods, by killing the good men who performed sacrifices. Then the gods, deprived of their food, would die.

But Krishna was destined to save the world from the fiends. His miracles began in infancy. His foster-parents were cowherds. Near them lived the demoness Putana, the child-killer, who took children to her breast to suckle. Whatever child she nursed instantly died. Such a tragic reason was invented by parents who saw their little brown babies slipping from life, and did not know why. The demoness had poisoned them. But Krishna was the avenger of all dead babies. No wonder anxious ignorant mothers love the figures of the child Krishna. For when the fiend took him up, asleep, he lay hold of her breast with both hands and sucked so violently that he drained out her life. People came running at the sound of her horrible cries and found Krishna in her arms. His foster-mother snatched him and waved a cow-tail brush over him to avert evil, while his father placed dried powdered cow dung on his head as protection. But the huge carcass of the demoness already lay harmless and dead.

Krishna and his brother grew like normal children, crawling everywhere, often into ashes and filth. They got into the cowpens and pulled the tails of the calves. His mother tried to punish by tying Krishna to the household mortar (a sacred thing, hymned in the Vedas), a huge wooden bowl cut from, and still joined to, a solid log. But Krishna simply crawled away with the mortar and dragged it until it caught between two trees and pulled the trees down! 'Thereat the child laughed and showed two little white teeth, just budded.' The cowherds grew frightened of the portents of the place and decided to move. They set off with their wagons and cattle toward Vrindavan (Brindaban, where they still worship the flowing river as Krishna's wife). Here the grass was sweet even in the hot season, so the cowherds formed their wagons in a crescent and settled. The two boys grew up, making crests of peacocks' feathers and garlands of flowers, and musical pipes of leaves and reeds, and driving the cattle to pasture.

The idyll of Krishna's childhood is full of the sights and sounds of the Indian seasons. 'Then came on the season of the rains, when the atmosphere laboured with accumulated clouds, and the quarters of the horizon were blended into one by the driving showers.' 'The bow of Indra held its place in the Heavens all unstrung, like a worthless man elevated by an injudicious prince to honour. The white line of the storks appeared upon the bank of a cloud, in such contrast as the bright conduct of a man of respectability opposes to the behaviour of a scoundrel. The ever-fitful lightning, in its new alliance with the sky, was like the friendship of a profligate for a man of worth. Overgrown by spreading grain, the paths were indistinctly traced, like the speech of the ignorant that conveys no positive meaning.' Krishna played in forests that echoed with the hum of bees and the peacocks' cries.

His wonders continued. Near-by was a lake inhabited by a dreadful serpent who was blasting the countryside. Venomous, and breathing out fumes that withered the trees, the copper-coloured snake king was attended by other 'powerful and poisonous snakes, feeders upon air, and hundreds of serpent nymphs, decorated with rich jewels, whose earrings glittered with trembling radiance as the wearers moved along.' Into this lake Krishna stepped, grasped the serpent, and, in spite of its writhing coils and the attacks of the other snakes, strangled it, and rid the country.

One of the most popular stories is his defiance of Indra. A very dry season had come: 'Autumn, when the lotus is in full bloom. The small fish in their watery burrows were oppressed by the heat. ... The peacocks, no longer animated by passion, were silent in the woods, like holy saints who have come to know the unreality of the world. The clouds of shining whiteness exhausted their watery wealth, deserted the air.' Lakes dried up, the moon was bright in a starry sky. Rivers and lakes retired from their banks.

The cowherd was about to sacrifice to Indra the rain god. But Krishna persuaded him instead to worship his own cattle, reasoning thus: 'We are sojourners in the forest. Cows are our divinity. The object that is cultivated should be one's chief divinity, venerated and worshipped.

'We are not shut in with doors,' continued Krishna, 'nor confined with walls. We wander happily in our wagons. The spirits of the mountains walk the woods, and sport upon their precipices. Let us worship the mountains and sacrifice to our cattle.'

So the herdsmen worshipped the mountain, presenting it with curds and milk and flesh. They fed hundreds and thousands of Brahmans; and they walked around their cows and bulls. Krishna sat on top of Mount Govarddhana, saying, 'I am the mountain,' and ate much food offered by the cowherd's wives. At the same time, in his form as a youth, he climbed the hill and worshipped his other self.

But Indra was furious at losing offerings and worship. He called up his cohorts of clouds to destroy the cattle. 'Clouds roared aloud. The earth was in impenetrable darkness. The world was water.' In this predicament, Krishna simply picked up the mountain with one hand and held it aloft, calling the people with their herds and carts and goods to come under it for shelter. That deed has pleased countless Indian listeners and been the subject of dramatic miniatures.

Another Krishna story which delights believers and inspires miniature painters is of the Gopi women, wives of cowherds. Krishna was a youth 'dark as the leaf of a full-blown lotus.' And his brother was white as a jasmine, a swan or the moon, and dressed in blue raiment. 'Krishna, observing the clear sky bright with the autumnal moon, and the air perfumed with the fragrance of the wild water-lily... felt inclined to join with the Gopis in sport.' So he and his brother began to sing low sweet strains, and one by one the Gopi women left their homes for him.

They hunted through the forest. 'See, here are the marks of

Krishna's feet, the impression of the banner, the thunderbolt, and the goad ...' 'What lovely maiden has been his companion, inebriate with passion, as her irregular footmarks testify?... Here a nymph has sat down with him, ornamented with flowers, fortunate in having propitiated Vishnu in a previous existence.'

When they found him, he came smiling. One exclaimed, 'Krishna, Krishna,' as if unable to cry anything else. Another frowned, as drinking with the bees of her eyes his lotus face.

They made the circle of the dance, and it seemed as if Krishna took each by the hand. They danced to the music of their clashing bracelets, and considered each instant with Krishna a myriad of years. In vain their husbands, fathers, or brothers protested. They went at night to sport with beloved Krishna.

When he left to go to Mathura (Muttra), they were jealous of the city women, and bewailed: 'His ears will be regaled with the melodious and polished conversation of the women of the city.... Expressive smiles, graceful airs, elegant gait, and significant glances belong to city women.' The two boys, sportive as colts, went to meet the demon wrestlers sent by Kansa to kill them. The brothers contorted and overpowered fiends, and Kansa was vanquished.

Krishna married Rukmani, and seven other graceful women. He had sixteen thousand additional wives, but he loved best of all Radha, wife of a cowherd, the loveliest and the most devoted. The tenderness of Krishna and Radha is the subject of many a miniature — an idyll slightly but not materially lessened by the sixteen thousand wives. Radha is the soul in the ecstasy of devotion to God, in some ways a lovely figure for all times and places, in some the inspirer of the orgies of the erotic sects.

Eventually Krishna had to die. While he was sleeping, he was shot by a hunter and became one with the universal spirit. Arjuna came to burn the dead. Eight queens, with Rukmani at their head, embraced the body and entered the funeral pyre. And the blaze was cool to them, happy in their contact with their lord. Arjuna performed the last rites and then led away the thousands of surviving wives.

But with Krishna dead, the powerful, dark-bodied Kali age descended upon the earth and thieves set upon the wives. Arjuna's invincible weapons became flaccid and his arrows were spent. He was helpless against the sticks and stones of the peasants who carried away the women. Arjuna wept. In his despondency, a sage consoled him, saying: 'The prowess of mortals is the gift of time. Time effects the production and dissolution of all creatures.'

As for the wives, they got no more than they deserved. For in a former incarnation they had flattered an ascetic who was in bathing, won his promise that they would all marry the best of men, then mocked him as he came from the water and they saw his crooked legs. He grew furious and cursed them with thieves for second husbands. 'And so,' the sage continued, 'there is no occasion for you, Arjuna, to regret it in the least.'

The story of Krishna, like most things Indian, is an incredible blend of profundity, enormousness of conception, of intuition which modern science approaches to corroborate — and the most childish ideas, told with a matter-of-fact literalness. In a sentence, the conceptions shift. 'The prowess of mortals is the gift of time,' says the sage — and who can make a better statement? But in the next breath a saint, sensitive about his crooked legs, orders women to be captured by thieves.

Vishnu, the Vedic god, in all his phases and stories continues to be widely worshipped and pictured in stone, usually a gigantic conception. Krishna, however, is portrayed as smaller, the amorous lad with a flute, the baby with a butter-ball. Although benevolent, and immensely loved in his special incarnations, the protecting god cannot quite hold his own over India with Siva of the terrors. Siva is his rival, followed in the main by different sects of worshippers.

Siva is the fearful one, the Vedic storm god of destruction; the Dravidian fertility god, who rides Nandi, the humpbacked bull; the passionless ascetic, who smears himself with ashes; the terrible ghoul, who dances in burial grounds and destroys gods themselves, the poetic conception of the dancing force that stirs the universe; eternal reproductive power under symbol of the lingam; the lord of ghosts and goblins and patron of thieves; the learned philosopher sitting on Mount Kailasa and discussing metaphysics with his wife; a wild, jolly, drunken hunter. As Kala, Time, he is lord of the world; as death he commands all.

He is married to Parvati, or Uma, who in that aspect is a lovely maiden, daughter of the Himalayan Mountains. She, too, has her thousand names. She is the frightful Kali or Durga or Deva, with a lolling tongue and a necklace of skulls and a victim's dripping head — the image of all nightmares, a creature to propitiate. She is the reproducer, symbolized by the yoni; and she is the mother of the universe.

The two children of their union are Kartikkeya, the god of war, and Ganesh, the elephant-headed god of wisdom, who is usually a most ingratiating god and blesses the beginnings of things.

Siva is most frequently worshipped as the lingam, rationalized in many ways. When he is carved or painted as a god, he may have five faces or one. He has three eyes to see past, present, and future. The crescent moon is on his forehead. His neck is dark blue, from swallowing poison at the churning of the ocean to save the earth. The serpent around his neck means the endless cycle of recurring years, and the necklace of skulls symbolizes the successive destruction and rebirth of men. He wears a tiger skin and carries a spear, bow, battle-axe or trident, or perhaps a rattle, drum, and begging-bowl. He has fewer legends than Vishnu, but he has one thousand and eight names.

The dance of Siva keeps the universe alive — he is all energy. He dances in the burning ghats. As a Dravidian god he would revel in things considered filthy by the early Aryans. The symbolic interpretation is that the burning ghat is the human heart.

Siva as an ascetic sits covered with ashes, motionless for ages, meditating. As a nature god, when the Ganges fell from Heaven and would have bored a hole through the earth by the force of its descent, Siva caught it in the thick snarls of his hair — the foothills of the Himalayas, entangling the course of rivers. Parvati loved him long, and fasted and did penance with heartbreaking rigour, her tender body wasted, that she might gain power to break his attention from his own contemplation and shift his concern to her. In these two forms Siva and Parvati are like human beings, the ideal youth of the race, noble and tender. The marriage carved at Elephanta is appealing. Perhaps the most beautiful human representation is at the caves of Ellora — Parvati, a graceful woman, afraid, touches Siva's arm as many-headed Ravenna, the earthquake, shakes the mountain beneath them; Siva, equally strong and quiet, presses one foot down to hold the earth steady for her — very human, and godlike only in the serenity and perfection of type.

When Siva's wife turns into Kali or Durga, she becomes terrible — the Dravidian demoness, the devouring matriarchal fiend — personifying all the fears of helpless men in a land of swift horrors of storm and disease and famine. But a cultured explanation of this gory figure is that she is Time, who devours all things. Whatever she is, she still laps goat's blood. She is also worshipped tenderly and devotedly as the mother of the universe. Again, she is illusion of the senses, which flings a veil over reality. The cruder later sculptures, with some influence from northern Mongolian neighbors, give her open mouth and lolling tongue and necklace of skulls and a fiendish expression. That hideous figure is a literal illustration of a Puranic story. If her horror is directed against an emeny, it is easier to understand the devotion she inspires — rather like an ugly watchdog. The Markandeya Purana, most popular in Bengal still, tells the legend which this frightful figure images.

In the days of the hundred years' war between the gods and demons, the gods were so overwhelmed that they left Heaven and wandered about the earth as mortals. In their extremity, they decided to create a saviour for themselves.

The saviour idea has an appeal for people who are feeling be-

DANCE OF SIVA, ELLORA CAVES

wildered and helpless against the oppressing ills of life. Any saviour will do — this time the terrible Kali. The gods began to manufacture her from their essence. 'An immense mass of light proceeded from the bodies of... all... the devas, and conglomerated.' This effulgent lustre appeared as a flaming mountain, 'and the phenomenon was transformed into a woman extending through the three worlds. The energy of Siva created her face... her two breasts were made by the moon, the space between them by Indra, her thighs and the calves of her legs by Varuna.' The gods armed her with weapons, and gave her jewels and a necklace of snakes, and Indra gave her the bell from his elephant.

'She shouted frequently with a terrible voice, the sound of which filled the sky.' 'She indented the earth, occupied by her foot, her crown struck the sky; the sound of her bow-string terrified the whole subterraneous world. She grasped all the space of the regions by her one thousand arms.'

The demons came toward her with a thousand chariots and elephants, but the goddess was equal to them single-handed. She sportively cut the fiends in pieces by the showers of her arrows. Then, by a sigh, she produced thousands of Amazons, who sounded conches and kettledrums and other instruments in the festival of war.

She rose on her lion over the peak of the stupendous golden mountain. She became terribly angry — rage changed her face into a hideous black. She wore a wonderful string of human skulls, and a tiger's hide; her flesh became dried. Her mouth expanded, she had a lolling tongue, a horrible, red-tinged eye. Her front filled the regions. She furiously destroyed the foes of the deities and devoured their faces. 'The troopers' chariots with their drivers, she threw them in her mouth, and chewed them with her teeth horribly.... She crushed some with her foot, and broke the bosoms of others with her trident.'

Such a creature, though useful, would hardly seem easy to love and worship, but the Hindu mind can accomplish the most impossible span in two sentences.

'The magnanimous goddess,' the story continues, 'devoured and crushed all the forces of the valiant Asuras.'

'O goddess,' the ecstatic worshipper cries, 'thou hast a beautiful golden-hued body.... The virtuous, by faithfully performing every day the different divine services and consecration, depart to Heaven, and thereby reap the fruit of their labour in the three worlds.' 'O Durga! all creatures lose their fear by praying to thee — thou dost grant abundance of prosperities, thou dost release from pain and grievous distress... All the universe was made happy by the death of the giants.'

The terrible face of the goddess is to frighten the foes of mankind. Nevertheless, her worshippers feel she is not to be trifled with, and propitiation from fear must be more lavish than gratitude for favours. When she is ecstatically worshipped as the mother of the universe, however, a saint of modern days may go into a trance in contemplation of her.

As the great illusion who shackles the world through the force of love, 'The divine goddess possesses irresistibly the heart of even the wisest, and forcibly leads into great deception. By her the universe consisting of animates and inanimates was created.' This is the way Brahma himself prays to her: 'O goddess of the universe; mother of the earth! creator of matter and destroyer of it... thou art the sustainer of all things, thou hast created all things, thou governest all things... thou art the principle of creation, thou art the preserver, thou art the destroyer in the end, thou pervadest through the universe.... Thou art the supreme knowledge, thou art the great illusion... the great love, the ample light... thou art the wisdom that creates understanding, thou art modesty, strength, and gratification, thou art mildness and forgiveness... thou art placid, the greatest among the meek, beautiful, excellent... thou art the great goddess.'

With this more flattering picture let us leave the pantheon of gods.

6. *The Epic Heroes of the Hindus*

INDIA'S two epics, the Mahabharata and the Ramayana, are more alive to Hindus than the Iliad or King Arthur's legends to us. They penetrate into life as the Bible and Shakespeare do and serve as religion and moral and drama and tall story. They inspire many forms of art, and slip into the daily thoughts of men and women.

So far away as the island of Bali, dancers still act the warriors of the Mahabharata. Strong-armed Bhima fights again in the posturings done in a reed-built hall in a little palm-sheltered village. The epic heroes are carved on rocks from Mamallapuram in South India to the distant temples of Java and Angkor. Delicate Rajput miniatures draw scenes from the Ramayana; the monkeys capture Ceylon in a balance of colour.

Places associated with Rama's life are pilgrimage spots. His birthday is a festival of rejoicing when his image and his wife's are worshipped with fast and vigil. Today a little bride is told to be faithful as Rama's wife Sita, who is the ideal of perfect wives — an ideal, it must be admitted, a little like patient Griselda, a reiterated teaching that makes women accept suffering as their lot. Servants should pattern on Hanuman, the type of faithfulness, and noblemen on Rama, the perfect, gentle knight. Savitri's devotion to her husband is the theme of a yearly festival for Hindu women. Thin-boned listeners today sigh wistfully at the strength of the gusty fighters of the Mahabharata. During the World War, there was a widespread conviction among certain simple Hindus that the Allies would win because King George had five sons, like the five sons of Pandu in the Mahabharata.

Wandering story-tellers still chant the epics to rapt listeners, most of whom cannot read, and who depend upon this ancient declamation that feeds their thought and senses. The arrival of the bard makes an occasion. A household brings rugs into the courtyard, and by the smoke of incense and sputtering lights the men sit motionless and intent under the deep sky. Behind the lattices they may hear the women breathe and mutter and exclaim, and shift an anklet or a silken sari as the story-teller chants on.

THE MAHABHARATA

'If it is not in the Mahabharata, it is not in India.'

A library called the Mahabharata grew from unknown time until about A.D. 400. The kernel is a swashbuckling epic of hard-hitting heroes and crafty gods. Savage and racy and rationalizing polyandry and primitive morality; in another part chivalrous and full of glitter and such pageantry as King Arthur's court loved; now tender and sensitive and compassionate, or rising to heights of religious inspiration—such is the great collection of the Mahabharata.

The original tale of the five sons of Pandu who fought the sneering Kurus was probably based upon the battles of two rival kingdoms near the site of Delhi, about the twelfth century B.C. The story of rivalry grew to some twenty thousand couplets. To that was added and mixed, in centuries of changing civilization, other stories and treatises and speculations, until the whole is now over a hundred thousand verses.

The dramatic force of the warrior's saga could carry a mass of moralizing. Brahmans used it to send along their teaching. The Bhagavad-Gita, which many know in the translation of Sir Edwin Arnold's 'Song Celestial,' rises to philosophical heights that profoundly influence Indian thought and is as dear to Hindus as the Psalms to Christians. The whole epic is so tied into religion that even the original tribal legend can be interpreted mystically if one knows how, and the five sons of Pandu made into man's five senses, at war with illusion.

The Kurus were an aristocratic race and the Pandus were upstarts who strengthened themselves by alliance with the Panchala, and decided to have the ambitious horse sacrifice. This ancient rite to the sun god served as a means for enlarging a kingdom. A horse representing the sun was released to wander for a year at will. He was followed by an army. Anyone who stopped the white horse in his browsing over borders had to fight the army. Anyone who did not dare stop him had to submit and pay tribute. At the end of a year the horse was sacrificed with great pageantry, and the submissive tribes were invited to come to the triumphant capital to pay.

The Kurus, civilized and effete, resented having to yield to the rude young Pandus. They thought of a clever scheme to retaliate, merely to win back all the kingdom by the gentlemen's game of dice — loaded.

That is the probable historic basis of the main story.

In the epic the five Pandu brothers were being brought up at the Kuru court with all tenderness by their uncle the king, as heirs to half his kingdom. But the oldest of the king's hundred sons, Prince Duroydhan, was bitterly jealous of his cousins.

A tournament was held in all splendour. The field was surrounded by lily-white towers, on which passing gods alighted, and hung with cloth of gold and curtains of woven pearls. As the crowds gathered, Brahmans chanted their hymns. The young heroes advanced in golden armour, wearing girdles of jewels, and they flashed swords like wreaths of flame. They aimed at targets racing, and shot the wild boar at gallop.

The five sons of Pandu, oddly enough, had one mother, Pritha, but each had a different god for father. Wise Yudhisthir, the eldest, was the son of Virtue. (Wise is an epithet which he does not seem to earn, being apparently simple-minded.) Mighty Arjuna was the son of Indra; Bhima the bulky, the son of Wind; and the two youngest were sons of the twin gods of the morning.

A strange mighty warrior came to the lists, Karna, who moved like a cliff, supposedly the son of a humble chariot-driver, of too low rank to enter the tournament. Actually he was the son of the incorrigible Pritha and the sun god. But as he was born before her marriage, Pritha felt an intense shame about him. Though she paled to see him battling with his brothers, she never acknowledged him. She would have saved much trouble if she had.

Karna fought as champion of the Kurus, in gratitude to Prince Duroydhan, who raised his rank to admit him to the tournament.

The epic rivals were Arjuna, born of Rain, and Karna, child of Sun — tiger-waisted Arjuna who could shoot arrows into the mouth of the wild boar, and Karna, who had muscles of iron and was blest with every manly virtue. When the two fought, Indra's black thundercloud hung over Arjuna and the sun god sent the full blast of his rays upon Karna. Arjuna won.

Later came the ceremony of the 'bride's choice,' of the Panchala princess. Eligible kings gathered from all sides. The Pandus, because of Duroydhan's attempt on their lives, came disguised as Brahmans. The princess was lovely Drapaudi, fragrant as the blue lotus. She had no mother. She sprang from the altar. Her father made an enormous bow to test the strength of her hundreds of suitors, and hung a whirling disc before the target through which arrows must pass.

The multitudes gathered — actors, dancers, wrestlers, minstrels, and Brahmans. Kings came from all the powerful lands to try to win the fragrant princess. One by one the kings stood up to the mighty bow — and one by one were thrown backward by its force, their necklaces awry and robes tumbled, and their tempers as agitated as their clothes.

When disguised Arjuna stood before it, the real Brahmans, admiring, wondered how a Brahman, 'weak by nature' and untried in arms, dare attempt it. The kings were snobbishly indignant that any but their caste should try. But Arjuna bent the bow with ease and shot straight through the whirling disc to the mark. When Drapaudi flung the bridal wreath about his neck, the kings were furious and rushed against him. Bhima, coming to help, had just time to uproot a tree and stand at bay; but only the god Krishna finally saved them.

Then a curious thing happened. Drapaudi became the wife of all five brothers. This is explained by some scholars as a probable survival of polyandry, told with simplicity at first and later rationalized as perfect filial devotion. (The brothers told their mother they had won a great prize, and she commanded them, like good brothers, to share the gift in common. They could not disobey their mother.) Although later some of the heroes acquired more private wives, Drapaudi was the one over whose sufferings they grieved.

After this marriage alliance, the brothers were strong enough to demand their rightful share of the kingdom. Although Duroydhan managed to keep the fertile valley land and allot to them scrub-jungle, the Pandus cleared the thicket like pioneers, and built themselves a fine city in Indrapat... and at that point in the story they decided to have the horse sacrifice. Kings yielded like toppling ninepins to their browsing stallion, but the Kurus, who had to come as inferiors to the ceremony, were bitterly jealous, and challenged to a game of dice.

No man of honour could refuse to play. The oldest, serious Yudhisthir, was no match for the wily court gambler. He plunged; he staked his wealth and his slaves. He offered his kingdom. Then he put up the lives of his brothers and himself — and finally, when all was gone, he staked his wife.

The lovely princess was dragged disgracefully by her sacred hair into the hall of men. She was pulled down onto Duroydhan's knee, like a slave girl, and told she could easily win the love of others now that her husbands were slaves.

The old king of the Kurus, ashamed of such actions and fearful of consequences, asked her pardon and offered to grant her any boon. She begged to have her husbands set free, and they were released from slavery to banishment, with these curious conditions: for twelve years they must live in the forest, and on their return, must hide for a year in disguise. If they were recognized, they would have to be exiled for another twelve years.

The time in the forest was not dull. Gods came to visit them. Saints told them tales and legends — the story of Nala and Damayanti, of Savitri, of Parasu Rama. Once the princess was carried away and rescued. And once Arjuna performed a penance so long and severe that he forced the god to grant him invincible weapons.

After the twelve forest years, they had the most difficult task to live in disguise. They went to a strange kingdom. Wise Yudhisthir pretended to be a Brahman, skilled in dice (which hardly qualified him as wise). The other brothers cooked, or groomed the king's horses, and Drapaudi served the princess as waiting-woman. Big Arjuna was so outstanding that they could only hide him by making him absurd. They dressed him as a eunuch, with conch bangles and earrings and braided hair, and he acted as dancing-master.

Unluckily for their concealment, Duroydhan went cattle-raiding — a princely sport — and carried off some sixty thousand of their master's fat kine. The prince was too timid to go after them, offering as his excuse that he had no chariot-driver. At which Drapaudi forced him into action by saying that his eunuch dancing-master had once been Arjuna's charioteer. Disguised Arjuna led the prince to a grisly place where wrapped corpses hung. But the corpses were only the hidden weapons of the Pandus, their gigantic bows, gold-tipped, their quiver of arrows, their scimitars, and long swords in scabbards of tiger skin. Arjuna, aiming his mighty bow from a distance, drove off the marauding Kurus. The rescued cattle ran with uplifted tails.

Then the Pandus openly claimed their own kingdom. But stubborn Prince Duroydhan would not restore the land. In council the great chiefs weighed conciliation versus fighting, and all wanted harmony. The old Kuru king and his warriors and priests saw that it was better to yield than to have a frightful war. But Duroydhan was the sort of person who thought there was a plot against him, everyone taking the side of the Pandus. He refused to give up his gambler's loot, or even a town, or a village, or a spot that a needle's point could cover.

Nothing but battle could follow that answer, and all the nations of northern India prepared to take sides in the world-rending war.

But when Arjuna (in the ranks of enemies lined up against him) recognized his old playmates, he could not bear to shoot. That was the occasion for the sermon by his charioteer, the god Krishna. Krishna argued that it was Arjuna's duty to shoot because he was a warrior. The fact that death would result was neither here nor there. Death is nothing in the eternity of God, upon whom the universe is strung like pearls — the Eternal, who is the fresh taste in the water, the smell of the earth, the gleam in fire, the sound in space, the light in sun and moon. The man who thinks he kills and the man who thinks he dies are equally deluded. Nothing that is, ever was not, nor will ever cease to be. The man new-dead is, like the man new-born, still living man. Duty, according to the caste into which one is born, must be the guide in life. For a Brahman, that duty is to meditate. For a prince, that duty is to fight.

Whereupon, after the great volume of doctrines and celestial poetry of the Bhagavad-Gita, Arjuna fought.

The chiefs came in their battle chariots, their horses grey or pibald or ivory white; their standards rising with the device of each warrior, a red deer on burnished gold, a silver lion, a water jar on a deer skin, a silver swan with bells, a golden peacock. Arjuna carried the monkey standard.

The tide of battles shifted. The slaughter was terrible, but not decisive. The Kurus were led by Bhishma, who could not be conquered. Arjuna, as a child, had climbed upon his knee, and once more he tried to stop the slaughter by appealing to their ancient love. Loyal Bhishma could not break his promise to fight — but he made one reservation. He would not attack a wounded foe, or a woman.

That gave wily Krishna an unscrupulous idea. A certain warrior had been born a woman and only lately changed by the gods into a fighting man. The god suggested sending him against Bhishma. Arjuna was appalled. He was constantly full of tender feelings and honour, but since the deity gave the command, he had to obey. (This is an instance of a later sense of honour explaining away some savage ancestral trickery.) At sight of the man-woman the fine old enemy warrior simply dropped his weapons and shield, and died unresisting. Quixotic honour and faith to a principle, no matter how far-fetched its application, contrast with knavery and cruelty.

When Karna at last took command of the enemy, the rivalry between him and Arjuna reached its height. Arrows fell like monsoon rains and came back like hissing serpents. Suddenly Arjuna's bow broke, and he asked for a truce to mend it. Karna, scorning honour, still aimed. Arjuna mended his bow in the thick of arrows and came back like a wounded tiger. Yet still the two were so evenly matched that only an accident decided the combat.

Karna's heavy chariot wheel sank into mud and the car listed sharply, caught to the axle. Now it was his turn to ask for truce and Arjuna's turn to scorn it. While Krishna pointed out all Karna's past misdeeds, he took up his celestial bow and killed Karna.

That ended the war. Bhima incidentally killed all that were left of the enemy princes, tracking escaping Duroydhan to a hut by the lake and challenging him at last for his insult to their wife. And as a final gesture also, a Kuru prince slew all of Drapaudi's sleeping children.

All was over but the funerals, and the lament of women, women throwing away their jewels, loosening hair and robes — the tramp of wailing women. The Pandus gave all pious rites to their foes. They had the shattered cars and splintered lances neatly hewn into firewood and heaped into funeral pyres. The princes and nobles and warriors were laid out according to their rank. Then rich libations were poured on the fire — which burned up a hundred kings.

At last, when all was over, Pritha confessed that Karna was also her son and grieved that he had died by his brother's hand. The Pandus admitted that if they had known, it would have stopped the war.

THE STORY OF SAVITRI

One of the tales interpolated into the Mahabharata is the theme of a yearly festival of Hindu women — the story of Savitri's devotion, which conquered fate. That it is based on the inevitable cult of the dying god and tree worship does not lessen the nobility of the legend.

Savitri was the goddess-granted daughter of an old King of Madra, and she grew in lovely grace with slender waist and rounded bosom like burnished gold. But she was so appallingly lovely that she terrified suitors and none came. Therefore, the king sent her out on pilgrimage, in her chariot and surrounded by courtiers, to seek a husband of her choice.

She chose Satyavan, the Soul of Truth, brought up in the forest retreat of his kingly father. He had every virtue. But there was one fatal barrier, he was doomed to die within one year.

All pleaded with her to give up the doomed young man, but she only replied that once a maiden had chosen, her troth could not be denied. Whether his life were long or short, his virtues great or few, he was her husband, and she would follow him into the wilderness. So in the forest hermitage they lived gladly for a year, Savitri performing all the duties of a daughter-in-law to his parents and wearing a suitable bark-skin garment. But she was reckoning the days until the time when death was due.

Four days before the fatal time, she began to fast — a three-day penance and vigil, which gave power with the gods. On the dread day she saw her husband, stately and calm, start for the forest with a huge axe over his shoulder for firewood. She begged as a whim to go with him, and his parents finally agreed, although she seemed so pale and weak from fasting, to let her go to the forest with her husband.

The woods were glowing with flowers and wild fruits, and they went from tree to tree filling a basket, when the prince complained of a dreadful pain in his head, and swooning lay with his head in her lap.

Then a terrible vision came from the shadows of the forest — Death, with a noose in his hand, and looked silently at the two.

Savitri rose, and worshipped him — the god Yama. He told her he appeared before her because of her devotion, but he must carry away the spark of her husband's mortal life in his noose. From the prince's pale body he drew the vital spark, 'purusha,' smaller than the human thumb, and went his way, leaving the body cold.

But Savitri followed him. 'Turn back,' said Death, 'and do his funeral rites.' Savitri only answered that she might not choose but follow, for eternal law did not divide man and wife, and said, 'The final goal of virtue is truth and deathless love.'

Death appreciated her courage and devotion, and offered to bless her with any other boon than her husband's life. She asked him to grant sight and vigour to her husband's father... But still she walked with Death and would not leave. He offered her another boon, and she asked restoration of her father-in-law's kingdom... which Death granted, crying, 'Turn, Savitri... living mortal may not go with Yama.'

But Savitri, meek and faithful, followed Death.

She begged the boon of many sons, and when Death granted that, he was trapped, for he must restore her husband.... He gave back his life, saying that a woman's troth abides longer than life, and a woman's love can conquer the doom of death.

THE RAMAYANA

'He who reads and rereads this holy life-giving Ramayana is liberated from all sins, and exalted with his posterity to the highest Heaven.'

The Ramayana is interpreted as an epic of faithfulness and honour. It is less racy, more polished than the Mahabharata, and attributed to one author, the saintly Vilmiki.

Rama is a form of the sun god, and Sita was born from a furrow of the earth. Rama drew a mighty bow to win her, a bow which no mortal could bend, and he shot an arrow that spun seven times around the world, while the bow broke with a sound of thunder. The prince was also an incarnation of Vishnu, born to save the gods from the demon Ravanna.

Rama was the oldest, beloved son of the King of the Kosalas. But his aging father had three wives, and the youngest and most beautiful could do what she pleased with the doting old king.

All went well in an ideal land until her jealousy. Each caste continued in its due observances. The Kshatriyas bowed to the Brahmans (who bowed only to God); the Vaisyas bowed to the Kshatriyas; and the toiling Sudras lived by labour, presumably bowing to all. The soldiers never turned in battle and no man ever lied.

The people loved Rama and his bride Sita. But when the old king decided to resign in their favour, his young queen made a scene. She knew exactly how to twist the elderly king's emotions. He found her weeping on the hard floor, intoxicated by grief, not to be comforted, and promised her anything to dry her tears. At which she sat up and asked to have Rama banished and her own son Bharat put on the throne. The old king was stricken, but could not change. A promise was a promise in those heroic days. Everyone acted with exacted nobility.

Rama instantly accepted the situation, and agreed to fourteen years' banishment in the wilderness so that his father could keep his word. Sita, the soft, lovely princess, insisted that she would go with him and share the dangers of wild India. Lakshman, the younger brother, decided to go to protect them. Even Bharat, when he was recalled to take the throne, sweetly begged Rama to keep it, and, reluctantly reigning, always kept a pair of Rama's shoes on the throne to show that he was acting as his regent. A promise, even a blind promise to an hysterical queen, bound them all.

Sita and Rama and Lakshman wandered out into the forest. The path of their long journeyings is carefully mapped out by the pious, and pilgrimages are made devoutly along their route yearly by thousands. On their sixth day they came to the hill Chitrakuta, where lived the saint Vilmiki, who is the supposed author of the epic. This hill is the very holiest spot of the sect devoted to Rama — every scarp has some legend — and devotees with naked feet walk the path around it.

They went into the pathless jungle, through the Vindhya mountains and across rivers. In time they crossed the dark and eddying Jumna by a raft bound with scented creepers, and Sita prayed to the goddess of the river. The forests were beautiful with honeycombs on every tree, luscious fruits, the sal tree, the date, the palm, the mango, trees sparkling in the light. Ancient, gentle hermits lived in the groves. Rama recited mantras and built a house in the forest.

All seemed well, if sylvan, when unfortunately a Raksha maiden, one of the demon tribe who can wear many shapes, saw Rama, and fell in love. He refused her, and, furious, she threatened to kill Sita — at which Lakshman cut off her ears and nose. With a howl for vengeance, the demoness rose in the air.

She turned herself into a radiant deer, and Sita begged Rama to catch the lovely creature. When he chased and finally shot it, the dying deer called for help, imitating his voice. Sita begged Lakshman to hurry to his rescue.

Hardly was he gone when on came Ravanna, king of the demons of Ceylon. He was disguised as a Brahman, but he had a restless eye. Sita received him, unsuspecting. He praised her beauty and offered to make her queen of all his empire, with five thousand maidens to serve her. She protested, and cried for help, but he carried her off in the air in his chariot drawn by asses. Sita called to the forest creatures as she flew over the endless woods, and a vulture tried to save her, but was dashed to the ground. She was carried over the ocean to Ceylon, and, as she still refused the king's wooing, was shut up in a garden watched by female furies.

Rama was devastated, but as the rainy season came on, he did not attempt to hunt for her until after that. It seemed an odd hindrance to so powerful a hero, but in India rains can still stop riots — they are something evidently beyond even a sun god at times.

The two brothers meanwhile restored a banished king to his throne, who, in gratitude, promised armies to help find Sita. When clear weather came, he ordered his generals to search in every part of India. His monkey general, Hanuman, leaped the channel to Ceylon, and saw Sita in her garden, guarded by the furies. She asked anxiously if Rama was gathering his great forces to rescue her. Hanuman reassured her and as he sped back with his news, set fire to Ceylon.

Ravanna, with his city blazing, called a council of war. All his chiefs agreed to it except his youngest brother, who said calmly that Ravanna had wronged Sita and that righteousness would prevail. He was banished, and went over to Rama's side.

The battles of the siege of Lanka were such as demons and half gods and monkeys and magicians could fight. The demons themselves invoked the gods by sacrifice. The monkey troops came at them with rock and tree as missiles, but even when they threw great rocks the stone splintered against demon iron limbs. Ravanna shot seven bright arrows, keen and whistling, but as each came Lakshman split it with his dart.

A demon magician did the most deadly fighting. Rama and Lakshman, strong in every young strength, could not protect themselves against his bewildering spells. He wrapped himself in a cloak of invisibility, and he threw a serpent's noose, which sucked the life-blood from the heroes, and left them lying apparently dead, until Vishnu's fabulous bird Garuda cured them. There seemed no end to the demon's magic, but fortunately they learned his secret. He could be killed if caught before finishing the sacrifices which made him invisible. Lakshman stole upon him as he was piling weapons on the altar, using the head of a black goat in his evil rites, and put an end to him and his unearthly spells.

There was a certain system or order of strength in the combats. Ravanna was able to kill all the monkey generals, and only met his equal in Rama. The single combat between them seemed dubious, but at last Rama took Brahma's arrow, tipped with smoke and flame, and shot Ravanna to the heart.

The demon king of the underworld, who makes earthquakes, was killed. Heaven rained down flowers and the gods applauded, and Rama piously gave him a funeral pyre.

Then Rama was troubled by dark suspicions. Sita had been in the clutches of the demon all this time — could she have maintained her virtue? He doubted. Sita asked him, rather reasonably, why he had rescued her if he felt that way. She told Lakshman to build a great fire to test her purity, and walked through the flames unscathed, while the very god of fire in person came out and assured Rama that she was faithful.

That should be the ending, the happy reward of loyalty and courage. But a late addition tells that when Sita reached home, the people began to murmur, and again suspected her purity. Rama, listening to their suspicions, weakly banished her. She took refuge in the wilderness with Saint Vilmiki, and there Rama's two sons were born, to return to him after many years as handsome youths, and recite Vilmiki's stanzas of the Ramayana. Lonely Rama recognized them as his sons, and begged for Sita. But he could not seem to drown his suspicions. He asked her to go through another ordeal, just for form's sake, to convince the people that she was pure. Patient Sita, unable to bear any more, asked the earth to swallow her, which it obligingly did. After all, she was the spirit of the plough.

But Rama remained the ideal knight of India, inspiring his many worshippers by thoughts of his saintliness and chivalry — and 'if you could search the hearts of nine tenths of the women of India, you would find that they have as ideal Princess Sita.'

7. *Some Mediæval Saints*

NOT every man revered in India as a saint appeals to western thought; so much ancient magic is encrusted in saintliness, deeply as many saints were encrusted in dirt and anthills. But among the stories of slaughtering kings and bad-tempered, fantastic ascetics, it is a relief to find simple people who had lovable dispositions and shrewd human sense, along with a deeper gift of penetration, men like the genial and homely Tiruvalluvar and the wise Kabir. To quote an unsatisfyingly few stanzas from them, and from saints of rather different leaning, can scarcely give their flavour, but can at least point in their direction.

Some time probably after the second century, and before the rivalry between sects grew bitter in the seventh century, the low-caste poet called Tiruvalluvar lived in the tolerant land of the south. Little is known of him, but he is supposed to have been a weaver belonging to the humble Valluvars who acted as priests of the outcastes.

Tiruvalluvar knew an active and vivid land. The Dravidian kingdoms of the south, the Cholas, the Ceras, and the Pandyas, were exporting spices and jewels and cloth to Egypt, Greece, and Rome. Near the sea at storehouses and platforms, goods were stamped with the tiger seal of the Chola king, and surf boats rode crashing breakers from trading ships to the sands. Vendors of flowers and incense and fragrant pastes, traders in sandal and coral and pearls and gold, and the more prosaic tailors and fishermen and blacksmiths, were busy at their work.

The Aryans had little influence as yet in the south, and life was simpler than it became after contact with their elaborated culture. The Dravidians were not yet divided into rigid castes, although fellow craftsmen tended to live near together. Men were classified by place — as desert-dwellers or mountaineers; or by work — as herdsmen or fishermen or cultivators. Each class had its own social customs, and expressed itself in its own peculiar type of poetry.

All sorts of people were writing poetry — farmers, foresters, herdsmen, women, merchants, and kings. They added to the richness of a growing Tamil literature. In a time and place of such vitality, Tiruvalluvar wrote shrewd and homely verses which have become almost a Bible to followers in the south. A legend tells that when he, humbly born and unpretentious, offered his verses to the learned men of the Madura Academy, they were scornful. The pundits were sitting on a raft floating in the golden-lily tank of the temple, very proudly. But when Tiruvalluvar put his manuscript before them, the raft shrank to such small size that the scholars were all splashed into the water, and only the palmyra-leaf manuscript had room.

It now is a bulky book of 1330 couplets — the sayings of a very sturdy person, honest, self-reliant, believing in sincerity and kindliness and harmlessness, in one all-perfect God, and laughing at ascetics as rogues and impostors. He took what he liked from Buddhism and Hinduism, and perhaps also from Christianity which Saint Thomas had brought to the surf-beaten shores of Madras. He is more often ethical than religious — very literally a homespun philosopher. A few of his couplets chosen at random do not give the cumulative effect of his work, which moralizes on many aspects of life, but especially thinks of the average, home-dwelling person.

> He who lives home life worthily
> Shall first among all strivers be.

Of a wife, he wrote:

> If she be worthy, what doth ever lack?
> If she be worthless, then what else remain?

And

> They cannot walk with lionhearted pride
> Whose wives guard not their name from mocking eyes.

And of children:

> 'The flute is sweet, the lute is sweet,' say those
> Who've never heard the pretty prattle of their little ones.
>
> . . . .
>
> To make him first in the assembly of the wise
> Is all a father for his son can do.

He wrote temperately:

> He holds the world in fief
> Who knows the measure of the sense five.

But he had an amused scorn for ascetics who grew bad-tempered from their negative excesses:

> E'en for a moment it is hard to check the wrath
> Of those who've climbed the mount of saintliness.

Rather he praised various generous virtues:

> All for themselves the loveless spend:
> The loving e'en their bones for others give.
> . . . .
> Both loss and gain must surely come to all
> An unwarped mind the wise man's jewel is.
> . . . .
> Forgive always the ills that others do;
> But to forget them — this is nobler still.

People who followed the teaching of Tiruvalluvar would not wander far afield. He is a common-sensible saint, rather than ecstatic.

Many other saints were primarily emotional, caring only for an ardent love of God, often expressed in passionate human terms. Such worship, called Bhakti, is like devotional Christian worship, especially that of the Middle Ages. A personal love of God was everything to them. But, unfortunately, they chose different gods to love.

After the tolerant age in which Tiruvalluvar lived, when all religions borrowed freely of one another's thoughts and gods, a revival of Brahmanism somewhat martially swept out corrupted Buddhism from India. Yet the Brahmans did not agree together. There was bitter rivalry between those who worshipped Vishnu and those who worshipped Siva. Poets called *Alwars* had sung since the second century in praise of Vishnu, and in the seventh century Saivite saints began to sing equally violently in praise of Siva. They were distinctly crusading and partisan, and it was boasted that one poet sang Buddhism out of southern India.

The hymns to Siva in the Tamil tongue are so closely woven to intricate music, so packed with imagery which needs a long explanation in mythology and legend to an alien mind, that it is hard to choose one to show their fresh force. These are from the translations in The Heritage of India Series — The Hymns of the Tamil Saivite Saints. They had in their time a mighty influence, and are still chanted in temples of the south, and taught to children like Bible psalms.

> His ears are beringed, He rideth the bull;
> His head is adorned with the crescent moon's ray;
> White is He with ash from the burning ground swept;
> And He is the thief who my heart steals away...

begins one song by Sambandar, a lonely pilgrim of the seventh century. Siva seems a very stylized God to love so ardently, but, with all the many images and associations in the minds of his hearers, Sambandar had a powerful effect. He reconverted the King of Madura from Jainism back to Hinduism, and, it must be admitted, allowed him to impale eight thousand of the stubborn

Jains who preferred their own religion. As a person, Sambandar would not have been so agreeable to know as Tiruvalluvar. But he is a poet of ecstatic worship, of no matter how involved and curious a god.

He is our only Lord, conjoined still
To her whose breast no sucking lips have known...
Our great one who is lord and lady too...
. . . .

Thou art right and Thou art wrong,
Lord of holy Alavay...
. . . .

Those Buddhists and mad Jains may slander speak.
Such speech befits the wanderers from the way.
But He who came to earth and begged for alms,
He is the thief who stole my heart away.
The raging elephant charged down at him;
O marvel! He but took and wore its hide;
Madman men think Him, but he is the Lord
Who in great Brahmapuram doth abide.

A rather humbler saint, named Apparswami, sang:

Thou to me art parents, Lord,
Thou all kinsmen that I need,
Thou to me art loved ones fair,
Thou art treasure rich indeed.
Family, friends, home art Thou,
Life and joy I draw from Thee,
False world's good by Thee I leave,
Gold, pearl, wealth art Thou to me.

But the religious leader who expressed this emotional worship, Bhakti, most singly and madly, who began a great revival of Vishnu worship in Bengal and the north, who danced and sang and went wild for love of his God, is Chaitanya.

Chaitanya lived in Bengal from 1486 to 1534, and the stories of his violent ecstasies are many. The turbulent, unlettered boy became a scholar and scoffer. From that he suddenly changed, made a pilgrimage of several hundred miles to a temple to Krishna at Gaya, where he experienced rapture and became for life a devotee. Crying, 'Where is my God Krishna?' and telling his visions, he would be so overpowered that he would fall unconscious. He would spend days and nights reciting the name of God, singing and dancing with a particular music and instruments that excited all hearers to a religious intoxication. He had no respect for castes or creeds, but said he was a friend to all; and so his caste-bound native village sent him out, and he walked and walked thousands of miles over India, singing and dancing like a madman. The mere sound of the name Krishna, or sight of anything that reminded him of Krishna stories — such as milkmaids' jars — would send him into a delirium. In this love affair with God, he took the feminine rôle. Dasgupta writes of him in Hindu Mysticism, 'He described God's love as being like love of woman in deep attachment to man, so deep that all sex considerations have ceased,... only an insatiable desire of union in love remains. Love is God's very nature, so it is only through a passionate love of him that we can enjoy his deep love for us.' He felt that the highest worship was to consider God as dearest friend, or lover — especially to love him as a woman does her beloved.

The worship of Krishna, with ramifying legends of love-stricken milkmaids, inspired erotic and sensual extremes, as did that of Siva and goddess sects. An ancient worship of woman and sex maintained itself covertly in mediæval times under many explanatory rationalizations. And even today very primitive sex orgies are furtively carried on by the left-hand Sakti sects, with the rather slimy decadence that sophistication gives — orgies for city babus, frowned on by other sects of Hindus.

Chaitanya was erotic but idealistic, sincere though perverse. He must play the rôle of a woman in his devotion. 'The sweet love of Krishna as lover, husband, and lord was the most important feature of his life.' Chaitanya had great influence in founding a revival of Vishnu worship in Bengal, and his religious sect continues with somewhat dried-up ritualism today, and he himself is worshipped in places as a god.

The most interesting tree of saintly succession in India begins with the austerest of pure philosophers, Sankara, and ends, in one branch, curiously with a modern martial sect.

Sankara is the giant. His commentary on the monistic philosophy of the Upanishads is the basis of Vedantic philosophy, which has had the greatest influence and most numerous followers among thinkers of India, down to the present. This sketch cannot touch the fine precisions of philosophers. But the line of saints diverges from him.

Sankara was born in the coconut-grove land, in North Travancore, about A.D. 788, near the Malabar coast where Phœnicians and Greeks and Romans, and Chinese of the Tang dynasty and of Kubla Khan's kingdom, had all come over the warm foam seeking spices or sandalwood. He was of purest Aryan stock, his caste being the Nambudri Brahmans, the proudest and holiest in southern India, before whose approach untouchables used to flee and stand waist-deep in the mud of a rice-field, if need be, to get to sufficiently unpolluting distance.

The boy was precocious and wanted to be a sannyasi, but, as this was not proper for an unmarried youth in his locality, he had to leave home, and finally studied in Benares, whence he became widely known. He wrote the oldest extant commentary on the Upanishads, which amplified and made firm the scattered wisps of obscure monistic thought in that early holy book. His hymns and poems and commentaries make twenty-two volumes, of the greatest Sanskrit poetry and prose. He aimed metaphysical arguments against Buddhism, and helped to weaken that faith in India and to swell the power of Brahmanism. After several years at learned Benares, he passed most of his life as a wandering philosopher, founding houses of learning to win men from Buddhist thought. And in the Badrinath Temple in Himalayan snows he wrote his great commentary on the Vedanta Sutras.

He was a rigorous monist. He believed in only one reality in the universe — God (Brahman) — a complete abstraction, an unthinkable Being of whom one could only say, 'No, it is not such.' All else was an illusion; the earth and stars merely the mirage of ignorance, not man's ignorance alone, but Cosmic Illusion.

Sankara excluded all women and low-caste men from his Higher Knowledge. For them he admitted a Lower Knowledge, in which God had definable qualities, and, in association with Maya — Illusion — became the creator, preserver, and destroyer of the world. The bright deceit of sights and sounds and tastes and loves and hates he then provisionally allowed as real. For these men with less-developed minds — and women — he wrote beautiful hymns in praise of the gods.

For he believed mankind proceeded through the cruder ancestral ways of worship — the ritual in the 'way of the fathers' and the offerings in the 'way of the gods' — to the final stage when the world meant nothing, space, time, and thought were gone, and the individual soul became one with the universal soul, the all-pervading, single Reality, the ultimate Brahman without qualities.

The chilly spaces of Sankara's philosophy were not for the masses of people in India. A satirical legend tells of his meeting with tribesmen who sacrificed human skulls to Kali, and who asked him for the gift of his head — since that trifling illusion must be valueless to him.

Sankara stands apart, but his teaching influenced the next saint of the line, Ramanuja, born at Madras near the end of the eleventh century, who studied at Conjeevaram under a teacher of the school of Sankara. Ramanuja, however, tried to reconcile absolute monism with the idea of a personal God who could be loved. He could be hot-tempered as any scholar, and lanced against what he called Sankara's 'fictitious foundation of altogether hollow and vicious arguments.'

For Ramanuja the ultimate God was not without qualities, but 'compact of auspicious qualities.' And creation was real, not an illusion, and God, individual souls, and matter existed.... They existed in subtle form in God in his quiescence, and in creation they came forth in visible expression. Creation to him was a wish of the creator, who pervades the universe in which he has expressed himself. The individual had separateness, but his soul became one with Brahman by attaining divine qualities, and when released from transmigration, enjoyed Paradise with a personal God. This conception made it possible for Ramanuja to call his personal God Vishnu, and to claim that the worship of Vishnu was a direct fulfilment of the teaching of the Vedanta texts. So he gave to the followers of Vishnu much stability and dignity.

The next of the line is Ramananda, who absorbed the message of Ramanuja, but who was also influenced by the Persian mystic poets, Sadi, Hafiz, and others, who were having great influence in India then. He hoped to reconcile intense Mohammedan mysticism with Brahmanism. Perhaps, too, he was influenced by Christianity. Several streams of thought poured into his ample mind, and he in turn influenced the most delightful of all saints, Kabir.

Kabir was a small Mohammedan boy living near fifteenth-century Benares in the home of a weaver who was his real or adopted father, and he learned to work at his loom. But he knew that in Benares the great Ramananda was teaching, famed for holiness and wisdom. Kabir chose him as master. A young Mohammedan weaver would have great difficulty in passing the barriers between himself and a learned Hindu. Both Mohammedans and Hindus would object bitterly. There is a story that he hid on the steps of the Ganges down which Ramananda walked to bathe, and the master, stepping upon him, cried 'Ram! Ram!' and the lad declared he had received the mantra of initiation from Ramananda's lips and could not be refused as disciple. A more sensible explanation is that Kabir, by the mere act of trying to bridge the chasm between Mohammedans and Hindus, was the very embodiment of the tolerant teaching of Ramananda.

He became his disciple and heard great Ramananda's discussions with Brahmans and Mullahs. Then he himself sang. He chose thoughts from all sects — from the Brahmans and the Sufis, from the Vedantists and the Vaishnavites. He said of himself that he was 'at once the child of Allah and of Ram.'

Rabindranath Tagore has translated his songs. As scornful heretic to the quibbling, sectarian Benares of the fifteenth century, Kabir said boldly:

> There is nothing but water at the holy bathing places; and I know that they are useless, for I have bathed in them.
>
> The images are all lifeless, they cannot speak; I know, for I have cried aloud to them.
>
> The Purana and the Koran are mere words; lifting up the curtain, I have seen.

That was enough to hurl him bodily from the cult-encrusted town.

I laugh [he said] when I hear that the fish in the water is thirsty.

You do not see that the Real is in your home, and you wander from forest to forest listlessly.

Here is the truth! Go where you will, to Benares or to Mathura; if you do not find your soul, the world is unreal to you.

. . . .

The Lord is near [he said to the yogin], yet you are climbing a palm tree to seek him.

Kabir did not find life a joyless thing or a burden to be escaped. He did not care to thin his consciousness into Nirvana.

Dance, my heart! dance today with joy.

The strains of love fill the days and the nights with music, and the world is listening to its melodies.

Mad with joy, life and death dance to the rhythm of this music. The hills and the sea and the earth dance. The world of man dances in laughter and tears.

Why put on the robe of a monk, and live aloof from the world in lonely pride?

Behold! my heart dances in the delight of a hundred arts; and the creator is well pleased.

And when the world seemed less warmly happy to Kabir, and there seemed no certainty in a misty landscape of existence, he still kept his balance and a self-reliance such as Buddha taught.

To what shore would you cross, O my heart? There is no traveler before you, there is no road:

Where is the movement, where is the rest, on that shore?

There is no water, no boat, no boatman is there;

There is not so much as a rope to tow the boat, nor a man to draw it —

No earth, no sky, no time, no thing is there: no shore, no ford!

There, there is neither body nor mind: and where is the place that shall still the thirst of the soul? You shall find naught in that emptiness.

Be strong, and enter into your own body: for there your foothold is firm. Consider it well, O my heart! Go not elsewhere.

Kabir says: 'Put all imaginations away, and stand fast in that which you are.'

Kabir seemed by turns to his bewildered contemporaries to be a Vedantist and a Vaishnavite, a Pantheist, a Transcendentalist, a Brahman, and a Sufi. He chose what he thought good, and his own suffusing wisdom made a unity. Later Emperor Akbar was to try to fuse the wisdom of all religions and to succeed only in mixing formulæ and rituals. But Kabir's wisdom was that of one loving and spiritual person who separated wheat from chaff.

It is needless to ask of a saint the caste to which he belongs.

For the priest, the warrior, the tradesman, and all the thirty-six castes are alike in seeking God....

The barber has sought God, the washerman and the carpenter....

Hindus and Moslems alike have achieved that End, where remains no mark of distinction.

Kabir had neither the erotically emotional love of God, visualizing him as Krishna playing a flute or Siva on a bull, nor the Vedantist conception, abstract as stellar spaces, that exigently called for the obliteration of personality in a qualityless God. Kabir is described as one of a small group of supreme mystics, who resolve the perpetual opposition between the Absolute of philosophy and the 'sure true friend' of devotional religion. Kabir says that God and creature are ever distinct, but ever united.

> O servant, where dost thou seek me?
> Lo! I am beside thee.
> I am neither in temple nor in mosque: I am neither in Kaaba nor in Kailash:
> Neither am I in rites and ceremonies, nor in yoga and renunciation.
> If thou art a true seeker, thou shall at once see me: thou shalt meet me in a moment of time.
> Kabir says: 'O Sadhu, God is the breath of all breath.'

> I do not ring the temple bell [he said in Benares, where temples had elaborate rituals].
> I do not set the idol on his throne.
> I do not worship the image with flowers.
> It is not the austerities that mortify the flesh which are pleasing to the Lord.
> When you leave off your clothes and kill your senses you do not please the Lord.
> The man who is kind and who practises righteousness, who remains passive amidst the affairs of the world, and considers all creatures on earth as his own self,
> He attains the Immortal Being, the God is ever with him.

Such a saint and thinker, with his feet on the ground though his head might reach the sky, has a practical wisdom not unlike Buddha's teaching, though his philosophy differs. He takes a middle path, flinging out excess and superstition.

But India most beautifully illustrates what other lands show in scarcely fainter intensity — that only the great minds are simple; and that no matter with what lucidness and wisdom they speak, so that a little child might understand, the lesser minds want elaboration and the encrustation of their old cults. They also want definite and literal ritual and small divisions.

For Kabir was followed by another sweet-natured wise man, Guru Nanak, who was the founder of the Sikh religion. That is too long a story to tell, but the point is this: His teaching is in their holy book, the Granth, aiming to do away with caste and with idol worship.

But today, in the Golden Temple at Amritsar, the Granth is clothed and covered with flowers, and worshipped itself like an idol, by throngs of people. And the followers of the man who did not believe in caste divisions became merely one more sect in India, in time divided from others by fierce hostility. Under the Moguls the principal sect was persecuted until its leader, in self-defence, turned them into a well-disciplined military unit. The Sikh brotherhood of saints became a warlike flying wedge, competent, and capable of their own cruelties when they captured Kashmir of alien faith. It is too long a story to sum up, but that was one end path of the teachings of tolerant Kabir, just as the Inquisition was one end path of the teachings of tolerant Christ.

> So long as man clamours for the I and the Mine, his works are as naught [said Kabir].
>
> When all love of the I and the Mine is dead, then the work of the Lord is done.

Such brief and random choice can do little more than suggest that, amid the wildest extremes in India, among the mythology and half-disguised savage cult, there were thinkers who had not only the extreme of spirituality that is assumed to be Indian, but also men who had sound human wisdom, daily sweetness, and healthy good sense.

Part II
THE WAY OF KINGS

The map of India is a story book, and railroads take one from chapter to chapter, and roads turn the pages.

8. *Alexander and the Ascetic*

326 B.C.

TAXILA

THE ruins of Taxila have three layers of age... and the earliest city welcomed Alexander the Great.

Taxila now lies uncovered to view, about ten miles northwest from Rawalpindi on the way to the frontier. Sharp-lit hills encircle the valley, and the snow peaks of the Murree Range rise in the distant air. The moon is electric and whitely disturbing over the sleeping cities, the half-Greek reliefs on the blurred buildings of the later citadels. The mound called Bhir, which saw Alexander, is now only a spur of hill above the brook-bed, still showing the line of its boundary wall on two sides, and elsewhere washed down into obliterating bays and gullies.

East and west had one sharp meeting. Alexander the Great decided to conquer Hindustan. The spoiled half-god laid his irresistible plans during winter in the Afghan mountains. When Greece came to touch India, what might have flowered from such a union of alien genius?

India was developing her passive ascetic; Europe, her man of action. With Alexander, the contact was to be made between rational West and mystic East. To be sure, the warriors in India resemble the warriors anywhere else, and the sages of India are more akin to the mediæval philosophers of Europe than to the princes of their own land. But the characteristic attitude of the two continents, the emphasis, the centre of gravity, is opposite. When Europe bred her active Alexander and India her passive ascetic, each was expressing her *n*th degree.

Taxila lay on the caravan route between Asia and India, sunning itself, a city grown great under the Persian rule of northwestern India. It had a sheltered, favoured situation with fertile soil and freshening water from the hills, and it throve on the caravan route as a town thrives on a river. Camels grunted and knelt to unload in the bazaars. Merchants with strange tongues and Mongolian faces brought in the wares that had come over high passes. In the market-place a crowd gathered about a girl put up for sale as a slave, because she was too poor to be married. By the burning grounds, a jewelled, wide-eyed widow, hysteric with excitement, made ready to jump on the flames that burned her husband's body. A grave student from a distance came inquiring for the university, which bore a reputation in far lands as the most learned in India, famed for its arts and sciences. In the busy city people were contented with prosperity and learning and the steady rule of their rajah; and not greatly bothered by their usual border warfares.

The Rajah of Taxila, however, was not pleased with the way his customary wars were succeeding. The king of the neighbouring state, gigantic 'Porus,' was far too dogged. It might be a wily thing to make friends with the oncoming Greek Emperor. It was a matter that bore considering...

For India was no nation, with a single loyalty. It was fenced off into little states of despotic petty rajahs, struggling with neighbouring tribes of democratic freemen, or of bordering princes, jealous of boundary marks and the rights to rivers. The whole continent was developing in its slow, meticulous way, little conscious of dying Persia, undreaming of a Mediterranean Sea and the upspringing strength of Europe.

Gorgeous Alexander cast his eyes toward India. He had conquered the whole Persian Empire, which had been overlording the civilized world. With that colossus tumbled, he made a small boy's gesture of defiance and set Persepolis on fire. That was glory — to burn the proud Persian capital in flames and leave her columned stateliness a ruin. He dreaded an anticlimax to life after that.

From Persepolis, the way to India lay over wide Persian deserts of many colours, and over the bleak mountains and plateaus of Afghanistan. As he marched, he founded cities. He named them for himself — Alexandria among the Arachosians (now Kandahar); Alexandria under the Caucasus. He left in each a garrison of his troops, and managed to fill the walls with natives to populate and make rich his base cities. In the winter of 329 B.C. he pushed his troops over the mountains toward Kabul, a painful march of men up bitter snows in a hostile land, trying to keep fed by the slow establishment of supplies.

He had cavalry from Greece, sporting young aristocrats trained to finesse of manœuvre; spearmen who had been Macedonian peasants, plodding afoot heavily loaded; and agile Balkans from their mountains armed with spears and bows. He had Persian cavalry — gilded youth picked up from the court of Darius; and dirty Mongolians who could ride hell-for-leather on tough ponies and aim true as they rode. He had sharp-eyed, bargaining Phœnicians who could have been sailing to India; and black-skinned Egyptians who had preceded the Indians in hollowing out caves for the sake of their religion, and left behind them waning glories. All these he united in his strange invading army, plus a few Afghanistan tribesmen who thought it wise to join the winning side.

The news of his victories spread by word of mouth, by wandering hillmen coming down to the plains of India to trade, by all the amazing ways that news still travels in India without the use of letters or wires. The story spread that the conquering Greek king was coming into India, bringing armies. Descendants of the Vedic Aryans who had once poured over those passes to master the land, now owners of rich cities on the plains, puzzled and debated.

Encamped in the Kabul Valley by the summer of 327, Alexander sent messages ahead to the chieftains and princes of northwestern India to submit. The son of the Rajah of Taxila had already sent envoys across the Hindu Kush Mountains to offer to march beside Alexander against any Indians who resisted; and the old Rajah, apparently persuaded that the overwhelming foreigner might help to flatten their troublesome neighbour, King Porus, travelled to Kabul to offer pliant submission. Before Alexander had cleared all the hornets' nests of hill tribes in those bitter mountains, the old Rajah had died, and his son, with oxloads of silver, welcomed the conqueror and yielded Taxila to him in 326 B.C.

The soldiers of Alexander poured in friendly fashion through the streets, and the bazaar tenders were busy feeding these strange men in outlandish clothing, of all colours and tongues. The soldiers in turn were open-eyed for all the surprises of the alien city, with the Rajah's elephants swaying through the lanes. The most amazing of all the fresh sights which these seasoned travellers came upon was that of some fifteen ascetics, ten miles out from the city, sitting naked upon rocks so hot under the sun that one could not endure to pick a way barefoot over them.

Naked, narrow-backed men, deliberately spoiling their bodies — a strange idea to the athletic Athenians, who gloried in their perfect strength and well-being. The Indians sat motionless and silent, enduring the torturing rays of the sun. The Greeks, in their broad-brimmed hats and high-topped boots and their sweeping cavalry wraps, came up to watch them. But the Indians did not move a muscle. Ever curious, the Greeks wanted to know the reason for this needless endurance, and carried the question to Alexander. The pupil and patron of Aristotle commanded the professors of this school of thought brought before him. But the ascetics evidently had no fear of a conqueror — no curiosity concerning a foreigner; and, in fact, no interest at all in the Emperor of the world who was in their city. They sat on their hot rocks and refused to go to Alexander.

Then Alexander sent an interpreter. Through three languages his message was translated to the holy men. The Greek King would like to learn their wisdom. The ascetics replied that the only way to begin to understand was to sit naked on the hot rocks beside them.

The Greeks evidently had no desire to do that, and the conversation seemed closed. Then a more conciliatory ascetic said it was very creditable of Alexander to want to learn wisdom, but that since all thoughts must pass through the words of three interpreters, who were men of mean understanding, it was like straining clear water through mud.

The talk, once begun, progressed, and the Indians asked if there were similar teachings among the Greeks, to which a man who had studied under Diogenes (a most sympathetic figure to the Indians) replied that their country had Pythagoras, Socrates, and Diogenes. The ascetics were pleased, but regretted that the Greek philosophers clung to such meaningless compromise with this world as clothing.

Then, strangely enough, one of the ascetics, whom the Greeks called Kalanos, left his hot rocks to join the court of warriors and philosophers surrounding the sulky and glorious Alexander. His fellows considered him an apostate, and continued to blacken and shrivel their bodies in the sun, but Kalanos stayed with Alexander. When Alexander left Taxila on his conquering path, Kalanos went with him.

Why did an ascetic who renounced the world attach himself to an Alexander who was trying to conquer it? Was there some strange kinship between the two men? The Greeks do not tell. The Indians have no chronicles of the affair.

Alexander marched on eastward into India. Kalanos stayed in his train, retiring when he chose to lie on his back exposed to sun or rain, then again joining the discourse of philosophers, comparing wisdom, imparting his doctrine to the inquiring Greeks.

At the Jhelum River, Alexander met with an Indian of different spirit from the Rajah of Taxila, or from Kalanos. The Rajah of the Pauravas, whom the Greeks called Porus, when summoned to Alexander, sent word that he would meet him on his own frontiers, in arms.

The two armies drew up on opposite sides of the powerful stream. The Indian war elephants were as bulky as battlements on the far shore. The Greeks made wooden boats to cross the swollen river, which was flooded into whirling rapids. They must row under the shower of arrows from the Indians, and climb the bank against elephants. Alexander's genius was equal to the attack. He made constant pretence of activity, now in one part of his camp, now in another — alarms at night, sudden singing of battle-songs, forming of cavalry — all planned to wear out the nerves of the enemy, who had to be ready at every point. The monsoon came on, and heavy black rains thickened the view and lashed the backs of men and horses. Porus did not relax. He sat a huge elephant at the centre of his lines, ready to meet the conqueror of the world.

At last, twenty miles downstream the Greeks found an undefended shore. Hidden from sight by a wooded island, in the thick of a gale and among frequent bolts of lightning that killed men, the Greeks somehow got their boats across to a strip of land cut from the mainland by flood. The Indians, learning of it, raced against time to the place. The Greeks still had to get men and horses across a last treacherous ford, while the enemy bore down toward them. Alexander had just time to place at the head of his troops the archers from the Asian steppes, who could shoot riding. His hard-bitten, battle-tried cavalry overmatched the horsemen of Porus, who were not trained to such shock of attack. The Indian archers were at a disadvantage, for they had to place their tall bows in the ground to shoot and could find no firm base for them in the slippery mud. Then Porus flung his elephants into the fight — the terrible elephants to crush Alexander. They were the last means of his own defeat. They stampeded in their ranks so madly that Porus had to give way.

Bleeding from a wound, he rode off defeated — and a horseman spurred after him, the wily young Rajah of Taxila, gloating undoubtedly, who came with a message from Alexander asking him to surrender. Porus found strength to throw a javelin at him by way of reply.

A more friendly envoy persuaded Porus to turn, and at that, Alexander, who could admire a gallant enemy, galloped out to meet him. The Greek was pleased with the bold, romantic fighter and asked what terms he would like. 'Act as a king,' said Porus, and refused to amplify his words, saying that included all things. Alexander reinstated him as ruler of his own lands under the empire, and added large pieces of neighbouring ground to his former kingdom.

Still an unsatisfied passion drove Alexander on to more conquering, more stamping of his personality on the world. What morbid hunger made him push his heterogeneous army over new deserts and treacherous rivers — what was the pull of the horizon? He played a thrilling game of conquest by his own rules. Now courteously magnanimous, now savagely slaughtering, he pressed on.

He organized as he went, unifying northwestern India, leaving in charge its own kings — to whom he added power — or his generals. His cities were planned to serve as bases for trade, and the whole framework of empire was planned, far-reaching for the thin line of his invasion, but possible.

There seemed for a time no limit to his pushing on. The check came finally from his own army, rather than the enemy. He was near the strong state of Maghada, prepared to attack, when his troops, worn out by heat and fatigue, refused to go farther. Alexander sulked in his tent for three days in classic fashion, but had to yield to the inevitable. Before he reached the Beas River, he turned his unwieldy army homeward.

The return was a march of genius and endurance, of wooden boats sailed down rivers to the Indus and the Persian Gulf, then of wilting marches through death-giving desert toward Persia. Alexander marched by land, while part of his force sailed up the Gulf. He crossed blazing sands where nothing grew but aromatic shrubs, and his men dropped and died. As he retreated from India, tribes had submitted, or cities had fought and been massacred. The Brahmans of some lands stiffened the resistance against Alexander and were hanged. Nothing had stood against him. He left behind him the scaffold of an empire, great satrapies under his generals, local units ruled by their own princes, a string of fresh-built cities to serve as trade centres and quicken the pulse of the East. All was to build the power of Alexander and spread his triumphant ego.

Kalanos, the ascetic, strangely drawn into the vortex of the ruddy conqueror's magnetism, could in no way compete. Alexander won the glory of all places and years. But Kalanos had his moment.

When the army finally reached Persia, Kalanos, honoured among philosophers of the Emperor, decided to die. Had the same dog bitten both the man who acquired and the man who renounced? Suicide was an honourable tenet of Kalanos's faith; but he did not simply go out into the desert and die unobtrusively.

He told Alexander that he had decided to die, and though the conqueror protested and argued, Kalanos was inflexible. So Alexander helped him to do it properly. He had a suitably huge funeral pyre built. Kalanos stepped into a litter, garlanded with flowers. He chanted hymns in praise of the gods as he went. The whole army was drawn up in battle formation around the pyre. The faggots were covered with precious brocades to make them as elegant as possible, and gold and silver vessels of rare workmanship were placed about. Kalanos mounted the pyre and gave away the precious things to his friends. Then he stood in sight of the whole army and adopted the correct and prescribed posture for death by fire. As the faggots were lit, the Greek brasses shrieked all at once, the troops shouted a mighty battle-cry, and even the Indian elephants, well trained, trumpeted to add to the glory. Kalanos stood motionless in the sight of all, while the heat from the flames rose. The army watching him might have conquered the world. But he was doing a thing which not even their general, Alexander, cared to do. He was burning himself up, and to the sound of trumpets.

What is left in India of Greece and of Alexander's conquest? Perhaps the justness of proportion of a temple in Kashmir. Perhaps an added felicity of sculptors' tools. Certainly the whole school of Ghandara carving which flourished in the northwest, and is now gathered into galleries in Peshawar, Lahore, Muttra—figures with half-Greek faces, the Indian interpretation of Greek. The strongest influence of Alexander on India may be the folds of a Buddha's garment.

For within two years Alexander died in Babylon, and his tentative empire, which might have held had he lived, crumpled. After him came the Seleucid and Bactrian kings who held the northwest, and through them filtered a Hellenic civilization to that corner of India.

Possibly Alexander's unifying influence may have helped the coming Indian conqueror, Chandragupta, to found his empire, for he broke up the rigid tribal loyalties. But if Alexander had depended on the Indian invasion for his glory, the desert marches and the struggles with floods and walled cities were as wasted as water poured into sand and as obliterated as the featureless mound of Bhir at Taxila.

9. *Asoka, the Amiably Glancing*

Reigned from 274–237 B.C.

OUTCROPPING boulders, chiselled with writing, rise in widely separate parts of India. They are variously regarded by the simple people who live near them. One is called the 'letter rock' and believed to have magic medicinal powers. The peasants wash the rock with water and give the result as a drink to sick man or beast. Another inscription on a shady ledge is the favourite seat for goatherds in the heat of noon. These rocks, found at such distances as from Peshawar district to Madras and Mysore States, are edicts of the first Indian Empire, written by the Emperor Asoka.

The same letters are on sandstone monoliths, polished like satin, so finely burnished that once they were mistaken for brazen pillars. In the fourteenth century impetuous Feroz Shah dragged two of them to Delhi. One is set up on the famous Ridge, the other is in Ferozabad, the dead capital near-by, where its incised letters tell the laws of Asoka, and the certain truth that 'it is difficult to secure both this world and the next.'

In the museum at Sarnath, near Benares, stands the capital of another column. Strong-maned, curly-haired lions squat, back to back, in Persepolitan spirit and style and precision. Below them a beautifully carved horse and elephant and bullock move around the monolith. The perfection of the workmanship at that time, the silken finish of the rock, and the clarity of the conception suggest Persian workmen imported into India, but point also to the intelligence and force which employed them.

Of all the mighty building of Asoka, known to legend, little is left. The traveller who has the Bombay–Delhi train flagged at Sanci may stop there to see the huge Buddhist stupa with its four incredible gateways. The core of that was begun by the Emperor Asoka, the earliest Indian architecture in stone. His capital, Patalipatra, so magnificent that Fa-Hien thought it the work of genii and spirits and no mortal hands, lies sunk beneath the silt where the modern city of Patna sprawls its nine miles along the Ganges. In the village of Kumrahar near-by, scattered shafts of polished stone were uncovered, from a great hall of columns. Underneath Patna, prosaic and dusty, underneath part of the East Indian Rail-

Copyright Archeological Department of India

LION CAPITAL OF ASOKA PILLAR

way and the civil station of Bankipore, lie buried unknown remains of the capital of the Emperor Asoka.

Once in many ages a personality rings clear as a bell or unmarred porcelain, and all who hear realize that the sound comes from the wholeness of a man. Broken and inwardly dissenting characters often stamp their fame on the centuries from their very discord, a strong brain or ego ill-matched with some weakness silly as a penguin's wings. Fame comes less often from the simplicity and the stately proportion of a character. So that one may say — as one says, that is a good Percheron horse, a good Baldwin apple — that, without distortion, is a good man.

Asoka might serve not only as a good specimen of mankind, but more especially as a good type for an Indian ruler. Most of the kings of India too readily followed the dictates of Manu, that their function was to slash the enemy and uphold the *status quo* of the castes; leaving thought to the Brahman priests. The two worlds, of thinking and acting, readily separated. Asoka undertook to combine them. He united a spiritual attitude and a practical ability in a proportion rare in India — or elsewhere. He might stand — and has stood — for what the desirable and fitting ruler should be for the dreaming medley of India, a mild and fatherly monarch, with his eye on both worlds.

Asoka, the 'amiably glancing,' sat at his daily massage listening to suppliants. Four attendants with ebony rollers were rolling briskly and artfully up his smooth brown arms as he listened and gave judgment. There was a reason for this intrusion of the private toilet into the public day. It was not ceremonious, no sanctity had accrued to it as to the occasion when the king shampooed his hair, and gifts came to the great and joyous court festival on ox-wagons and chariots and elephants gay with gold and silver. This was a practical matter of keeping physically fit while getting through the mass of work of the empire. To be chief justice and legislature and executive of the loosely bound country took most of the waking moments, and the Indians had evolved this passive exercise. It was amazing to the athletic ideal of the Greek ambassadors. But it had its purpose and skill, and achieved its end.

Asoka's seat was in a stately palace. Power and spaciousness had been achieved in an Indian empire by the time he was born. He was the grandson of the conqueror and strong man, Chandragupta.

As he sat and listened to the appeals, one may imagine the moment, the period in his life, when his mind was pulled elsewhere by an inner crisis. The powerful man — still in his youth, trained to grace and swashbuckling, with most of the map of India his to do with as he chose or could, massaged and tended, with an army for his toy and a distinct flair for using it successfully — had nevertheless a horror in his mind. Perhaps in the crowd of suppliants he saw the orange robe of a Buddhist monk, which turned his thinking. He was seeing vividly before his eyes dying and groaning or decaying men piled into heaps on his recent triumphant battlefield.

He was too sensitive and inquiring to accept a tradition which lay at hand to excuse the Brahmanical doctrine which Krishna preached, that death was an unimportant change from one life to another, that each man must fulfil his predestined duty, and the duty of kings was conquest. Asoka could not silence his horror with that reasoning. How much he was influenced by some Buddhist monk is a matter of legend — but he had the conflict to solve.

Two very different men affected Asoka's life: his triumphant grandfather, Chandragupta, who founded the Mauryan dynasty; and Gautama Buddha, whose teachings had spread only to a small group of strolling monks and mendicants. Those two warred within him.

Chandragupta had been nobody in the state of Maghada, a land nearly as large as France, and as strong as any kingdom then in India. It lay in the northeast on the Ganges plain and its people were apparently more Dravidian than Aryan. Some said that Chandragupta was the low-born son of a barber; others, with perhaps a later flattery, related him to Buddha's knightly family. He seems to have been an adventurer, and one story tells that he saw Alexander, and, being observant, carried away several useful ideas. After Alexander's death, the border tribes rose in revolt against Greek rule, and Chandragupta may have taken advantage of that to lead them. In Maghada, his opportunity came through a revengeful prime minister, various scheming malcontents, and one or two strategic murders. At the right moment Chandragupta was at the capital gates with his army, and the throne of Maghada toppled to his hand.

He did not stop with Maghada. He added one state after another until he had a solid bloc in northeastern India. Then a rival appeared from the West — the satrap of Babylon, Seleucus, who had inherited part of Alexander's shattered empire. Seleucus also planned to take a page from Alexander's book. The two armies drew up for battle on opposite sides of a river. The Greeks glittered with helmets and spears. The Indians were behind their massed war elephants. But a curious thing happened. There was a beautiful anticlimax, and no battle. Perhaps Seleucus learned for the first time of Chandragupta's strength — some nine thousand war elephants and five hundred thousand men. Perhaps a revolt had begun somewhere in the rear of his far-flung kingdom. In any event, he made this surprising bargain — he gave up to Chandragupta his lands as far west as the Kabul Valley in Afghanistan, and took in return five hundred war elephants. The low-born king returned to his capital the emperor of a wide country, and the Greeks saw fit to send ambassadors to his court and Megasthenes wrote his observations.

Perhaps it is not to be wondered that the stout conqueror, who so quickly pieced rival kingdoms together into a patchwork empire, intimidated foreign armies and held the strong schemers of his court at bay, should feel the desirability of a few secret stairways and hollow pillars in his palace.

He fortified his town of Patalipatra on the confluence of the Ganges and Son Rivers. He built of wood, as was the custom, and the long narrow city followed the river for nine miles, enclosed by a high wooden palisade with loopholes for archers to aim through, with five hundred and seventy lookout towers, with sixty-four great gates, and a moat two hundred yards wide.

Chandragupta proceeded to organize his unwieldy empire. India — as it is today — was a country of villages, linked then by trails through forest or scrub desert, worn by the feet of pilgrims, traders, or soldiers. Most of the people were cultivators, with minds so simple and duties so well defined by caste that even if a battle began in a neighbouring field they would plough their own rice patch unconcernedly. Each village, a self-sustaining unit, was ruled by a headman with a council of elders, the panchyat, who oversaw the farming and tax-collecting, and decided upon the duties and privileges of the village barber, washerman, potter, and blacksmith.

Above the village headman, the rule converged through the overseer of five villages, through district officials maintaining revenue and police departments, through the great viceroys up to the ministers of state, who obeyed the emperor. All power focussed to him, and his rule was absolute, so long as his arm was strong.

The Hindu theory was that a king must be an unlimited monarch, guarding the social order, and that the need for kings arose because people had grown wicked and needed to be punished.

By the time of Chandragupta, the regulations of life and trade had grown detailed. In towns and cities people had to stay indoors during the night hours between trumpet calls, they had to sleep in the front of their houses because of fire hazard, they could not build windows that looked into another house, and their property and persons were registered. The traders who took caravans through India had to have passports, and pay duty at port and frontier and at city gate. The prices of ordinary goods were fixed and proclaimed daily by officials. To watch over so large a country so minutely, Chandragupta kept an army of spies watching for wrongdoings, which the king might have punished by fines or whipping, mutilation or death, with or without torture.

Chandragupta, as king, traditionally owned all the land of India. The peasant who ploughed might assign a share of his acres to another man, but the title still remained with the king, who took as revenue one quarter of the produce of the land, plus the rent. Whether or not Chandragupta was oppressive is uncertain, but Sanskrit writing on polity tells a king not to shrink from severity, and the people to 'bear like strong bulls' the burden of taxation. In return for the money his people paid him, the king must take care of the land, see that fertile fields were tilled, wasteland brought into bearing, and dry places irrigated.

Chandragupta ruled for twenty-four years by making strong men fear him, while he himself lived in fear. He passed the empire down to his son Bindusara, Asoka's father, who held it for twenty-four years without change. Little is known of him. Poor man, his only immortality was a blunder of taste. He wrote to a Greek king asking if he might buy some figs, sweet wine, and a sophist. The Greek sent the figs and wine, but wrote that it was not their custom to sell their philosophers.

Asoka, his son, played as a child in the gardens of the spreading wooden palace built by his grandfather at Patalipatra — a place of many courtyards and many secrets. It was so noble and stately that the Greek ambassador declared it rivalled Persia's cities of splendour — Susa and Ecbatana.

The child knew for his playground the enclosed gardens lying open to the eye of the sun; the trees trained formally to elaborate interlacing, birds flying thickly, green parrots flocking to the mango trees, or screeching to his shoulder; and the particular privilege of small princes, that of swimming in the great pools of the garden, the oblong tanks that lay warm and shallow below the trees, full of fish so tame that the naked little boy could scoop them up with his hands.

The men about him wore robes of shining white linen, and with white ivory earrings against their dark skins; they dyed their beards blue or green or purple or orange, so that they moved as brightly as the parrots themselves about the garden. In the forecourts of the palace, Asoka knew the strange mock bodyguard of his father — the dwarfs and hunchbacks in armour, the wild men of the forest, and the women armed with spears. Beyond that was an actual bodyguard, very much in earnest, to protect the emperor.

Asoka was heir to an India grown complicated. A child must sense the fear and precaution — the terror of being a king — from the prudence of that palace. No attendant inside could talk to any outside. The palace women could not have their own families visit them, except at illness. Any employé coming to the palace, from messenger to dancing-girl, must be bathed and massaged and put into fresh clothes before entering. Asoka must have known from some terrified nurse or palace woman the underground passages, the secret staircases and hollow pillars — all the paraphernalia of escape. The kitchens were in a secret place, and many tasters had to sample each dish for possible poison before it was sent to the king. Female slaves had to handle all his clothing to see if they sickened from the touch, and beauty specialists had to apply their cosmetics to their own faces first. The king as a last precaution slept in a different room every night.

The boy Asoka was tutored by Brahmans in the traditional kingly lore. He studied the Vedas and the pithy commands of the Sutras. He was taught that he must gain control of his passions by considering the famous men of the past. He must never be off guard or lacking in force. He was also trained in the science of polity, elaborately thought out. Although a king was considered the father of his people and taxes as payment for his defence and care, yet other teachings were far from spiritual. For example, the familiar policy that the nearest state is one's enemy, and the state beyond that, the ally. Also that a monarch should consider four means of gaining his ends — by war, by conciliation, by bribery, or by sowing dissension among the other peoples. And technique was also given in planting suspicion between allies, treason in other peoples' armies, and revolt in their cities.

The boy studied it all and absorbed what suited his nature. He was strong, and on leash to begin some conquering of his own. His territory was already enormous, and by his further conquest he was to unite more of India under one rule than any single power did again — even Akbar the Great Mogul or the crafty Aurangzeb — until the British in the nineteenth century. His land began in the far northwest, with a good share of Afghanistan, and went to the Bengal coast in the east. The northern limit was the wall of the Himalayan Mountains, and he finally ruled as far south as an imaginary line between Pondicherry and Cannanore. Only the southern tip of India was left beyond his ultimate rule.

Young Asoka, heir to all this land and system, trained in polity, philosophy, and mathematics, a strong and poised young man, bred in the way of courts, tasted power. He felt more than equal to some conquering of his own. His great army included the fine, old-time warriors of the Kshatriya caste with their high traditions, as well as hirelings and guild levies and subdued wildmen of the forest. Perhaps he had some strain of cruelty still unconquered in his nature. A legend of some centuries later tells that in his youth he decided he would have a hell. He made a strong enclosure, into which he threw all criminals to be tortured by a horrible brute.

Finally he threw in every passer-by. This curious monkish tale, designed to show the great power of Buddhism over his spirit, might have a trace of foundation in his youthful severity or warlike nature. His sound and lovable character seems a strange base for such a legend. But he did have a zest for battle.

He led his armies against the Kalingas in the ninth year of his reign. Their state lay to the south, along the eastern ocean, by modern Orissa and northern Madras. Asoka attacked them magnificently, after the tradition of heroes, until the dead bodies of the Kalingas were heaped up in piles. That was as a conquering king should do. He had been trained to it by sacred and profane teaching. Slaughter was incidental to the glory of kingdoms.

Then, riding over the battlefield made hideous by the dead and dying, he suddenly saw that warfare was piteous and terrible. Asoka, flowering from the rich soil that Chandragupta's conquests had prepared, felt only pity for the broken men his battle had left and shock at their suffering. Through the ugliness of the slaughter he realized that nothing after all had been gained, but that something had been wasted and interrupted by battles — man's thought and piety.

Buddhism lay at hand, with its doctrine of mercy to all. His thinking left him no peace until he adopted the Buddhist doctrine of Ahimsa — doing no hurt to any.

Asoka's instinctive revolt and disgust at warfare was the turning-point of his attention. He looked into the religion of these strolling priests who taught gentleness to all creatures, both great and small, and the rather steadying doctrine of doing one's duty in the present world.

Asoka studied Buddhism as a lay disciple, and two years later, in the eleventh year of his reign, he became actually a monk of the Buddhist order. But here an interesting balance shows in his character. He did not, so far as one knows, consider giving up his kingdom to become a recluse or leave unregarded the affairs of his kingdom and his people. He translated his religion into action and undertook his responsibilities whole-heartedly.

'All men are my children,' he had carved in stone. 'As on behalf of my own children I desire that they may be provided by me with complete welfare and happiness in this world, and in the other world, even so is my desire on behalf of all men.'

This was the theme of his reign.

Out from the pomp and triple guarding of his wooden palace he went as a simple monk, and travelled far into his forest kingdom, through the packed and footprinted trails, stopping at villages of clay or bricks or boughs to discuss and talk with his people — here a Brahman to whom he gave reverence and alms, there an old man for whom he had gifts; instructing the village groups that gathered about him — in what? Very simply, the king instructed in religion and morality.

Moreover, he felt the importance of that so greatly that he told his officials to do the same thing. The government was not to be merely an affair of tax-collecting and improving farming, so that bigger crops produced bigger revenue; or even of judging between man and man in excitable, involved feuds. The government was to lead the mind and character of the people into happiness and spiritual rightness. Mild and unquestioning, Asoka tried to blend mind and matter to best uses.

Over the space of India from Afghanistan to Bengal, Asoka had need of a means of communication. He began to write his edicts on stone pillars of an incredible polish. Amazing, gentle words he had carved and set up in all parts of India, to be studied by the officials and any learned men who might be able to decipher the incised stone.

His first rock edict at Girnar still tells, 'Here no living thing must be killed or sacrificed.' This is in the Buddhist tradition of sparing all life. Then he sets a personal example of abstinence — and abstinence with a certain amount of difficulty, which he admits. He is speaking with no veils and without indirection, frankly to his people. He is trying as hard as any to follow right actions, and admits that he finds it gradual. 'Formerly in the kitchen of the king,' the edict confides to the dead centuries, 'many thousands of animals were killed daily for the sake of curry. But now, when this rescript on morality is written, only three animals are being killed daily for the sake of curry — two peacocks and one deer — but even this not regularly.' That curry, flavoured with peacock and venison, was hard to give up. But Asoka was bracing himself and his household to it. 'Even these animals shall not be killed in the future.'

'It is difficult to perform virtuous deeds,' wrote Asoka, his workmen carving it on stone in a far country. 'He who starts performing virtuous deeds accomplishes something difficult. Now, by me, many virtuous deeds have been performed.' A king should not minimize himself, and Asoka spoke the truth.

Some of the virtuous deeds were very gracious. He had groves of mangoes planted, and along the highways he set trees to give shade for travellers from the beating Indian sun, banyan trees whose branches drip their fringes of roots toward the ground, making a green twilight over the highway. And he had wells dug at intervals to relieve the thirst of travellers, indeed, to make travel possible in the days when a journey must go from water to water. Very likely the wells were like spacious rooms surrounding the pool, with steps leading down to the water, a shade-giving space under which pilgrims or merchants could sit, resting and discussing with agile, expressive hands. He ordered medicinal herbs planted, to help cure the many diseases that were besetting India. And he arranged for medical treatment for men and cattle throughout his land.

But he was chiefly concerned with the individual happiness of his people, which would come from right thinking and right acting. 'All men are my children.' Paternal, certainly — even more nearly maternal in his yearning for a sweet-growing and healthy personality for his 'children.' But India has always thrived on paternalism; it suited the strange and varied medley to have itself fused and interpreted by a benign king.

In the fourteenth year of his reign, he undertook seriously this matter of character, of right and releasing understanding which would help his people live. He appointed high officials who, beside redressing wrong or misfortune and making gifts to the poor, were to teach piety. The governors were to hold assemblies in which its law should be discussed — conferences, so to speak, on ethics; not too bad an idea for the officials of a present democracy. His lesser officers (although not to the neglect of their duties) had to attend these conferences. He wished to have his officers free from envy, harshness, or impatience. He wrote that they could not hope for favour either from Heaven or their sovereign if they did not obey his commands.

If the people of India had relaxed into slacker fibre from the more complex and luxurious life of the empire, Asoka undertook to restore old standards. These are the laws of piety which he had carved on rock. Every man should cultivate self-control, purity of mind, gratitude, fidelity. He should abstain from rage, cruelty, pride, and jealousy, and — oh, wise Asoka — practise self-examination constantly. He should be strictly truthful, treat all living beings with kindness, obey parents, reverence elders; be generous and decorous to friends, relatives, ascetics, and Brahmans, and treat servants and even slaves with kindness. He should be tolerant of other religions, as all creeds, in India at that day, agreed on the essentials, and all aimed at purity of mind and self-control. A man should respect his neighbour's faith.

Asoka, although suggesting tolerance to all faiths, nevertheless began to send missions to preach the gospels of Buddhism to other lands. Before he was converted, Buddhism had lived for two centuries in the valley of the Ganges as a sect of Hinduism. It had been an affair of monasteries and strolling monks in orange robes with their begging-bowls. The simplicity with which any man might retreat to the forest and become a saint rather brought down upon it the jealousy of the Brahmans, who had hitherto held that as a prerogative of their caste alone. But Buddhism was not a serious rival to Brahmanism until Asoka's reign.

He began in the eleventh year of his reign to send missions charged with preaching to Ceylon, to the kingdoms at Madura and Trichinopoly, to the Malabar coast, to Bombay, to the Mahratta cities, to the Himalayas and Kashmir.

The conversion of Ceylon (one of the last strongholds now of pure Buddhism) is attributed to Asoka's son Mahinda. The story goes that he gave up his right to the throne of India and put on the yellow robes, to his father's delight. Mahinda had studied all the arts and sciences necessary to a prince, but he cared only for religion and philosophy, and he was moved by a yearning to help poor, lost peoples. He heard of the ignorance in Ceylon, where men still sacrificed animals to their gods, and he went there, sailing across the warm choppy seas with the flying-fish starting at the bow of his trifling boat.

And in Ceylon, near where the ruins of Anaradhupuram now bare their noble proportions, Mahinda stood at the top of a great rock in the forest, while all the king's hunt was coming that way. And he called out in a loud voice, frightening the stag, and presumably the king: 'Tissa, live and let live. Kill not. It is an unworthy act.' When King Tissa turned, startled, to see what this might be, Mahinda continued calmly: 'All good people must refrain from causing pain to others, whether man or beast. If you are king, you should set a good example to your subjects.'

That is how Ceylon became Buddhist.

A daughter of Asoka, too, according to legend, gave up the glitter and prestige of her royal life, and, becoming a Buddhist nun, carried to Ceylon the slip from the sacred bo-tree under which Buddha had sat during his enlightenment. Today it is still shown, the oldest tree of history, growing gnarled and enormous.

Asoka himself, however, did not give up his kingdom's work for the religious life. After a period as a strolling monk, in which he learned to understand all kinds of people, he continued his steady work of administration. He was the supreme judge in India to whom all appeals rose.

His day was scheduled, traditionally and minutely. The water dripping through a water clock divided the day into eight parts. Music and drums woke him. His priest came first to salute him; then the doctors, who talked over the health of the palace people; and the kitchen attendants, who told him perhaps — before his conversion — how many deer and peacocks were to be roasted in the kitchen that day. For a little space he was left alone, to consider his policies. Then he called his secret agents, whom he sent about their business (this was the system of spies which Chandragupta had developed; Asoka enlarged the plan, using them as a human telegraph system to report to him the happenings in all parts of the empire), and his military advisers, who made their report.

After that he went to his hall of public audience, where any of his subjects might come to appeal to him.

By that time the heat of noon would be pouring into the palace — the sultry, sleepy, oppressive heat — and he would bathe and eat and perform his religious devotions. Then he was at home to those bringing him gifts; every day is Christmas to an Indian emperor, since it is not courteous or politic to approach him empty-handed.

After his correspondence with distant ministers, he had a few more moments of quiet to consider his policies. Toward the cool of the evening, his animals were led past for inspection, his horses and elephants in their trappings. He talked with the commander-in-chief of the army and inspected his arsenal, and when the sun sank, he performed the imperial religious ceremony. After dinner he had little relaxation for the spies came in with their reports. The day finally ended with another bath and a space for religious meditation. Then the drums struck up as he went to bed.

Such a stern routine left little time for the dalliance and self-indulgent pleasure that one popularly pictures in a pearl-hung Eastern emperor. Even so, Asoka felt that he was not working hard enough. He had another rock edict engraved, his sixth:

> For a long time past business has not been disposed of, nor have reports been received at all hours.
>
> I have accordingly arranged that at all hours and in all places, whether I am in the ladies' apartments, in my bedroom, in my closet, in my carriage, or in the palace gardens, the official reporters should keep me constantly informed of the people's business, which business of the people I am ready to dispose of at any place.
>
> ... for I am never fully satisfied with my exertions and my dispatch of business, than which nothing is more efficacious for the general welfare. And for what do I toil? For no other end than this, that I may discharge my debt to animate beings, and that while I make some happy in this world, they may in the next world gain Heaven.

For Asoka's conception, magnificent and incredible as it may seem, was that the king should help the human stuff of his kingdom. He would not disregard the care of his own fields, and channels for water to wet the crops. There must be good harvests to feed the people, and taxes paid to keep the complex empire working like a hive of bees. But he was concerned beyond that. Can a government rise above the level of its human stuff? Of what value is it if people are shoddy and distorted? Its chief duty, he thought, is to help their happiness of spirit and integrity of character so that their lives may be full-flowered. That idea was Asoka's great originality.

For thirty-six years he reigned over India with its rich waste of jungle, its faint trails and threaded villages.

He put his moral and possibly dreamy policy into practice with a magnificent, undoubting simplicity. His empire held clashing elements. There were gruesome and strong-fibred savages whose minds were dim. There were half-subdued border tribes waiting a chance to rebel. His rule was not evenly established in all parts of the country. In the Kabul Valley, in the Deccan, or the lands of the Kalingas or Avantis at the south, his overlordship was remote and the chance of revolt was strong. But this is the way he dealt with troublesome tribes. He sent an edict to his officers in the Kalinga country, where mischief brewed.

> If you ask what is the King's command to us, or what truth is it that I desire the borderers to grasp? the answer is that the King desires that they should not be afraid of me, that they should trust me, and receive from me happiness, not sorrow. Moreover, they should grasp the truth that the King will bear patiently..., so far as it is possible to bear..., and that for my sake they should follow the Law of Piety, and so gain both this world and the next.

With all the generous sweetness and gentleness which Asoka felt, he kept his feet on the ground. He did not quite go up into the clouds of pure theory. After all, he was governing a motley empire and keeping it steady for thirty-odd years. He remarks that he will bear patiently so far as it is possible to bear patiently — but no further. Beyond the limits of patience, Asoka still had his army. However, there is no record of his using force again anywhere in his kingdom. That does not mean that he did not control the situation. But he was one of the rare kings — has there been another? — who put into practice a policy of peace.

On the foundation which Asoka laid, no man built a superstructure. Perhaps that was the inevitable weakness of his plan. It all depended on his strength, and no strong person inherited. After his death, the Mauryan dynasty weakened and crumbled.

His reign was followed by centuries of conflict in India. Little islands of power rose here and there above the waves of chaos: the Sunga dynasty, with its moments of peace and beautiful sculpture; the Andhras of the Deccan, with four hundred years of stability and art in their smaller realm; the Kalingas of Orissa and the Kushan kings of the northwest — the conquering White Huns. Kanishka, the Kushan king, was strong, he was a disciple of Buddhism, and he held the northwest. But elsewhere in India, and after his death, came marches and countermarches, and slaughter and looting. India was any man's oyster. For five centuries no one approaching Asoka's stature arose to give a measure of unity and peace until the Gupta kings, three centuries after Christ.

Asoka's political empire did not hold, but he acted as the Constantine of Buddhism. The force and fame which he gave to that religion brought pilgrims and devotees from far parts of the earth, until it had spread and filtered to distant countries, where it lived long after it had disappeared from India.

10. *The Classic Age of India*

320 A.D.–647 A.D.

THE golden time that Hindus love to recall, when her kings were mild and just, when her artists blended many foreign skills into their own noble expression, when the peasant song, 'Good King Vikramidyit gave us pearls to eat,' might almost be true, was the rule of the Gupta kings. They reigned in Elizabethan vitality and expansiveness from A.D. 320 to A.D. 480, over a wide empire. After that their kingdom was shattered and shrunken. But the mellow civilization still spread full tide over northern India, and the shaped and classic art called Gupta kept its integrity until the beginning of the seventh century, and the character of the period was not completely interrupted until after the death of King Harsa in 647.

While the Gupta kings reigned, Rome fell to the Visigoths, Attila scorned Paris as too trifling for his attention, Saint Patrick was converting Ireland, and wild Anglo-Saxons swarmed to the English shore. In Gupta palaces and courtyards life was moving very sensitively, very gently, with refinement of refinement. The great picture book of the age is in the caves of Ajanta in the Deccan, frescoes which, though painted after the empire's greatness and in a neighbouring state, give life to that time of flowering.

A wild country surrounds the Ajanta caves today — ravines and stiff forests under the blazing, sickening sun of the Deccan. A trivial stream once cut a hill to the curve of a crescent moon, and on the westward face a trail leads for three miles past cave after cave hewn into living rock deep enough to make monasteries and chapter halls for Buddhist monks. The earliest caves were begun about 200 B.C., and the work continued for nine hundred years. Then they were lost from memory until 1819, when a company of British soldiers on manœuvre came amazedly upon one dark opening after another. English Tommies stood looking at the silent Buddhas.

In some of the caves frescoes were painted, rich and vital ones from about A.D. 500 to A.D. 650, when Buddhism was putting forth its last impulse in India, trying to save its followers from the reviving power or fascination of Brahmanism. Kings considered it an act of piety to endow chapter halls at Ajanta, and nobles acquired merit by giving money. Yet a force of emotion drove the pious meditators, with simplest tools, to carve the untouched hills deep into their rinds, to cut great figures from the living stone, and to paint some halls with frescoes that seem to find the space all too small to tell their message of devotion and stories of a gracious and miraculous Buddha. Though the Ajanta caves were decorated by monks, they do not suggest asceticism, a loss of delight in the senses, or worship oblivious of the world. The rough, grey rock of the hills suddenly modifies into carving of refinement and certainty, the language of courts as well as of monasteries.

The centrifugal forces had been at work in India, and kingdoms had split apart as simply as lizards that drop their tails at a touch. But the second king of the Gupta line, Samudragupta, who in moments of peace dallied with a lute, brought many quarrelling states under the peace of one strong rule. He marched to the south until he met the Pallava kings. He marched to the north to the wall of the Himalayan Mountains. His kingdom finally made a wide band across India, from the Jumna River of the west to the Brahmaputra of the east, from the northern mountains to the Narbada River about two hundred miles north of present Bombay. Then he had time to compose verse and play his lute, and to proclaim his sovereignty by sending a white stallion wandering for a year, followed by armies, challenging any to dispute his reign where the white horse browsed. At the end of a year he performed the great ceremony of the horse sacrifice.

It was the son of the conqueror, with the empire founded, who became the beneficent and brilliant ruler and called himself Virkamaditya — Sun of Valour — besides his own name, Chandragupta the Second. He ruled from A.D. 375 to 413, and it is probably about him that tales have gathered of the Rajah Bikra, or Vikramadyit, who flung pearls for food in India's golden age. He went conquering also, and annexed Malwa, Gujarat, and Kathiawar. He gathered to his court poets, musicians, astrologers, mathematicians, painters, and sculptors — men of genius called the 'nine gems' of his court.

History knows too little of him. But the paintings of Ajanta of a century later, in an allied kingdom, give the liveliest sense of life in his age, the beneficent time to which Hindus look back fondly.

Inside an Ajanta cave it is easy to imagine banners and tapestries. But the tapestries are rich frescoes over the walls, graceful and enticing, both spiritual and sensuous. The people in those paintings give the impression of tropical ease, of a languid and unstrained life in a world of pervading warmth. Clothes are merely decorations, not necessities. The slender brown bodies are bare to the waist or curve through transparent veilings. Ornaments are applied importantly to people and things. A headdress is as careful as a cathedral. The women arrange their hair in ways that take hours of study. The fabulous Indian love of splendour is suggested gracefully. Strings of jewels dangle from canopies as the proper ornaments.

A long civilization lies behind the gestures of graceful wrists, and incredible fingers trained to expressiveness. Men and women move as carelessly and beautifully as dancers. Gentleness is there, and sweetness of mood. Nothing in the paintings is alarming. The lovers are appealing and the worshippers are putting their souls into the worship.

Here are the people of untouched and unconquered India in her warm prime, subtle, but before her subtlety elaborated into triviality. The king is no hawk-nosed frontier chief, but a slender, smooth-faced youth, with soft brown shoulders, baring all of his slender, rounded torso, hung with ornaments. Women are in attendance, bare to the waist, in their long, wrapped skirts with horizontal stripes — long-eyed women with slender wrists, wearing earrings and anklets.

A princess is making her toilet, swaying her hips below a heavy jewelled girdle while an attendant brings a tray of little ointment pots. Two high-born lovers are reclining on a couch together, he brown, she fair, leaning against him, while a black serving-woman in a figured velvet jacket is presenting a jug, and a dwarf stands below with an urn.

Ladies sit on their balcony, watching a sword festival; a king, in white tunic and leggings and white fillet, goes hunting, his elephants wearing white necklaces. Elephants in flat-bottomed boats are going to battle; elephants with striped saddle blankets, and attendants kneeling on the rump; elephants bearing archers or kings under umbrellas.

A rich civilization, beauty-loving, soft, seductive. But can the graceful princes defy the Huns pressing over the Afghan border, evil-smelling nomads with a leader as fierce as Attila? The Huns are massing to swarm down into India, while the wave of Gupta civilization rises to its crest.

Buddhism and Brahmanism both swelled its power. Behind the people of Gupta days was the background of the Vedic hymns, the groping, brilliant Upanishads, the code of the lawgivers, the epic poems, and now, the fairy story, religious Puranas, the storehouse of mythology. The original simplicity of Buddha, his teaching of kindness to all and the sparing of every living thing, his inculcation of self-control and duty in the world as it is, his democratic sincerity, were being elaborated by his followers into something rich and strange. Brahmanism was rising in a renaissance of strength. This mental background lay in the thinking of the cultivated few.

The many lived simply by the codes that were taught them, carefully watching out around their huts for Bhuts and rakshasas.

The art of the Gupta period drew from many lines of inheritance, and combined skill learned from Asia, Persia, and Greece with native ability, now all unified to express the classic mood of the period: strong, composed forms, without uncertainty or naïveté.

Kalidasa was the classic Indian poet, whose imagery was sensitive, but not so ornate as that of the later writers. He, too, expresses an age of gentleness, of sensitive perception and form. To quote, ever so sketchily, from him may help to imagine the period. Charles King gives this translation of Kalidasa's 'Cloud Messenger,' the appeal of an exile to a great cloud moving north to carry his thoughts to his wife in the Himalayas.

> Massed radiance and vapour, wind and water is a cloud; meet a message is for mortals.... For the lovelorn in their longing are distraught....
>
> With plantain flowers thy thunder the fruitful earth can clothe; the royal swans shall hear it sweet upon the ear....
>
> The speckle coats shall see the kadamba flower, all yellow and brown, with infant stems, and the plantain trees in the marshland whose firstling buds peep forth. Earth's savour they shall smell too, that is sweet, most sweet, with the scent of forests burnt....
>
> Though thou wouldst journey swiftly for the sake of her I love, thou wilt dally, I foresee it, friend of mine, on this mountain on that mountain, that with kutaja flowers is sweet. Thy welcome shall be cried by peacocks....
>
> Pray to survey Ujjain's palace balconies... the town-girls' eyes that quiver and shiver at the lightning's forked flash....
>
> The dancers' girdles twinkle with their dancing, and their hands are wearied as they wave in sport their fans... when on their nail marks thou dost shed the first refreshing drops of rain, they will cast on thee side glances long as rows of honey bees...

In 'The Birth of the War God' (translated by Monier Williams) he tells the story of the maiden Uma, daughter of the Himalaya, who falls in love with the ascetic god Siva, and wins him from his austerities by the strength of her own devotion. Siva as an ascetic is a terrible figure. But when Uma is asked,

> How shall thy tender hands
> Decked with the nuptial bracelet's jewelled band
> Be clasped in his, when fearful serpent's twine
> In scaley horror on that arm divine.
> How shall thy robe, with gay flamingoes glancing
> Suit with his coat of hide with blood drops streaming...
> Deformed is he — his ancestry unknown
> By vilest garb his poverty is shown

the astute and steadfast girl only replies:

Who is greater, he who strives for power
Or he who succors in misfortune's hour?
The spring of wealth himself, he careth naught
For the vile treasures that mankind have sought.
If on his brow the crescent moon he bear
Or if a shrunken skull be withering there
The funeral ashes touched by him acquire
The glowing lustre of eternal fire.

Kalidasa's most famous work is Sakuntala, a play of the love of a king for a forest maiden, in which they are separated by the wrath of an irascible holy man whom the girl offends, and only brought together by the plot of the ring swallowed by a fish and found by a fisherman. The plots of plays at that time were likely to run in well-worn grooves. The hero was usually a king with one or more wives, who fell in love instantly with a lovely woman, sometimes a nymph. After many trials, the happy ending came. Sakuntala was no exception.

There were three classes of actors — the inferior, who spoke a patois called *Prakit*, in a monotonous tone; the middling; and the superior, who spoke Sanskrit. Women were ranked with inferior creatures, and even the heroine spoke Prakit, but the hero spoke mostly in Sanskrit verse. Apparently there was no scenery, but there were elaborate costumes worn. The device for opening the play was first a benediction pronounced by a Brahman; then a dialogue between the manager and one or two actors, giving an account of the author and flattering the audience; then introducing one of the cast. After the benediction, in Sakuntala, the manager calls:

Lady, when you have finished attiring yourself, come this way.
Here I am, sir, what are your commands?
Manager: We are here before the eyes of an audience of educated and discerning men, and have to represent in their presence a new drama composed by Kalidasa, called Sakuntala, or the Lost Ring. Let the whole company exert themselves to do justice to their several parts.

The learned men of Vikramaditya's day listened to the play of Kalidasa — or perhaps they went to 'The Little Clay Cart.' Their minds were stimulated by the imagination of the playwrights and poets, and the exchange of trade and thought with other lands.

To ask how Vikramaditya was governing his kingdom leads to another story. The only record of the actual condition of the state, curiously enough, is Chinese — the diary of Fa-Hien, traveller to India, who casually mentioned the rule of the Indian emperor.

Fa-Hien was a Chinese Buddhist monk who lived in Shan-hsi. When he was twenty-five years old, he decided that he would go to India to hunt for certain Buddhist books of monastic discipline. And that was all that interested him.

To travel from China to India in the year four hundred was terrifying. His route is still the way of explorers only. He had to cross the Gobi Desert *and* the Himalayas, and after that had a thousand miles to travel to his particular holy cities.

But he was not to be diverted. He was a man of decision. At the age of ten he had made his choice between his family and the monastery, in which he decided to stay. 'I did not quit the family,' he wrote, 'in compliance with my father's wishes, but because I wished to be far from the dust and vulgar ways of life.' Later, as a young man, he was cutting rice with several fellow disciples of the Chinese monastery, when some hungry thieves flung themselves upon the defenceless monks to steal the grain. The others ran, but Fa-Hien stood his ground, and talked to them simply. 'If you must have the grain, take what you please. But sirs, it was your former neglect of charity which brought you to your present state of destitution, and now again you wish to rob others.... I am afraid that in the coming ages you will have still greater poverty and distress.... I am sorry for you beforehand.' As one might reason with Chinese or Chicago bandits today.

Such a man was not to be stopped from his journey of piety by distances or devils. India to him was simply the birthplace of Buddha. He was concerned only with the miracles of his lord in that land — only incidentally he mentions the government of Vikramaditya. But he was willing to undergo the terrors of devils and tortures of travel to reach India. He set out across China, so ploddingly slow that two years found him still working his way across the Chinese map. And according to Buddhist custom, he spent each summer in retreat and meditation, while the rains beat down outside.

Then he had to face the matter of the Gobi Desert, with his little company of four friends. Before setting out he was told fearful stories of its sand-storms. In one gale, the wrinkled wise men told him, such great waves of sand shifted that three hundred and sixty cities were buried in a day. Fa-Hien must have felt pitifully small to face such a force. He was given some advice about the best route to take across that place of 'many evil demons and hot winds.' And he found it as terrible as the warnings. 'There is not a bird to be seen in the air above,' wrote Fa-Hien, 'nor an animal on the ground below. Though you look all round most earnestly to find where you can cross, you know not where to make your choice, the only mark and indication being the dry bones of the dead.'

But by the white bones of dead men, Fa-Hien made his way across the Gobi Desert.

In the uninhabited countries he had to find ways to get across the rivers that he met. In a bleak rock land, imagine the microscopic figure of an earnest Chinese monk on the bank of some great stream that gnashed a way through the land, trying to think a way to master the mighty water. Besides rivers, there were mountains. He came to the northern barrier walls between Kashmir and China, and wandered among them for twenty-five days, trying to find a way. It is uncertain just where his path went, but for a month he worked his way over ranges of mountains. 'Snow rests on them both winter and summer. There are also among them venomous dragons which, when provoked, spit forth poisonous winds, and cause showers of snow and sand and gravel.' The microscopic figure was climbing up the heights among the dragons, his robes puffing and flapping, making his way up a crenellated wall.

For fifteen days he followed the course of a river. 'The way difficult and rugged, the bank exceedingly precipitous, which rose up there — a hill like wall of rock, ten thousand cubits from the base.... When one approached the edge of it, his eyes became unsteady, and if he wished to go forward in some direction, there was no place in which he could place his foot, and beneath were the waters of the river called the Indus.' What better description could there be of a precipice? — 'If he wished to go forward in the same direction, there was no place in which he could place his foot.'

He found in some places paths chiselled along the rocks, and ladders by which to climb up or down. He went up some seven hundred of such ladders built 'of old' and in unsteady repair. He crossed the Indus by bridges of rope — those things that began to sway and get momentum as one is over the centre of a torrent.

By way of Afghanistan he came down into India, through Peshawar, Muttra, to Benares, and to Patalipatra, where he saw Asoka's palace still standing like columns built by genii — and surely by no mortal hand.

As he was chiefly bent on finding books of monastic rule, he was chiefly observant of the miracles of Buddha. Taxila he records as the place where Buddha — as a Bodhisattva — gave away his head to a man (who seemed to need it). Two days' journey farther, he notes the place where the Buddha gave his body to feed a starving tiger.

Marvels and wonders. In Peshawar was Buddha's begging-bowl, which the monks brought out daily before the monastery. But when an invader tried to steal it and harnessed his elephant to it, the elephant could not move it. Neither could a four-wheeled cart, yoked with eight elephants. At noon the seven hundred monks of the monastery brought out the bowl and made offerings to it. When poor people threw in a few flowers, it was full. But very rich people might throw in hundreds of thousands of bushels, and yet not get to the top.

Fa-Hien found India partly Buddhist and partly Hindu, in

a great struggle between faiths. To him the Brahmans were heretic, and had ruder manners. He called them 'the Brahmans with their contrary doctrine, full of hatred and envy.' He told a legend to show how inferior their religion was.

A Buddhist and a Hindu temple stood side by side. When the sun was in the west, the Hindu temple was entirely covered by the shadow of the Buddhist. But when the sun was in the east, the Hindu shadow bent aside in order not to touch Buddha. The busy Brahman priests burned incense and lighted lamps to shine all night before their gods. But in the morning, the lamps had vanished. The angry Hindus stayed up all night to see who was stealing their lamps. They only saw their own gods rise from behind their altars and pick up the lamps and carry them over to place at the feet of Buddha.

That was a legend to bolster a losing cause. The birthplace of Buddha was by that time a place of ruins, a 'scene of great desolation.' Fa-Hien found neither king nor common people, only a few monks. He saw great mounds where buildings had stood, and on the roads, wild elephants, and lions. India always had its dead cities.

But Fa-Hien found the kingdom of Vikramaditya benign and prosperous and tolerant, truly a kingdom of a golden age, when pearls to be eaten were not too incredible.

This is his description of the 'Middle kingdom,' the Ganges Valley, which Vikramaditya ruled.

> In it heat and cold are finely tempered — no hoar frost or snow. The people are numerous and happy. They have not to register their households, or attend to any magistrates and their rules. Only those who cultivate the royal land have to pay (a portion of) the gain from it. If they want to go, they go. If they want to stay, they stay. The king governs without decapitation or corporal punishments. Criminals are simply fined, lightly or heavily. In cases of repeated attempts at wicked rebellion [which happened even then] they have their eight hands cut off. The king's bodyguards and attendants all have salaries. In the whole country people do not kill any living creature, nor drink intoxicating liquor, nor eat onions or garlic.

The only exceptions were the outcaste Chandalas.

> These are held to be wicked, and live apart from the others. When they enter the gates of a city or a market-place, they strike a piece of wood to make themselves known, so that men know and avoid them, and do not come into contact with them.

They were relegated to the ancient position of lepers, shouting unclean, unclean. The good castes did not deal in intoxicating drinks or live stock. They would not sell pigs or fowls or cattle, and there were no butcher shops in the town bazaars. Outside the city the outcastes who were fishermen and hunters sold their meat, though to what buyer is not mentioned.

At Patalipatra Fa-Hien marvelled at the palace of Asoka, 'all made by spirits, which piled stones and reared walls, gates, and executed the elegant carving and inlaid sculpture work which no human hands in this world could accomplish.' Buddhism was flourishing there, both in its purer form, Hinayana, and in its elaborate development, Mahayana. Both sects had their monasteries, but there was as yet no religious bitterness.

'The cities and towns of this country are greatest of all in the middle kingdom. The inhabitants are rich and prosperous, and vie with one another in the practice of benevolence and righteousness.' A Brahman procession bore 'figures of devas with gold, silver, and lapis-lazuli grandly blended, silken streamers and canopies — a structure of bamboo five stories high; twenty cars of niches with Buddha seated in each.' During this procession the rival religions seemed to join. 'The Brahmans come and invite the Buddhas to enter the city.'

In this benign city there were charities and hospitals.

> The heads of the Vaisya families establish houses for dispensing charity and medicines. All the poor and destitute-orphans, widowers and childless men, maimed and crippled and diseased, go to these houses and are provided with every kind of help, and doctors examine their diseases. They get the food and medicines which their cases require, and are made to feel at ease; and when they are better, they go away of themselves.

The same sweet courtesy prevailed in the monasteries. This is the way Fa-Hien, the dusty, strange-looking Chinese pilgrim, was received by the saffron-robed Indian monks: The old residents went to meet him, carried his clothes and his almsbowl, gave him water to wash his feet all cracked and sore from travel, and oil with which to soothe them. They served him the liquid food which his vows permitted him to take out of regular hours. Only after he was rested and refreshed did they ask him how many years he had been a monk, to decide the delicate matter of his precedence in sleeping-apartments.

For three years Fa-Hien stayed at Patalipatra, where he finally found the copies of monastic rules he had sought. He learned Sanskrit and copied the monkish laws, and then sailed away in 'a large merchant vessel,' travelling fourteen days to Ceylon, and three years back to China.

How much Fa-Hien's transcript of monastic rules benefitted the monks of China is not known. The thing upon which he set the greatest store and spent such tremendous effort has dissolved and vanished. But the few paragraphs he threw in accidentally about the rule of the Gupta king — whom he did not even name — have been the delight and joy of Western scholars, trying to penetrate the past of India.

Two more Gupta emperors — Vikramaditya's son and grandson, continued the mild, wide rule of the golden age. Then the tempest broke.

The White Huns encamped in the Oxus Valley. They made one vicious attack on the Gupta kingdom, and were driven back. Then they conquered Persia and killed the Sassanian king. They came down through Afghanistan and took Kabul, and, with all resistance from that side gone, swept down in irresistible flood into India. Their leader, Toromana, was like Attila.

The Huns broke up the political power of the Gupta empire. It split again into kingdoms, with wars and counter-wars, and the kings ruled a little area. Until Harsa arose, the sixth century was utter chaos. The family and clan traditions, the stories of dynasties were lost. If it had not been for Fa-Hien, and the poets, and Ajanta and a few coins and sculpture, nothing would be known of India's golden age, and the pearls to eat.

11. *King Harsa, Who Marched to Golden Drums*

Reigned A.D. 606–647

HARSA, the last great king of the Gupta period, moved in enormous, if sometimes dusty, splendour.

Today, when an old-fashioned prince travels to Delhi with two or three hundred retainers, when he has himself weighed in a balance against gold and silver to be scattered in largess to the crowds, the lavishness and cumbersome habits of grandeur are only scant remnants of the glories of past kings.

King Harsa worshipped the Sun, Siva, and Buddha with a gracious inclusiveness. He was born near the end of a classic period, when taste had begun to weaken into excess and prettiness. He was the imperious elegant, the amateur who turned his hand to Sanskrit drama, the pedant who wrote a treatise on grammar. He was also brave and decisive, a conqueror, and a benevolent autocrat, who does not entirely deserve to be seen through the flowery, overwrought style of the court dramatist, Bana.

As a boy of sixteen, he was faced with a state in chaos, and begged to set it right. He might well have thought the time was out of joint. Think of any sixteen-year-old boy asked to save his country, not as a puppet rallying-point, but as a real dictator. A kindling spark of courage was needed — a leader. It was always to be the great Hindu need in fighting — a focus, one person to follow like a banner, be it an untried boy.

He was reluctant at first to take the empty throne of the State of Thaneswar, near Delhi, which his father had ruled. But danger and the threat of chaos spread farther than his own borders. Northern Indian states were struggling in a discord that meant anarchy. The grief-stricken boy of sixteen was called on to save the situation.

Bana, the Brahman playwright, was one of two writers who left manuscripts about Harsa's reign. The other was the stately Chinese scholar, Yuan Chwang (also called Hüan Tsang). The Chinese stories are straightforward and clear; Bana's are mannered and imaginative and precious. Of the two, however, Bana's give greater suggestion of the way it felt to be a privileged Indian of the time of Harsa — how one lived (with slightly Hollywood ideas of luxury) and above all, what was the fashionable attitude of a period.

Bana wrote two plays which give background to Harsa — scenes of lordly, late Gupta India. One, called the 'Kadambari,' although fiction, draws vivid pictures. The other, the 'Harsacarita,' is the actual partial story of King Harsa. In spite of its adjectives and fulsome figures of speech, scholars find it based on truth.

'Who is not carried captive by tales fashioned in freshness of speech, all alight with similes and the lamps of glowing words?' asked Bana.

From the 'Kadambari' comes the ideal of a king. He sat

> on a couch studded with moonstones, beneath a small silken canopy, white as the foam of the rivers of Heaven, with its four jewel-encrusted pillars joined by golden chains, and enwreathed with a rope of large pearls.... His left foot rested on a footstool of crystal... that was adorned by the brightness of his feet, which yet were tinged blue from the light rays of the sapphire pavement, as though darkened by the sighs of his conquered foes.

The sighs — or the widows — of conquered foes, were the conventional attributes of a king.

Bana is more realistic in describing the king's longing for a son:

> When will my queen gladden me wearing yellow robes, and holding a son in her arms... with his curly hair yellow with many a plant, a few ashes mixed with mustard seed on his palate, which has a drop of ghi on it as a talisman, and a thread bright with yellow dye around his neck, as he lies on his back and smiles with a little toothless mouth.... When will he adorn my courtyard, as he toddles around it, followed by my heart and eyes, and gray with the dust of the court... and when, running about at will in the courtyard, will he run after the tame geese... and weary his nurse who will hasten after him, following the sound of the bells in his golden girdle.

This is the way a barren queen secured the desired son — a queen with wide hips and slender waist who attended to her 'usual duties, such as putting on her ornaments.' The queen slept in the temples of Durga — a custom not unknown today. She

> bathed under a cow adorned with auspicious marks.... Every day she would rise and give to Brahmans golden mustard leaves adorned with every gem; she stood in the midst of a circle drawn by the king himself, in a place where four roads meet, on the fourteenth night of a dark fortnight, and performed the auspicious rites of bathing, in which gods of the quarters were gladdened by the various oblations offered... with a sunrise turn she worshipped the pipal and other trees... she offered daily to Goddess Durga a sacrifice of parched grain; she besought, with mind prostrate with adoration, the naked wandering ascetics... she made the Brahman chant the Veda; she heard sacred stories constantly repeated; she carried about little caskets of mantras filled with birch leaves written over in yellow letters; she tied strings of medicinal plants as amulets; she daily threw out lumps of flesh to

the jackals; she told the pundits the wonders of her dreams; and at the crossroads she offered oblation to Çiva.

Harsa's own parents, according to Bana, had no need of such magic. According to Bana, the father of Harsa descended from an ideal ancestor in an ideal land. It was a land 'peopled by the good, where the laws of caste are forever unconfused.' It had sugar cane, corn heaps, rice crops extending beyond their fields. It was all things to all men.

> Sages called it a hermitage; courtesans a lovers retreat; actors a concert hall; sons of the sword, the soil of heroes; scientists, the great artificer's temple; good men, the gathering of the virtuous; libertines, the rogues' meet; quietists, the Buddhist monastery; lovers, the apsaras' city....

This ideal ancestor wrestled unarmed with a goblin in a cemetery to defend an ascetic, and in return was promised that his line would bring forth King Harsa.

Harsa's father was a worshipper of the sun, who had an eye for effect:

> Day by day at sunrise he bathed, arrayed himself in white silk, wrapt his head in white cloth, and kneeling eastward upon the ground, presented for an offering a bunch of red lotuses set in a vessel of ruby and tinged, like his own heart, with the sun's hue....

His mother had 'the gait of hamsa, voice of cuckoo, full bosoms of rainy seasons, laugh of wine, adorableness of twilight....' She was 'honey in converse, ambrosia in delight, rain to her servants, bamboo to her elders....'

The queen could scarcely move before the portentous child was born; all day her downcast eye was on her zone, and she 'set her feet on the laps of her handmaids and the heads of her co-wives' — a pleasant tradition. When Harsa was born, Bana writes, the country went mad with rejoicing. In the saturnalia of celebration the Brahmans who came to chant the Vedas were overshadowed by the revelry. The prisons were flung open, and 'away ran disorderly crowds of freed persons, their faces hairy with long matted beards, their bodies black with miry smirch.' The scrupulous rule of the palace was gone, masters and servants reduced to one level, and entrance to the harem in no wise criminal. Wives of neighbouring kings approached from every side like 'Krishna's mistresses on the march,' followed by servants bearing garlands in wide baskets, dishes laden with bits of camphor, jewelled caskets of saffron scents, and ivory boxes.

> Young people of noble houses, unused to dancing, frolicked for love of the king. Drunken slave women allured the favourites, while the monarch himself looked on with a secret smile. Respectable old

> feudatories clasped the necks of intoxicated bawds, naughty slave boys, set on by a glance from the sovereign, betrayed in songs the secret amours of the ministers of state. Wanton water girls embraced aged ascetics.... In eagerness of ardent rivalry thousands of slaves carried on a war of foul language.

This curious liberation of the obscenities is a thing still caught in little shells of custom here and there today.

> Smash went the pearls on the ornaments of young princes slapping each other in their play... men tripped on heaps of pearls that fell from necklaces broken in collisions... harlot women danced to instrumental music... tambourines, cymbals, gourds, lutes, jingling anklets kept time.... They sang the words of vulgar mimes, ambrosia to their lovers' ears... they lashed the young folk with great wreaths of flowers.... As to what was proper to be said and what not, they were as void of discrimination as the childish play of happiness.

The king's wives were dancing under white umbrellas, with red lac on their feet. Even old ladies shouted like maniacs. Harsa's elder brother, just big enough to walk, was stained yellow over his body, and wore on his head a mustard amulet, and a necklace of tiger's claws and gold. The king, in the lavishness of the East and his rejoicing, gave away a fortune.

The two boys grew up stout of thigh and with arms like iron bars. They were given, as attendant, the eight-year-old child of a conquered prince, 'a naturally courtly child.' As they grew older, their father told them that the first essential of sovereignty was to secure good servants, and warned them of the difficulties, since the world is strewn with mean persons, fools, impostors, the low-born, and cheats. And he selected two sons of the conquered Malwa king, untouched by any taint, to whom they were told to show consideration. A more exotic servant was the little betel-bearer, the captured princess, at Prince Harsa's side, day or night.

This was the education of a king's son according to the 'Kadambari' of Bana: one might compare it with hunting and aviation and cornerstone-laying and all modern princely accomplishments: skill in word, sentence, proof, law, and royal policy; in gymnastics, in all kinds of weapons, such as bow, quoit, shield, scimitar, dart, mace, battle-axe, and club; in driving and elephant riding and knowledge of a horse's age; in painting, leaf-cutting, the use of books and writing; testing of jewels, carpentry, the working of ivory; in architecture, physics, mechanics, antidotes, mining, crossing of rivers, leaping and jumping and sleight-of-hand; in stories, dramas, romances, poems; in the Mahabharata; the Puranas, the Itihasas, and the Ramayana; in all kinds of writing, all foreign languages, all technicalities, all mechanical arts, in metre, and in every other art: 'in all the arts of gambling, knowledge of the cries of birds, and astronomy.'

Harsa, it is to be presumed, had some such an elaborate curriculum of study. Whether or not he had to master gambling (a gentlemanly art from ancient days) and the knowledge of the cries of birds, his later prowess implies that he certainly mastered royal policy and warlike skill, and his erudite tastes and compositions that he was a deep student of India's literature.

By sixteen, it is assumed that the prince had mastered the study of the Shastras, and now the women's quarters, the zenanas, are longing for his sight. This is the hyperbole of the prettiness and easily excited emotions of the fluttered palace ladies — and withal a graceful flattery to a prince. When the prince of the 'Kadambari' went out on horse, shaded by a huge umbrella, the women ran up to the rooftops to see him, leaving their work half done. Some had mirrors in their hands, some were 'robed in rainbow hues like the beauty of a day in the rainy season; some raised feet that blossomed into the white rays of their nails... some held strings of pearls in their hands.' The women's graceful speech became straightway mirthful, confidential, confused, envious, scornful, derisive, coquettish, loving, full of longing. 'Hasty one, wait for me! Drunk with gazing, hold thy mantle!... Love distraught, tie up thy hair! Heartless one, pick up thine earring. Eager in youth, thou art being watched! Cover thy bosom.... Artfully artless, go on quicker! Envious girl, why block up the window?... Bereft of sense by the stroke of love's arrow, place the end of thy silken robe on thy head to keep off the sun's rays.'

Admittedly, when women fluttered so and suffered sunstroke for a sight of him, a prince was in a fair way of losing his sense of proportion.

To counterbalance that, the guru, the spiritual teacher of the prince, warns him of pitfalls:

> The madness that arises from the senses is violent, and not to be counteracted by roots or charms.... Thus thou must often be told at length.... Birth, fresh youth, peerless beauty, superhuman talent, all this is a long succession of ills... this mirage of pleasure always ends in sorrow. Extreme clinging to the things of sense destroys a man, misleading him like ignorance of his bearings.... The teaching of a guru is calming, able to cleanse all the stains of man.... They are especially needed by kings, for the admonishers of kings are few.

With such teachings, a young prince was steadied.

Harsa's little sister was growing up, swiftly mature, and she, too, was expert in the desired graces of a princess, so that kings from all sides sent envoys for her hand. It was decided to give her to the King of the Mukharas, and on a day carefully selected by astrologers as being of good omen, the betrothal water was poured upon his envoy. The astrologers must have miscalculated, for tragedy lay ahead.

Villagers came with loads of gifts. There were trains of troubadours, courtyards of elephants and horses, throngs of astrologers studying the characteristics of various moments; gold-workers noisily hammering gold; skilled artists painting auspicious scenes; modellers making clay figures. Crocodile-mouthed conduits were spouting scented water into a variety of pleasure ponds.

Footmen with gold-studded fly-fans ran before the bridegroom. The king and Harsa and his brother went out to meet him. He did not enter the house until the astrologers decided which was the auspicious moment. Through thousands of glances of curious women, he went to the door of the bride's house, then waited. The little girl, 'not too tightly embraced by womanhood,' was choked with fright, bashful, and trembling as she submitted to the rites of the women. Then the bridegroom took her by the hand to an altar whitened by new plaster, and surrounded by earthen dolls with auspicious fruits in hand. Brahmans were busy kindling the marriage flame. The bridegroom ascended the altar and walked to the right, and poured the oblation of rice, ignoring the weeping of the bride and howling of her women. When the rites were completed, the husband bowed with his wife to the parents, and they entered their chamber, supplied with a 'fair, well-upholstered bed with pillows, a golden rinsing vessel, a golden figure holding an ivory box, and a night bowl of silver bedecked with lotuses.' 'The bashful young bride slept with her face averted while the bridegroom spent the night gazing at her images in the mirrors of the jewelled walls.'

All was happiness and fitting prosperity until Harsa was nearly sixteen. At that time he was in the Himalayan hills hunting tigers, while his older brother was attacking the persistently menacing Huns, when a messenger came to him: the king, his father, lay in violent fever. On the hurried journey home, Harsa met bad omens — a crow, a naked Jain bedecked with peacock feathers, and such portents of calamity.

When he reached home, he found the family doing their utmost to save the king's life. They were giving away all their goods, worshipping the family gods, cooking the ambrosial posset, milk, ghee, and rice, offered to the gods to preserve from death. Buttermilk was freezing in pails packed with ice; a collyrium stick cooled with camphor powder was placed on a moist white cloth; whey was ready for gargle, boiled water was cooling, and lustral water was being scattered by feed Brahmans. Sympathetic magic was lavishly used in the cure of sickness. 'Attendants were drinking streams of water from uplifted cups in order to distract the pain in the king's dry mouth, and gourmands were being fed to relieve his craving.'

To cool his fever, servants were dusting the poor king with pearl powder, smearing him with sandal, and incessantly applying petals of red, white, and blue lotus. His queen sat fanning him, but giving him little peace, touching him on head and breast and crying, 'My Lord, are you asleep?'

The king looked up and recognized Harsa, and with fatherly tenderness said, 'My son, you are thin.'

Then the fever burnt him up again and he cried out, 'The heat is terrible — bring pearl necklaces... place jewelled mirrors on my body... apply a moonstone to my eye, set a blue lotus on my cheek... bind tight my whirling head.'

From the women's apartments a messenger of grief ran to Harsa. Her hand was swollen and dark from beating her breast. 'Help, help, my lord — though her husband lives, the queen has taken a certain resolution.' Running to his mother, Harsa heard cries 'like those from queens resolved to die.' From queens resolved to die — with what strange ease people slipped from life... with impulse so fixed that the very cries were conventional and recognized? Add to the list of recognizable cries, the cheering of crowds at a sport, the applause after a play — the cries of queens resolved to die.

'Beloved Mango,' she was saying, 'take thought to yourself, your mother is seeking another home. I am going, darling jasmine ... bid me farewell.... Forget me not, brother parrot in the cage.... To whom shall I entrust the tame peacock that clings in my path?'

Harsa found her, dressed in saffron robes, smeared with saffron paste and wreaths of flowers, holding a picture of her husband in her hand. She was determined, like Sita, to enter the fire before her husband's death.

He begged her not to kill herself. She wept and cried aloud, addressing her absent son, 'Alas, darling, that I see you not!' To her daughter, 'Defenceless are you now.' She reviled Death. 'Remorseless one, thou hast stolen me away.' But it never occurred to her that a woman of honour could live for her children, rather than die with her husband.

'I am the lady of a great house,' she said to her sixteen-year-old boy, 'born of stainless ancestry, one whose virtue is her dower, the lioness mate of a great spirit. Daughter, spouse, mother of heroes, how otherwise could such a woman as I act?' 'Upon the heads of rival wives these feet have been set, fanned by chowries waved by captive wives of foes. I would die while still unwidowed.... Compared with the flame of wifely sorrow, fire itself is chilly.' And after worshipping the flame, she plunged into it.

Harsa, watching his mother burn, then had to see his father die. These grim words were the king's dying plea: 'Make prize of feudatory kings, support the burden of royalty, protect the people, check levity, annihilate your foes...' The lad was soon to need to act on that advice.

When the king's body was burned by the river Sarasvati, his favourite servants, friends, and ministers could not be restrained from abandoning their wives and children and dying with the king. A few compromised by taking to the forest as hermits. Others plunged into the fire, or jumped from precipices, or starved themselves to death — a classic Indian accomplishment. After the deaths and the holocaust of mourning suicides came the horror of the days of impurity, when the household was corrupted by death, when the sons and servants were unclean until time and ceremonies purified them.

Harsa's older brother had hurried home from the war by forced marches, and arrived worn and sleepless, and bandaged for arrow wounds from the Huns. His army had these significant gaps in the force: 'The umbrella-bearer was wanting, the superintendent of wardrobe lagged behind, the pitcher-carrier had collapsed, the spittoon-bearer was prostrate.'

Danger threatened, now that their strong father was dead. The Lord of Malwa killed their sister's husband, put the princess in prison, and was planning to march against Thaneswar. Women screamed, and the Brahmans with uplifted arms wailed with horror. The people started patiently with their children and aged to the safety of the forests. In the days of sudden wars and abandonments, the whole population flocked out for safety. Bana, describing the reign of a strong king, said, 'Chess alone made empty squares.' Deserted cities and silent market-places inspired that play upon words.

Harsa's brother marched against Malwa and routed his forces with ridiculous ease, but was no match for guile. He accepted the courtesy of the king of central Bengal. Weaponless and confiding and alone, he was murdered.

The boy Harsa was left, to defend his people. He had endured grief for his father, mother, and brother, the horror of the carnivals of emotional mourning, and the practical loss of trusted ministers by suicide. Now he had to rely on himself. All men appealed to his youth and inexperience to lead.

His action was at once decisive. 'He ordered the elephant herds hastily called out of pasture.' Gorgeous giganticness of elephant pastures.

But his guru warned the high-willed boy to learn, from his brother's death, not to trust people too easily. 'This gives you some inkling of the despicable characters of vile men,' said the sage. 'Thus national types vary, like the dress, features, food, and pursuits of countries, village by village, town by town — dismiss therefore this universal confidingness, so agreeable to the habits of your own land... The Mathura king was killed digging treasure; another, fond of drama, was attacked in the midst of actors. One king was fond of music, and men disguised as musicians cut off his head with sharp knives hidden between the vina and its gourd.' Queens had been known to poison, and there were mirrors with razor edges. Young Harsa was warned.

A troop of hundreds of astrologers — in no wise discredited by the bad moments they had chosen for the little widowed princess — were set to work to calculate the auspicious day for starting to march. After that was decided, Harsa bathed in vessels of gold and silver, worshipped Siva, fed the fire, gave Brahmans precious gifts, and sat on the throne covered by a tiger skin. Then, from a large temple built of reeds near the river, he gave orders to break camp.

An enormous mass of people and animals had been gathered, and the start to war was an incredible medley. As an instrument of destruction such an army sounds as improbable as a village of civilians on the march. But Harsa was to contend with armies organized in the same mixed fashion, like two big bumblebees fighting. It was not until the Mohammedans came with focussed onslaughts that Hindu tactics failed. Harsa's army had its own unseen order, loose system, or habit, its own gigantic effectiveness. As Bana describes it, this is Harsa's army breaking camp, and on the march.

Eight sharp strokes were given on a drum, marking the number of leagues in a day's march. Then:

> The drums rattled, trumpets brayed, horns blared, noise of camp increased, officers roused courtiers... and thousands of torches made inroads on the darkness. Loving pairs were roused from sleep by the tramp of women of the watch.... Shrill words of command... noise of mattocks uprooting ground fastenings.... Servants were rolling up awnings and cloth screens of tents and marquees,... clusters of cups and vessels lifted upon many elephants.... Savage elephants trumpeted, bells jangled, camels bellowed as sacks were set upon their backs. ... Carriages of high-born nobles' wives thronged with roguish emissaries sent by princes of rank.... Footmen led the fine horses of the King's favourites.... Stablemen dragged along half-eaten shoots to be eaten at morning's manœuvres.... Low people of the neighbourhood, running up as the elephants and horses started, looted heaps of abandoned grain.... Crowds of carts with creaking wheels... in front were the kitchen appliances of the great feudatories.... First ran the banner-bearers.

The elephants were on the march. The poor people whose hovels were crushed by the animals' feet, flung clods at the elephant-keepers and wretched families fled from grass huts ruined by the collisions. Despairing merchants saw oxen bearing their wealth flee before the tumult. 'The whole world was swallowed up with dust.'

The warrior nobles would look most amazing to the age of soldiers of khaki and steel — chieftains mounted on female elephants, their saddles curving with scimitars and bristling with golden arrows. Javelin-keepers guarded their sheafs, and a betel-bearer fanned the heat and flies away. The officers' uniforms, though soiled by war, were rare as butterfly wings. 'Their shanks were covered with delicate tinted silk, their copper coloured legs checkered with mudstained wraps,... their tunics darkened by black diamonds.' They wore Chinese cuirasses, and shawls of the shade of parrots' tails, and their coats and doublets showed clusters of bright pearls. But the most foppish details were taken for granted. 'Servants ran up to loose dangling earrings which had become entangled with pearl necklaces tossed by their movements.... The stalks of ear lotuses were fixed in their turbans, inlaid with bits of crestgems.' Yet the ear lotuses and necklaces had survived long travel, which had bedabbled the elephants' housings. All this delicacy was part of manly and soldierly equipment. They were 'proud, restless warriors with round shields of various colours, and chowries tossing in front of them.' The king reviewed his troops, sitting on a female elephant under an auspicious umbrella with a turquoise rod. He wore a tunic of raw silk, and his lips were smeared red with betel and vermilion.

He himself was surprised at the size of his forces — the army starting out from its encampment seemed like 'the animate world trembling at an æon's commencement from Vishnu's belly.'

As the army got under way there was a babble and chatter from all sorts of people passing and bumping.

'"March on, my son." "Friend, you hobble like a lame man, while the vanguard is coming furiously on us." "Don't you see, you pitiless brute, the child lying there?" "Laggard, you can suck sugar cane on the way." "Quiet your bull." "The road is all ups and downs, old fellow, see that you don't break the sugar kettle." "Quick, slave, cut a mouthful of fodder from this beanfield — who can tell the fate of his crop when we are gone?" "Keep away your oxen, fellow, this field is guarded by watchmen..." "Oh, friend of the distressed, raise this ox from the mud." Groups of elephant men, knaves, donkey boys, camp followers, thieves, serving men, rogues and grooms, sated with an easily acquired meal of plentiful, readily pounded remnants of grain, expressed their approval in bold jubilation.'

When they reached camp at evening, Harsa sat to receive tribute. Servants in due order displayed the gifts of kings — pearl necklaces, silken towels, sapphire drinking-vessels embossed by artists, leather bucklers, volumes of fine writing, luscious milky betel-nut fruit, camphor, aloe flowers, carved boxes, musk deer, birds in gold-painted bamboo cages, partridges in cages of coral. The present practical mind pauses at the idea of adding all this to the camp luggage, but such things were details to lavish Indian ways.

Before this enormous army needed to do battle, however, Harsa was distracted by news that his sister had escaped from the guards of the King of Malwa, and was wandering helpless in the jungle of the Vindhya hills.

The news came through his dead brother's general, Bhandi, who brought back the army that had routed the forces of Malwa. Bhandi came mourning for his murdered master, riding on a single horse followed by a few nobles, and his breast 'filled with the points of enemies' arrows, like an array of iron pins implanted to restrain his heart from bursting.'

Behind him was the captured army and loot — 'elephants in thousands, moving as great boulders, with muddy cheeks... horses swift as antelopes... wondrous pearl necklaces... beauteous women like Apsarasas.' The followers of the Malwa king marched with iron chains on their legs.

When Harsa heard that his brother's army was returning, he was stabbed by grief, and went into the darkness of his tent, refusing to see anyone. But at word of his lost sister, he became energetic and practical. He turned the captured prisoners, army, and loot over to overseers; he commanded Bhandi to lead the whole army in vengeance against the Bengal king who had killed his brother. But he himself set out to the mountain forest to find his sister. He was told that many searchers had failed to find her, but the boy replied, 'What care I for other searchers?'

He rode on horseback toward the Vindhya forest. After a few days he came to a village on the outskirts, grey with smoke. There were tiger-traps about, and there were cowpens fenced with dry branches around some huge banyan tree. In the little rice-fields the soil was stiff as black iron, and the peasant farmers were whacking and spading with vigorous language. Under wayside trees Harsa rode through a drinking-arbour, the cool shelter grey with the dust of travellers' feet and scattered with the seeds of apples they had eaten.

He met hunters with intricate snares, women with baskets of fruit on their heads hurrying to a village market, and men with strong axes going into the forest, carrying their lunch and wearing ragged clothes for fear of thieves. The place was alive with the activity of the simple people who made the majority of India, strange to the luxury of Harsa's court.

Here a forest chieftain brought a mountaineer, his hair tied into a crest above his forehead with a creeper, his dark forehead like night, to guide the king into the forest.

They sought a certain hermitage where a particularly all-knowing sage lived who might have news of the princess. It was a flowery forest place where all animals were at peace. Birds were flying, parrots pecking fruit, hares basking on rocks, antelopes playing free from fear, and even 'polecats making a low noise in the shrubs.' As Harsa rode up, he saw Buddhists from various provinces perched on pillars, or sitting on rocks, or squatting on the roots of trees or living in bowers of creepers, 'devotees, dead to all passion.' There were also Jains in white robes, and followers of Krishna; ascetics who pulled out their hair, followers of the Upanishads; believers in God as a creator; assayers of metals; students of the Puranas; and adepts in sacrifices requiring seven ministering priests — 'all diligently following their own tenets, pondering, urging objections, raising doubts, resolving them.... Even the monkeys were gravely busy performing the ritual of the Çaitya, while some devout parrots... were explaining the Buddhist dictionary... even tigers had given up eating flesh under the calming influence of the Buddhist teaching.' All were gathered as disciples of the holy man whom Harsa sought.

Hardly had the proper compliments been passed between the sage and Harsa when a mendicant came up in what seems almost breathless haste for the Orient, and said that a young woman was about to mount a funeral pyre and that nothing could dissuade her. He begged the holy man to use his influence. Harsa at once asked what the woman was like and how far away. Whereupon the mendicant described the scene for four pages, and begged them to hurry.

As they drew near, they heard the cries of women all anxious to die, and they came upon a dishevelled band of ladies, their feet swollen from fatigue and bleeding from sharp stones, their silken skirts and jackets torn, their thighs wounded from the spines of shrubs. Harsa's sister lay among the women, her feet bleeding, her face pale, but determined to go into the pile of bonfire which stood ready.

Harsa brought his sister from her swoon and the reservoirs of her grief overflowed. He was able to persuade her not to die; but she declared that if she lived, she would put on the red robes and become a Buddhist nun.

With his sister rescued, Harsa went back to command of his army — the great horde of people and animals, the confused organism, marching thousands of miles over northern India. Back and forth they travelled in conquest. For five and a half years the elephants were not unharnessed nor the soldiers unhelmeted. No one tells about the number of cooking-pots and servants and hangers-on. And no one mentions whether the pearl necklaces and ear lotuses of the officers had to be replaced. The simple fact emerges that it was a victorious army. It grew, also, like a snowball, as conquered lands were added, until at the end Harsa had one hundred thousand cavalry.

The boy conquered upper India, excluding the Punjab, a belt from the eastern waters of Bengal Bay to the western waters of the Persian Gulf, and as far south as the Narbada River. He tried to conquer the Deccan, but met his only defeat from the Chalukya king, Pulakesin the Second, of the marvellous country in which the Ajanta caves lay — a king who had several hundred champions whose habit was to intoxicate themselves with wine to such a pitch that one man with lance in hand would challenge ten thousand, and who inebriated their elephants and turned them loose against the enemy.

After his five-year campaign, Harsa rested, and tried to put away the lances and store the trappings. But he did not entirely give up further conquest as Asoka did.

In 612, after the weary years in camp, he was crowned king. He was grown to full manhood, sinewy and tested, and he took on a fuller personality, amplified into the strongest king in India. He ruled wisely over a subdued and calm and splendid country, the patron of poets and artists. He was a builder, and made his capital of Kanauj (not far from Lucknow) agreeable with gardens and tanks of still water. People flocked to the peaceful city, and the temples of both Brahmans and Buddhists increased to more than a hundred each, when the land became secure.

This is the way Bana expressed such safety and peace:

> While he, having subdued the earth, was guardian of the world, the only mixing of colour [varna, meaning caste] was in painting; the only pulling of hair, in caresses; the only strict fetters, in laws of poetry; the only care, concerning moral law; the only deception was in dreams.... Banners alone trembled... elephants alone were rampant... lattice windows alone sent messengers; dice and chessmen alone left empty squares.

The city of Kanauj is left now without a trace, except a few mounds. The Mohammedans of later centuries destroyed all the buildings of Harsa. But Yuan Chwang (Hüan Tsang), the Chinese pilgrim, saw and described his city and land.

Yuan Chwang came travelling into India from China of the T'ang dynasty. The way had not improved, nor the Himalayan mountain passes lowered, since the time of Fa-Hien — nor had the earnestness of a Chinese pilgrim's purpose decreased. Yuan Chwang was a man of substance and dignity, a devout and learned Buddhist, called the Master of the Law. He travelled over the mighty mountains, 'over hills and across gullies, ascending the Indus by hazardous pitch through gloomy gorges, across bridges spanning precipices, or climbing by means of pegs for steps.' In India he had to cross deserts; his way was blocked by a mountain of ice falling across it; he was captured by Thugs to be killed as a sacrifice — but he only asked time to meditate in order to meet death joyously, and fortunately a storm came up which convinced the Thugs he had the gods on his side.

As he went through one kingdom of India after another, Yuan Chwang observed. Kings came out to meet him. He was treated with great courtesy and aroused much interest by his discussions. His mind was fixed on the theory of the greater Buddhism, the Mahayana doctrine, which he upheld; but he nevertheless observed very candidly.

He saw India as a diverse land. In Taxila, he decided, the people were sturdy. In Kashmir, they were good-looking but deceitful, timid but boastful, and they felt very superior to their neighbours because they had a dragon to guard them. In Mathura — a rich region — the people had bad, rude ways and vulgar speech and few were Buddhist (which might influence a pilgrim's opinion).

The country of the Kalingas had flowers and fruit and tawny wild elephants. The climate was burning, the people rough and uncivilized, but true to their word, the population sparse and insufficient for the land. But in Kosala the population was dense, the men were 'violent, brave, and impetuous, earnest in study and of high intelligence.' Chola was deserted wild marshes and jungle, with troops of brigands going openly through the country, and the people dissolute and cruel. In Dravidia, however, near present Madras, the people were courageous, deeply attached to principles of honesty, and esteeming learning. In Malwa the soil was rich in vines, flowers, and fruit, the men virtuous and docile, the language elegant and clear, learning profound, and the people polite and tolerant. In Baroch, with a salty soil, the people were crooked and perverse, did not cultivate study and were 'wedded to error.'

Such was the variety on the continent of India, in which King Harsa ruled the largest section.

Yuan Chwang rode on his red nag into walled cities with towers of wood or bamboo. Outside of the cities he saw the quarters of the unclean tradesmen — butchers and fishers and dancers, executioners and scavengers — who were not allowed to live in the town. He saw them coming inside the walls on their errands, slinking along on one side of the street, so that they might not defile their betters. He rode through crooked, dirty lanes, and bazaars with stalls and signs to catch the eye, and under the balconies of brick or tile houses, plastered with lime or mud and cow dung. On festival days he saw the people scattering flowers about.

The people walking in the street wore white garments of silk or hemp or cotton or goat's hair, and the Brahmans and Kshatriyas were cleanly. The women wore flower wreaths and necklaces, and robes that fell from the shoulder to the ground, even as now. Non-believers mixed with the crowd, wearing odd things like peacock feathers, skull-bone necklaces, leaves or bark.

Yuan Chwang thought the ordinary people were 'naturally light-minded, yet upright and honourable. In money matters they are without craft, and make light of the present world.'

Harsa he observed governing them with a light rein. There were few regulations. The merchants came and went freely so long as they paid a small tax at road barriers and river passages. Families did not have to register themselves, and if called out for forced labour, were paid for it. Taxes were light because of the crown-owned lands which paid for state sacrifices and various charities and expenses. There were few criminals, and Harsa took care that those discovered had the fullest justice of the day — the evidence sifted, and, failing that, the guilt definitely established by the ordeals of walking on hot iron or through fire, being weighed in balance with a stone, eating poison or being thrown into water. If a man could not prove his innocence by such clear tests, he was imprisoned and left to live or die, no longer counted among men. But that was the custom — and Yuan Chwang found much gentleness and sweetness and rectitude in the behaviour of Indian kings.

The Chinese pilgrim and Harsa were destined to meet. When they did, the figure of Harsa jumps from the hyperbole of Bana into the realism of the Chinese narratives — Yuan Chwang's and his biographer's.

Harsa had been ruling nearly thirty years — a man getting toward fifty, to whom everyone bowed, whom no one dared defy. In his later years he had grown more and more religious. He had always maintained publicly the sun worship of his father. He also sacrificed to Siva. And finally he grew deeply interested in Buddhism. One would think that such a cautious — or liberal — investor in religions would find place for all varieties of Buddhism. But Harsa was most strongly attracted to the Greater Vehicle of Buddhism, the Mahayana, and contemptuous of the simpler sect.

For Buddhism had, by that time, split into about eighteen disputing sects in India. The widest schism lay between the group that followed the Hinayana (or lesser Buddhism, which was the purer, and nearer to the original teaching of Gautama) and the disciples of the Mahayana (or Greater Vehicle, which enlarged Buddhism to include magic and yoga and marvellous metaphysics).

Harsa liked the elaborate Greater Vehicle, but he was shown a treatise of seven hundred verses against it. It was written by a Hinayana scholar who defied anyone to answer his seven hundred stanzas. Harsa remarked scornfully: 'I have heard of the fox, accompanied by the meadow rats, boasting he was able to contend with the lion, but as soon as he saw him, his heart failed him, and they were all scattered in a moment. You, sirs, have not seen the priests of the Greater Vehicle.'

So he sent a messenger to the monastery at Nalanda, asking to have four scholars sent to him who could refute the Hinayana treatise. Now Yuan Chwang was stopping at Nalanda, the guest of the Buddhist monks. Wherever he went in India he had won great renown for his learned arguments in defence of the Mahayana doctrine. There was no need to find the three other scholars. Single-handed, Yuan Chwang answered the seven hundred verses with a treatise of sixteen hundred verses. There could be no doubt who won that argument.

Imagine the delight of the kings who heard of that triumph, kings who were patrons of religion and art, and who sought Yuan Chwang much as ambitious hostesses seek their lions.

Kumara Rajah of Assam wrote a letter to the head of the monastery, saying: 'Your disciple wishes to see the great priest come from China. I pray you, respected sir, to send him, and so gratify this imperial thought of mine.' That invitation was rather embarrassing, for Yuan Chwang was promised to visit Harsa, although Harsa had been courteously lenient about the date. The monk made excuses.

Whereupon Kumara Rajah wrote angrily: 'When I heard the name of the priest belonging to the outside country, my body and soul were overjoyed, expecting the opening of the germ of religion (within me). But you, sirs, have refused to let him come.... I have again sent a messenger. If necessary I will equip my army and elephants, and like the clouds swoop down and trample to the very dust that monstery of Nalanda.'

So the monk advised Yuan Chwang to take the slight trouble to go to Assam.

Yuan Chwang visited at the court of Kumara Rajah for a month, made welcome with ceremony, with music and banquets and flowers and incense. But Harsa, returning from a campaign, raised his eyebrows, remarking: 'I frequently asked him to come here before this, and he did not come. How is it he is now living there?' And he sent a messenger requesting Yuan Chwang.

Kumara Rajah replied saucily, that Harsa could take his head, but could not take the Master of the Law.

To which Harsa tersely answered, 'Send the head by my messenger.' One did not bandy words with Harsa.

Kumara Rajah, alarmed, equipped thirty thousand ships to escort the Master of the Law up the Ganges toward Harsa. He stopped some distance away, and built a pavilion of travel in which he left the Chinese Master, while he and his ministers went on. Harsa greeted him kindly, and promised to call on the Master.

In the first watch of the night, men working up the river heard the beat of drums and saw thousands of torches.

'That is Harsa coming,' explained the slightly nervous Kumara. 'He marches always accompanied by several hundred persons who beat golden drums at each step the king takes.' The modest boy, who at sixteen hesitated to take the throne, in his middle age refused to let any other king have golden drums beaten for him. His own anxious drummers watched each pace to announce it to a waiting world, and the thousands of torches reflected in the dark river and spattered over the land turned the stars cool. Kumara Rajah hurried out to meet him.

The Chinese monk stayed with dignity in his pavilion. Harsa entered, bowed at his feet, scattered flowers before him, and recited many long verses in his praise, then thoughtfully considered his guest's fatigue, and left early. Such was the respect paid to religious learning.

Next day at the palace the Master of the Law, after offerings of choice food and music and strewn flowers, showed the king his sixteen hundred verses. Harsa was delighted, and said: 'When the sun rises in splendour, the light of the glowworm is eclipsed... so with the doctrine which the Master offers. The priests have not dared offer a word.' There proved to be an excellent reason why no priest offered a word, as it developed later.

While the king and scholar were discussing the treatise, a woman sat behind them, listening with great intelligence and delight. It was the lost princess, Harsa's sister, who had wanted to burn herself up, but who now found her compensation in the theories of the Greater Vehicle. She praised Yuan Chwang repeatedly.

Having captured his scholar, Harsa called a great convocation of all religions at Kanauj to investigate the treatise of Yuan Chwang. Eighteen kings came, three thousand priests of the great and little Vehicle, three thousand Brahmans, and a thousand priests from the Nalanda monastery. They came on elephants, in chariots, in palanquins.

Harsa had built two great thatched halls which could seat a thousand people each. And at dawn the procession started toward the halls. Harsa and Kumara Rajah, wearing tiaras and flower wreaths and jewelled ribbons, rode on elephants on either side of a golden image of Buddha which they were conducting to the hall. Yuan Chwang and three hundred princes, ministers, and priests followed on elephants, chanting verses as they rode — an earth-shaking procession.

With great ceremony the Buddha image was installed in the hall, and the most learned priests entered. All were fed, including Buddha. The Master of the Law sat in front, to expound the Greater Vehicle. A placard outside the hall announced that his head was offered to anyone who could refute his arguments. That seems an effective way of silencing opposition. Harsa had a still better way. When jealous Hinayana priests threatened Yuan Chwang, he commanded that anyone who hurt the Master would be beheaded; and anyone who spoke against him would have his tongue cut out. That is reverence for scholarship.

At the end of the one-sided discussion, Harsa told Yuan Chwang to mount an elephant and proclaim to all that he had established his doctrine. Yuan Chwang demurred, but Harsa, grown arbitrary with the years, said, 'It has ever been the custom, the matter cannot be passed over.' And, holding Yuan Chwang by the garments, proclaimed everywhere: 'The Master of the Law from the kingdom of China has established the principles of the Great Vehicle and overthrown all opposing doctrines; for eighteen days no one has dared to enter on a discussion. Let this be known everywhere, as it ought to be!'

Gautama Buddha's religion had travelled a great distance from his doctrine of self-knowledge and self-control, and a middle path in life. If he had seen the pomp and fanfare and heard the elaboration, he might have thought, wearily, that it would be as well if his religion did fade from India. Simplicity is the gift of few.

Yuan Chwang at last wanted to go back to China and take the holy images and manuscripts he had collected. The Indians tried to dissuade him. The priests reasoned that India was the land of Buddha's birth, and one should not leave it, after coming so far. Moreover, they remarked, with an intolerance and certainty not unknown today, 'China is a country of barbarians, men of no importance, and shallow as to religion.' The king also begged the Master to stay a little, for he was regretting the small increase of his own religious merit — and wanted to do something about it.

Harsa went off the stage of history with a last grand gesture. He invited Yuan Chwang to the Great Largess. Once in five years Harsa gave away all his wealth. The place chosen was the site of the present Allahabad, by a confluence of rivers, on a sunny strip of sand. Scores of thatch-roofed buildings were put up to house his treasure. Harsa went in state from Kanauj — the golden drums beating their pace music.

At this sacred place, numberless people came to die in the river, hoping to be reborn in Heaven. On the day when Harsa came, even a monkey starved himself to death. Ascetics were there too — the ancestors of flagpole sitters — each on his high pole, holding on with one hand and foot, while the other leg was stretched at full length, as with bloodshot, blinded eyes each followed the sun from dawn till sunset. At this holy place King Harsa held the ceremony of giving away his wealth, which lasted for days and weeks.

He gave first to Buddhist images, then to Siva and to the Sun.

He gave to monks, to those conspicuous for great learning, to the scholars of all religions, to the poor and kinless.

He gave away the wealth and jewels accumulated in the last five years, everything except the horses and elephants and military equipment. Bewildered monks went away holding a hundred pieces of gold, a pearl, a cotton garment, food, flowers, and perfume. Still King Harsa kept on giving, in due order, until he finally, with a gesture, stripped off his own jewels and clothing, and to cover himself borrowed a garment from his sister.

He did not quite achieve simplicity, however. The lesser kings went around among their subjects and bought back some of Harsa's belongings, and restored them to him.

Harsa and Kumara were both truly grieved when Yuan Chwang had to go. The Indian kings arranged to send his treasures by a military escort on horseback to China, and Harsa gave Yuan Chwang a large elephant, and enough gold to pay his expenses on the way home, although the Master protested that he required nothing. They parted with tears and real sorrow forever. But three days later, as Yuan Chwang's procession was travelling, Harsa and Kumara Rajah came galloping up like happy schoolboys with a large body of swift cavalry, bringing letters, sealed in white cotton with red seals, to present to kings along his way for conveyance. The two Indian kings rode with the Chinese monk for some time, before they could bear to part.

In time the Master of the Law came to the snowy mountains and sharp-pointed peaks. He was no longer able to go on horseback, and dismounted and took up his staff. On he went over passes through snowdrifts and ice, through freezing winds, while his company dwindled and left. The mountains were so high that when the wind rose the birds could not pass them in their flight. Yuan Chwang travelled back through Kashmir and across the Gobi to his home in China, and when he reached his own courtyard, his own pine tree bowed to welcome him.

Harsa, brave, lavish, imperious, and a little diffuse — Harsa, who could hold all the grandeur in place — died without heir. After his death, picture mourning if you will such as surrounded his father's body, or greater — for Harsa was a greater king. Then picture fear penetrating the grief, and disorder and confusion, and families taking to the safety of forests at news of an enemy approach — and empty squares, not made by chess.

Harsa's kingdom fell with him. The great period of the Gupta age had ended. All over India for three centuries there was confusion and chaos, with little peace or order, in few places.

The Moslems had already tasted India; they had touched on the west coast at Barouch in 636, and Sindh had become an Arab province after 643. The kingdoms of India lay leaderless, their only continuity of civilization in the little villages, and the caste life. Separate and passive, the people, enervated by warmth, were following detailed elegancies, carving statues more embellished, dreaming, sacrificing. These were the people, and this the civilization, to which the swift-slashing Moslems came.

12. *The Rajputs, Knights of the Hindus*

IN THE obscure centuries after King Harsa, the Rajputs were rising, a sword-arm for defence of the Hindus — warriors who might have strength to meet the shock of Moslem attack.

The sun race, ruling today at Udaipur, and the moon race, at Jessulmer, are the only Rajput dynasties which have survived the stormy centuries still striding their own thrones. Though there are Rajput princes now in pink stucco Jaipur, in camel-raising Bikaner and elsewhere, their houses were reinstated later under alien conquerors.

But the Maharana of Udaipur, chief of the proud Sisodia Clan, is heir to unbroken rule and most distinguished tradition. He takes precedence of all. He can boast descent not from such parvenus as William the Conqueror or Charlemagne, but from the Sun, the very sun, in lineage traced in black and white from the beginning of the world. His clansmen, who part their beards crisply in the middle and carry always a curving sword, and who — if they are great nobles — never leave their doors without an escort of lesser noblemen, know the pride of being Rajputs of the most ancient line.

They live now at Udaipur, the city of glistening lake palaces that blind the glance at noonday, but the tragic fortress of Chitor was the ancient and sacred home of their race. A fort rises on a long promontory, like a ship riding the misty, undistinguished land. High within its walls, bleak sides of palaces have empty windows, stone temples await worshippers who do not come, and the many-tiered Tower of Victory, with its staircase and thick dark carvings, is an isolated finger rising from sun-dried grass and bramble.

Who were the Rajputs who have such pride of race that the poorest, in flapping cotton, who hops a ditch to chase his buffalo, may wear a curving sword, insigne of birth?

To place them, it may be clearer to go back to the beginnings. After colossal King Harsa died, his empire fell to fragments. For more than three centuries all the states of India were very busy changing frontiers and making history which no one put into a book. But it does not follow that people were less active or lazy, that weavers stopped weaving or farmers ploughing, or storytellers spinning yarns that went on with the fabulous Pancatantra, or flowed into the 'Ocean of the Streams of Story'; nor that fewer women prayed by stream or tree for a son, or burned alive with a departed husband.

During this time — between A.D. 650 and A.D. 1001, the unnamed sculptors of India carved such immensities as the temple cut from living rock at Ellora, the mighty figures in the Elephanta Cave, and the stones at Mamallapuram shaped into animals or shrines. Early mediæval sculpture had scarcely waned in power from the classic Gupta serenity and combined grace with strength. The careful adherence to sacred rules of art, the growing richness of detail had not yet stiffened the essential life.

During this time elaborated Buddhism faded from India — Mahanaya Buddhism such as King Harsa had loved, with its Heavens full of compassionate Buddhas and Hells full of demons; with its mystic interpretations of ancient cult; with its tree of life, lotus, and wheel turned into subtle allegory — Buddhism with its many monasteries of gentle, hair-splitting, miracle-hoping monks. It was driven from India by the renaissance of Brahman power, and found its home in the groves of Java, the weird highlands of Tibet, and under the roofs of China and Japan, to grow, encrusted with myth and metaphysics, until Siddartha Gautama would have needed an introduction.

During this time, while the many small states of India made their wars and crowned many unimportant kings under umbrellas, there came to be a certain cohesion of power, a practical unity of strength, in clans called Rajput.

How or why Rajputs came to be Rajputs is not known certainly, although the stories are many. The word means king's son, or noble. In the fifth and sixth centuries, invaders from over the Afghan mountains, the Sakas and Hunas whom King Harsa fought, the Gurjuras and Maitrakas, won footing in that much-trampled northwestern corner of India that always fell first to invaders. Some tribes penetrated to the stony hills of Rajputana, the desert and tiger-infested thickets, and there strengthened their courts and their vigorous codes of chivalry and war. Strange tenacious customs suggested Viking habits. They built up the states of Mewar, Jodhpur, Jaipur, and Bikaner. By the eighth century these clans had grown strong and important and apparently indigenous. Though they bound into their code and custom people of various races, both Indian and foreign, yet in the course of time strict laws of intermarriage built up a certain cousinship among them, with men of good foreign descent in the upper ranks, and in the lower fringes the cultivating Jats, and some wild men of the hills. Their rule spread in time from Rajputana to the central Himalayan hills, to the Punjab, and even to Kashmir.

Though their subcastes were as many as the hairs of the head, yet the word Rajput acquired a single significance. Hinduism accepted them as Kshatriyas, the traditional kings and warriors of their ancient system, which had been dislocated by stormy wars. The Rajputs believed themselves to carry on Hindu tradition without a break since the time of Rama, then back to the sun or moon or — belatedly and less aristocratically — to a firepit.

Each mythical division — sprung from sun, moon, or fire — was in turn split into many branches, and most branches had many clans. Each had its own genealogy, accurate back to its astronomical origin, and a creed of its own custom and belief and laws of intermarriage. Every Rajput in theory should be able to recite his genealogy and creed, but, failing that, he might turn to a bard, who could supply him with all the glory any ego might need.

The Rajputs were kings in most of the northern and central states of chaotic, picture-puzzle India before the Mohammedans invaded. Unluckily, they had jealous natures and many feuds. In the rivalries, certain kings won land and tribute from others. Power grouped into four states, including Delhi, Mewar, and Kanauj. The smaller princes paid homage to the more successful.

Because they were to stand their ground against Moslem attack, and in later centuries, under alien rule, to provide a strength for the submerged Hindus, it is clearer to get a picture of them at this point, even though the stories of their actions come later, for they become strong characters in the drama of India. The Rajputs almost said, 'They shall not pass.'

Near the beginning of the nineteenth century, a discerning English officer named Lieutenant Colonel James Tod, who had mapped and campaigned in Rajputana wilds, and who lived for years as English Resident at their courts, had translations made from the vast and mildewing library at Udaipur — chronicles, Puranas, songs of bards. These, with his own long and intimate observations, he gathered into his rich 'Annals and Antiquities of Rajasthan.' He felt that he was observing tenacious fragments which suggested the complete system of the past of pomp and power.

The Rajputs were anything but introverts. They did not care for sitting in groves renouncing the world, nor for spinning delicate arguments in metaphysics. They loved action and war and had a sensitive code of honour, for which they often gave their lives.

A Rajput worshipped greatly and chose lusty things to honour — his sword, his horse, the sun. Once a person of not unsimilar temperament, a Western cowboy, remarked that he cared for just three things in the world — his horse, his rope, and his hat. He is hardly to be compared in glamour, but has the same active, outward turn of mind. The Rajput 'swore by his steel,' and had a definite public ceremony of worshipping the two-edged sword. He bowed himself to the ground before his shield, lance, sword, and dagger. He was buried fully armed, with his shield on his back and sword in hand. His horse a symbol of the sun, although not sacrificed at its master's funeral, was given to the priest. His women, however, had no such alleviation, and regarded burning themselves at his death as incidental. But the sati spots, where the gallant women died, were a little feared as the resort of harpies.

The women of the Rajputs, from girlhood, must have accustomed themselves to the idea that at any moment they must be ready to step into the flames. For each slain soldier a woman, or several women, burned. And when a city was besieged without hope of relief, honour demanded that people put on the saffron robes of sacrifice, that the men rush out to die upon the enemy's spears, and the women burn alive rather than be captured. Whether drugged and dazed-eyed, or hysteric with excitement, trembling with terror or exaltedly calm, women of honour usually ended their lives in flames.

The Rajput inherited many sun-worshipping cults. At the ceremony of the returning sun, or Spring personified, the prince and his chieftains chased the wild boar, reckless of danger, galloping over jungle wastes until he was speared, killed, and eaten — which meant that the Great Mother, Siva's wife, would not refuse her gifts that year. The boar, who is all mixed up with the sun and sex in the cults of many lands, was eaten in the same way that totem worshippers ate the sacred animal to renew their life and the fertility of the years — all very obscure but rather magnificent and dashing in actual habit. Today the wild boar is not regarded simply in Udaipur. Flocks and droves roam the hills, state-protected. The ugly predatory things would root out all the farmers' crops, so at every sunset the Maharana has them fed amply. They come snorting in, raising clouds of dust, and gobble up their share of the state's income in their appointed place as the sun goes down.

The image of the sun was placed on the Rajput's banners; the chief bastion of his fortresses was dedicated to the sun; and the palace of the Maharana of Udaipur today still shows a gold gypsum sun raying out on the white wall. The pipal tree, sacred to the sun, could not be cut down, and the bull of Siva was in its grove.

Besides the sun and horse and sword, besides Siva and Indra, battle-loving gods, and the Great Mother, the Rajput worshipped lavishly. As Colonel Tod said, 'No object was too high or too base... from the sun to the paring-knife of the shoemaker.'

The reckless and ardent Rajput loved gambling and his hearty cups. Without either battle or hunting, he was at a loss, and might grow lazy or slothful, since he did not care for mental activity. He could apparently slip into apathy for years, and then, when a wild occasion arose, rise to ride the tempest.

In mediæval days the princes lived in great splendour. Though a desert might surround the State of Mewar and hills covered with scrub-jungle where aigrettes flew and panthers sprang; and though on the stony outskirts on three sides of the land lived tribes of marauding Bhils, ready to swoop down with skilful arrows, yet the Maharana at the core of the state maintained his large and fine dignity. He was head of a martial system like that of feudal Europe. He was a patriarch to whom his people claimed blood relationship, from the proud sixteen nobles of the first class to the man who only owned so much land as he could plough in a day.

Family counted chiefly in the rule of the state. The absolute ruler had officials who inherited their places as cup-bearer, steward of the household, master of the wardrobe, of the kitchen, of the horse. Chieftain relatives of different rank held the districts of the state. The land at the centre, near the capital, was a great prize. The land at the circumference, subject to hillmen's raids, was given strategically to the best fighters.

According to their nicely graded rank and rent-rolls, each type of nobleman had his duty at court. The great sixteen 'first-class noblemen' need only come for solemn ceremonies. The next class must always be there, on call as army officers. The petty nobles, who owned only a village or so apiece, had to attend the prince's person, and clogged the palaces and camps with their numbers.

In their smaller way, the haughty chieftains of the first class maintained their own courts and hereditary cup-bearers, their minstrels to precede them, their palaces and terraces. But proud though he was, if such a noble had been a little laggard in his duty to the Maharana, he might one day see a royal herald riding up to his castle, with a warrant for him to entertain the herald and twenty or more horsemen as long as they cared to stay. That device was an accelerator of the age.

The Rana supported his state by taxing chiefly the land, but also by making people pay for battles, horses, ploughs and weddings.

Each city had its hereditary chief magistrate, but much minor and local government was done by the caste councils. Merchants had to pay transit duties on their goods, but such was the simple honesty of the people that 'our ancestors tied their invoice to the horns of the oxen at the first frontier post, and no questions were put until the last, when it was opened and payment made.'

In great crises of war, the first chieftains formed the Rana's advisers. At other times he might balance the smaller vassals against their too great insolence. So long as the prince was strong and tactful, the system worked well. When he weakened, each part separated and moved in its own course, following each jealous chieftain. The wise ruler kept his hostile factions all balanced, and walked his tight-rope of dignity and power.

13. *Moslem Attack*

BLACK met white and night met day when the Moslem met the Hindu. Desert thought met jungle thought; a religion of wild spaces, empty except for sun on sand, met a faith rich as tree-fern thickets. The *élan* of one prophet proclaiming one God unified followers who bore down upon Hindus divided and subdivided.

The Moslem conquered the Hindu by sword, not persuasion. Outwardly bending, inwardly tenacious, the Hindu kept his ramifying ways, for centuries a subject civilization. The Mohammedan at his side stayed contemptuously Puritan.

Mohammedan singleness contrasted with Hindu multiplicity. Allah, the one abstract God, hater of images, scorned the millions of anthropomorphic gods and their sculptured shapes. The Moslem believed that all men were equal, brothers under Allah. The Hindu separated human beings inexorably into a hierarchy of caste. The Moslem thought this world good, a place for swift action, whose reward would come in a houri-tended Paradise when the curtain went down. But the Hindu brooded that this world is an illusion — which the seeker for truth must ignore and escape — enmeshed in millions of lives.

Moslem architecture severely subordinated detail to central unity. Hindu building let violent details riot over a less important pattern. A southern Hindu temple, with scattered, god-covered gopurams and courts, live peacocks, dancing-girls, stone chariots, rearing horses, and bazaars with sewing machines in the courtyard, contrasted with the emptiness of a mosque, hollow of all but stately space, and a floor to pray on.

The stern regimentation of Moslem worshippers, athletically bending heads and hands to earth, kneeling, rising in focussed devotion, differed from Hindu worship, where each man had his private necessity of rite. A Moslem congregation was a unit; a Hindu, a chance gathering of intent individuals.

The Hindu mind, even when it turned outward toward life, did not like singleness and synthesis; it wanted to analyze and split apart. The Hindu wanted more and more castes and sects and gods and sanctities. The Mohammedan sought a single principle to dominate his action.

The Moslem was fanatical and intolerant. The Hindu was foggily tolerant of all beliefs, but bitter and violent when his purities were defiled. The Hindu reverenced the cow. The Moslem killed it to eat. The Hindu fed graven images. The Moslem smashed them. So it went for centuries. Humble neighbours found means of *rapprochement* in daily living, but a trifle might start deep volcanoes of hate.

The great Arabic civilization imposed itself upon an India such as King Harsa knew. Islam did not come empty-handed. It had swept since the seventh century through Persia and over North Africa to Spain, and the treasures of its art grew as the centuries advanced, and it gathered to itself the genius of the conquered lands. To think of Islamic civilization is to see the arches of the mosque at Cordova, a Moorish palace at Fez, the courts of Granada, galloping horsemen throwing lances, illuminated manuscripts, glazed tiles, and domes of heaven-blue.

Swordarms, stateliness, simplicity, intensity, cruelty, passion, scorn of women, and a belief that a straight line is the shortest distance between two points — these are the attributes of the sensual, hard-riding Puritans. They bred thick barbarians and degenerate despots, but they also bred strong, intelligent men.

The invasion of Turks, Arabs, Afghans, Moguls, and all the Mohammedan peoples who passed through the highlands of Afghanistan into India, began in the eighth century as an episode, threatened strongly in the eleventh, and lasted from the twelfth to the eighteenth as the varying but chiefly dominant power over most of India.

MALMUD OF GHAZNI

997–1030

Loaded with Spoil and Encumbered with Captives

The city of Lahore, with a tangle of rooftops — high-walled flat roofs where families sleep in the heat, and the hidden women find fresh air by day; Lahore, where the well-born women, shrouded in white even over the eyes, peer through embroidered meshes when they go abroad, and through carved lattice and curtains when they stay indoors — Lahore is mostly Mohammedan now. The city's crumbling palaces were built by Mohammedans. Her geometric mosques, white-domed or Persian-tiled, today express that single civilization.

Lahore in the heart of the Punjab, the home of Aryan tribes, a land that once knew the Vedic song-makers, and in mediæval days the kingdom of pearl-hung Hindu princes — Lahore lay in the path of the first great Moslem conquest.

The Hindu cities of the plain were as tempting as a heap of jewels to a bandit. The Punjab dust was trampled by the mountain raiders. Back and forth the pillaging armies marched, and women and girls who could not hide in the openness of the brown plain or behind the useless walls of fallen cities went back as slaves to Afghanistan.

During years or maybe centuries of fear, after the Moslems were the accepted rulers, Hindu women learned to shroud themselves into limp balloons of cloth or to keep indoors. Possibly they copied the fashion from the veiled Mohammedan women, who were now the court ladies. To translate into modern vernacular, 'My dear, *when* are you going to learn to veil your face? Positively *nobody* lets herself be seen. They say the Sultan's women never stir outside of the palace.' Fashion can make a virtue of incredible necessity. Today a limp balloon of cloth means a woman who respects herself, whose family is in some degree proud. The screens put up at a railway station to allow a high-born lady to take a train without being seen of men are the fastidiousness of propriety.

But they say that an undersized, pockmarked mountaineer was the ultimate cause of the fashion of purdah for Hindu ladies.

Mahmud of Ghazni, of the Afghan hills, looked into the glass and found himself ugly. He was shorter than most of the tribesmen whom he ruled, and his face was spotted with scars. He remarked to a courtier that a king's face should gladden beholders, while his was positively forbidding. To which the courtier made a suave reply. But Mahmud knew that to command admiration he had to act fast.

One pictures Mahmud — a speeded film of him — with a sword in his hand, flashing on all sides, now front, now back, now raiding India, now turning back to enlarge his mountain kingdom or to subdue a rebel; lunging here and there, chiefly for the fun of the thing — his whole life a campaign. If he had been handsome and the rightful heir, he might have relaxed.

The fun of the thing, the greed and the glory, and the freedom to smash, he translated into religious duty. He believed that he felled idols for the sake of Allah and the destruction of false religion, not to mention his own reward in Heaven. He could find Koranic text for his idea that he was ensuring himself a lasting place in Paradise.

Mahmud was not a savage chieftain. He was a cultivated man who enjoyed the turn of a phrase and who patronized genius. His family story was rich in adventure.

His father, Sabuktikin, was brought from Turkestan to be sold as one of a string of slaves in the newly made mountain kingdom of Ghazni. Though travel-worn and abased, he had the blood of the last Sassanian kings of Persia, and his bearing caught the eye of the self-made ruler, who took him into service. At his death, Sabuktikin was chosen by the chieftains to reign. He conquered Afghanistan and a part of Persia, and a trifle turned his attention toward India.

A Rajput prince, Jaipal of Lahore, haughtily undertook to punish his army for destroying some Hindu shrines.

Jaipal ruled all the Punjab and land as far as the Hindu Kush Mountains; he had a weighty army, and had not tasted Moslem attack. No soothsayer told him what he was bringing on himself and his country. For when he faced the barbarians, his huge army was shaken to the roots of its superstition by a violent storm when the sky seemed to fall in one lump of water — they thought the gods were angry, and ran. Jaipal had to surrender, and Sabuktikin soon found pretext to take part of his kingdom.

Mahmud of Ghazni was heir to this feud. He was not his father's chosen successor, but the son of a concubine, who had to see his younger brother inherit. Being an experienced soldier and governor at twenty-seven, he quickly pushed his brother from the throne, imprisoned him for life, and proceeded to be king of Ghazni.

It was an unlucky day for India when Mahmud's attention was turned that way. Of course the clash between the neighbouring civilizations was inevitable, and an osmosis from Indian wealth to Afghan dearth. Other wire-muscled mountaineers beside Mahmud liked loot. But if Mahmud had been the handsome, legitimate heir to a cushioned throne, he might not have exerted himself so much. The degree of first terror in India might have been less sharp.

Jaipal's unfortunate move brought a vengeance from the hills out of all proportion to the cause. The Hindu princes should have been quiet; they should have used protective colouring to escape the notice of that energetic fanatic, Mahmud of Ghazni.

In August, 1001, Mahmud, with his kingdom well organized at home, started the first of his many attacks upon India. He made a holy vow that he would invade the country once a year for the glory of the Prophet. And although he did not quite carry this out, because of interruptions at home, he did his best.

He marched first against Lahore. He took fifteen thousand chosen horse, and met Jaipal near Peshawar, on the bleak brown land. He was outnumbered. The Rajah of Lahore had twelve thousand horsemen and thirty thousand infantry and three hundred elephants, and was waiting for more reinforcements. Mahmud forced an attack before these could come. His headlong horsemen were irresistible, his archers better marksmen, and the Hindus who were not dead were flying for their lives. Jaipal was captured. And Mahmud ran his fingers through sixteen necklaces of jewels taken from the great Hindu princes, and gloated.

But Jaipal was shamed, his Rajput honour sullied, by two defeats in battle. When he was released from confinement, he gave his crown to his son Anandpal, and climbed onto a funeral pyre to burn.

Mahmud was doughty enough to lead his battles in person when need be, and there is a tale of a dramatic scene when the time came to inspire his men to final energy. Once, when his troops were falling back, Mahmud at sunset turned his face toward Mecca, prostrated himself on the ground in sight of all, and called upon the Prophet. Then he sprang up dynamically and cried, 'Advance, our prayers have found favour with God.' The soldiers shouted and rushed the enemy into the walls of the town.

In 1008, Mahmud decided to punish rebellious Prince Anandpal of Lahore, who now realized his danger, and sent ambassadors to all sides for help. The Hindu kingdoms made one cause against the Moslem. Ujjain, Gwalior, Kalinjur, Kanauj, Delhi, and Ajmer gathered an army so enormous that the problem of paying for food arose. The Hindu women melted their golden ornaments and sold their jewels to buy provisions for the army.

For forty days the enemies camped in full view on the bone-bare plains in the province of Peshawar, neither side caring to attack. Mahmud, the little smallpoxed man, saw the Hindu forces increasing daily and tried to provoke them to aggression. He sent out archers to irritate them to battle.

Thereupon from the Hindu lines came thirty thousand Khokars, wild men with head and feet bare, charging both flanks of Mahmud's army, passing the entrenchments, laying five thousand Moslems bloodily dying. Such a shock of attack might turn a less tenacious man than Mahmud, or one with less invention. But he had naphtha grenades thrown among the Hindu elephants, and to his luck, the beast that carried the commanding general, uncontrollable, ran away. The Hindus, with an eye out always for the leader, seeing him apparently in full retreat, turned and fled in disorder. Again and again in Indian history the elephants are unruly perils to their masters. Again and again the greatest sacrifice and courage scatters to nothing when the leader has mishap.

Mahmud harried the running army day and night, and sent thousands of Hindus into their next incarnation. The terror of being pursued by mounted Turks and Afghans and Khiljies would last for years, and wake a man cold in nightmare.

In 1013, he finally annexed Lahore. He learned that Thaneswar — the ancient kingdom of King Harsa — was considered sacred, a Mecca for faithful Hindus, and that its king was reverenced by the idolaters. He decided that such things must not be.

He required the Rajah of Lahore to give him a safe passage

through the kingdom. Being fated to live as the corridor of Mahmud's armies, the Rajah had no choice. He had learned to be polite and conciliatory. He sent a message saying that he was the subject and tributary of Mahmud, but he begged permission 'to acquaint His Majesty that Thaneswar is the principal place of worship of the inhabitants of the country; that, if it is required by the religion of Mahmud to subvert the religion of others, he has already acquitted himself of that duty in the destruction of the temple of Nagrakoti.' He promised tempting tribute if Thaneswar were spared. But Mahmud now preferred treasure in Heaven to treasure on earth — or perhaps he intended to have both, for he only replied, 'The religion of the faithful inculcates the following tenet: That in proportion as the tenets of the Prophet are diffused, and his followers exert themselves in the subversion of idolatry, so shall be their reward in Heaven.'

Therefore he declared he must root out the worship of idols from the face of all India. Hercules had a smaller task. But Mahmud felt that he was making headway.

The Rajah of Delhi sent messengers throughout Hindustan that Mahmud, without provocation, was marching to destroy Thaneswar, and that all must unite to save the holy city. Mahmud did not give them time. He fell upon the helpless place and plundered and broke the temple carvings. He led a cityful of captives away. Two hundred thousand went from Thaneswar as his slaves. When he returned to Ghazni, his capital looked like an Indian city, and the meanest soldier had money to spend, and a Hindu to order about as a slave.

Slightly inflated, Mahmud wrote to the Caliph of Baghdad, mentioning that, as long as he held the greater part of Khorasan, he might as well have the rest. The Caliph thought it prudent to oblige him. But when Mahmud, his camel's head in the tent, demanded Samarkand also, the Caliph wrote a sufficiently sharp letter to puncture this trial balloon. Mahmud found the direction of India simpler.

His lesser invasions do not bear recording. In the spring of 1018 he pointed his armies toward Kanauj, the city of King Harsa, full of the glories which Bana described, excluding perhaps the sapphire pavements.

Kanauj lay three months' march from Ghazni. Mahmud, who started soon after the rainy season in September, had to cross seven formidable rivers, swollen and unbridged. They were straws in his way. His army had bodies of leather and bellows for lungs and liked rocks for pillows.

On his way to Kanauj lay great Muttra, undefended, the sacred homeland of Krishna, a treasure-chest of a city, piled with architecture given by devout Hindus. His soldiers broke down and burned the images of the gods and carried away the melted gold and silver Mahmud looked at the temples with an eye to their destruction. He may have decided that the labour of unpiling the stone temples was too great, or, as the Hindus believed, he may have been awed by their beauty. If so, it was the first thing which awed or deterred him. He stayed at Muttra twenty days and did all the damage he could by fire and loot. He unearthed some five hundred and forty-eight pounds of gold. The people living there shrank into their houses when they could not escape beyond the walls, and prayed to their hidden idols that Mahmud's men, spurring down their streets and bursting into doorways, might pass them by.

In time Mahmud's army came to Kanauj, 'a city which raised its head to the skies.' Seven detached forts guarded the ramparts. Its prince affected the greatest state and splendour, but he was not expecting Mahmud, and could not collect his troops. Terrified, he withdrew and left his city to the Moslem — and sued for peace in order to save it from destruction. One story says that he submitted so far as to embrace the Mohammedan faith.

'Loaded with spoil and encumbered with captives,' Mahmud returned to Ghazni. He began work on his upstart capital with wealth sucked from India and taste learned from Persia. Neither labour nor money was lacking for his projects. The Hindu captives were so cheap that they sold in camp for a few coins apiece — Hindus of all castes and abilities and sensibilities; and the surplus slaves were sent on to the markets of Iraq and Persia.

He built a mosque of granite and marble, furnished with rich carpets, such as museums dream about, and he named it the 'Celestial Bride.' He attached a university, with a vast collection of curious books in various languages, and a museum of natural wonders. He was concerned with education, and established a fund for the maintenance of students and proper persons to instruct them in the arts and sciences. Excited by his example, the nobility of Ghazni began to build, until the city rose with mosques and caravanserais, and colleges, fountains, and reservoirs and aqueducts, beyond any city of the West.

Mahmud was not a mere bandit. He regarded India as his natural bank account, and, luckily, the land also of a heathen cult which the Prophet called upon him to destroy. India was the convenient source of treasure upon earth and treasure in Heaven. He valued both.

The buccaneer, at home, became the liberal patron of arts, though always with the uncertain temper of an Oriental despot. He could order his poets about and have the literature created which he wished. It was his idea to put into verse the stories of the kings of Persia, which became the great epic 'Shahnamah' — earlier than the 'Chanson Rolande' and European epic cycles — the

'Shahnamah' endlessly copied in rare calligraphy and coloured as Persian miniaturists can.

He had so many poets in his court that he ordained a superintendent of literature to sift all verse and bring only the best to his attention. One of his favourite poets was named Unsury, a most discreet man, who wrote an heroic account of Mahmud's actions, a flattering mirror into which he could look with delight at his own deeds. This poet could soothe his most troubled mood. One morning Mahmud was most perturbed. In a drunken debauch he had cut off the long black hair of his favourite mistress. That troubled him more than any number of rebellions. He could not get over it. He paced the floor. He sat. He rose. And nobody dared come near him, except the poet Unsury, who walked up to him with a few apparently extemporaneous lines so unctuous, so relievingly appropriate and just, that all the sting went from Mahmud's heart. He was so delighted that he stuffed the poet's mouth with jewels. Ah, welladay!

He did not treat Firdausi quite so well. Mahmud, to glorify his own reign, projected a monumental history in verse of the early kings of Persia. He chose seven stories of kings from a manuscript plundered from a Persian library, and gave them to seven of his poets to be turned into verse. The poet Unsari, who took the story of Rustam, won the contest.

But meanwhile, in distant Khorassan, Firdausi had been making a name as a poet. He heard of Mahmud's edict, and put some of the story of kings into verse which was so much admired that the fame reached the ears of Mahmud, who promptly invited the poet to his court. Brought before the sultan and challenged to extemporaneous verse, Firdausi could flatter with the best.

> The cradled infant [said he], whose sweet lips are yet
> Balmy with milk from its mother's breast,
> Lisps first the name of Mahmud.

He wrote the stories of Isfendiyar and Rustam so surpassingly that Mahmud without hesitation transferred to him the appointment, promised to pay lavishly, and gave him the surname Firdausi, which meant Paradise, because the beauty of his speech spread Paradise throughout the court.

Unsari, put aside, did not apparently make trouble. But a certain favourite of Mahmud grew very jealous. He tried, almost successfully, to prove Firdausi a heretic and ingrate. The poet still rose in honour and esteem. At the end of thirty years he had completed his work of sixty thousand couplets, and Mahmud ordered him rewarded with an elephant load of gold. The jealous favourite managed to get this order changed to sixty thousand silver coins. Firdausi was in the public bath when the money bags were brought to him. When he saw it was only silver, he was so furious that he gave twenty thousand to the keeper of the bath, twenty thousand to the seller of refreshments, and twenty thousand to the slave who brought them. Naturally, this could be interpreted as insulting to Mahmud, who thereupon ordered Firdausi trampled to death by an elephant. A man needed every wile to live under an Oriental king. Cunning and conniving and cringing were bred into brains. Firdausi hurried to Mahmud, prostrated himself at his feet, and begged mercy, composing breathlessly an elegant eulogium on the glories of his reign and his innate generosity. Mahmud was touched and rescinded the order. Firdausi made haste to be clear of the kingdom, but before leaving he managed to get from the king's librarian the presented copy of the 'Shahnamah,' and he rewrote his flattery into a scurrilous satire calling Mahmud a bastard, and remarking such things as

When charity demands a bounteous dole,
Close is thy hand, contracted is thy soul.

Long afterward, one story says, Mahmud was sorry for his meanness, and sent to Firdausi a present of money and a robe of honour, which reached the city just as Firdausi's funeral procession was leaving the gates.

From these home occasions and the diversifications of life in Ghazni, Mahmud was always ready to march for India. His energy was inexhaustible.

The separate Indian princes met the danger of Mahmud variously. Gwalior, a sheer-walled fortress on a hill, could buy him off with only thirty-five elephants. But the Rajah of Kalinjur was more ingenious. First he loosed his elephants, riderless and maddened by drugs, against the Moslems. Mahmud ordered his fearless Tartars to mount some, and drove them all off. At that the Kalinjur king, thoroughly frightened, tried literature. The story goes that he sent Mahmud a panegyric on the bravery of his troops, which proved more effective than drunken elephants. Mahmud's courtiers admired the verse so much that Kalinjur was given the government of fifteen forts.

The most famous of Mahmud's raids, to Hindus the most scandalous and stamina-breaking, was his attack on the holy temple of Somnath. This stood by the sea in Kathiawar, so sacred that Hindus believed their souls after death went to Somnath to be changed into the next incarnation. They said that the ebb and flow of tides at the foot of the temple was the obeisance paid by the ocean to this shrine of the moon god. In time of eclipses two or three hundred thousand people flocked to the temple. The princes of Hindustan had given two thousand villages to maintain the priests, who were so pure that they washed daily in Ganges water brought a thousand miles. There were two thousand priests and three hundred musicians, and three hundred temple barbers who shaved devotees before admitting them; and five hundred dancing-women whose posturing worshipped the phallus of the god, and whose prostitution served priest and pilgrim. A king did not think himself demeaned to give his daughter to this temple service.

The temple stood fortified, on a narrow peninsula, washed on three sides by the sea. Mahmud, from his Afghan mountains, decided to destroy it. He chose fifty-four thousand horsemen and thirteen hundred elephants. A great desert lay before him. He ordered each trooper to carry fodder, water, and food for several days, and in addition he loaded thirty thousand camels with supplies — and mastered the desert.

By rapid marches he came to Somnath, and could see on its battlements crowds of people, armed and jeering, who signalled for a herald to approach, to say that their great god Somnath had drawn the Mohammedans thither to shrivel them in one blast, to avenge the gods of India.

The Hindu gods battled against Allah's desert prophet.

Mahmud had no fear of the crash of destruction which the Hindus believed would consume his troops. He advanced and began assault. His sure-aimed archers cleared the battlements of the swarm of people. The Hindus, astonished that Moslems had power to break through the spell of their gods, rushed down from the walls and into the temple, prostrating themselves in tears before the lingam of Siva, praying for help. Mahmud took this chance to put scaling-ladders against the walls, and the Moslems climbed, crying, 'Allah! Allah!'

The Hindus at that rose to a spirited resistance and fought so hard that Mahmud's men fell back from fatigue. As fast as the besiegers scaled the walls, they were hurled down. On the third day of battle, large reinforcements of Hindus approached. Mahmud attacked them to prevent their entering the walls, and before their fresh strength, his troops began to waver. Quick to sense the psychology of his men, he leaped to the ground and did his public prayer. Then, mounting, he took a general by the hand and advanced toward the enemy. The sight so cheered his troops that, ashamed to abandon their king, they gave a loud shout and rushed forward. Their charge broke the enemy line into a general rout.

Over the walls of Somnath, the Moslems fought through the streets, driving the Hindus toward the temple. Some tried to escape through a gate toward the sea, but Mahmud quickly found boats and had them pursued even on the waves.

Then he, with his sons and nobles and chief attendants, entered the superb temple. The roof was supported by fifty-six pillars curiously carved and set with precious stones. A great chain of gold held bells to call the priests to prayer. The pendent lamps reflected in all the jewels to lighten the place and fell on thousands of small golden and silver images.

In the centre stood the lingam, three yards high, and embedded two yards deep into the ground. The priests, according to the tale, begged Mahmud to spare the sacred image and offered him huge sums. Mahmud replied that he did not wish to be known as a seller of idols, but as a breaker of idols. He lifted his mace and smote the lingam. When the stone broke, some say, a heap of jewels tumbled out.

Somnath is fallen, is fallen! There was no revenge, unless it is true that the guide on the way home purposely led the Moslems through wastes of the Sind Desert, where many died or went raving mad from heat and thirst before they discovered that the guide was a priest of the temple of Somnath, trying to avenge its fall.

This was the climax of Mahmud's idol-smashing, the uttermost attempt to gain treasure in Heaven. The Calif of Baghdad sent him flattering titles and recognized him as ruler of Khorassan, Hindustan, and Seistan.

But when the time came to go to his stored-up wealth in Paradise, Mahmud found it hard to pry himself from this world's goods. He was dying in bed. His kidneys or intestines prosaically did what all the united armies of the Hindus had failed to accomplish. When Mahmud knew himself near the end, he commanded all his gold and caskets of jewels brought to him. He wept at the sight, and sent them back to the treasury. He ordered a review of his army, the elephants and camels and horses and chariots. He feasted his eyes upon them, and again he wept. For he could not carry his loot through the barrier of death.

The Punjab was the only Indian province which Mahmud organized and held, but he was the first to carry Islam into the heart of India — the geographic heart, not the emotional centre. He was the first of the terror-makers who struck in the name of Allah and obliterated pious cities and carvings.

The Ghazni dynasty which he founded included quarrelsome kings, mostly of smaller stature than Mahmud, who in time lost all their Afghan and Persian lands, and retreated to their last province, the Punjab. By 1190 the Ghazni dynasty fell before the upspringing power of Muhammad of Ghor.

14. *Rajput Resistance*

THE Rajputs in the twelfth century had their chance to save India for the Hindus from such aliens. Prithvi Raj was the darling hero of their bards, a young Lochinvar with the advantage of princely descent. He ruled Ajmere and Delhi, where he built a stronghold named after himself, whose crumbling ruins can be seen today, marching out to guard the ghosts. Under his daring leadership, the Hindus might have built a single bulwark against the tides of Mohammedan mountaineers, spilling over from Afghanistan.

A rival Rajput king, however, was even stronger. Jaichand, Rajah of Kanauj and Benares, was haughty. He was very near to delusions of grandeur. When he had made eight lesser kings of India prisoners, he decided to hold the very ancient ceremony called 'Bride's Choice,' for his daughter. This was nearly as arrogant and dangerous an undertaking as the horse sacrifice, since it assumed sovereignty of the earth and divine honour. He invited all kings to come as suitors for his daughter. Prithvi Raj was too spirited to accept an invitation which implied obeisance.

Jaichand's palace was emptied of all but kings, who each took the place of some servant. The halls had princes holding basins and placing cushions, each delicately ranked in the household hierarchy by the importance of his state. To insult the absent Prithvi Raj, a mean and unflattering statue was made of him and set up as horseboy, the lowest of the low.

The climax to the long ceremony was his daughter's supposedly free choice of a husband. The little princess, stepping from her quietness into all this confusion of strange youths and bearded men obsequiously waiting for her choice, slender but sinewy warriors sending quick glances at her from imperiously velvet, hot eyes, might excusably have been bewildered. But she did not hesitate. Probably she had never seen Prithvi Raj, but news always travels swiftly in India, and she knew all about him. She ignored the young men present, and went directly to the mean little statue, and flung her wreath around its neck.

Prithvi Raj was at her side, carried her off from her father and the rival kings, set her on his waiting horse, and galloped off. His small band of followers guarded the flight, slashing down pursuers.

The romance is a favourite of Hindu song, and Chand Bardai tells of it in many cantos. But it had the disastrous effect of further estranging the difficult Jaichand, too confident of his single power —a king who could hear his bards singing that the van of his enormous armies reached the sunset goal before the rear could move.

Meanwhile, in the small kingdom of Ghor in the Afghan hills, a man called Muhammad Ghori was rising, with greed in his veins and cunning and courage. He was given his start in the world by the acts of his uncle, an unpleasant man called the 'World-Burner,' who captured Ghazni in seven days of slaughter and fire and added it to Ghor, and in whose reign people felt that 'pity had fled from the earth.' This horridly won kingdom was left to Muhammad's elder brother, but Muhammad (Mu'izz-ud-din Muhammad bin Sam) was his energy. The relationship of the brothers showed the one trait that lifted Muhammad from the ruck of cruel, capable conquerors — he was loyal and had a distaste for killing his own family. The brother ruled with title and prestige of king, while Muhammad went conquering and adding lands, and looked toward India. The weight and power of the Rajput princes, living in slow pomp in their fortresses on hills, or on plains behind miles of walls, well armed and delighting in warfare, would check to prudence any but a fanatical Turk, bred in Afghanistan. It would seem sheer insanity to push into the heat and desert and armoured elephants of India.

But Muhammad Ghori had a gadfly which sent him in. By guile and craft and shrewd soldiery he made his way. One method of taking a fort was by offering marriage to its unscrupulous queen if she would kill her husband and let him in. Another method — against the benevolent and kindly last king of the Ghazni dynasty at Lahore — was to promise to send back the king's six-year-old child whom he had captured, and then to delay the child's coming so long that the eager father came out of his fort to meet him — and Muhammad cut him off. By such methods, and others, he made his way toward the territory of Prithvi Raj, and threw down the gauntlet by capturing the fortress of Bhatinda in 1190.

The bard describes the clash between Rajput and Moslem. The message came to Prithvi Raj, the young elegant at his sport, that Muhammad had offered 'pan' to his heroes; and when a king in durbar had a dish of pan placed before him, and called on any chief who dared follow him to eat it, it was a storm signal to enemies. The Moslem drums were beating and Muhammad was boasting: 'I have taken Lahore. I shall also take Delhi, while the king amuses himself hunting.'

Prithvi Raj called a council of his chieftains. Some spoke in favour of sending letters to allies for help, while others wanted instant action.

'Wah! wah!' cried one old chieftain, rising noisily. 'Listen, all. The Shah is come, a brave man like an elephant and a lion. Wherever he is brought to bay, there he fights. Our chieftains know nothing of councilling. They hold but one counsel... to die a hero's death.'

So the horses were brought out, in their quilted or leathern mail, looking, according to the bard who told the story, like birds with wings folded. The warrior-poet was still further put to it for comparison when he called the rearing horses 'broad as bedsteads placed on end.' He was trying to be free with Oriental metaphor as became one who inherited a literature like Bana's, but he was a little stiff and creaking. 'The horses have frills down their faces, just as women of good family put on veils when they walk out.'

The elephants came, with knives fastened to their tusks.

Prithvi Raj set out to relieve Bhatinda. He passed beyond it and met the force of Muhammad at the village of Taraori, eighty miles from Delhi. He had prayers said to avert evil and obtain luck. He considered the position of the stars and set out at an auspicious hour, at the rise of powerful Saturn, when Mercury and Mars were ready to do their bit. The prince drew his troops up in one of the positions dictated by Manu, with some thousand years of sanctity behind it. Hindu generals felt bound to follow the battle positions which these sacred scriptures prescribed, to draw up their troops in the shape called vulture, snake, staff, or cart, needle, or thunderbolt. Prithvi chose for this moment the shape called the crescent. But Muhammad, unbound by ancient sanctities, formed his army as he chose for the instant..

'On came the Shah's warriors. They drew their glittering swords, the Hindus and the Mlechhas encountering each other.... Some pulled out the elephants' tusks, just as, to put it in a figure, the Bhils procure turnips.' The poet of battle describes it with gusto. The drums beat, the swords are lightning, piercing clouds. Horrors are only delight. 'On spears striking heads, brains are scattered about, appearing like rice on which crowds of crows feed. The gallant warriors cry, "Slay! Slay!"' All seemed sufficiently bloodthirsty, but in case of flagging zeal, the Rajputs had runners to go beside the soldiers singing war songs to encourage them.

Armour flashed in the sun. Flowing plumes on the helmets gave shade from its fierceness and tossed over the heroes like ships in a storm. Yellow umbrellas swung to and fro. Men cried with eager shouts. Heads fell off, but did not care. Blood ran in streams. 'Blood made the ground beautiful, as with a carpet of scarlet flowers.' If a leg of a rajah was broken, he still rushed on, using his sword as a prop. 'Trunks danced about, and heads shouted aloud.' Whenever a head fell off, Siva and Indra, like gallery gods, beat their kettledrums, and Siva danced on the battlefield.

Such absolute delight in killing or being killed — even though some of it was propaganda for the timid — is far from Asoka's pity, from the Buddhist or Jain doctrines of gentleness which Rajputs might inherit. It is even far from Krishna's moral to Arjuna, that a warrior's duty is to fight because it is his Karma, but that the result of fighting, the death, is nothing at all. Here is real joy in the slaughter itself. How good is man's fight, the mere killing and dying. A trunk dances about, and a head, somewhere else, shouts aloud.

In such zest for war, the Rajputs matched the Mohammedans, and behind them the more timid castes of the Hindus went their peaceable ways.

As more and more trunks and heads fall apart, with the insouciance of sawdust dolls, the bard makes the scene operatically familiar. The curtain is rising — the Walküre are hurtling with Wagnerian yodles down to the battlefield.

The Rajputs call them Apsaras, uniting this idea with the name of the river or air goddesses of Vedic hymns. The Apsaras are waiting to take the fallen heroes onto their laps. Before the battle they make their homes ready and hospitable. Each chose a beloved. One Apsara mourned because Indra's queen had chosen her coveted hero. 'Today has come the day of entertainment,' she bewailed. 'Sitting in cars the guests are ascending, but I have caught no sight of my beloved.' That was because she had chosen too brave a man, for a man who never bows in battle goes even beyond the Apsaras, straight up on a chariot of the gods to be united with the sun. Such a steadfast soul will never suffer rebirth.

At the first battle in Taraori, the Rajputs pushed with such *élan* and weight into the Moslem lines that they forced back the enemy flanks, and Muhammad Ghori, in the centre, was in danger. A frightened messenger rode up to warn him to look to his safety, but Muhammad hacked down the messenger of prudence and charged with a few followers straight at the Rajputs. Prithvi Raj's brother drove at him with his war elephant. Muhammad, seeing the grey monster bearing down, threw his lance straight, hitting the Rajah in the mouth, and knocking out his teeth.

Muhammad himself was struck so forcefully that he was faint and would have fallen from his horse and been trampled, had not a quick-witted servant jumped behind on his horse and guided him to safety. Enormous things turn on trifles. The nameless and unimportant man lost India for the Hindus.

Muhammad was galloped away to recover from his wounds, and went back to rest in Ghor and Ghazni, spending a year in merriment, but keeping India in mind. He disciplined his deserting officers by making them walk around the city with their horses' nose-bags, filled with grain, hung from their necks. The shamed officers walked around munching and masticating.

At the end of a year he had recruited an army of over a hundred thousand horsemen, Turks and Afghans, many of whom had their helmets set with jewels and their armour inlaid with silver and gold. He marched back to India, 'determined to recover his lost honour.' And he was generous enough to allow his disgraced, nose-bag officers to join the new army to wipe out their shame. As he marched on toward Lahore, he sent an ambassador to Prithvi Raj, ordering him and his followers to embrace the true faith of Islam.

One can imagine how Prithvi Raj felt, to be told by the vile, intruding, cow-killing Mohammedan to give up his religion — or to do anything at all at another's command.

Prithvi Raj sent this letter back:

> If you are wearied of your own existence, yet have pity upon your troops, who may still think it a happiness to live. It were better, then, you should repent in time of the rash resolution you have made, and we shall permit you to return in safety; but if you have determined to brave your evil destiny, we have sworn by our gods to advance upon you with our rank-breaking elephants, our plain-trampling horses, and bloodthirsting soldiers, early in the morning, to crush the army your ambition has led to ruin.

A fair and honourable letter.

Prithvi wrote to neighbouring Rajputs to gather together, to be ready to meet the Moslem refusal, and the Rajput chiefs responded. They gathered three hundred thousand strong, well mounted, and with three thousand of the earth-trampling elephants. One hundred and fifty Rajput chieftains swore by the water of the Ganges that they would conquer or die martyrs to their faith. The great mass of Hindus camped across the river from the waiting Mohammedans, again at Taraori.

But Jaichand, feeling invincible, chose this time to be jealous of Prithvi Raj. He and his armies stayed at home.

Muhammad, knowing himself outnumbered in a hostile country, again tried one of his psychological moves. He had played upon a woman's greed and a father's tenderness. Now he played upon Prithvi Raj's straightness and honour. He replied to the letter:

> I have marched into India at command of my brother, whose general only I am. Both honour and duty bind me to exert myself to the utmost in his service. I cannot retract, therefore, without orders; but I shall be glad to obtain a truce till he is informed of the situation of affairs, and till I have received his answer.

Guileless Prithvi Raj took him at his word. The Rajput was bound by his gentleman's honour. He began a battle, as one begins a tennis serve, when his opponent was ready. An answer from Afghanistan would take some time to arrive, weeks at the fastest. Meanwhile, the strain of an expected battle was postponed — and the cups were ready. The Hindus spent the night in revelry, ready to sleep at dawn. But at dawn Muhammad forded the river, drew his army up in the sand spit, and was silently entering part of the actual Hindu camp before the alarm was given.

There was confusion among the sleepers, cries of 'To arms! To arms!' — lamps flaring up at scattered points. Horses were neighing and plunging. Amazing as it seems, the mere size of the Hindu forces gave time to form part of the cavalry, and get into action in time to check the intruders and give the huge mass a chance to get into order.

In spite of heavy lids and giddy heads from the night, the prospect of battle wakened the Rajputs to keenness. They sent forward four lines, with great resolution.

Muhammad at this halted and began different tactics. He charged at their centre from dawn till sunset. Then himself leading twelve thousand of his best horsemen, he plunged against the weary, staggering army. Like a great building it tottered to a fall. In a general panic, Prithvi Raj's brother fell — and after the battle his body was identified by the broken teeth which Muhammad had given him the year before. Prithvi Raj, the focus of the Rajputs, was killed.

The fall of Prithvi Raj was momentous. It was well to believe that Apsaras took him to the sky, that he went to unite with the sun. And the princess, whom he had stolen from the elaborate, gilded 'Bride's Choice,' burned herself to a cinder. The prince was a symbol and a centre of power. When he and his kingdom fell, Hinduism as a fighting force in northern India was mortally wounded.

The usual camp equipment, elephants, horses, and armour, fell to Muhammad. The forts surrendered before him. He went to the city of Ajmere, and put all the inhabitants who opposed him to death and took whom he chose as slaves.

Raja Jaichand meanwhile stayed aloof, thinking he was far enough away and sufficiently terrifying to anyone. But Muhammad came nearer. His faithful slave and general, Kutb-ud-din Eibak, in 1193, took Delhi and all its districts, and from that day onward it was never again in Hindu hands. The saying went, 'The Empire of Delhi was founded by a slave' — of whom, more later.

Muhammad Ghori marched at last toward Kanauj, definitely against Jaichand, who saw too late how he had been weakened by the fall of his rival, Prithvi Raj. Although Jaichand's elephants were as the clouds and his horses like locusts, he was defeated by the army of Ghor, under Kutb-ud-din. He himself was killed by an arrow in the eye, and his corpse lost on the battlefield, until searchers found and identified him also by the teeth. He wore, apparently, a set of false ones, devised to be held in place by golden wires.

Muhammad marched briskly off and took the fort where Jaichand's treasure was stored and gathered the gold and jewels. Then he went on to the ancient sacred city of Benares, and had a marvellous time breaking the images in a thousand temples and righteously smashing. 'He purified and consecrated,' wrote Ferishta, 'in the name of the true God.' So completely did the Moslems 'purify' Benares that it has today nothing left of ancient Hindu architecture.

Then, through the activity of the faithful slave general, Muhammad cleared out the remaining knots of Rajput strength, Bhim Raj of Gujarat fell, and the hill-crowning fort of Gwalior, after a long siege, and Kalinjur and Budaon...

Between himself and his generals, Muhammad did a tidy piece of conquering, and the countryside all about Delhi was forced to acknowledge Islam from that time on.

All this time he had been acting in the name of his brother, who still reigned nominally as King of Ghazni and Ghor. Not until 1196, when his brother died, was he himself crowned king.

From that point his luck seemed to change. Revolts and betrayals and loss of his own city he met, and an attack of wild mountain Gukhurs on Lahore. Having settled their affair, he was marching back to Ghazni dreaming of further conquests. It was very hot weather with the air like a heavy hand. To get any breath of breeze at night, the king ordered that the screens which usually surrounded the royal tents in the form of a large square be taken down. A small band of Gukhurs bent on revenge could see inside the tent, where the sleeping king lay, fanned by two slaves. They stabbed the sentry, rushed in, frightening off the slaves, and knifed the king in twenty-two places. That was the end of the man who conquered northern India for the Mohammedan religion.

'He bore the character of a just monarch,' says Ferishta, 'fearing God and having the good of his subjects at heart. He paid great attention to learned and devout men.'

This man ended Hindu mastery of northern India. After his time the Rajput power was broken. They were the dissenting or rebelling minority. Sometimes they served faithfully in the conqueror's armies. Sometimes they revolted and gained a local freedom. But they were never again supreme masters in their homeland. The peasant people who ploughed the rice-fields, the women who plastered the walls of their mud houses with dung cakes to dry for fuel, the potters and washermen and all the simple people, when the armies had passed their villages, knew or cared little who ruled at Delhi, for each had his little caste group whose wise men told him what to do; and there was always more or less grain to pay to some remote tax lord; and droughts came and their cattle died, and fever took their babies, so they propitiated their godlings and were careful not to eat with caste outsiders. It was the superior people who were kidnapped to the alien court, the artists and craftsmen, the lordly, subdued warriors, the Brahman prime ministers who schemed for a foreign prince — such people, in the north of India, now knew continually that a civilization with different emphasis and values was bound to their own.

Perhaps Muhammad of Ghor was killed by Gukhurs, perhaps by the plot of slighted Shiah Mohammedans. But the Rajput bard decided differently. It was Prithvi Raj, who had not been killed in battle, but who had lived, imprisoned and blinded, and at last escaped to avenge the Hindu defeat. It was Prithvi Raj who killed the conqueror of Hindustan.

15. *The Fierce Sultans of Delhi*

A.D. 1206–1526

DELHI, the capital of India today, the heading of news despatches — what sort of point on the map is that? The city that Muhammad of Ghor and his slave captured from Prithvi Raj has been longer than any other the capital of an Indian empire. Now a New Delhi houses the government in a landscaped place of distances, of spreading stateliness to maintain prestige in rivalry with the past.

For the past in Delhi is formidable. There have been eight Delhis altogether, and six of them are dead. Legend says that there will be nine.

Scattered over the brown plain by the Jumna River, the dead cities lie. Ambitious sultans did not like to be crowded, nor to be held within the limits of another man's ego in stone. So the great fragments of cities, the mosques and tombs, the forts and universities, tell the story of their changes. The turbulent men who built them cannot realize their silence now — left to lizards and tourists and turbaned caretakers. An opulent Mohammedan woman in yellow trousers and curly-toed shoes, with her burka thrown back for a moment, carrying her baby on her hip; a man with a bed on his head; a sweeper with his faggot broom for the gravel paths; three tourists in white topees — such are the passers-by. The afternoon light falls in fulness on rose and yellow stone, green lawn and flowing trees, where spearmen once marched past enslaved Hindu columns, where open-handed Kutb-ud-din, riding his devoted elephant, scattered coins to the crowd; where quizzical, able Iltutmish raised his sea-plant tower.

Whatever the men were who built these dead cities, they were not weaklings — and they were not trivial builders. The Mohammedans who broke up Hindu temples to make their mosques, who forced Hindu workmen to carve their magnificences, but checked the fluency of their carving into the patterned restraint of Islam — these mediæval kings conceived of cities with boldness. The clash of Moslem severity of design with Hindu fertility of invention made a new style of architecture, once popularly called Pathan — the style of the Turkish sultans come down from Afghanistan, who held the space of plain that bore so many Delhis.

From 1260 until 1526, Delhi was ruled by four dynasties of Mohammedan kings, Turks or Afghans, who varied, as despots do, but who, with one or two exceptions of kindlier beings, were as bloodthirsty a lot as one would care to meet. The early Moslem creed divided all unbelievers into the People of the Book — Jews and Christians — who need not be slaughtered; and idol worshippers, who could be killed because they were an insult and offence to Allah. Many of the sultans, however, being far from unintelligent, discovered that they could not kill all their subjects, and that it was more profitable to make them pay extra tax for being Hindu. Of these sultans, some ruled with a firm hand, established order, and left a degree of local independence, so that one historian remarks that the rule of the Slave Kings was probably no harder to bear than that of the Norman barons of England.

Their exploits have an oddly familiar sound. American racketeers of today seem to revert to their type — a survival of an earlier approved fashion of man, pushing up through the cooling surface of civilization. The racketeer is very degenerate. He is below the surface of society, rather than above. He is not moved by religion, nor is he a mighty builder or æsthete — but in single-minded, callous grabbing, he has his resemblance.

Picture such a grabber with a gorgeousness, a swagger, retinues of splendour, manuscripts from the Persian, and often energetic prayers and a conviction of righteousness. Then imagine one thing more — a stirring of trouble sometimes within him, a very infrequent, faint consciousness that the seething mass of people called subjects were swayed by some laws he could not grasp, and for which the code of Islam had no rules. The Sultan of Delhi had to face those eternally modern things — the mass emotions of people, their hunger and hate, or food and contentment. He had to deal — he who had no textbook on economics — with standards of money, and prices, the distribution of wealth among the people, with the violence of all their excesses, and the excess of their taste for drink. To meet this his only training was the Mohammedan code, and his own particular experience in stealing or managing armies. No wonder that some of his ideas had an originality that the longest-haired or shortest-moustached legislator of today cannot equal. By the measure of these Sultans of Delhi the greatness of Asoka grows — maturity, once found, and lost for centuries.

The kingdom, of which Delhi remained the capital for these three centuries, expanded and contracted following the ability of succeeding sultans, like mercury in a thermometer — or values in a stock market. Under Muhammad Tughlak, the Delhi sultanate spread almost to the southern tip of India. At other times it dropped apart until only small districts around Delhi were actually held.

The first of the sultans who ruled at Delhi, driving out the Rajputs, was the slave, Kutb-ud-din Eibak, founder of the dynasty of Slave Kings which ruled from 1206 to 1290. The second dynasty of the Khiljis produced Ala-ud-din as its strongest, and lasted only from 1290 to 1318. Next came the dramatic Tughlaks, whose sultans ruled from about 1321 to 1388; then a time of feeble confusion, burst into by Timur's raid, and last the emergence of the Afghan Lodi dynasty from 1451 to 1526.

Obviously one cannot tell, in a book of this sort, all the intrigue and dramatic conflict of each reign, all the changed boundaries and fallen cities or sudden revolts, but a few brief episodes suggest some personalities of those sultans, and the way they governed.

THE SLAVE KINGS, WHO BUILT THE KUTB MINAR

Eleven miles southwest of Old Delhi rises an amazing tower. If the plain were the bottom of the ocean, the Kutb Minar would seem a plausible sea plant; or its fluted sides might suggest the cactus of the California desert — red sandstone, rising and constantly tapering to a height of over two hundred feet, banded with severe decoration of Arabic letters interwoven in flat relief; a tower massive at the base, yet seeming to sway like a whip when one looks to the top against the moving depths of the sky. The Kutb Minar was named for a Moslem saint, and built by the Slave King Iltutmish. At its base, a ruined arch, a magnificent gate to air, is all that is left of the Mosque of the Might of Islam, whose walls used the fragments of twenty-seven mutilated Hindu temples.

Kutb-ud-din Eibak is the nickname of the first Sultan of Delhi, who built the great arch of the vanished mosque, the conqueror who helped pull together this Mohammedan empire. Eibak referred to his broken little finger, and Kutb-ud-din meant 'Pole Star of the Faithful.' So the name of the conqueror and first Sultan of Delhi was 'Pole-Star-of-the-Faithful-with-a-Broken-Little-Finger.'

He deserved the name Faithful, for he served his master, Muhammad Ghori, loyally. He was one of the lucky ones of earth; obstacles cleared from his path as before a good hockey player. As a child he was brought from Turkestan and sold as a slave. But his master, seeing his genius, sent him to school to study science and Persian and Arabic. Then luck seemed to fail, only to grow brighter. His good master died, and he was sold with the estate, like a clock or table or bale of silk. But he was profitable stuff, and a merchant made a tidy sum by investing in him and selling him again to Muhammad Ghori.

Steadily he made his way into Muhammad's favour, until he was master of the horse, then commanding general of the armies in India, then viceroy of the Indian provinces, and finally Sultan.

From the time of his conquest of Delhi in 1193, when the Jumna River ran blood, until his death, he maintained the state and dignity of a king, although he was not formally crowned until 1205. He ruled well according to Mohammedan ideas, for he had a brave and virtuous disposition and was generous to friends and courteous to strangers. In fact he was so liberal that it became proverbial to say 'open-handed as Kutb-ud-din.' Nevertheless he had the usual prejudice that a captured city was a place for massacre, and if 'his gifts were bestowed by the hundreds of thousands, his slaughters likewise were by hundreds of thousands.'

He rode always on a white elephant. This was one of three hundred which he had captured from the Hindu Rajah Jaichand, and offered to Muhammad Ghori, with a flourish. It was the only elephant of the three hundred which refused, at a given signal, to salaam before the king. Usually docile, it nearly killed its rider. Muhammad gave it back to Kutb-ud-din, who ever afterward rode it. Kutb-ud-din escaped the usual assassination, being killed in 1210, by a fall from his horse while he was thoroughly enjoying himself, playing polo. At his death, his elephant is said to have pined away within three days.

ILTUTMISH

His slave Iltutmish did not pine like the elephant. He was so promising that Kutb-ud-din had married him to his daughter, and the powerful nobles put him on the throne in place of Kutb's own feeble-witted son.

Iltutmish had a Joseph-like story. His own jealous brothers had stripped him of his noble clothes while they were out hunting together, and sold him as a slave to a band of travelling merchants. That might easily have been the end of him, but purchasers evidently often treated their bargains kindly. One master had him well educated, and he seemed to survive the apparent ignominy of passing through several hands in sale. Muhammad Ghori heard of his beauty and talents, but haggled over the price. Nobody else dared buy him, however, until Kutb-ud-din, getting his master's permission, had the merchant bring the handsome slave to Delhi, and there paid fifty thousand pieces of silver for him, later giving him his daughter in marriage. Why a man of Iltutmish's ability submitted himself to the buying and selling is hard to understand, even accepting the Oriental figure of speech which assumed that every subject was the slave of the monarch. At that time and place, however, it was no disgrace, but a pride and a stepping-stone, to be a king's slave, and the best way for a young man to rise in the world.

Iltutmish was the ablest of the dynasty called Slave Kings, and was kept entirely busy conquering. He had to reconquer many parts of the empire, which had set up for themselves at Eibak's death. By 1232 he had reassembled the kingdom which Eibak had ruled, and undertook to enlarge it, and spread his rule fairly firmly over most of Hindustan. It is he who has that most beautiful tomb near the Kutb Minar, built by Hindu workmen under Moslem direction, rich in exquisite interwoven carving applied flat to its severe walls.

But Iltutmish, good conquerer though he was, had only one unique claim to distinction. When dying, after a reign of twenty-six years, he named a girl, his daughter Razziya, as next sultan. It is only when one remembers the scorn which was the lot of Moslem women — closeted breeding-machines — and that society was expurgated of them as though they were indecencies in the novel of life, that this act gives Iltutmish such originality and perhaps humour.

RAZZIYA

The girl really was the best man of the next generation. But the chieftains were sceptical, and tried first her brother, Rukn-ud-din Firoz, weak as a stalk of narcissus, sensual and foolish, who left the government to the jealousies of his mother. She had been a harem slave, so she took her chance now to put the well-born wives to death — while her silly son rode about the streets on his elephant, scattering gold to watch the rabble scramble.

The people of Delhi finally revolted and raised Razziya to the throne. It was none too soon, for the empire was dropping to pieces again, states were rebelling, and affairs were in a shocking state of palsy. The governors of Lahore, Hansi, Multan and Budaun formed a confederacy not ninety miles away and were marching on Delhi, threatening the central power. That was the situation which the young girl Razziya was called upon to meet.

She was a girl of amazing ability and coolness. 'She read the Koran with correct pronunciation, and in her father's lifetime employed herself frequently in the affairs of government' — which he encouraged. Once he left her as his regent. When asked why he appointed her instead of sons, he replied that sons gave themselves up to wine and every excess, and the government was too weighty for their shoulders, but that Razziya had a man's head and heart, and was better than twenty such sons.

She had no one but herself to help her, for the formidable chieftains, the Forty, were against her. During the reign of Iltutmish the Turkish nobles had formed themselves into a college of Forty, which divided among its members all the great fiefs and highest offices of state. Iltutmish was strong enough to hold them in order. Could a young girl like Razziya do as much?

The leagued armies besieged Delhi, and the young woman was forced to leave the city and camp on the plain outside with her soldiers, too weak either to attack or repulse. She used her head without too great scruple. She connived to get two of the enemy confederates to come to her tent, to discuss betraying the rest. Then she sent her own spies back to their camp to circulate the rumour of treason, until each man feared his neighbour, and none knew whom to trust. In a panic many fled, and her cavalry pursued. Thus by her cunning she broke up the league, and established her rule in Hindustan and the Punjab. The governors of Bengal and Sind, finding her strong, voluntarily sent their allegiance.

All this she had done in her lady's graceful silks, with her face discreetly hidden. Now she stepped out, dressed like a man, a sword at her belt, and with her face bared to the public. The great chieftains apparently accepted that, and the people followed. It must have been a relief to the clear-headed woman to feel her face free, not to pretend weakness when she knew she was strong.

In one thing she failed to foresee the emotions of her truculent forty chieftains. An African, a man named Yaqut, caught her fancy, and she advanced him to the position of master of the horse. She may have had good reasons for this. He may have been more honest and loyal than others. But the proud Turks did not care to see a black outsider enjoying her favour, and when the rumour spread that she allowed him to put her on her horse, by lifting her underneath the armpits — she might as well have resigned then and there.

'How,' says Ferishta, the Mohammedan historian, 'are we to reconcile the inconsistency of the queen of a vast territory fixing her affections on so unworthy an object?' — and one and all blandly ignored the unworthy objects upon which kings of vast territories had fixed their affections. The cards were stacked against Razziya, 'possessed of every good quality which usually adorns the ablest princes; and those who scrutinize her actions most severely will find in her no fault but that she was a woman.' She stooped in her favouritism. It was, as Manu would have known, 'against the hair.'

In her brief time, her energy and wit were all absorbed in skirmishing to hold the irritated and ambitious officers. When the governor of Bhatinda rebelled, he caught and imprisoned her, killed her African master of horse, and made her brother sultan. But he decided soon that he had not got his fair share of the spoils, so he took the lady out of prison and married her, in order to reinstate her as queen and incidentally himself as king. Their hired Hindu troops, when they had lost the battle for Delhi, set upon the girl and her husband and murdered both.

She had ruled three years and a half — in the opinion of a contemporary historian 'a great sovereign and sagacious, just, beneficent, the patron of the learned.' She might have been the Queen Elizabeth or Victoria of her time and place — if she had followed the policy of either in the matter of private affections, if she had kept all suitors guessing, or had supplied herself early with an impeccable prince consort, and never allowed an undefined African to lift her on her horse by the armpits.

BALBAN

After Razziya came two weak brothers and turbulence, from which a strong man arose, one of the Forty, named Ghiyas-ud-din and called Balban.

Balban ruled until he was eighty with an amazing combination of severe justice, rigidity, pomp, and splendour, Puritan prohibitions, and a devilish cruelty in punishing rebels and maurauders, which brought a certain security in his kingdom.

This sultanate of Delhi was never a solid empire. It was a grouping of great fiefs of land, under fief-holders. Across the Ganges, the Moslem governments were mere outposts, making expeditions now and then against otherwise untroubled Hindus. The lands lying nearest Afghanistan were always the pathway for Mogul raids, sudden as thunderstorms. Even around Delhi, under a few years of weak and dissipated sultans the jungle grew up again, and the woods made hiding-places for certain tribes of Hindus whose livelihood was brigandry and murder along the roads to Delhi, and even within the city walls. When they were audacious enough to rob the army transport camels, Balban made after them with determination, offering a bounty of a silver piece for each head. He exterminated the brigands with twenty days of slaughter, and had prisoners trampled by elephants and a hundred men flayed alive, their skins stuffed with straw, and hung at the city gates as a warning. It is too horrible to imagine these blowing in the wind at the great gates that all must pass, day and night. Yet it is one of the few things that slightly encourage one about civilization today.

It was an undesirable time to be living. Yet, on the whole, perhaps the ordinary non-combatant, the woman water-carrier and the thin-legged man on the street, were safer under Balban.

He ruled his court in gloomy splendour, with a Prussian rigidity of etiquette. His favourite companions at meals were Islamic theologians, which rather discouraged gaiety. There were also fifteen refugee kings at his court, exiled from Turkestan, Khorassan, or Irak by the raids of Genghis Khan. These kings stood solemnly to the left and right of his throne, except two of the race of the Caliph of Baghdad, who were allowed to sit. His court was esteemed far beyond his frontiers as the most magnificent and learned in the world, and his son entertained a circle of musicians and dancers and actors, while he patronized the group of intellectuals, graced by Amir Khusru, the poet.

Because he punished friend as well as foe unsparingly and did reward merit, he was renowned as far as Persia and Tartary for his justice. But the penalties of Balban were not to be sought. When, in his old age, he had to go after a rebel in Bengal, he had the man's followers impaled on stakes, a row two miles long on either side of the street, neatly spaced.

Perhaps because Balban had been a winebibber in his youth he was later very strict, and forbade the use or manufacture of fermented liquor throughout his land, enforcing his orders so exactly that it was said that for one disobedience he would send an army to the remotest parts of the empire. The old man frightened his people into compliance.

But the usual swing in fashions of morals followed him. His grandson, Kaikobad, who came to the throne, had been a pleasant young man, brought up most strictly in his grandfather's principles. So as soon as Balban died, he began a riotous orgy, and everyone followed. 'Every shady grove was filled with women and parties of pleasure... streets rang with tumult and even magistrates were seen drunk in public.' The end was that Kaikobad, finally paralyzed from his excesses, was rolled in his bedding, kicked in the head, and thrown into the Jumna River.

That was the end of the dynasty of the Slave Kings of Delhi.

THE KHILJI DYNASTY

At the base of the Kutb Minar stands the Alai Darwaza, a warm red sandstone mosque which is a small treasure of Islamic architecture, built by Ala-ud-din, the strongest of the Khilji dynasty.

The first of the line, Firoz Shah, was an old man when he ended the matter of Kaikobad. Fortunately, when one family of kings grew sufficiently weak or vicious, a new family arose to end them. Though Firoz Shah had not been a weak soldier — he had conquered an invasion of some hundred thousand Mongols — he was so old when he was crowned, so civilized and tender in his feelings, that he did not seem natural to his followers, and caused great resentment. He would not flay people alive. When rebels were brought before him in bonds, quaking knees in fear, he wept for them, and released them with a cup of wine. Perhaps he did carry the matter too far. There was a Hindu tribe of fanatical brigands called Thugs, bandits by holy hereditary law. When one of his officers captured a thousand Thugs, he could not bear to kill them, but shipped them in boats down the Ganges, passing them on to the people of Bengal — where the river Thuggee has lasted to modern times.

If Firoz Shah had been younger and stronger, he might have brought a period of peace and mildness like the Asokan, and introduced a consideration of life and feeling to his ably killing contemporaries. But he was not young and strong and wise — only kind and a little doddering, and far too trusting.

He trusted his nephew Ala-ud-din. This brilliant young man's best exploit, which he concealed from his uncle by various good stories, was to travel southward (with seven or eight thousand horsemen) for two months, by devious and little-used trails, through strange forest countries, pretending when he reached civilizations to be a disaffected noble seeking service at some Hindu court. By this means he reached the Deccan, the hitherto untouched Hindu land. At this time the Deccan held two strong, rich Hindu kingdoms — Deogir in the west, and Warangal in the east. The capital of Deogir is now called Daulatabad, and its amazing fort still stands, an isolated hill, sliced down to bare rock so smoothly that not even a snake could climb up it. The only passage, cut through the rock, could be blocked by lighting a fire which would heat it like an oven. A moat surrounded it, and a wall guarded the moat. Though not large, it is a picture-book illustration of the word Fort.

Ala-ud-din surprised its Rajah with his forces away. The Hindu king hastily drew a few thousand men into the citadel, and to provision the fort, seized the camel bags from a passing caravan. When the load was opened, the bags were found to be filled with salt. The bravest soldiers cannot live on salt. Deogir had to yield. With other stratagems and fights, Ala-ud-din soon forced terms, and made off with seventeen thousand pounds of gold, two hundred pounds of pearls, twenty-eight thousand pounds of silver, one thousand pieces of silk, and a province.

A somewhat guilty-feeling Ala-ud-din went back toward Delhi, knowing he had exceeded authority, but contemptuous of his old uncle. The headstrong, inventive liar very nearly holds the record for baseness.

He let the story precede him that he was afraid of the sultan's displeasure, and did not dare approach. So the kindly old king, who had been out hunting near Gwalior, sailed down the Ganges to meet him, letting his army go by land. When he reached the place where Ala-ud-din's armies were drawn up, another message came that his nephew was still afraid, and begged him not to let his troops come near for fear of bloodshed. As though cringing, he even asked that the king dismiss his armed attendants, explaining that his own army was merely a guard of honour. Poor old Firoz Shah went unprotected to meet the strong youth — very likely with tears in his eyes. As he approached, his nephew fell to the ground in abasement. Firoz Shah stooped to lift him, embraced him, and chided him gently for doubting his affection and forgiveness. While he was saying his fond words, Ala-ud-din signalled to the assassins to strike. Firoz Shah realized the treachery and died. Ala-ud-din had his white-haired head raised on a spear-point, as occult proof that armies had better seek another leader.

He had to meet other claimants to the throne, but their division helped him, and so did his treasure. It was not hard to persuade lukewarm soldiers by well-given gold. He was enthroned at Delhi in 1296, in the red palace of Balban. He won followers by his lavish gifts, and then, mistrusting such shifty devotion, he took away the treasure and land of these nobles, blinded some, imprisoned others, and made their families beggars.

For a time the Rajputs in Rajputana, Malwa, and Gujarat protected the south of India from his ambition. But in 1297 he began to expand his kingdom. Gujarat fell to his generals, bringing in with the driftwood a low-caste Hindu eunuch named Kafur, who was to become the king's 'vile favourite,' and sending its Rajah and his beautiful daughter, Deval Devi, flying to Deogir for refuge. The lovely girl, whose family were too proud to wish her to marry the Deogir prince because he was of a Mahratta race, was to become the plaything of chance and changing princes.

After Ala-ud-din had conquered a Mongol invasion, he began to wonder whether he might not become both an Alexander the Great and a prophet at the same time. Thereupon a very, very fat adviser — too fat to come to court more than once a month — was brave enough to tell him honestly that a king had better not try to be a prophet unless inspired, and that, with Mongols likely to invade, and no Aristotle to govern during his absence, it was prudent to give up the idea of being Alexander. Ala-ud-din was able, at that time, to accept wise advice.

He was the target for the sort of rebellions he had tried himself. Once a nephew, seeing him alone while hunting, sitting on a stool awaiting for attendants, ordered his archers to aim. Ala-ud-din quickly used the stool for a shield, and a lucky chance saved him. Other nephews rebelled, but were captured and he watched them have their eyes cut out.

These insubordinations convinced him that something was wrong in his kingdom. He thought, and decided that the reasons were that he had too few spies; that people drank too much wine which loosened their tongues and caused mischief; that the nobles strengthened their families through intermarriage; and finally that people had too much money and leisure, which left time for plotting.

This naïve reasoning was the best product of the great conqueror's brain. He acted upon it. He had so many spies that people looked over their shoulders if they talked in an open field, and what they said at breakfast was known in the palace by night. To prevent leisure, he had his tax-collectors extort gold from any who owned it. To prevent talking, he tried, like Balban, to enforce prohibition. He forbade liquor or drugs under penalty of fine or banishment or prison. He had the wine vessels broken and skins of wine poured out at the city gate. But those human beings whom he ruled set up stills in their houses, or smuggled liquor into the city under other goods on pack-animals, or crossed the border of the Jumna River and travelled twenty-five miles for a drink. Though offenders were flogged and confined in pits, where many died, still the people drank. At last Ala-ud-din relaxed so far as to permit its private manufacture and use, but forbade its public sale, and convivial gatherings. The nobles dared not yet whisper together.

In the Doab certain high-caste Hindus had grown rich and arrogant as revenue collectors, shifting the burden of taxes to the poor. The sultan decreed that they must pay also, in proportion to their incomes, and that no one should keep enough money to ride a horse, carry arms, or wear rich clothes. To make the collectors work at their unrewarding tasks, he had them driven with ropes around their necks to the villages where they must collect taxes.

Once the sultan was a little doubtful whether his laws followed those of the Prophet. He asked a fearless holy man, who first replied that it would spare time and trouble to be executed at once; and then, reassured, said that it was quite lawful to persecute the Hindus, and sacred writings recommended it for unbelievers, but that cruel punishments were unlawful to the tradition of Islam. Ala-ud-din accepted his words and rewarded him.

Conquests, which were mere incidents to Ala-ud-din and regarded as a detail of glory, were of course deep tragedies to those who suffered. The people who fell were not always articulate, but there is a record in Rajput bards of the first sin of the sack of Chitor, which from the Mohammedan point of view was something that Ala-ud-din took in his stride in 1302–03.

Ala-ud-din, said the bards, besieged the great fortress of Chitor for love of its beautiful queen, Padmani, so beautiful, with skin so delicate that when she ate, one could see the food slip down her throat. Ala-ud-din had never seen Padmani; he had simply heard of her, and stories seemed to be very inflammatory in those days.

Chitor rises like a ship from the plain, a rocky promontory, three miles long topped by walls. It gives the illusion of parting the waves of land like a flat ocean. The only approach is up a steep lane a mile long, shut in by walls, and blocked at intervals by seven massive gates. Some of those gates are still set thick with spear-heads at the height of an elephant's forehead, to keep elephants from battering them down. There is a story of a Rajput who once, for the glory of giving to his clan the capture of such a fortified town, held his body over the spear-points and told the drivers to push on against him, a cushion between spears and elephants' foreheads. Such courage was in the defenders of the fortress of Chitor. And a certain amount was in Ala-ud-din.

Chitor held all that to the Rajput Clan was precious and untouched.

Ala-ud-din besieged it for months, on the rumour of the lady's beauty and to add her to his already well-stocked harem. But his armies had the defenceless position on the plains and gradually Ala-ud-din lessened his demands. He no longer asked for possession of Padmani, only for a sight of her. Finally he offered to give up the siege if he might look at her reflection in a mirror.

This was arranged in all honour. Ala-ud-din knew he could rely on the faith of a Rajput. He climbed the hill to the bristling fort only slightly guarded, and was led into a room with a mirror in which he saw the exquisite Padmani, ready to hide in gauze gold veils from the greedy, hawk-faced infidel — but true to her promise. Ala-ud-din looked as long as he chose and then went down the hill. The courteous Rajputs went with him to the last gate, while Ala-ud-din offered many compliments. Of course he had prepared an ambush, and took the ruler of Chitor, demanding Padmani as condition of release.

There was despair in Chitor, which could only fall by such foul means. Should they give up their beautiful queen to the horrible Moslem? Padmani learned and agreed to go, but she and her kinsmen thought of a way to save her honour.

The city sent word to Ala-ud-din that on the day he withdrew from his trenches, the fair Padmani would be sent to him, but in a manner befitting her high station. Her women should accompany her, ladies-in-waiting and servants and kinswomen. No one should violate female decorum. And Padmani's state was such that seven hundred tightly closed litters were carried into Ala-ud-din's camp, past the murmuring soldiers, under strict orders to honour these swaying silent packages of Hindu ladies.

The royal tents were enclosed by long walls of cloth, and here the litters were set down, and the Rajput prince given half an hour to say good-bye forever to Padmani. Ala-ud-din grew jealous of the long farewell and came rudely to interrupt. Then out from each litter sprang an officer of the Rajput army, and each of the six porters was a soldier in disguise, and they cut a way of escape for the queen and king. They saved their leader and the flower-like Padmani, but at a terrible cost, for Ala-ud-din would not let them escape without reprisal.

The youths of Chitor rushed to the gates to beat back his renewed attack. One boy of twelve, who did his share, had this conversation with the widow of a fallen chieftain. 'He was the reaper of the harvest of battle,' the twelve-year-old boy told her. 'I followed his steps as the humble gleaner of the sword. On the gory bed of honour he spread a carpet of the slain.'

'Tell me, Badul, how did my love behave?'

'Oh, mother, how further describe his deeds, when he left no foe to dread or admire him?'

She smiled farewell to the boy, and adding, 'My lord will chide my delay,' sprang into the funeral flames.

The city, weakened by loss of its strongest men, had to resist a more violent attack when the Moslem entrenched on a threatening southern hill.

At this point the Rana of Chitor, father of twelve fine sons, had a dream. Or was it a dream? He was in bed, wondering how to save at least one of his children, when he heard a dreadful voice say, 'I am hungry.' By the small light of the lamp, advancing between the granite columns, he saw the goddess walking — the guardian goddess of Chitor.

'Are you not fed,' he cried, 'when eight thousand of my kin have been slaughtered for you?'

The unmoved goddess answered, 'I must have royal victims, and if twelve who wear the diadem bleed not for Chitor, the land will pass from the line.' Then she vanished.

The king called together his bearded chiefs in the morning and told them his terrible dream. They laughed and cajoled him, and the next night he went to bed reassured. But at midnight he heard the steps of the goddess — stone walking on stone.

'Twelve of royal blood must be sacrificed to me, or I will leave Chitor. Each prince must be placed upon the throne and proclaimed, and given the insignia of royalty — and for three days every decree of his will be supreme — and on the fourth day he must go to meet the enemy, and his death. Only then will I remain.'

Each prince begged to be the first to sacrifice himself to the goddess, and one by one eleven sons were crowned and died blindly fighting.

The Mohammedan armies still lay ominous as a cobra. The Rana, calling his chiefs around him, said, 'Now I will devote myself to Chitor.'

The women must first be saved from the besieger. A funeral pyre was lighted in an underground chamber cut into the solid rock, and a procession of women and girls entered the cave. The fair Padmani came last, and the opening to the cavern was closed upon them forever, and smoke seeped through the door, and a great serpent came to guard the place.

Now from the citadel the Rana called his last chiefs, and with a rush they threw open the gates and plunged at the enemy, meeting death before defeat. Ala-ud-din, the impious, climbed to the empty fortress, and saw not even an image in a mirror — only the thin smoke coming from the crude cave entrance.

But the twelfth prince, saved by his father's sacrifice, had escaped with a small band of followers beyond the enemies' camp to carry on the line of the House of the Sun and Rama. And the oath, 'By the sin of the sack of Chitor,' became the most solemn a Rajput could take.

Rajput bards saw no objection to making a good story better, or a bad story good. Severe historians accuse them of inventing a tale of enemy treachery to excuse their own defeat. That is a thing which races and individuals have done and probably will continue to do. It seems too bad to puncture the soaring balloon of a romance which makes villains bad and heroes good and everything on our side as noble as possible. When the romance is a stirring tale, which incited generations to courage and comforted them in exile, when it is a composition as perfectly balanced as a structure of music, it seems to have an intrinsic merit, a place with all ballads.

There is an anticlimax, the sharp little instrument of fact will pierce this lovely balloon. But it is a beautiful balloon, and a race capable of flight must have made it.

Other chronicles were kept by Moslems, in which Chitor is only one campaign, not a ghastly pity. It is true that Chitor fell to Ala-ud-din. But though the rite of sacrifice may have been performed, Ratan Singh, Rana of Chitor, was taken alive to Delhi, and there bargained with Ala-ud-din about his fair Padmani. There was an old Rajput maxim which said that a man might surrender his wife to preserve his land. The Rana had been imprisoned for two years, and his worn, starved body and mind played with the idea of freedom. But his noblemen, who had escaped and were wandering in the intricate hills of Mewar as outlaws, heard about the bargaining and sent him messages begging him not to disgrace the name of Rajput, and conniving to get poison to him to save his honour by death. He was actually saved by the scheme of the litters carrying armed men who leaped out and killed his guards.

Be it all as it may, the little white palace of Padmani still rises like a swan from the waters of a lake within the fortress walls of Chitor — graceful, feminine, shining in the sun above the dark water. Ala-ud-din did not destroy it.

Once back in Delhi, weakened by the siege, Ala-ud-din had to bear one of those swift raids of Mongols — one hundred and twenty thousand camped near the river, and dashing into the city streets to rob as they chose, shutting Ala-ud-din up in his own fort for safety, and then suddenly, as if whimsically, leaving — some said, due to the prayers of the holy men. Ala-ud-din had to repair forts and strengthen his army, and he had no money. Nothing was left possible to tax. So he decided to fix prices and make everything cheap and easy to pay for.

He decreed the cost of slaves, horses, silks, arms, and simple necessities. Then, when he reduced the pay of his armies, his soldiers suffered no hardship. The money of the kingdom was centred in Delhi, and difficult transportation made the city an artificial laboratory for the experiment. The enormous wealth he had stolen had cheapened money and inflated prices, so his ruling was less amazing than it seems. He could actually make it effective. When grain merchants objected to the low prices he set, he ordered everyone to buy grain at the state granaries until the merchants were forced to sell it at even less than he had commanded. Outside the capital revenue was largely collected in kind, but if the scarcity of grain anywhere threatened to raise its price, he could flood the markets with his own stores and lower the value. His remarkable edicts worked so well that he managed to pay a standing army of nearly half a million men.

In 1308, he decided to be thorough about his southern conquests, and sent a large army to Warangal, driving the people of the country before the army, and getting inside the two miles of breastwork of Warangal, forcing surrender. Then Halebid, capital of the kingdom that is now Mysore, fell. Finally his general marched to the kingdom of the Pandyas in the far south, went into Madura, stole and smashed in the storied sprawling carven temple, and went to Rameswaram to loot treasure. This was the farthest south of the Mohammedan conquests. Below that on the very tip of India the Hindus could, if they liked, be peaceful under their palm trees.

After this climax of power, Ala-ud-din's judgment began to fail, and his naturally fierce temper grew more bitter and black. He refused to listen to advisers and tried to administer the whole vast empire himself. Of course the horrors piled up, and the rebellions. In one the Rana of Chitor threw the Moslem officers over the walls of the citadel.

Ala-ud-din, though not a fountain of wisdom or kindliness, had at least groped. When he died in 1316, a hideous reign began: his son Mubarak, lewd and degenerate, wore women's finery and jewels, raised a Hindu scavenger to be his favourite, killed twenty-nine relatives, and put his brother's captured wife, lovely Deval Devi, into his harem. He was finally murdered by his own outcaste favourites. All the outcastes broke into the palace, and murdered, and a scavenger stole Deval Devi for his wife.

It was time for another cleaning-up. Strong Ghazi Malik, a fine old man, a conqueror of Mongols, a loyal officer and a strict Moslem, overcame the rabble, and the citizens gave him the keys to the palace. He loyally asked if any descendant of Ala-ud-din remained, but since the family was extinct, he was persuaded to take the throne, and established the Tughlak dynasty.

THE TUGHLAKS

1320–1413

The tomb of this officer, who ruled as Ghiyas-ud-din Tughlak, stands in his departed city of Tughlakabad, one of the many Delhis, an expression of stern simplicity and strength. The city has little left but its giant grey ramparts, with splayed-out bastions and narrow loopholes and steep entranceways. But the tomb stands like a walled island beyond. Inside its battlements rise the powerful red sandstone walls, eleven feet thick at their base, slanting inward — two inches to the foot — toward the light white marble dome. There are no elaborate carvings such as the Slave Kings had, only the force of the mass and warmth of the red and white. This tomb unites closely the three first and greatest Tughlak kings, holding the graves of the good father, the half-mad son who killed him, and the spot where the pious successor tried to make expiation.

Ghiyas-ud-din Tughlak, old but vigorous, began to bring order and a degree of common-sense and kindness. He had the kingdom pacified within forty days. He punished the scavengers who had married lovely Deval Devi to the outcaste Hindu. He returned to the people their confiscated property and gave lands and employment to all the faithful. He stopped highway robbery and built forts of refuge from brigands for the farmers, and tried to develop agriculture by limiting the land tax to one tenth of the gross produce and collecting it with due consideration of the farmer. He even realized, and told his officials, that the surest way of increasing the state's money was by making the farms prosperous, not by bleeding them with extortion. He had gardens planted, restored ruined villages, and allowed Hindus to live in moderate, though not too luxurious, comfort. Being a punctilious Moslem, he forbade the manufacture and sale of wine, but this had less emphasis than under Balban. His two innovations for welfare were to begin canals for irrigation and to start an interesting postal system.

From most ancient days there had been some sort of mail in India, but in the frequent times of wildness the thread snapped. He had the post carried by horsemen or runners. The horsemen galloped seven or eight miles, where they found the next rider to take the pony express. The runners had only to go about two thirds of a mile, but at top speed. They lived outside villages and had to be ready to start at a moment's notice, and each carried in his hand a staff tipped with copper bells to warn the next man to be ready.

The people, who began to breathe again under this king, had little time to regain strength and security. In these dynasties the horrors seem so crowded that one would not be surprised if such a period had originated the Hindu doctrine that life is a malady to escape. The people were at the mercy of anyone who by force or guile could steal the throne.

The sultan sent his son Muhammad to subdue Warangal, which was trying to drop from the southern tail of the empire. An army in the hands of a king's son usually meant trouble for the king. Muhammad, conquering Warangal with catapults and ballistæ, and taking the triple-moated fortress of Bidar, had a dangerous taste of power. When his father had to go in person to Bengal and left his son as regent, the prince began to plot.

He had astrologers predict that the king would never return to Delhi; then he took practical steps to see that the prophecy was fulfilled. When his father was coming homeward, Muhammad had the city of Tughlakabad elaborately decorated in hypocritical welcome, and a few miles down the road on which his father would come, he had built a temporary kiosk for rest and refreshment, of wood, with one projecting beam. He welcomed his father at the kiosk, gave him a meal, and then begged him to allow the elephants to be paraded in his honour. The projecting beam was arranged so that when an elephant touched it, the whole building toppled down upon the king and his favourite son. The sultan's body was found in the debris, bending over the boy as if to protect him. Most people say that the king was still breathing when he was found — but not for long. He was soon put into the magnificent tomb, with walls eleven feet thick.

Now Muhammad Tughlak sat upon the throne, without a qualm. He had amazing qualities blended in the instability of a madman. He could be brilliantly able, lavish, and scrupulous to observe Islamic law. He could utterly disregard law in public matters and concoct the most fiendish cruelties. He was so insanely haughty that he punished the slightest deviation from his rule by death, and so cringingly obsequious that he grovelled before the meanest relative of the Calif of Baghdad, and invited him literally to set foot upon his neck. Sometimes he quixotically allowed his subjects to make legal complaint against himself as against any other citizen. Three times he appeared as a culprit in the court, and accepted meekly the verdict, even to twenty-one strokes of the lash. Yet he murdered his brother for no other reason than that he was handsome and popular. He proceeded to devote himself to the details of government, to register the income and expense of the empire, and to try to set a uniform land revenue. And he had a rebel cooked with rice and offered to the elephants — and to his own wife.

His most totally despotic and wild act was to order all Delhi to move to Daulatabad, some six hundred miles south. He decided that it was more central as capital of the empire, which it may have been. But he treated his people like paper dolls. At first he ordered only his great officers there. Two years later, however, when the people of Delhi threw reproachful anonymous letters by night into the hall of audience, he took his reprisal. He ordered everyone to move toward Daulatabad within three days. The journey would take a month by camels or donkeys or human foot. Naturally people tried to evade, but he had his soldiers search for all who hid. His slaves found two men who had not left the city. One was lame and the other blind. He ordered the cripple shot from the mouth of a ballista, and the blind man dragged the forty days toward Daulatabad. The blind man was rubbed to pieces on the way, and only his foot reached Daulatabad. Even to tell such insane insensibility would be too terrible — except to show what humble people bore from their despots.

Muhammad wanted to be not only Alexander and a prophet, but King Solomon also. However, he rivalled only Nero. He stood on the roof of his palace looking at the empty city of Delhi, without light, without smoke, and he said, 'Now my heart is content and my soul is appeased.'

Thereupon he tried to persuade other people to move in to fill Delhi, but they had the wit to avoid doing it. He raised the taxes of the discontented Hindus of the Doab so high that the farmers gave up their lands and took to brigandage, and then he took such reprisals that in a short time he had made one of the most fertile districts of his kingdom a wasteland of war. He began to think that his subjects were his enemy, and treated a restive province like a hostile country. He put rows of Hindu heads on the battlements. Those who escaped to the jungle he had hunted like wild beasts, the circle of beaters narrowing around the king's quarry.

And yet, when the traveller Ibn Batuta came unknown to India, the sultan showed him the most fantastic courtesy and generosity, gave him a grant of three villages for income, and ten slaves and money.

His economics being slightly faulty, he thought he could fill his emptied treasuries by simply coining money. He was king and owned the mint! He made brass or copper tokens which had to pass for one hundred and forty grains of silver, and thought he saw himself buying the whole world. Unluckily, foreign merchants refused to take the tokens, and, still worse, his subjects promptly used them to buy gold and silver, but paid taxes with tokens. They were so easy to counterfeit that a clever workman could make them at home, and the saying went that every Hindu house was a mint.

To add to the pity of his reign, for seven years the rainfall in India was slight, and a famine came on the land, the most severe of which there is record. Everyone has heard stories of even mild Indian famines. In this, whole villages were emptied, and people ate horrible things, and human flesh was common food. It is true that Muhammad did issue a daily ration of grain to the people of Delhi, and too late lent the farmers money to sink wells and buy cattle and seed. By that time men were too weak to hold a plough. If they spent his money to restore their frail bodies, he punished them severely. At last he had a really good, if characteristically high-handed, idea. The province of Oudh was prosperous under a good governor. But so many thievish tribes ravaged the roads that he could not get food between the two places. Finally he shipped the people to the supplies, and they settled in Oudh with a degree of comfort.

Another of his reforms which had a germ of brilliance was to create a department of agriculture. He divided the kingdom into thirty districts of about eighteen hundred square miles each, in which the land was to be entirely cultivated and the crops raised in rotation. It was good, except that he did not understand which crops to rotate or take into consideration forest or desert. His unscrupulous district superintendents feathered their nests.

Bengal freed itself; so did Madura in the south, and Warangal. The Deccan was dubious. The revenues there had fallen ninety per cent, and the sultan could not see the reason. He appointed a very skilful extortionist, who told him the former tax-collectors were at fault, so he had eighty-nine tax-collectors put to death. Even those who groan over taxes would not want to go that far, but Muhammad thought it a plausible solution. Of course the Deccan revolted from his ravages and punishments, and it too won freedom. The Moslem rebel who freed the Deccan founded the Bahmani dynasty there, which ruled for a hundred and eighty years before it split into the brilliant Mohammedan kingdoms of Bidar and Golconda, Bijapur, Ahmednagar, and Berar — all sprung from the extortion of Muhammad Tughlak.

He could not understand what ailed his kingdom. He called his historian to him, and said sadly his India was like a sick man with a variety of diseases, and the remedy for one aggravated the rest. He really thought he had done his best. But his people *would* disobey, and he must wield the sword of punishment. Luckily he died in 1351.

His cousin Firoz Shah, who came to the throne in middle age, did his best to restore order and plant the land again. He lowered taxes and abolished the squeeze system, gave up the heavy road tolls, so that farmers had some return for their efforts, and in time, near Delhi alone, he had twelve hundred garden villages growing fruit. His originality was to begin schemes of irrigation: he started five canals, and one of them, five hundred miles long, leading the water of the Jumna into arid land, still carries its waters into a part of the modern Western Jumna Canal. He was a great builder, and made, among other things, two hundred caravanserais, thirty palaces, five reservoirs, five hospitals, a hundred bridges, and a hundred tombs. Most travellers who visit Delhi remember him for the city of Firozabad, whither he carried the polished pillar of Asoka; from his severe and massive tomb; and the college at Hauz-i-Alai, whose cloisters give an uncanny sense of the dignity of the life that moved there, of students with focussed minds walking down the vaulted stone corridors. Now one may see only a peacock walking up a grey dome.

Firoz Shah had moments of massacre in the name of religion: he used capital punishment for fanatical unorthodox belief, but he was kindly enough to abolish torture. He offered to any Hindu who was converted to Islam freedom from the special poll tax on Hindus, and 'great numbers of Hindus presented themselves and were admitted to the honour of Islam, day by day from every quarter, adopting the faith, were exonerated from the tax, and were favoured with presents and honours.'

At this time, when Firoz Shah tried to tax Brahmans, who had hitherto been exempt from the Hindu poll tax, they gathered and fasted near his palace until they were at the point of death, to force a reduction in their tax rate. Gandhi recently tried to enforce his will in politics by similar methods. Probably Muhammad would have let them starve, as an easy means of reducing his enemy, the public. But Firoz Shah split the difference in their taxes, and they began to eat again.

The proportion of space given to the almost always good Firoz Shah is not measured by his importance to the people, who under him had thirty years of comparative order and calm. But he could more nearly fit into another period and is a less striking extreme of his own. It was he who went to the red sandstone tomb at Tughlakabad, carrying a manuscript of testimony from the heirs of Muhammad's victims, now appeased by gifts, that he had atoned for the sin of Muhammad. He placed the duly witnessed document in the tomb, for the good of the soul of Muhammad, who lay beside his murdered father.

When he died in 1385, senile at eighty-three, there was practical anarchy. The feebleness of Hindustan more than invited the raid of Timur, who swooped down from his Samarkand in 1398 with ninety thousand horsemen, taking cities and killing as he came; who proclaimed himself king at Delhi, with a general massacre and looting, and carried off wealth and women and skilled artisans to beautify his Samarkand. He went as he came — a blighting flash of lightning.

Delhi was numb — could not arouse. For more than fifty years there was no real strength, no centre, not even a very good bandit. Finally, in 1450 an Afghan of the Lodi tribe named Bahlol Khan caught the throne, and founded the dynasty of Lodi, the first Afghan or Pathan rulers, who lasted none too pleasantly until the Great Moguls.

There was a miasma over the Hindus, the depression of failure, the temptation to retreat more and more into the past and dreams, and to cling to their own customs and social barriers — a situation which forced the Moslems into an isolation of their own, and even influenced them into a pseudo-stratification of castes.

These are the highlights of the story of three centuries of one dominant kingdom in India, expanding and contracting. As rich details, and as important (for none of them were really lastingly important), could be found in the other contemporary kingdoms of India — in Moslem Bengal, Malwa, Gujarat, and Kashmir; south in the Deccan where the high-stepping, hard-drinking Bahmani sultanate began, far south where the Hindu states were being sucked into the power of the last great Hindu rule in Vijayanagar. But Delhi's childlike rulers are a fair example of the Moslem despots of the day — and the misery they succeeded in making; men, failing other dangers, brewing their own poison.

16. *Vijayanagar, the Last Empire of the Hindus*

1336–1565

VIJAYANAGAR means 'City of Victory.' Today the glory is gone. One finds it in the guidebook under its old name Hampi, in the district of Bellary, over the southern border of the Deccan. It is in an overgrown wilderness of banyans and vines and palms growing through gigantic piled hills of black stones, queer outcroppings of rock which the gods are supposed to have thrown there when they finished building the earth.

The pediment to the king's throne still stands, dominating an upland of jungle. On its stone sides are friezes. Full-breasted warrior dancing-girls, bare-bosomed, full-skirted, clash swords with their upflung arms. Below them a line of foot soldiers march. Below them grooms lead strong-necked, resisting horses — the horses bought from the Portuguese at Goa — and below them march the wrinkle-hided elephants, mastered by little fat mahouts. On the platform above this stood the throne, on which a king might sit only when he had not told a lie.

This was the capital of the last great Hindu empire. This wilderness, where the only life now is the occasional traveller to the dak bungalow made over from a little temple, or the occasional pilgrim to its broken shrines, was a triumphant and peopled city from the fourteenth to the sixteenth century. More than a million Hindus lived in this welter of black hills behind their seven lines of walls. It was the capital of a kingdom that included all the land from the river Krishna to Cape Comorin, the southern tip of India. Here flourished a civilization and glory strange to our minds, the culture of the Telegu and Kanarese Hindus. By 1565 the city was dead.

While the sultans of Delhi had been imposing themselves upon the north, the Dravidian Hindus of the south had rich kingdoms and dynasties as thick with story as any, but the history that is left of them is stripped to the bone, gathered from the inscriptions of boastful kings, from coins, from grants of land engraved on copper, — a dismaying list of boundaries changing like the lines of waves on sand, of kingly names that have few shreds of personality.

Perhaps it did not matter to the people how their frontiers changed or which family of kings governed. Their social life was static, ordered by holy law or hoary custom. The village or town or

THE KING'S THRONE AT VIJAYANAGAR

caste group carried on their local government with routine method, needing from a king or emperor only military protection from foreigner or angry neighbour. Except for the actual battlefields and looted cities, it seems only a matter of a king's pride or luxury when one dynasty conquered another.

But the southern dynasties have sonorous names befitting their pride. Of the three most often dominating, the Pandyas held the far south, the Cholas, succeeding the Pallavas, were strong chiefly in the southeast, and the Chalukyas in the southwest. The names come to life when one sees their expression in stone, such as the seaside rocks at Mammalapuram carved into temples under the Pallava kings, the graceful human or god figures made at Ellora by Chalukyan sculptors or the storied tower of Tanjore temple, built by a Chola conqueror. And when the doughty mountain chiefs of the Hoysalas rose in the eleventh century to power, and took lands including most of modern Mysore — their intricate minds may be imagined from the rich, intricate temples that they left at Belur and Halebid.

It was a king of the Hoysalas, whose beautiful city Halebid was sacked by the Moslems, who founded Vijayanagar, a phœnix from ashes, a last outpost against the north. For the several dynasties of shifting power meant, in late mediæval days when the Moslems were coming, that the Hindu south was divided into continually fighting rivals, with no sense of unity against an alien race or faith.

The first threat was Ala-ud-din of the Khiljis, whose plundering general marched and looted through Chola and Pandyan lands, and brought back elephant loads of treasure and left submitting Hindu kings as distant vassals. Muhammad Tughlak, terrible and fantastic, was a greater menace, for he meant to consolidate all his empire, which at its greatest reached as far south as Madura, and moved the protesting, cowed people of Delhi to Daulatabad, to centralize his rule. He was the man whose delicate fancy had rebels flayed alive and their skins stuffed with straw.

At the danger from Muhammad, Vira Ballala the Second, the last king of the Hoysalas, began the fortress city of Vijayanagar in 1336, as one of a series of defences against the north.

A fighting rabbit was the appropriate omen for the building of the city. Hindu forts had fallen and flamed. A chivalrous Hindu king had, by his own hand, killed his fifty wives, his sons and little daughters, before he opened his gates to the conqueror and died fighting. It was well to apply to the site of Vijayanagar this hopeful legend.

One day, when the king went out hunting with his fierce dogs who dared attack a lion or tiger, a hare rose up before him, which, instead of running from the dogs, ran toward them and bit them. The king asked a holy hermit to interpret the wonder, and the sage replied that the courage of the feeble hare at that place showed that the site was so salubrious and favoured of the gods that a city could be built there which would never be conquered. The king ordered work begun on the walls at once.

'Its fort walls were like arms stretching out to embrace Hemakutta. The points of the battlements like its filaments, the suburbs like its blossom, the elephants like bees, the hills reflected in the moat like stems. The whole resembled the lotus on which Lakshmi is ever seated.' So the growing city of Vijayanagar appeared to one of her poets.

It was a warrior city. The king who founded it was killed soon after in battle, but his generals carried on his work of defiance. Harihara and Bukka, two brothers, were the city's early rulers. Bukka, according to his own admission, was 'beyond the reach of scandal, a thunderbolt... a lion to the rutting elephants of hostile kings, firm as Mount Meru, delighting in battle.' And, 'as Bukka danced round the field of battle... the Andhras ran into their holes ... the Kalingas suffered defeat.' A pleasing title of a victor was 'Bestower of widowhood on the wives of hostile kings.'

With such leadership, Vijayanagar began to conquer, gradually consolidating the old tottering Hindu states of the south under her new energetic standard, the last great Hindu offence against the Mohammedans — the biting rabbit.

The great City of Victory would be strange to our eyes today, stranger than the cities of most other civilizations — a wildly imaginative, uncouth expression of a people who loved to 'story-tell' in stone, carving their way as priestly canon perscribed and as their luxuriant fancy budded. In that background of piled rocks and monstrous-shaped hills, imagine the nine-storied truncated temple carved on its way to the sky with giant human figures of gods and goddesses. Before such a temple was dragged the tiered, high chariot of Jagganath, under which worshippers flung themselves, to the sides of which they hung by ropes through their own skins, in religious ecstasy. In that temple the Brahman priests maintained their ritual, killed their goats, made offering to their particular deities, lighted the many butter-lamps for the feast of lights, stored their jewels and gold in dark stone recesses. And to that temple from the carved stone street of the dancing-girls came the hundreds of temple prostitutes, whose traditional posturing dance was a part of the ritual of worship. The king prayed in a tiny temple shaped like a warrior's chariot in stone, with wheels and a convenient stone ladder to reach the high sill; or the king sat under a stone canopy supported by pillars up which life-sized horses rear back, mounted by confident horsemen. Snake goddesses, the enormous Narsingh — the man-lion incarnation of Vishnu, looking rather like a giant bullfrog — and the largest lingam and yoni in all India, brought crowds of pilgrims. The city at its largest was sixty miles in circumference; its walls were carried up into the mountains and enclosed valleys. It had 'great and fair palaces, water-tanks, gardens of trees, and sweet-scented shrubs.'

To support its kings and warriors, thousands of humble people lived in their palm-thatched huts beside the rapid, rock-enclosed river, or on the slopes of the precipitous queer hills. Caste by caste they followed their hundred trades as their fathers and grandfathers had done. The weavers wove, the potters made beautiful cheap clay vessels which could be broken after each meal and never pollute the pure. The brass-makers made for the high-caste Hindus brass bowls and plates which could be scoured with sand and charcoal until they shone palely, like the gold vessels the goldsmiths were making for the kings. The hereditary grooms looked after noblemen's horses, and the hereditary mahouts looked after the elephants — fifteen men to a royal elephant. The nobles were gorgeous in silks and armour and ladylike finery, but the common people seldom needed or used more than their bare, sun-blackened skins under that dominant heat. The peasants, who cropped the land which the great lords held in fee from the king, were little more than part of the vegetable cycle of the crops. The lives of the simple went on samely. The mountainous variety was in the lives of the kings.

In the climax of its power, Vijayanagar had swept under its rule all the land to the south. To the north its great rival was no longer Delhi, but the Bahmani kingdom founded by a soldier who rebelled against Muhammad Tuglak in 1347 and took the Deccan from that puzzled despot. After nearly two centuries it had split into five separate and magnificent Mohammedan states — Golconda, Bidar, Bijapur, Berar, and Ahmadnagar, usually enemies of the southern Hindu empire.

Vijayanagar did not fear them. Her riches and display were fabulous. In those days the Portuguese, who had made their little dent into India on the coast at Goa, were growing rich from trading with the city, shipping up thousands of horses from Ormuz, elephants from Ceylon, camphor from the Punjab, fine silks from China.

The elegants and litterati of the city were writing Sanskrit drama and romances, and epic poems of battles in which showers of flowers and sounds of music from Heaven tell of the approval of the gods for Vijayanagar's heroes. The great king, Krishnadevi, was a patron of letters, and two of his dramas have survived to this day. Learning was treasured, and Brahmanical schools and colleges flourished for the high-born.

Vijayanagar could muster an army of at least a million and some two thousand elephants. A Persian ambassador tells of its eleven hundred thousand troops. He goes on to describe the city: 'The space which separates the first fortress from the second, and up to the third fortress, is filled with cultivated fields' irrigated by elaborate water channels. 'From the third to the seventh one meets a numberless crowd of people, many shops, and a bazaar.... Roses are sold everywhere. The people could not live without roses, and they look upon them as necessary as food.... Each profession has shops contiguous... the jewellers sell publicly in the bazaars pearls, rubies, emeralds, and diamonds.... In the king's palace are several cells like basins filled with bullion, forming one mass... the king is dressed in robes of green satin, the colour of pearls of beautiful water.' He has an olive complexion, and is tall and thin, with a pleasing expression. So says Abdur Razzak, ambassador from Persia.

Nicolo Conti, the Italian travelling in Vijayanagar in the reign of Deva Raya the Second, about 1420, tells of the king's wives. First he mentions that the men in general marry as many wives as they please, who are burned with their dead husbands. One still sees the gruesome tablets, standing beside some tree — a flat stone carved naïvely with the figures of women, each with a hand aloft, standing beside the husband. For some reason it was the husband who was called the hero, rather than the ladies who jumped into the flames after him. But where the modest man's tablet shows only three or four women, the king, according to Nicolo, takes 'twelve thousand wives, of whom four thousand follow him on foot wherever he may go, and are employed solely in the service of the kitchen' — a rather cumbersome scheme. 'A like number,' says Nicolo, 'more handsomely equipped, ride on horseback. The remainder are carried by men in litters, of whom two thousand or three thousand are selected as his wives on condition that at his death they should voluntarily burn... a great honour.'

Whether or not Nicolo took an accurate census of the king's marriage lines, one gets an impression.

Fernao Nuniz gives slightly different figures, but a similar testimony to lavishness. 'Five hundred wives, and as many less or more as he wants with whom he sleeps, and all these burn themselves at his death. On journeys he takes twenty-five to thirty favourites, each in a palanquin on poles... the principal one covered with seed pearls.... Within the palace he is served by five hundred women and eunuchs. Each wife has her own retinue. As the king goes to rest, he passes through cloisters of wives, and each stands at the door to call him in.... These are not the principal wives.'

'When the king rides out,' continues Nuniz, 'he takes two hundred horsemen and a hundred elephants and forty captains,' besides 'two thousand men with shields — all men of good posi tion.' Think of the gradual dents worn in the stone-paved street when the king rode out. 'Behind with the rearguard go the master of the horse with two hundred horsemen, then one hundred elephants ridden by men of high estate, five elephants for himself, and twenty-five horsemen with banners, drums and trumpets. Whoever is missing is severely punished and his property confiscated.'

These were the daily lavishness — stools and vessels and basins of gold, mattresses of silk and bolsters worked with seed pearls. The nobles, who held the land from the king as renters, paid him one half of the value of the crops, and as the nobles were frequently tyrannous, the peasants who worked the land often suffered hardship. But they could watch the glory; they could see state festivals which went down their stone streets with all the pageantry which we of today have confined to our theatres. These were the days when gold and jewels were not ostentatious in daylight, and when night brought the riding king his hundred and fifty torch-bearers.

In the great nine-day feast of Dasahara in September, to celebrate the victory of Siva's wife over the buffalo of Evil, and the march of Rama against Ravanna, the captains came to pay their land rents to the king. Gold was the theme. The king seated himself upon a throne of gold and precious stones, mounted upon the carved stone base, where he sat only once a year, and only when he had told the whole truth.

Before him his nine greatest captains had built nine great castles, hung with rich cloths, glowing with scarlets and gold, woven with vivid Indian pattern. Nine horses and nine elephants, covered with roses, made salaam. The slow, swaying elephants, ornamented and rose-covered, wearing anklets, bowed and raised trunks before the king, while hieratical priests brought rice water, fire and scent, and offered prayers and sprinkled the horses and elephants. A holocaust of animals was incidental to the religious ceremony, nine buffaloes, nine sheep, and nine goats being sacrificed the first day, and double the number each succeeding day.

One thousand women went past, dancing and posturing before the king, who was no doubt weary with this overture, unless he were a keen connoisseur of the dance. The climax must have been the stately, heavily laden parade of thirty-six of the most beautiful of the king's wives, each carrying a flaming lamp, and so weighted by the pearls and gold and jewels in their garments that they barely moved. Behind them came all the other wives and female servants with torches burning, proceeding slowly under the splendid pressure of their gold and jewelled garments.

Elephants, yoked oxen, and all the horses of the king marched by, and some thousand wrestlers contorted together. Three arrows were shot ceremoniously, and, according to Nicolo, it was the custom of Deva Raya to make war on the kingdom lying in the direction of the farthest arrow.

That is as sensible a way as another to decide where to make war.

Vijayanagar had many places to turn to for an advantageous battle. After the weaker Hindu kingdoms had been conquered and combined under her rule, there remained the rival states in the Deccan — Golconda, Bidar, Bijapur, Berar, Ahmadnagar — strong cities on hills with underground passages to plains, with crenellated ramparts, towering stone arches, triple gates studded with spear-heads, triple moats, carved bronze cannon.

They were civilized, those strong Mohammedan kingdoms of the fifteenth and sixteenth centuries. A university in Bidar brought students and professors from all the Oriental world. Behind bulwarks of walls rose cities of refinement and taste. There were mosques of severe simplicity, mosques that were a sturdy forest of columns or small gems of quiet. Finely chiselled flat decoration that understood its geometry was applied to the building. Bold domes arose — one greater than Saint Paul's. In a Bijapur palace, in a room with low-arched windows, proportioned to those sitting on the floor on cushions, the black marble walls are alive with Persian writing in mother-of-pearl, in severe and graceful design, expressing such tender and sensitive feeling as this:

> Since in my eye dwells always the image of my lord,
> It is my prayer that my sight may remain only as long as that vision.

Two violently opposed temperaments, two alien views of life, were expressed in the opposing cities, Vijayanagar and its Mohammedan rivals — Hindu diffuseness, Mohammedan singleness; Hindu exuberance, Mohammedan restraint. Alike in glory and pomp, the two civilizations must split, must battle.

Vijayanagar, with the arrow falling northwest, perhaps, had fought in a way that called for revenge. In 1419 her king 'broke down mosques and holy places, and slaughtered the people without mercy... seeming to discharge the treasured malice of the ages.' He massacred Moslems and made a platform of their heads. About a century later, Rama Raya, the last acting king of Vijayanagar joined Bijapur for a while against the rival sultanates, but in doing so he desecrated Mohammedan mosques, whereupon Bijapur went back to the side of her own religion.

Bijapur called upon her former enemies to ally with her against the Hindu forces, too great for any one Moslem city to fight. Four princes of four kingdoms met on the plains to unite their armies.

The City of Victory was not afraid. Rama Raya, an old man, 'ninety-six, but brave as thirty,' was haughty to the Mohammedan ambassadors. He sent them away scornfully, and gathered his huge forces to swallow the enemy. The city people went about

THE FORT WALLS OF BIDAR

their daily work with no precautions. Strings of pack-bullocks started out to the seaports with their usual loads, the peasants worked in the fields, the priests in the temples, and the bazaars continued to sell roses and pearls, while the army went out to meet the four princes at Talikota.

Old Rama Raya sent out his two brothers with armies of a hundred thousand or more to strategic points, while he himself led the main forces of the empire to the point of attack. His troops were all the conquered tribes and Hindu nations — Kanarese, Telegus, Mysoreans, Malabarese, and Tamils, each tribe under its own captains. Altogether he had about twice as large a force as the Mohammedans.

He was haughty. He ordered his men to bring him the head of Hussein, and they set about to do it. Lords in silks and silver armour and sharp swords, in pale blues and water greens and sensitive yellows. They attacked the Moslems.

But Rama Raya presumed too much. He forgot the old Hindu habit of disintegration. He was the only focussing point of that army; in that warfare an individual rather than a system mattered. To encourage his troops, he left the litter in which he had been carried, and seated himself on a throne of gold and jewels. There he directed the battle, a frail old man under a canopy of crimson velvet and pearls. He ordered his treasurer to bring him heaps of money, and sat surrounded by piles of gold, to show his captains the reward for victory.

The Hindus were attacking boldly when the Moslems fired bags of copper coins from their guns, which killed about five thousand Hindus. To direct the disorganized battle, Rama Raya took to his litter again.

But as the Moslem cavalry were charging the Hindu guns, an elephant went mad with excitement. It bore down upon the litter of Rama Raya, and his terrified bearers, instead of trying to save their king, dropped the litter and ran for their lives. Rama Raya was surrounded and captured by the Moslems.

That instant decided the battle — the capture of one old man. The Hindus were in panic. They ran in such confusion that they could not take up a second position in the hills. They did not even try to make a defence for Vijayanagar. They ran.

Vijayanagar lay in the path of the fleeing princes. They came through, bringing terror. Instead of trying to organize defence for the city, they took what loot they could scramble together and fled on five hundred elephants. The poor people were rooted to the place. All the oxcarts and animals had gone to the coast or with the armies. They could not go except on foot to starvation. There was nothing to do but stay and wait for the slaughter.

On the third day the Mohammedans reached Vijayanagar and

killed and looted and burned. They bashed the great stone temples, they broke the faces and legs of idolatrous images, they crashed down stone buildings until they were weary, and then they left.

They left the city to monkeys and lizards and cobras. With it fell the last great Hindu kingdom of India. Today one may go and read, from the carved stone wrestlers and dancing-girls and prideful elephants, the story of a haughty civilization—then watch the sunset over cactus and heaps of rubble.

17. *Babur, the First Mogul Emperor*

Ruled 1526–1530

IN THE next conqueror, trampled Hindustan might lift up the sick head and weakly rejoice. He promised better things than those begun by Muhammad Ghori—not unmitigatedly promising, but better.

East of Samarkand, west of Kashgar, lay an exhilarating small kingdom named Ferghana. A strong bird flying northwest from Kashmir would reach it after lifting himself three or four miles high in the air over the snow-deep crests of the Hindu Kush. But birds are lost against those mountain-tops, and a sensible one would approach from Russia. The kingdom is now a spot in Russian Turkestan nearly as inaccessible as any left in the travelled world. Ferghana was the source of the line of Great Mogul Emperors of India, whose fable spread to Europe and excited the imagination of Shakespeare's time. Babur, the founder, exiled in desiccated brown Hindustan, remembered Ferghana with longing.

The Emperor Babur was delightful, the first Moslem invader who seems three-dimensional, a nearly mature man after the spoiled-children despots. He was born ten years before Columbus discovered America, when the Western world was stirring. Heir to Mongol hardihood and to Turki civilization, he seems to catch, too, some of the Western renaissance temper — a blithe, full, curious mind, an accurate eye, enormous ability, strong affection, sensitive taste, and, now and again, unnecessary honesty and humanity. Although he sometimes followed the time-honoured habit of making piles of enemy skulls, he did it more as a convention for the well-bred conqueror than for pleasure. His tastes were those of a country gentleman — gardens, a mass of tulips blowing in the wind, the qualities of fruit and land, the accent and eccentricities of people, the skill of a verse, and also wine-bibbing parties on the rivers. But his versatile pleasure in the small things of civilization never weakened his hardiness, the leathern strength of a boy thrown on his own resources at the age of twelve, in a mountain kingdom, with an enemy coming — a boy able to survive and take a city when he was fifteen years old.

He came fairly by his strength. He descended, on his father's side, from Timur, and on his mother's from Genghis Khan — hard to better as family tree for a conqueror. But although he was of Mongol stock, his father's family had been settled for two centuries south of Samarkand, where the Turkish language and manners prevailed, in cities of elegance and civility.

So he was heir to two traditions, that of Mongol tribesmen who grew strong in their tents on the deserts of Central Asia, who bucked biting winds and sandstorms and lived on scarcity, and whose ancestors in the thirteenth century, under Genghis Khan, had swept over India, most of Persia, and a large part of China. (Babur was remote cousin of Khubla Khan of Xanadu.) His maternal uncles were still chiefs of Mongol tribes, half savage, half sumptuous, who inherited the traditional body of law called the Institutes of Genghis Khan, which Babur at first respected. These uncles, with their horse-tail standards, and their gold-threaded caps and embroidered robes of state, their ceremonious greetings, their tents messy with harness and melon seed, sometimes helped the desperate boy with the loan of bodies of horsemen, and sometimes let him shift, with as much liveliness as he could, for himself. On the Mongol side his most steady friend was his grandmother, wife of the old chief Yunis Khan. She was the sort of woman who, when captured and given as spoil to an enemy, received the intruder calmly in her tent, stabbed him, and told her captor that he could kill her if he chose, but it was not lawful to give her to another man than her husband, and she would stab as many as he sent.

Babur had little good to say of the shifty, disloyal Mongols upon whom he had to depend for help as a boy. His sympathies and tastes were Turkish. No one ever described the Mongols as beautiful; rather as hideous and graceless, with slanting eyes, big outstanding ears, fat lips, and the crude ways of nomads.

Babur himself was a man of elegance and distinction. The Turks among whom he lived were considered even by the Persians as handsome men with cultivated manners. The near-by States of Herat and Khorassan were more sumptuous than the courts of Europe. Khorassan, influenced by Persia in her prime, could compare favourably with the later court of François Premier. Her poetry, history, the grave study of morals and metaphysics, of music and the fine arts, were as learned.

But the times were very unsettled. To survive, a man had to adapt to sudden shifts of fortune. Babur took his rough and smooth with equal, fascinated interest. The death of a strong man then and there was the signal for a free-for-all contest, since there was no fixed rule of succession to any throne. Every chieftain marched as best he could for the toppling prize. Since loyalty to a leader was not thought a necessary virtue, troops might shift sides with the simplicity of present-day Chinese soldiers who wear arm bands of two armies. A nation meant less to the affection than the religion of Islam, whose laws prevailed regardless of dynasty in the various kingdoms, and whose holy sheiks formed the court of the lands, and could sometimes force the hands of kings. Sometimes a sultan was very scrupulous in his observance of the law of Islam, religious or secular. Sometimes, well-armed, he felt he could take it or leave it.

Babur, brought up on alarms and intrigues, had an enormous zest that seldom failed — a Robert Browning sense of 'How good is man's life, the mere living.' Even when exiled and deserted, he decided that this was a chance to visit China, which he pathetically could not do when he had to stay at home and be a king. His gusto could carry far into an India mortally weary of life, and was a strange hypodermic into that civilization which saw the world as an unhappy fantasy. Babur's vitality lasted through the first six of the Great Moguls. Then it wasted.

Babur kept a journal — diary notes jotted down during his camp days, and sometimes polished later, for he had great regard for style, and wrote in the Turki language with clarity and grace. The man seems to derive some qualities of freshness and vigour from the country he loved. When he writes of his Ferghana, one wishes to move there at once.

> The country of Ferghana is... on the extreme boundary of the habitable world... a country of small extent, but abounding in grain and fruits; and it is surrounded with hills on all sides except the west, toward Samarkand and Khojend, where there are none; and on that side alone can it be entered by foreign enemies....

Andejan, the capital in the centre, was alive with the noise of flowing water.

> The watercourses of the mills by which the water enters the city are nine. Around the fortress, on the edge of the stone-faced moat, is a broad highway covered with pebbles. All round the fort are the suburbs.... The district abounds in birds and beasts of game. Its pheasants are so fat that the report goes that four persons may dine on the broth of one of them, and not be able to finish it. The inhabitants of the country all are Turks. The common speech of the people... is the same as the correct language of composition. The inhabitants are remarkable for their beauty.

As for the melons, they were so plentiful that they were given away at the beds. Babur was a connoisseur of them. 'At the time when I took Samarkand, I had melons brought from Akshi and Bokhara, and cut open at the entertainment, when those of Akshi were judged beyond comparison the best.' One sees the turbanned and scimitared young warriors gravely considering the merits of melons.

Of all the districts of Ferghana, none was better than Ush. Here Babur built himself a hillside palace where the whole town and suburbs were seen stretched out below. On both sides of the river, which flowed through the suburbs, 'there are gardens, all of which overlook the river. Its violets are particularly elegant.' It abounds in streams of running water. In the spring its tulips and roses blow in great profusion. From the hill comes a great and wide stream of water, which flows past the mosque, where 'there is a meadow of clover, sheltered and pleasant, where every traveller and passenger loves to rest.' Such sweet, invigorating, and somnolent countries grew pomegranates and apricots that the people dried and stuffed with almonds. Other districts had good hunting and hawking, and in a small desert the white deer were numerous.

> All around the country of Ferghana, among the mountains, there are excellent summer stations.... The revenues of Ferghana may suffice, without oppressing the country, to maintain three or four thousand troops.

In such a small Paradise, Babur might have lived happily. Men worked to make it delightful — then worked to destroy it as fast as they could, by all the fights they could achieve.

Babur's father, Omer Sheikh Mirza, tried to do a little conquering, when he might have known from the nature of things that he was not fitted for an heroic rôle. He had gone after Samarkand, which his elder brother was ruling, and consequently this elder brother, allied with another of Babur's uncles, was marching to invade Ferghana. This is the way Babur, with an accurate but just eye, described his father:

> Omer Sheikh Mirza was of low stature, had a short, bushy beard, brownish hair, and was very corpulent. He used to wear his tunic extremely tight; insomuch that as he was wont to contract his belly while he tied the strings, when he let himself out again the strings often burst.... He never neglected the five regular and stated prayers, and rigidly performed the prayers and fasts. He devoted much time to reading the Koran.

He read elegantly, and liked certain Persian poetry, especially the Shahnamah.

> His generosity was large, and so was his whole soul; he was of excellent temper, affable, elegant and sweet in his conversation, yet brave and manly... in his later days he was much addicted to Maajun [an intoxicating comfit, prepared with a drug]. Of his three great battles, he lost two.

He had a large household of wives and concubines, and was fond of backgammon and of training pigeons. He made his capital at Akshi, where the castle was built on a high precipice, with the river flowing below its walls and the steep ravines serving as a natural moat. He scarped some of the ravines outside of the fort, to make it safer from armies, not knowing that the greatest threat to his life was pigeons. For, like many other Eastern kings, he was a great lover of pigeons trained to circle and to tumble in the air.

Amiable and a shade ridiculous, he died an amiable and ridiculous death, leaning out from his precipice castle to play with the pigeons. His stout, cumbersome figure and the pigeon cotes fell together over the side of the scarped cliff. His fall left the kingdom to the twelve-year-old boy.

'In the month of Ramzan, in the year eight hundred and ninety-nine [our 1494] and in the twelfth year of my age, I became King of Ferghana.' Babur wrote this simply at the beginning of his journal, as though it were a natural thing to be an independent king at twelve and one for which he was ready.

The amiable nonsense of his fat father translated instantly into melodrama. Babur learned of his father's death when he was in Andejan, in the palace of Four Gardens. 'I immediately mounted in the greatest haste, and taking with me such of my followers as were at hand, set out to secure the castle.' The boy did not question his ability to save the fortress. That he was still regarded as something of a child is shown by the action of a faithful chieftain just as he reached the gate, who caught his bridle and turned the horse's head to the open, thinking that Babur might be safer to get north to the hills with his mother's Mongol relatives. For Uncle Ahmed Mirza, Sultan of Samarkand, was advancing, taking cities as he came, and preparing to besiege Andejan.

The officers of Babur's father, who were in the citadel, grouped faithfully around the boy, and 'applied themselves to put the fortress, with its towers and ramparts, in a state of defence.' Other officers returned and took service with Babur. 'And all of them, with one heart and soul, set themselves zealously to maintain the place.'

The boy wrote an astute letter to his oncoming and conceivably victorious uncle. 'It is plain that you must place some one of your servants in charge of this country; I am at once your servant and your son; if you will entrust me with this employment, your purpose will be attained in the most satisfactory and easy way.' Babur had correctly judged his uncle, who would have agreed, but, 'as Sultan Ahmed Mirza was a mild, weak man, who was implicitly guided in all his opinions and actions by his begs; and as they were not favourably disposed to this proposition, a harsh answer was returned, and he marched forward.'

This was Babur's first battle. The soldiers of his own home rallied around him, resolute. The unquestioning pluck of the child, his attractiveness and mature good sense, undoubtedly made him a better centre for his troops than some other twelve-year-old. Luck also helped — the enemy horses had an epidemic of disease, and many were bogged fording the slimy river. Luck at that moment helped Babur, or, by his account, 'Almighty God, who, of his perfect power, has in his own good time and season, accomplished my designs in the best and most proper manner.'

When free of danger, Babur began to attend to the 'administration and improvement of the country and to placing everything in proper order.' He never saw himself as of schoolboy age, but as king, with certain work to do. He gave the important strongholds of the country to various tried men, and a district or estate suited to the rank and consequence of each of the begs and younger nobility.

He observed and estimated the men about him, and his writings about them give an instant sense of the values of the period.

There was a black-hearted creature who succeeded Ahmed Mirza on the throne of Samarkand. Indirectly, this man was the first cause of Babur's long exiles and vicissitudes, for he was so evil that the people pushed him from the throne, which fourteen-year-old Babur decided to take.

This sultan, 'equally devoid of courage and modesty,' had had the indiscretion to murder a prince or two.

> Another circumstance which added to his unpopularity was, that though his plan of government and general arrangements were laudable, and though he was naturally just and qualified to direct the concerns of revenue, being well versed in the science of arithmetic, yet his temper had something in it tyrannical and profligate.... What added to these evils was that the prince himself was tyrannical and debauched, his begs and servants all faithfully imitated his example... constantly engaged in debauchery and drinking.... None of the townspeople or shopkeepers, and not even the Turks and soldiers, could leave their houses, from a dread lest their children should be carried off for catamites. The people... who had lived in ease and tranquillity under Ahmed Mirza, were stung to the soul....

Babur quotes Sa'adi:

> Beware of the smoke of internal wounds:
> For a wound, though hidden, will at last break out.
> Afflict not, if you can, even one heart,
> For a single groan is sufficient to confound a world.

The wounds broke out, the people proclaimed another man as king, who attempted the throne.

This news reached Babur, 'and in that same month I, too, mounted and set out with my army to attempt the conquest of Samarkand' — aged fourteen. Three sultans were besieging it from three sides, with not quite the seriousness of a game of golf, and they finally decided to ally, and, moving nearer together, 'had an interview on horseback in the midst of the river.' But as winter approached and supplies were scarce, Babur went back to Andejan, and the Sultan of Bokhara went home, and the Sultan of Hissar, 'being deeply enamoured of the daughter of Sheikh Abdullah Birbas, married her, and renounced schemes of ambition.... Nay, this was his only object in advancing against Samarkand.'

Next year, allied with the Sultan of Bokhara, he again went to besiege green-domed Samarkand. Babur's horsemen were in many sharp skirmishes, high-spirited, but Babur's discipline in successful times was good. While encamped near the bordered pleasure-ground, traders from town came to the camp bazaar, to buy and sell.

> One day, about afternoon prayers, there was suddenly a general hubbub and the whole of these Mussulmans were plundered. But such was the discipline of my army, that, on my issuing an order that no person should... detain any... property... so seized, but that the whole should be restored without reserve before the next watch of the day was over, there was not a bit of thread or broken needle that was not restored to the owner.

That, in spite of the fact that on other occasions he plundered the nomads' flocks to feed his armies.

The blockade of Samarkand lasted from summer to cold weather, when the starving town gave up. Babur found himself at fifteen, 'by the favour of God,' in possession of Samarkand. He ruled there just one hundred days. The town was so distressed that 'it was absolutely necessary to furnish the inhabitants with seed corn and supplies, to enable them to carry on the cultivation till the harvest. How was it possible to levy anything from a country that was in this condition?' The soldiers began to desert, by twos and threes, and all the Mongols left. Babur, desperately holding on with about a thousand men, heard that his home, Andejan, had been seized by a rebel. His mother and grandmother wrote him, in danger. He himself fell so ill that for four days he could not speak or eat. High and low, despairing of his life, began to shift for themselves. At last the boy weakly struggled to his feet and rode out of Samarkand to try to relieve Andejan — on the very day when it fell. 'For the sake of Andejan, I had lost Samarkand, and found that I had lost the one without preserving the other.'

'Separated from my country and my followers... since the day that I had known myself, I had never experienced such grief and suffering.' He tried to get help from his uncles to retake both cities, but failed. Although still weak from illness, he was 'reduced to a very distressed condition, and wept a great deal.... I would not, on account of one or two defeats, sit down and look idly around me.'

For two years he was able to do little but stay in Khojend and skirmish a bit.

> Khojend is but a small place; and it is difficult for one to support two hundred retainers in it. How, then, could a man, ambitious of empire, set himself down contentedly in so insignificant a place? There, however, I remained with my whole family for a year and a half, or nearly two years.

His fortunes changed like the crests and trough of waves, and as suddenly. One day, 'about afternoon prayers, a horseman was descried at the bottom of the valley.' He came as messenger from a repentant chieftain, who offered Babur the town of Marghinan. Babur, at sunset, mounted and rode all night and until noon the next day without a stop. Marghinan opened its gates to him. He skirmished near Andejan, and very soon the garrison declared for their rightful king, Babur.

> And thus, by the grace of the Most High [and in June, 1499], I recovered my paternal kingdom, of which I had been deprived nearly two years.

This did not mean simplicity and peace. Strong rivals were outside the city, and Babur made mistakes that cost him many unstable followers. But he learned from his errors:

> When there was a rival like Jehangir Mirza at my elbow, it was a senseless thing to exasperate so many men who had arms in their hands.... In war and affairs of state... no matter ought to be finally fixed without being well weighed and considered in a hundred different lights.

Meanwhile, his emotions were beginning to disturb him, in one way or another. He had been betrothed as a solemn child of five to Aisha Sultan Begum, daughter of his uncle, the Sultan of Samarkand, and married her in 1500, when he was eighteen.

> In the first period of my being a married man, though I had no small affection for her, yet from modesty and bashfulness, I went to her only once in ten, fifteen, or twenty days. My affection afterwards declined, and my shyness increased; insomuch that my mother, the Khanoum, used to fall upon me and scold me with great fury, sending me off like a criminal to visit her once in a month or forty days.

From such a childlike and forced unripe marriage, he swung to the prevalent distortion of the age, and fell in love with a boy. Whether fashion alone, the influence of one mind on another sways a given society — sheer imitation of a degraded person with prestige; whether the racial chemistry or the nervous systems get out of gear in a mass, or whether the relation between men and women gets unbalanced — be it all as it may, certain states in Babur's time were completely on the bias. 'And such currency did this vile practice gain' in Samarkand, in Mahmud Mirza's time, 'that every man had his boy; insomuch that to keep a catamite was thought to be a creditable thing, and not to have one was regarded as rather an imputation on a man's spirit. As a judgment on him for his tyranny and depravity, all his son's were cut off in their youth.' Babur condemned the vice. Yet he fell madly in love, with a sort of romantic, distant love, with a lad belonging to the camp bazaar. 'Before this I had never conceived a passion for anyone; and indeed had never been so circumstanced as either to hear or witness any words spoken expressive of love or amorous passion.' But now the king was confused if he met the bazaar boy suddenly, and could not look him directly in the face. 'I composed a few verses in Persian. "Never was a lover so wretched, so enamoured, so dishonoured as I... etc." From the madness of my passion and the effervescence of youth... I used to stroll bareheaded and barefooted through lane and street, garden and orchard, neglecting... the respect due to others and myself.'

Luckily a new siege of Samarkand pulled him from his distraction, and wild travels with his men up steep and narrow mountain passes, where horses and camels failed. Samarkand was now held by the tribes of greasy Uzbeks.

The King of Ferghana, now nineteen, with two hundred and forty men, still felt it a sporting event to take a city. 'Come, let us hit on a lucky guess, and may God accomplish it! When shall we take Samarkand?' After a good-omened dream at midnight, he sent seventy men to fix scaling-ladders to the wall, get into the fort, then take a certain gate. They climbed silently without alarming anyone, fell upon the guards at the gate, broke the lock with axes, and threw it open — at the very moment that Babur came up, ready to enter.

> The citizens in general were fast asleep, but the shopkeepers, peering out of their shops... offered up prayers of Thanksgiving.... In a short time the rest knew it, and manifested great joy.... They pursued the Uzbeks in every street and corner with sticks and stones, hunting them down and killing them like mad dogs.

Babur went to the college and monastery and took his seat under the arched hall, while the streets were full of shouting and tumult. The chief people of the city came up to welcome him, with much joy, and offerings of food and grateful prayers. Success drew adherents, as failure threw them off. The Uzbeks abandoned forts to him, and all his affairs prospered, until in six months his army snowballed into such a size that he dared attack his greatest enemy, Sheibani Khan, 'A man full of talents, of deep experience, and in the meridian of life.'

His too sudden aggression against this seasoned warrior was the beginning of the lowest ebb of his fortune. He quoted Sa'adi:

> He who with impatient haste lays his hand on his sword
> Will afterwards gnaw that hand with his teeth from regret.

> The cause of my eagerness to engage was, that the stars called the eight stars were on that day exactly between the two armies; and if I had suffered that day to elapse, they would have continued favourable to the enemy for the space of thirteen or fourteen days. These observations were all nonsense and my precipitation was without the least solid excuse.

Sheibani Khan's Uzbeks, flying at breakneck gallop and shooting, turned Babur's flank. The wretches of Mongols, who had joined Babur, dismounted and robbed their own side.... 'If the Mongol race were a race of angels, it is a bad race,' wrote Babur. Victorious Sheibani Khan besieged Samarkand until the people were in distress, eating dogs and asses, feeding the horses on leaves or shavings of wood soaked in water. The soldiers began to desert, letting themselves down over the city walls. When the supplies were completely gone, Babur himself had to escape, by the dark of midnight taking his mother and eldest sister from the city he had so lately conquered. They were entangled in the great branches of the waterways outside the city, lost their way in the dark, and wandered silent and trying to avoid ambush — and Babur's sister was seized by Sheibani Khan's men.

But Babur's boyishness could not be depressed.

> On the road I had a race with Kamber Ali and Kasim Beg. My horse got the lead. As I turned round on my seat to see how far I had left them behind, my saddle girth being slack, the saddle turned round, and I came to the ground on my head. Although I immediately sprang up and mounted, yet I did not recover the full possession of my faculties till evening, and the world... passed before my eyes and apprehension like a dream.

The hungry group finally reached a town of friends and plenty.

> Here we found nice fat flesh, bread of fine flour well baked, sweet melons and excellent grapes in great abundance; thus passing from the extreme of famine to plenty, and from an estate of danger and calamity to peace and ease.... In my whole life I never enjoyed myself so much... enjoyment after suffering, abundance after want, come with increased relish, and afford more exquisite delight.

The next two years, however, were lean ones of exile. Babur spent a winter in a peasant's hut, on the side of a high mountain, where the Sart people pastured their sheep and mares. The headman's mother, a woman a hundred and eleven years old, told stories of a kinsman who had followed Timur Beg into India, and aroused Babur's first interest in the place. The exiled king walked barefoot that winter over all the hills, rugged enough to cross the winter desert.

> It was wonderfully cold, and the wind... here lost none of its violence. So excessive was the cold that in the course of two or three days we lost two or three persons from its severity. I required to bathe on account of my religious purifications, and went down for that purpose to a rivulet, which was frozen on the banks, but not in the middle, from the rapidity of the current. I plunged myself into the water, and dived sixteen times. The extreme chilliness of the water quite penetrated me.

He was still in the country of his Mongol uncles, but perhaps they had tired of giving him men, for he was shabby now. 'When I went to my uncle, the khan's divan, I was attended sometimes by one person, sometimes by two,' and he said to himself, 'It were better to retire in some corner where I might live unknown and undistinguished... to flee away from the sight of man.' He wrote a 'ghazel,' a poem of six couplets, beginning:

> I have found no faithful friend in the world but my soul;
> Except my own heart I have no trusty confidant.

Indomitable Babur, in his twenty-third year when he first, as he mentions, began to shave, was still fighting against odds.

> The followers who still adhered to my fortunes, great and small, exceeded two hundred and fell short of three hundred. The greater part of them were on foot, with brogues on their feet, clubs in their hands, and long frocks over their shoulders. Such was our distress that among us all we had only two tents. My own tent was pitched for my mother, and they erected for me at each stage a felt tent of cross-poles.

He had given up hope of regaining his Ferghana, and was on the way toward Kabul. From that time on his fortunes mended. Going through the kingdom of hated Khousrou Shah — a murderer who had killed a sweet and trusting young prince by strangling him with a bowstring — Babur managed to take away the allegiance of his shifty Mongol tribes. Khousrou Shah thereupon submitted to Babur. 'The pompous man now bent himself for twenty-five or twenty-six times successively, and went and came back and forward, till he was so tired that he nearly fell right forward.'

'I now left my encampment [in the year 1504] and marched against Kabul.' It surrendered soon to his well-planned siege, and from this time Babur was a king with a throne to sit on.

Kabul, too, was a gardened city in the thick of its hills, and its people had ice brought down from the mountains to cool their water, and a large river ran through the town, 'green, gay, and beautiful,' and it was the centre of two great caravan routes, from Turkestan and from India. Every year Hindustan sent up to Kabul from seven to ten thousand horses, pieces of cloth in the thousands, slaves and sugar candy and drugs and spices. Up they came through the Khyber Pass, and turned Babur's attention down it.

> Drink wine in the citadel of Kabul, and send round the cup without stopping;
> For it is at once a mountain and a sea, a town and a desert.

Babur at this period needed no one to tell him to drink wine or pass the cup without stopping. He enjoyed himself, and laid out his gardens, with a campaign or two going on most of the time, but not interfering with leisure and pleasure.

The gardens are to dream about, undoubtedly.

> I formed a great garden in the year 1508. It is called the Garden of Fidelity. It overlooks the river.... In the garden there is a small hillock, from which a stream of water... sufficient to drive a mill, incessantly flows into the garden below. The fourfold field plot is there. On the southwest part of this garden is a reservoir of water... which is wholly planted with orange trees; there are likewise pomegranates. All around the piece of water the ground is quite covered with clover. This spot is the very eye of the beauty of the garden. At the time when the orange becomes yellow, the prospect is delightful. Indeed, the garden is charmingly laid out.

Babur brought to it plantains from conquered Lahore, and sugar cane, which thrived. He knew all the details of trees and fruits, as well as inhabitants and animals, in his new kingdom of Kabul.

But he was on his way down to India. 'I had always had the conquest of Hindustan at heart.' He went down gradually, making five invasions — sometimes only down through the bleak brown Khyber Pass and back, or down as far as Sialkot on a raid to punish some Afghans. His final and conquering invasion was not until 1525.

Meantime, his campaigns down through the hills were varied by gardens and drinking-parties, especially on rivers, when there were rivers to float a pleasure boat. 'About the time of noonday prayers, I mounted to take a ride, and afterwards going on board of a boat, we had a drinking bout.' The party consisted of Dost Beg, Mirza Kuli, Muhammad Ali Jeng-Jeng, and many other stout Mohammedan warriors. 'We continued drinking spirits till bed-time prayers, when, being completely drunk, we mounted, and, taking torches in our hands, came at full gallop back to the camp from the riverside, falling sometimes on one side of the horse, and sometimes on the other.' Muffled figures must have skipped out of the way of the emperor's party on the dark road. 'I was miserably drunk, and next morning, when they told me of our galloping into camp with lighted torches in our hands, I had not the slightest recollection of the circumstance.'

One time, ill of a fever, he gave up wine for a bit, but allowed his

MINIATURE OF BABUR IN HIS GARDEN

shahs to drink. 'I said: "I never in my life sat sober while my friends were getting merry, nor remained cool and observant.... Come, therefore, and drink near me, that I may observe for a while the different progress and effects of society on the sober and the drunk"' — a detached and scientific interest. Babur teased a young soldier who rigidly abstained from wine, 'You, a soldier, young, with a black beard, and never drink! What sense is there in this?' But he added, 'It was never my custom, as I did not think it polite, to press anybody to drink who did not wish; so that this passed as mere pleasantry, and he was not induced to take wine.' Babur's descendants were not all so considerate.

These parties and pleasantries were in the midst of an invasion toward India — no more than a raid on the tribes in their mud-walled, watch-towered settlements in the Khyber Pass; gathering the harvest of others' rice-fields; and then going back to see his Garden of Fidelity in all its autumn glory, 'The grass plots covered with clover, its pomegranates hanging red on the trees... the orange trees green and cheerful, loaded with innumerable oranges.'

During the period of the early invasions, Babur's eldest son Humayon, child of his favourite wife Mahum, was growing up. By the time Babur seriously invaded India, Humayon was eighteen, had had his first shave, and was in command of some of his father's troops.

At this time, in 1524, the sultanate at Delhi was a trembling remnant of strength. The last of the Afghan dynasty of the Lodi — Ibrahim Lodi — was haughty and cruel, arrogant without sense. The whole empire was discontented... and he ruled only a little island with certainty. Bengal was independent, and Malwa and Gujarat. The Rajput princes had rallied in a threatening confederacy, led by Rana Sanga, of the Sun race of Udaipur.

A wily and fierce old Afghan governing the Punjab invited Babur to help overthrow the Lodis, but could not remain loyal, and by rebelling against Babur broke up his own plan. In November, 1525, Babur in his fifth and final invasion, captured the treacherous old governor with two swords hung on him, and when he was slow in bowing, Babur directed a man to push his leg and make him salaam. He cleared the first obstacle in his way to Delhi.

> I placed my foot in the stirrup of resolution and my hand on the reins of confidence in God, and marched against Sultan Ibrahim, the son of Sultan Iskander... in whose possession the throne of Delhi and the domains of Hindustan at that time were; whose army in the field was said to amount to a hundred thousand men.

Babur halted at Panipat, the inevitable battlefield near Delhi, and made everything ready. His troops were alarmed, and he did not blame them — two months' journey from home, and engaging an enemy whose language they did not understand. But Babur remarked that trepidation and fear are always unbecoming, and what Almighty God has decreed cannot be reversed. He connected his gun-carriages with twisted bull hides, and between every two gun-carriages raised defences for his matchlock men. After every part of this apparatus was in order and ready, he called together in council all the men of any experience and knowledge. Ibrahim Lodi, who was negligent, who marched without order and retired without plan, had no chance against Babur's experience and wisdom. 'The sun had mounted spear-high when the onset of battle began, and the combat lasted until midday, when the enemy was completely broken and routed.' The body of Ibrahim, the last sultan of the Lodis, was found in the field.

Babur, victorious, camped on the banks of the Jumna, visiting the tombs and palaces and the minarets of his predecessors, like any sight-seer, and drinking arrack on a boat, and appointing a military director of Delhi and sealing the treasury. At the Friday mosque in Delhi he sent one in to read the kutbeh in his name proclaiming him ruler, and to give money to fakirs and beggars, while he went on to Agra.

He observed the land he had conquered with a clear eye, as he had Kabul. He was not too well impressed. These are some of the notes scattered in his journal:

> The empire of Hindustan is extensive, populous and rich.... At the period when I conquered the country, five Mussulman kings and two pagans exercised royal authority. Although there were many small and inconsiderable Rais and Rajahs in the hills and woody country, yet these were the chief, and only ones of importance.
>
> The country and towns of Hindustan are extremely ugly. All its towns and lands have a uniform look; its gardens have no walls, and the greater part of it is level plain.... In Hindustan, if you except the rivers, there is little running water.... All these cities and countries derive their water from wells or tanks... filled in the rainy season.

Babur noticed the dirty wells where the bullocks raised water, tied by a rope to the bucket. 'Every time the bullock raises the bucket from the well, as it is let down again the rope slides along the bullock course, is defiled with urine and dung, and in this filthy condition falls into the well.'

The disorder and planlessness of Hindu ways struck him, accustomed to the formal harmony of a Persian civilization in its prime.

> In Hindustan, the populousness and decay, or total destruction of villages, nay of cities, is almost instantaneous. Large cities that have been inhabited for a series of years (if, on alarm, the inhabitants take to flight) in a single day, or a day and a half, are so completely abandoned that you can scarcely discover a trace or mark of population.

> And if they intend to settle, needing no watercourses or flood mounts... and the population of Hindustan being unlimited, inhabitants swarm in from every direction. They make a tank or dig a well... there is no need of building a strong house or erecting a firm wall, they have plenty of strong grass and timber of which they run up hovels, and a village or town is constructed in an instant.
>
> Hindustan is a country that has few pleasures to recommend it. The people are not handsome. They have no idea of the charms of friendly society, of frankly mixing together, or of familiar intercourse. They have no genius, no comprehension of mind, no politeness of manner, no kindness or fellow feeling, no ingenuity or mechanical invention in planning or executing their handicraft works, no skill or knowledge in design or architecture; they have no horses, no good flesh, no grapes or muskmelons, no good fruits, no good food or bread in their bazaars, no baths or colleges, no torches, not a candlestick. Instead of a candle and torch, you have a gang of dirty fellows... who hold in the left hand a kind of tripod... and a wick and gourd to pour on fresh oil.... If the emperors or chief nobility have occasion for a light by night, these filthy diwatis bring in their lamp, which they carry up to their master, and there stand holding it close by his side....

This was the impression India made on the first of the Great Moguls, the greatest line of kings of India since the Guptas.

Part of his distaste may have come from the fear and dislike which the natives felt for him, the villagers fleeing in terror and taking off their stores of grain, thieving from his army as they could, rebelling on the highways. Meanwhile the heat grew unbearable, and his mountain men died of sunstroke.

His men loathed it all; his whole army, down to the dregs, gave their 'stupid and unformed opinions.' 'What sense or propriety was there in eternally repeating the same tale in different words, to one who himself saw the facts with his own eyes, and had formed a cool and fixed resolution in regard to the business in which he was engaged?' Babur faced rebelling troops better than Alexander did in a similar situation.

> What force compels us, [he asked them] and what hardship obliges us, after having worn out our life in accomplishing the desired achievement, to abandon and fly from our conquests?... Let not anyone who calls himself my friend ever henceforward make such a proposal. But if there is any among you who cannot bring himself to stay... let him depart.

To hold the country he had still to march against the 'Pagans' — Rana Sanga of Chitor and his league of Rajputs. This old Rajput had been the hero of a hundred fights that had swelled his power. What was left of him was still formidable. He had lost an eye and an arm, and had a broken leg and about eighty scars. But he was the head of a hundred and twenty Rajput chieftains, and had eighty thousand cavalry to Babur's poor little twelve thousand followers, which number included servants and camp merchants.

Babur chose a camp site well supplied with water near the present Fathpur Sikri to await the aggressive Rajputs. He spent twenty-five days in fortifying his position — with guns in front, connected by chains, and with ditches. But more than material preparation was necessary to relieve his army's panic. It needed a moral gesture, and Babur found it. He was struck by the reflection that he had always intended to repent — and that the moment was ripe. He wrote a poem in Persian, beginning, 'How long wilt thou continue to take pleasure in sin?' and vowed never to drink wine again. But he had to make his repentance dramatic to have an effect.

He sent for all the gold and silver wine cups, and ordered them broken, and their bits given to holy men and the poor. He poured his drinks on the ground, and when the camel-load of wine came in from Kabul, he had salt put into it. That night and the next, numbers of his amirs and courtiers and soldiers, all repented and poured out wine on the ground. That helped — but there was still a very real terror in his men: 'not a single person who uttered a manly word, not an individual who delivered a courageous opinion.' He had to change this shrinking mass of men into a fighting unit. Calling an assembly, he spoke to them.

> Noblemen and soldiers! Every man that comes into this world is subject to dissolution. When we are passed away and gone, God only survives, unchangeable. Whoever comes to the feast of life, must, when it is over, drink from the cup of death.... How much better it is to die with honour than to live with infamy!... If we fall in the field, we die the death of martyrs; if we survive, we rise victorious, the avengers of the cause of God. Let us, then, with one accord, swear, on God's holy word, that none of us will even think of turning his face from this warfare, nor desert from the battle and slaughter that ensues, till his soul is separated from his body.

Galvanized by Babur, the men, great and small, seized the Koran and swore. 'My plan succeeded to admiration.'

'The heathen fell furiously upon the holy warriors... but the holy warriors cast them all out like their black fortune.' That is the gist of the battle. 'Many were slain... some turned to the desert of ruin, and became the food of crows and kites; and hillocks were formed of the slain, and towers raised of their heads.'

Nauseating pain, shock, and blank grief, and the snuffing out of lives that took years in building, did not stir a nerve of anyone. A new family had come to dominate Hindustan. That was all. Gay, kindly, and insouciant Babur, too tolerant to force a man to drink against his will, established his dynasty and continued building gardens, ordering such of the affairs of the country as could be touched — directing his battering cannon against hill fortresses, from which Rajputs flung down rocks and flaming things, and remarking calmly, when the last men of the city sacrificed themselves to the Rajput code, 'One person took his stand with a sword in his hand, while the others, one by one, crowded in and stretched out their necks, eager to die.' 'In this way,' said Babur, 'many went to Hell.'

A son of the brave Rana Sanga offered to surrender to Babur, who gave him back his father's throne in Chitor.

Babur's eldest son Humayon, who stirred his tenderness deeply, was now a graceful and cultivated man, older than Babur when he last took Samarkand, and fretted a little by subordination to his father and the greed of his bolder brother Kamran. Babur in his journal speaks little of any of his family, except Humayon. He had married probably five wives in all, one or two from affection; one who died soon of smallpox, one who quarrelled and left him, and Humayon's mother Maham, to whom he was devoted.

At this period he had living four sons and three daughters. The daughters were named Rose-Coloured, Rose-Face, Rose-Body — all children of Queen Heart-Ravisher. The sons were Humayon, Kamran, Hindal, and Askeri, strong demanders to partition the kingdom their father had won.

To Humayon, Babur wrote affectionate or slightly scolding letters with fatherly advice.

> To Humayon, whom I remember with much longing to see again: Thanks be to God, who has given you a child, and to me a comfort and an object of love.... Fail not to exert yourself strenuously to meet every situation as it occurs; for indolence and ease suit but ill with royalty....

He tried to be just to his sons, and keep the bounding ambitions in place.

> If Kamran thinks Balkh too small a government, let me know, and I will, by divine grace, remove his objection by adding something from the neighbouring territories. You know that you always receive six parts, and Kamran five.... Remember, too, always to act handsomely by him. The great should exercise self-command; and I do hope you will always maintain a good understanding with him.... You complain of separation from friends. It is wrong for a prince to indulge in such a complaint, for there is a saying: 'If you are fettered by your situation, submit to circumstances. If you are independent, follow your own fancy.' There is no greater bondage than that in which a king is placed.

Then the father was most modernly paternal. He complained of

Humayon's bad handwriting and ill-composed letters. 'You certainly never read them over.... It is excessively confused and crabbed.'

But to Humayon, Babur, who could raise piles of enemy heads without flicking an eyelash, showed the most extreme and selfless love. The young man, charming and easy and mainly compliant, seemed to him to have every princely virtue. Humayon, possibly realizing that Babur's boundless health was failing, decided to come to Agra, leaving Badakshan which he was ruling, to a subordinate who stole it. Babur forgave him and gave him another province. In six months the prince fell desperately ill.

Every medicine and herb, every doctor's method or holy man's prayers, failed. Humayon was dying, with no help for it. Then a pious and learned man told Babur that sometimes the Almighty was willing to accept, in exchange for a life, the most valuable and cherished gift which a friend of the dying could make. Babur instantly said that of all things his own life was dearest, and vowed to offer his life to Heaven in exchange for Humayon's. His nobles begged him to consider such rashness, and to offer instead the bulky diamond which he had won at the fall of Gwalior. But he said that no diamond could be valued in comparison to life. He walked three times around his dying son — which was a Moslem rite to avert misfortune — and then went aside to pray alone. After a while his appalled attendants heard him cry, 'I have borne it away. I have borne it away.' And Moslem chroniclers say that from that time, Humayon's strength began faintly to return, and, as life came back to the son, life went from the father. Babur actually died, apparently of this emotion and will, and his last words were to commend Humayon to the protection of his begs, and to ask him to be kind and forgiving to his brothers.

Then the genial, hearty man who had ruled Hindustan five years, and barely quieted it to his central power, died in his fiftieth year.

18. *Akbar, the Greatest Mogul*

Ruled 1556–1605

THE dark sky presses heat down on a silent red sandstone city — Fathpur Sikri, twenty-three miles from Agra. One may walk through the king's sleeping-apartments, called the House of Dreams; over a paved courtyard where tradition says the emperor played chess, moving long-eyed slave girls as pawns from square to square; through walled lanes, hiding his comings and goings to the palaces of the three principal wives; to the house of the little Turkish bride, carved thickly with wreaths and vines and fruit and birds; by the water pool, by the stable that tethered camels; to the strange audience seat on top of a pillar where once the learned men from each religion — Hindu, Parsee, Jain, or Christian — tried to explain its truths to the emperor, and better his rival's theology. A high Gate of Victory opens to the mosque, a noble arch, fairly sonorous of triumph. Yet one of its inscriptions tells: 'So said Jesus, on whom be peace! The world is a bridge; pass over it, but build no house upon it.'

The Emperor Akbar chose to build. His city expresses his manifold nature. Akbar, the inquisitive-minded, was the strongest Mogul emperor, and the ablest ruler of India since Asoka. No later king equalled him in tolerance and wisdom, in clear intelligence of rule. On his foundations the English built. He tried to penetrate the reasons of religion. And he kept in his red sandstone city, 'as they do credibly report,' said Ralph Fitch, a thousand elephants, thirty thousand horses, fourteen hundred tame deer, and eight hundred concubines (included in the list with cheetahs, tigers, and fighting buffaloes). The first letter that travelled from England to India came from Queen Elizabeth to him, addressed, 'The Most Invincible and Most Mightie Prince, Lord Zelabdin Echebar, King of Cambaya.'

Akbar — in his little turban and his belted, flaring gold-shot robe, whose scribes sat writing his every word, and whose liberal adviser, Abul Fazl, kept a detailed and fulsome history — remains, as a person, an enigma.

The white ants or human enemies destroyed all the volumes that the busy scribes wrote; but Abul Fazl's lengthy work remains, and the stories of other Moslem historians, the brief letters of the first

English merchant travellers, and the journals of the Portuguese Jesuits, who came to his court to convert him.

Akbar's story confounds most theories of education, and may comfort some schoolboys, for, although exposed to many tutors, he would never learn to read and write. He could ride an infuriated elephant, and, afoot with his sword, kill a female tiger guarding cubs; he could conquer half India and establish a sensible government; he could sift and weigh religious dogmas, and try to found a fusing faith — but he would not bother to learn the alphabet. There were others who could. Anyhow, as he remarked, the prophets were always illiterate, so it was well to keep one person in each family who could not read.

Akbar was the grandson of Babur and the son of agreeable weak Humayon, who had lost, temporarily, the Indian Empire. If Babur's adventures began at twelve, Akbar's began before he was born. Humayon, for whom Babur had willed to give his life, was an exile. He had lost the throne of Delhi to the Afghan Sher Shah, a strong and intelligent man. Graceful and opium-loving Humayon was a fugitive in the low sandhills near the blazing Sind Desert. And necessarily all his ladies and followers were in exile, too, for there was no safety in India for them. High-born women who had lived in the seclusion of carved palaces had to ride day-long on horse or camel in the heat, with scanty food and water.

While in the unsheltered desert, Humayon received his pleasant half-brother, Hindal, and saw among his followers a little girl of fourteen, daughter of a prince's tutor, of Persian descent. His Majesty asked, 'Who is this?' and although the thirty-three-year-old impoverished king was sufficiently married, he was persistent in sending for her again. 'My waiting eye is on the road,' he said. She had spirit, and replied to his summons: 'If it is to pay my respects, I was exalted by paying my respects the other day. Why come again?' And a second time she answered: 'To see kings once is lawful: a second time it is forbidden. I shall not come.' For forty days the discussions went on, with Humayon growing irritated at the suggestion that he could not pay a proper price, and Babur's widow Dildar telling the girl she must marry someone, and who better than a king — until finally the marriage was arranged that bore Akbar.

Several months later, in the suffocation of August, Humayon had to escape a Hindu army. His underfed horses sank to their knees in sand, and night after night they reached no water. When they found deep wells on the fourth day, the crazed people flung themselves so madly that they broke the bucket ropes and fell in; and at pools many of the sorely needed horses drank so greedily that they died. The unborn Emperor Akbar was taking this journey.

Beyond the desert the citadel Umrkot was beautiful to their eyes,

Copyright Archeological Department of India

AKBAR'S AUDIENCE SEAT, FATHPUR SIKRI

cooled by tanks and green with gardens, with plenty for the hungry. The Rajah made them welcome, and Humayon gracefully borrowed his money to present him with appropriate sword-belts and dresses. After several weeks, Humayon was sent on an expedition by the Rajah, and when he had been gone three days, in November, 1542, by the whiteness of a full moon, the baby was born.

Horsemen galloped with the news to Humayon, camped twenty miles away. The father bumped his head to the ground, thanking Allah, and named the child 'Full Moon of the Faith,' also Muhammad, also Akbar, meaning great. Then he was embarrassed.

When an emperor's son is born there should be rich ceremony and heedless largess. Humayon scarcely owned his tents and his travel-worn clothing and enough food to keep man and horse alive, yet he wanted to celebrate the birth of the heir to Hindustan. He asked his ewer-bearer to bring what treasure he had. There were two hundred silver coins and a silver bracelet, which did not belong to Humayon, so he gave them back to their owners. Only a pod of musk was left him, but the desert king was a glass of fashion and a mould of form. He called for a china plate, and, breaking the pod, gave some of it to the principal persons gathered, saying, 'This is all the present I can afford to make you on the birth of my son, whose fame will, I trust, be one day expanded over the whole world as the perfume of the musk now fills this apartment.' Then the drums beat.

It would not seem, by our present gentle theories, that blistering desert and escaping parents beset by enemies made the best environment for the care and feeding of an infant, or for the stamp of his mind — which proves, perhaps, how little we know. Great Akbar's babyhood was perilous.

Humayon was in danger from two of his brothers, Kamran who held Kabul, bold, restless and untrustworthy, and Askari, his loyal viceroy in Kandahar. When Humayon decided to ask help from the Shah of Persia, he had to pass the borders of Kandahar. The instant reaction of Askari was to gallop out after him with two thousand horsemen. Humayon had warning only in time to lift his wife Hamida to his own saddle, but with 'no chink of time' to take the year-old baby Akbar. Askari captured the child, but chose to treat him kindly. His wife and his aunt, Babur's sister, took careful charge of helpless Akbar. When the baby was two years old, the old lady took him through deep winter snow up the passes to Kabul. She delighted in him, kissing his hands and feet, which she said were shaped like Babur's, and hoping doubtless that he would entirely resemble that triumphant man.

Meanwhile Humayon, who had gone through snows and starvation, once killing a horse and boiling it in a helmet to feed Akbar's mother, reached Persia. He was lavishly received by Shah

Tahmasp. The Persian ladies had picnics for the Indian queen. The emperor gave gracious affairs for Humayon, feasts at which poets and wits gathered, and scholars and artists. Humayon's meeting with the Persian miniature painters was to be the beginning of the Mogul school of painting in India. The scenes of their entertainment still last in fading colours on the walls of the palace of Ispahan — gentle knights nodding their turbaned heads. The only string attached to the generous splendour was that Humayon must either be converted to the Shiah sect of Mohammedans, or be burnt alive. Such hospitality has not the qualities of endurance.

Armed by Persia with horsemen, Humayon took Kandahar and Kabul from his brothers. But while he was on a further campaign, Kamran slipped back into Kabul with the water-carriers' wagons, imprisoned the ladies and captured five-year-old Akbar, whom he had held up on the ramparts, exposed to the fire of his father's guns.

Brotherly love was not a telling phase in those days. Yet there was a later scene when Humayon welcomed Kamran with kettle-drums and tears, and the brother kings sat side by side on one carpet, eating sherbet. And a still later scene, eight years later, when Kamran, who was quite a bad egg and trouble-maker, was caught for Humayon and blinded by a lance thrust fifty times into his eyes ('such was the will of God'), with salt and lemon squeezed into their sockets. And Humayon (whom Babur had yearned over and asked to care for his brothers), hearing that the business was *quite* completed, called for his bath-water.

From the age of five, Akbar was given tutors equipped to teach him all the graces of Persian literature. But with toughness and originality he braced his small will against all the tutors and his father. The elegantly written page could not get access to his shut mind. Akbar's youth seemed a throwback to some Mongolian nomad ancestor. He preferred to use his will power on living and inscrutable things — animals. Few boys in the world had such playthings — horses, camels, elephants, tame deer, pet hunting leopards. No wonder he could not focus to the pale abstraction of an alphabet!

Animals fascinated him. As he grew older, he mastered that minor kingdom. 'He also applied his thoughts to the delight of an Arab horse, which is a grand subject of dominion and exaltation.' To be able to understand a skittish Arab, to forestall a snarling camel, or control the great emotional mass of a mad elephant, is not too bad training for mastering people, their obstinacies and fears and guiles. A camel and a stupid rebel have some common denominator. Akbar had magnetism, a quick eye, and a flair for sensing reactions. As for his muscle, which was after all no small factor in his endurance to conquer and rule half India, that grew iron. His education was more like that of a circus performer than a prince; but for Akbar, it succeeded.

Yet the strange, half-savage seeming boy had moments when he loved to listen to Persian poetry of the mystic Sufi school, whose singers longed for a union with God, and some part of his nature sounded in answer.

When Akbar was twelve, his father invaded India. Powerful Sher Shah and his son had died, and the passing of the strong men made Humayon's opportunity. They floated down the Kabul River on a raft, and, after crossing the Indus, Humayon tried to bless his enterprise by giving a solemn audience to his son. 'His Majesty was sitting, facing the setting moon; he ordered the prince to sit down opposite him; he then read some verses of the Koran, and at the end of each verse he *breathed* upon the prince, and was so delighted and happy it might be said he had then acquired all the good fortune of this world, and the blessing of the next.'

Humayon's invading army was under command of stout Bairam Khan. He regained Lahore and Delhi, and appointed thirteen-year-old Akbar as governor of the Punjab, with Bairam Khan as guardian. Humayon was restored as emperor, but had less than a year to live. In January, 1556, one sunset-time, he was talking with astrologers on the roof of the Sher Mandal, which he used as a library, when the voice of the muezzin called to prayers. Humayon, trying to bow down at the call, tripped on the skirt of his gown and fell headlong, fracturing his skull, and was never again conscious.

Fourteen-year-old Akbar was in the Gurdaspur district at Kalanaur, where the Hindu kings of Lahore used to be crowned. He was on campaign against Sher Shah's nephew, when word came of his father's death. He was crowned at once, on February 14, 1556, seated on a brick throne which still stands in its desolate garden. The first miniature of him, painted a year later, shows a rugged boy in a flaring lavender coat, golden-sashed, wearing high yellow boots and a curving sword. On his head is a turban set with an aigrette, and a curl hangs down his cheek. He is smelling a flower.

He was not actually heir to much. Humayon left him little more than the gesture of the pod of musk.

The fourteen-year-old boy on the throne at Kalanaur was simply entered in the competition to win northern India, a distracted and ill-governed country, where famine was emaciating the thousands who had lived in the path of armies. Against him were the heirs of the Sur dynasty, and also an upstart Hindu general named Hemu, formerly in their service, who now set up for himself as a king in Delhi. Akbar had only a precarious claim to certain parts of the Punjab. Even his small army, under faithful Bairam Khan, was not necessarily to be trusted. His seat on the throne was as delicately balanced and swaying as his seat on any of his wild horses or elephants.

But for the first four years of his reign, the boy apparently paid little attention to India. It was a strange country to him -- he had lived always in Afghanistan. He was not like his grandfather Babur, alert at twelve, with a sense of his own need to save a beloved homeland. Akbar's personality, until he was twenty, was strange and hidden. Abul Fazl's phrase was 'behind the veil.' Full of sports and animals, his mind was maturing, but he gave no sign. He left affairs in the hands of Bairam Khan. But, in rejecting all formal training, he was finding his own touch directly with life.

Possibly he might have exerted himself if Bairam Khan had been worthless. But the fine, solid old general worked for him, automatically as a steam roller, crushing opposition in logical progression.

This was the situation in India at Akbar's enthronement. Kabul in Afghanistan, under his younger brother Mirza Hakim, was practically independent. Kashmir, the Sind, and Baluchistan were free. Bengal, under ruffian Afghan chiefs, had been clear of Delhi for two centuries. Malwa and Gujarat were independent Moslem states. In Rajputana, the Rajput princes who had bowed to Babur had regained many of their fortresses. In the wild Gondwana regions, in what are now the Central Provinces, there were local chieftains. The Deccan Plateau, which the Moslems of Delhi had taken from the Hindus, had split into five strong Moslem states. From the Deccan to the southern tip of India the last great Hindu kingdom was at the height of its glory — Vijayanagar.

And in little bites on the west coast, and most proudly at Goa, the Portuguese ruled, and controlled all ships up and down the Arabian Sea, and forced annoyed Mohammedans to use passports stamped with the pictures of Jesus and Mary.

Akbar, the rebellious schoolboy, in his Punjab foothold, had far to go. Bairam Khan went steadily to work, first against Hemu, who had had himself crowned at Delhi as Vikramaditya — spotting the name. When, in the famine of 1555–56, starving people turned cannibal, Hemu let them die like flies, while he fed big supplies of rice and sugar and butter to his five hundred elephants. Hemu was fortunately shot in the battle of Panipat, and his followers saw no point in fighting after the paymaster was finished. It is said that Akbar had been at the rear of this battle, and that Bairam Khan told him to come forward to finish unconscious Hemu, thereby winning the title of Ghazi—'Slayer of an Infidel.' Victorious Akbar made a state entry into Delhi. The dazed inhabitants, who saw one king shifted for another, probably were too dulled to feel much. If any boldly original had questioned, he might not have been encouraged when Akbar's army built the usual commendable tower of heads of the dead.

Bairam Khan cleared the field of the heirs of the Sur dynasty, and made Akbar free of rival claimants in India. He added parcels of states. Gwalior surrendered to him, Ajmer, and Jaunpur.

Until Akbar was eighteen, he was very much under the influence both of Bairam Khan, who gave him his pocket money, and the women of the household, who had come down from Kabul in 1557, comforting Akbar by the reunion. These two influences became rival. The women decided to be rid of Bairam Khan.

A curious household system prevailed then. Babies were suckled by wet-nurses up to the age of three or even five; and these nurses, high-born women to care for the princelings, might gain an unholy ascendency over the child. Their own sons became foster-brothers of the baby — a relationship considered strong and binding. Akbar's chief nurse was Maham Anaga, a cunning woman who played upon his devotion and carefully inculcated respect. Her own obstreperous son was named Adham Khan. These two were the most conspicuous, but not the only wire-pullers among the foster-relatives.

Maham Anaga, working with Akbar's own mother Hamida, decided to be rid of Bairam Khan. Her ideas were congenial to the eighteen-year-old king, who was too much checked by the inelasticity and stubborn if faithful dominance of his general. It was a delicate matter to intrigue against the man who commanded both the army and the treasury. But the women manœuvred to get Akbar to well-fortified Delhi, whence the boy sent a letter to his guardian, his first declaration of independence.

> As I was fully assured of your honesty and fidelity, I left all important affairs of state in your charge, and thought only of my own pleasures. I have now determined to take the reins of government in my own hands, and it is desirable that you should make the pilgrimage to Mecca, upon which you have been so long intent.

Bairam Khan could only comply. But, unfortunately, Akbar did not quite leave him his dignity, sending an inferior officer to see that he left the borders. The old general was goaded into brief rebellion, was captured and forgiven by Akbar, and went on toward Mecca and his death.

About this time, Akbar, after a cup or two of wine, mounted an elephant called 'Like the Wind' — a wicked, vicious brute, whom he forced to go through all sorts of manœuvres. That being not excitement enough, he set his mount against another elephant named 'Tiger in Battle,' which ran, with Akbar's maddened beast after it. They plunged down the steep bank of the Jumna River and over a pontoon bridge. The boats swayed and went down under water beneath the impact of their weight. His excited servants jumped into the Jumna and swam alongside futilely to help. Miraculously across, the escaping elephants still ran wildly, but Akbar, suddenly using his power, brought 'Like the Wind' to a stop. This mad exhibition of force he linked in his strange mind with his sense of dependence on God. Later, he explained that he hoped God might end his life, if he had 'knowingly taken a step displeasing to the Most High. For we cannot support the burden of life under God's displeasure.'

Although he paid no attention to formal affairs of state, Akbar was studying people, talking to all sorts, questioning ascetics and fakirs, 'restless in his search for physicians of the soul.' He used to stroll out, like Haroun al Rashid, disguised, at night. Once in a dense crowd he saw a man recognize him, so he quickly made faces and squinted his eyes, and got away before the observer could be certain.

Now Adham Khan, the foster-brother, rose to power. He went as Akbar's general to conquer Malwa in 1560, and did it insolently, with rough jokes while prisoners were slaughtered, and outrages to women. Also, he did not send the spoils and the women to Akbar. The indifferent young king suddenly roused himself, galloped from Agra to Malwa in the hot season, so fast that Maham Anaga's swiftest messengers had no chance to warn her son. He recovered the women and then rode back, thirty-eight days in all. But he left one brutality unpunished. Adham Khan had managed to secrete two lovely ladies, who, his mother feared, might tell of his treachery. She quietly had them killed, for 'a severed head makes no sound,' as she prudently put it. Abul Fazl commented that Akbar overlooked this gross outrage, as 'the veil was not yet removed from his world-illuminating countenance, and he regarded the done as not done.'

Finally, Akbar turned on Adham Khan with the swiftness and force with which he set upon a tiger, and in so doing cleared away the cobwebs of harem intrigue and the abnormal power of Maham Anaga, who practically thought herself prime minister and appointed thievish underlings of unctuous embezzlements. She did not like a certain minister whom Akbar had appointed, and rowdy Adham Khan simply walked up to him in the palace and stabbed him dead. Then he tried to rush into Akbar's room, and, when Akbar snatched a scimitar and asked what he meant, grasped the king's sword. Akbar with one blow of his fist knocked him senseless, then told attendants to throw him from the terrace. When the timid attendants only half-killed him the first time, he made them drag him up and throw him to his death.

From that time there was no veil over Akbar's face. He acted entirely from within, which was fortunate for India, as he was greater than any adviser. He listened to advice and arguments and considered what men and women had to say. But neither harem intrigue nor the judgment of ministers made his decisions. As his grandfather remarked, 'Save my own heart, I have found no faithful friend.'

But he emerged from the veil, in his early twenties, with profound bitterness of spirit. Gloom was always his to be contended with. There is one suggestion that he was epileptic. In any event, some dark spirit connected itself with his religion, his sense of final personal inadequacy, and 'lack of spiritual provision for his last journey.' A wild and haunting need to feel his connection with an eternal God took many forms — a sudden focus into ecstasy or a squandering in trivial rituals.

Gloom drove him also into headlong diversions. One means of distraction was women. He was amorous, and in his youth did not care by what means he added desired ladies to his harem. At twenty-one he was scheming to take certain high-born Delhi wives from their husbands, when a well-placed arrow-shot in his shoulder brought him to his senses. He was never involved in scandal again — though he scarcely needed to be, with a zenana of five thousand women. Unlike his father and grandfather, his son and grandson, each capable of one great love among the lesser, he was passionate without any known outstanding devotion to one woman. His great interest and energy flowed outward toward his multifarious, bright-coloured, somnolent India.

The effect of an unconventional education is that one does not mind breaking tradition. Akbar's tradition was to treat Hindus as despicable infidels, who should be thankful to pay Moslems to be allowed to live. His forceful departure from this was his great originality and the key to his rule of India — the idea of treating all his subjects alike, and fairly. It was astute, it was enlightened selfishness, since the vast majority of his subjects were Hindus. He saw, with a great clarity of mind, that a firm government rests on the well-being of the governed. But the policy seemed to begin in some sympathy and fairness of his own nature.

For when he was twenty-one, he noticed a group of Hindu pilgrims all paying their coins to worship at a certain shrine. The tax on non-Moslem religious pilgrims was a regular source of income. The realization of it offended Akbar. He ordered the tax abolished, though it lost millions of rupees to his treasury — for India is always rich in pilgrims to shrines. The boy said it was contrary to the will of God to tax people assembled to worship, even though erroneously, the Creator.

At twenty-two he broke tradition again, and stopped the poll tax on Hindus, which had been a twist of justice for centuries. It was a loss to his treasury, but a gain to his strength.

He began to give high government office to Hindus, although not in proportion to their numbers. His court was essentially foreign, mostly families who had come to India with Humayon or later. And he appointed only twenty-one Hindus in the course of forty years to important place. Yet the presence of a few strong Hindu advisers flattered their people and strengthened him. He also began a policy of state marriages with Rajput princesses. A monogamous prince is very limited when he tries this, and can conciliate only one state, but Akbar could do it fluently. Such marriage was supposedly forbidden and despised by both Rajput and Moslem. But Akbar, marrying the Princess of Amber won the support of men of her family, Bhagwin Singh and Man Singh — two strong arms at his side. Later he married princesses of the desert states Bikaner and Jessalmer, adding more fighting Rajputs to his banner. The House of the Sun of Chitor, however, boasted that they never lowered themselves to give a daughter to a Mogul emperor.

One cannot compute the influence of his first Rajput wife, if intelligent and graceful and charming, as she more than likely was by her whole tradition, by her rich dyed veils and enamelled jewels, the caste mark on her forehead, her hennaed hands and toes, and her docile quickness of admiration. More than likely she had her share in interesting Akbar's grasping mind in the ways of her people. Fundamentally he wanted to know and to understand.

This primary policy of tolerance built the Mogul dynasty so sturdily that it held its strength for a hundred years after his death. Before him, the invading Moslems had assumed that the country was a milch cow to be drained, feeding the fewest straws to keep the animal alive. Akbar's originality lay in the idea that to feed the cow more generously might make it produce more milk. The principle held true in the animal world which he had understood as a boy. Complete altruism was not his. First catch the cow, then get all the milk you can (the hordes of his treasure and jewels when he died were staggering). But, if the cow is treated gently, and fed well, she will yield more.

First catch the cow. Young Akbar set out upon a steady and logical course of warfare in India, grabbing, with little pretext, more and more independent states. From his unsteady throne at Kalanaur he expanded his rule, until at his death he held Afghanistan, Baluchistan, and Kashmir, and all India as far south as the Deccan, where he had begun by conquering two states. Power was his intention — to subdue the beast India as he had once subdued horses and elephants. Once mastered, he handled it wisely.

'A monarch,' said Akbar, 'should be ever intent upon conquest, otherwise his neighbours rise in arms against him.'

The stories of battles grow monotonous — a mere list of hideous

AKBAR AT HOME

suffering, the tactics of elephants and men and guns. But some of Akbar's campaigns were striking: the swift camel ride to Gujarat, the river sail to Bengal, the great slow stately camp on the way to Kabul, and his last battle in old age against impregnable Asirgarh, a matter of money bags. A conqueror, by the mere effrontery of his selfishness, often achieves a dignity. Akbar's kingdom went marching on.

A good queen was ruling in the wild Gondwana country, a queen of the ancient Chandel House. She was an able Amazon, a general famous for her cavalry and five thousand elephants, a generous woman and wise ruler. There was no reason for attacking her. She defended her home well. Twice wounded, she led the charge against Akbar on her big elephant, and when she was defeated, killed herself. Her country went to Akbar. He added it to his map.

There was scarcely more pretext for going after Chitor in 1567, except the challenge of its pride and strength. Chitor, first sacked by Ala-ud-din, then by the King of Gujarat, was again in the hands of the Princes of the Sun.

Akbar stretched his camp for ten miles in a siege of four months. He oversaw batteries and mines, and the casting of a cannon which could throw a ball weighing forty pounds. But it was not this that took Chitor. Akbar chanced to see a man in a chief's cuirass busy directing defences. He aimed his musket, and the man did not reappear, but he had no idea of the effect of his single shot, the horror and despair. In less than an hour his men saw smoke rising in several places and realized that it came from the burning of women. His shot had killed Jaimall, the commander. Why, when the Rajputs had such courage that Jaimall's widow armed herself and her son's young bride with lances, and in saffron robes fought beside the men until death, why a courageous city assumed defeat at the loss of its commander is hard to understand. But it was traditional. The fall of a leader in India was always deciding the fate of enormous numbers of men. One would think they would build caves for their leaders and strong-boxes. But they never learned.

When Chitor accepted defeat, nine queens and five princesses and three hundred other Rajput women went to the pyre heaped with wood and grass and covered with clarified butter. When Akbar climbed the walled lane to enter the city, eight thousand Rajputs, vowed to death, rushed at him and fell fighting. Forty thousand peasants had helped during the siege. Akbar's huge temper, usually controlled, was excited by such resistance. He ordered their massacre, and killed about thirty thousand. They say that he estimated how many Hindus had died by collecting and weighing the sacred threads which the twice-born men wear. He took back to Agra the fortress gates and the big kettledrums that had sounded for miles the comings and goings of the princes. After this bitter waste, Chitor became a place accursed. and its eight centuries of shifting glory were ended.

After the burst of hatred or policy in which Akbar had slaughtered the humble Rajput followers, he turned the warm sun of his nature toward such as were left. He was honourably generous and flattering. He set up at the palace at Agra fine statues of Chitor's heroes, Jaimall and Patta, good enemies who had had the courtesy to lose. Colonel Tod wrote, 'He finally succeeded in healing the wounds his ambition had afflicted, and received from millions that meed of praise which no other of his race ever obtained.'

When he took Ranthambhor, for instance (and that is a picturesque story, walking up himself disguised as a mace-bearer to look over the Rajah), he made generous terms. So long as the Rajah recognized Akbar as overlord and gave up his fort, he could govern fifty-two districts, have the kettledrums beaten to announce him as far as the Red Gate, enter Akbar's hall of audience completely armed, and need not prostrate himself before Akbar. He need not lose face by serving under another Hindu, nor brand his horses with the imperial flower, nor give a bride to the royal harem. That shrewd consideration won loyalty.

When Akbar had reduced the four fortresses that gave control of Hindustan, he turned next toward Gujarat in the west, the richest state in India, touching the Arabian Sea at ports lively with commerce. Ahmadabad, its capital, was one of the fine cities of the world. Gujarat was then divided among seven warring kings, one guileless enough to ask Akbar for help. He came, and conquered. He saw the sea for the first time in his life. He saw Portuguese merchants also for the first time, and asked many questions about the wonders of Portugal, and the manners and customs of Europe. He came to a dead end against their naval squadron, ready to help certain rebels — so he made terms with their viceroy.

After he had conquered and apparently settled Gujarat, he showed his hard-hitting arm and adaptability. Usually he marched with a cumbersome camp in traditional Indian slowness, hunting as he went. But when Gujarat rose in an overwhelming rebellion, he struck with speed, though his army was tired out, his equipment shredded, and he disliked to waste money. Under an August sun that makes English soldiers wear spine-pads as well as cork helmets, Akbar rode a swift camel fifty miles without stopping. Perhaps his prenatal ride had conditioned him. Varying with a horse, or light cart, he went six hundred miles in eleven days. The rebels at Ahmadabad heard his trumpets, but could not believe it was Akbar. He would not let his weary men wait. He spurred his horse across the river and led a hand-to-hand fight, so wildly that once he was left on a wounded horse with only two troopers. He forced his three thousand men against the city's twenty thousand, reduced to such terror that Akbar's men reached into the quivers on their backs and shot them with their own arrows.

Akbar made a pyramid of the heads of the dead rebels and was back at Fathpur Sikri in forty-three days from the time he had left, riding proudly through the red sandstone gates, spear in hand. Gujarat stayed conquered.

The court had been living at Agra, which was then a fine city, fertile on its wide pale loop of river, with lovely gardens and a wealth of merchandise, and palaces of cunningly joined stones. There was no reason to desert it — except the ghosts. Father Montserrate said the ghosts were terrible in the fort at Agra, 'ghosts which rushed to and fro, tore everything to pieces, terrified the women and children, threw stones, and finally began to hurt everyone.' 'Then the cruel spite of the Evil One killed two of the king's newborn sons.'

Akbar grieved sharply over the loss of the infants, distressed that he had no durable heir. A holy wise man, Sheikh Salim Chishti, living as a hermit among the stones and wild beasts of the desert Sikri, promised Akbar a son if he would come to live near him. When the Rajput Princess of Amber actually gave birth there to his son Salim, Akbar decided, in 1569 (according to Abul Fazl), 'to give outward splendour to this spot which possessed spiritual grandeur.'

He began to build with a passion. Sometimes nothing would satisfy him but to quarry the stones himself. That was part of his insatiable curiosity and energy; he might have a whim for shearing camels, hewing wood, or hammering iron, as zealously as if it were his life-work. Akbar, without his terrific will to unify himself, easily could have been a jack-of-all-trades. The strange red city rose with fantastic speed. Both Moslem and Hindu architects worked at its design, Akbar advising, and the buildings admirably blended the two styles. He built schools and large public baths and gardens and mosques and houses for all sorts of people, as well as the court palaces. And to the north he made an artificial lake, six miles long, whose breezes at sundown cooled the tense air.

After about fifteen years he deserted his city, capriciously as one might drop a fan. Some say the Holy Saint tired of hearing the city noises, and that Akbar, always deferential, moved it away to leave him in quiet. Others claim that when the dam of the great lake burst, the city lacked sufficient water supply — but the court lived there three years after the lake had gone. Another reason may have been that, after 1585, Akbar found it prudent to live in the Punjab to watch the inevitable Afghan frontier.

However it may have been, for the fifteen years of its life, Fathpur Sikri was a sumptuous stage, a city bigger than London of that day. Here Akbar lived in his prime; from these gates he set out for great campaigns, and within its rooms he worked out his system for governing India, and toiled his way through religious disputes. Here the fine carts went past, carved and gilded and covered with silk or cloth, drawn by little bulls. Merchants came from Persia and all India, and the twenty-three-mile road between Agra and Fathpur Sikri was a continuous bazaar, selling drugs and spices, pearls and civet, cotton cloth, cloth of gold, woollen woven soft in Kashmir, carpets, velvets, wrought metal, and silks that museums would love to see.

In Fathpur Sikri the artists of the Mogul school were painting their miniature portraits, fusing Hindu and Persian art. And hordes of binders and gilders were working under the direction of these painters — and the calligraphers who ranked as equal artists — to make the beautiful books for Akbar's library.

In the stables stood five thousand elephants, ready to march, with heads covered with iron mail, with a sword attached to the trunk, and a dagger to each tusk; each elephant fed and scratched and tended by his own four servants. Here were lodged the tame deer, and the trained camels, and the elephants that dance. Here strolled groups of profligate men, dressed and jewelled like women. Here were grounds where polo was played, after sunset by lighted balls of Akbar's devising. Here elephants waited to fight, and gladiators to die, to amuse Akbar out of his gloom.

Here was the royal zenana, a town in itself, housing more than five thousand women. Each harem lady had her separate apartments and servants, and all was guarded in concentric circles, first by female guards, then by eunuchs, then by trusted Rajputs, and finally by other troops on all four sides.

Akbar's enormous household was managed in finest order by heads of departments who were great courtiers and perhaps personal friends — the master of the kitchen, of water, of the stables, and so on, all serving under a palace commandant, through whose hands all orders passed. And the courtiers imitated the emperor's splendour. One had his flagging appetite tempted by a thousand rich dishes daily. Another flared the city streets to light by his five hundred torch-bearers.

Daily, before the sun was up, a crowd gathered to see Akbar. He would appear unfailingly at dawn, a burly man strongly built, with a horseman's legs under his gold-threaded brocade coat. Under his bright-coloured turban the jewels hung on his brow, and his eyes twinkled and flashed like the sun on waves. If he laughed, his whole face contorted with mirth. He was clean-shaven except for a moustache; his nose was small and straight, with wide mobile nostrils. He radiated energy. He could be charmingly winning in manner, affable, genial, without losing the impassable dignity of a king. He might bend to take up some poor trifle that a peasant had offered, and hold it to his breast like a treasure, while he only looked from the corner of his eye at the rich gift of a nobleman. There were bells on the palace gate which any suppliant might ring, to get his attention. But it was advisable to have a matter worth his while.

At his formal audience, eight great officers presented the suppliants, who prostrated themselves and kissed his feet. If he felt only slightly gracious, he leaned forward and touched their necks — even when a king offered fifty camels trapped in green and crimson velvet and treasure worth thousands of crowns. Akbar never gave back the velvet-hung camels or the jewels. But he appreciated and was touched by simple honesty and high-mindedness when it came before him.

At Fathpur Sikri, Akbar evolved his final scheme for administering India — the assessment and taxation system which was rescued from oblivion by Warren Hastings, and even today is followed in some provinces. The record-room at Fathpur Sikri had its red sandstone shelves full of manuscripts on the details of administering India.

If Akbar's first great aim was tolerance, his second was the direct relation between subject and state or emperor. He tried to end feudalism — the system of letting middlemen control districts, squeeze what they could from the peasants, and return what they chose to the crown. He could not entirely succeed. Many places he had to leave under the feudal jagirdars — landholders, or kings or chiefs, as in the present Indian states. South of Bombay the country was mostly governed by nobles with freedom to act as they chose, so long as they came to court to do homage to the emperor, bring gifts, and help him in wars. At the height of his power Akbar had twenty such salaaming princes. But when he could, he collected taxes directly through salaried tax-collectors. Graft had been rampant and palms were still sticky. The position of jagirdar was popular, but the position of direct tax-collector was called 'rotten,' as it was not so enriching.

Akbar appointed sound and brilliant ministers. He did not need to be surrounded by puppets to keep his pride. He was under no compulsion to have any advisers, but he chose great men. He chose them capriciously, depending upon his own digging insight into character.

Among his 'nine jewels' were Rajah Birbal, the witty Hindu whose palace still stands in Fathpur Sikri — a trinket in sandstone; Tansen the musician, who adapted Hindu music to his ears; Todar Mall, the Hindu finance minister; and the Mohammedan family who strongly supported Akbar's policy of tolerance — sceptical old Sheikh Mubharak and his sons, Faizi the poet, and Abul Fazl, the king's 'Jonathan,' whose honesty contrasted with the treachery frequent in courts.

Rajah Todar Mall worked out a fiscal system, following brilliant Sher Shah, who, in five wild years' rule at Delhi, had begun an administration directly subordinate to the crown, and had surveyed the villages. First India must be measured, and a device for accuracy which Akbar introduced was a bamboo rod, fitted with iron rings. Before that, anyone who tried to survey India had done it with hempen ropes, which shrank when wet. The picture of Todar Mall's underlings laboriously measuring the Punjab and other provinces with bamboo rods, inching over the map of India, is too wearying. But it was done. A large part of conquered India was surveyed.

The crops were recorded in detail. The lands were classified, not by soil or irrigation, but as land continuously ploughed or left fallow. The ten-year average produce was made the basis for tax, with elaborately differing rates for each crop. Abul Fazl kept bulky statistics in the record-room at Fathpur Sikri. The tax was about one third the average gross produce. Though a peasant was supposed to have a rebate in a crop disaster, the humble man had a slow time collecting. There were certain difficulties and shortcomings, but for the peasant and his fields, the system was far better than the 'squeeze.'

Akbar's whole government was essentially military. About sixteen hundred officials — commanders of ten horse, up to commanders of five thousand — were paid huge salaries, even as salaries go today, from which they theoretically supplied their number of men and horses, pack-mules or elephants. A commander of one thousand had a salary reckoned three times the pay of a lieutenant-governor in India in 1914. These commanders were, interchangeably, generals, governors, masters of the royal household, or attendants at court. By 1580, Akbar had divided the empire into twelve viceroyal states, whose governors were also commanders-in-chief and supreme court judges.

There was no civil law in India — only religious law, Moslem or Hindu. There were no lawyers, but scholars versed in the Koran or Hindu Shastras. Akbar advised a judge to trust primarily to his own knowledge of psychology, for, he said, 'from the excessive depravity of human nature and its covetousness, no dependence can be placed on a witness or his oath.' He discouraged cruel punishments. He had no love of torture, and when he himself ordered a death penalty, wanted to be reminded three times — to check a tempestuous impulse. Regular penalties included impalements, trampling by elephants, a hand cut off for robbery, or strangling and crucifixion for highwaymen and adulterers; but 'the light of clemency and mildness shone forth from this prince.'

A city was a little despotism. The kotwal, appointed its chief, was police commissioner, revenue collector, chief of secret service, and judge. He kept registers of houses and people, watched strangers, and tried to carry out Akbar's special ordinances, such as the prevention of suttee against a woman's will. In a distant town a kotwal could do as he pleased; everything depended on his favour, and the scope of bribery was large. But on the whole travellers were favourably impressed by the order in towns.

The chief aim of the system was to collect enough money to maintain an army sufficient to keep Akbar in power.

His people either were enormously rich or raggedly poor. The raggedly poor, of course, had few needs — a mud or palm-leaf hut, a little grain, and a rag of cotton cloth. They could shiver, starve, and be drenched, certainly — and suddenly sicken and die; but a wretchedly poor person could get on in India more simply than elsewhere. There were no middle classes. Professions, such as law, secular teaching, engineering, had not developed. Learned men attached themselves to the court for patronage. The rich were the merchants who took the hazards of precious caravans, the tax-collecting jagirdars, and the great commanders of the court, much bejewelled and becamelled and fanned and fed.

Akbar, the sharp-striking soldier, the administrator who held a thousand trifles in his mind, the sportsman and builder, in time gave rein to the mystic urge in himself. He felt an infrequent mood when he could cast the world aside and turn anchorite. He had a sense of oneness with the Crèator. He did not know, in his later doubting days, which name to give to God, which life-history or which ritual, but apparently he always felt his dependence.

He had flashes of a philosopher's dispassionate searching for truth. He said once, 'Discourses on philosophy have such a charm for me that they distract me from all else, and I forcibly restrain myself from listening to them, lest the necessary duties of the hour should be neglected.'

After his campaign to Bengal, his religious interest took strange outward form. The campaign had been masterly. He went after a rebel general in the rainy season, when no well-tutored Indian army thinks of fighting until after the autumn Dasahara Festival. He sailed down the Ganges in Cleopatra-like splendour, in barges planted with beautiful gardens, and carrying two fighting elephants and the females to soothe them, while the army followed ashore so accurately that the land and river forces met at the appointed day and place. Over the flooded Ganges near Patna, many miles wide, and hiding the drowned columns of Asoka's city, Akbar fought, captured the town that supplied the rebel army and left his commanders to do the rest.

When Bengal was conquered, he had, for the first time in his life, no important enemy in the known world. He felt a surge of immense gratitude. He spent whole nights in praising God, and 'from a feeling of thankfulness for his past successes he would sit many a morning alone in prayer and meditation on a large flat stone of an old building which lay near the palace in a lovely spot, with his head bent over his chest, gathering the bliss of the early hours of dawn.'

Later, in 1578, when he had ordered a great hunt in the Punjab, and his beaters were converging from a circle forty miles in circumference, driving all the game toward him for ten days, he suddenly commanded the hunt to stop, lest so much as the feather of a finch be hurt. No one could tempt him out of his trance. 'A strange and strong frenzy came upon the emperor,' said Badaoni; and Abul Fazl declared he was 'nearly abandoning this state of struggle, and entirely gathering up the skirt of his genius from earthly pomp.' For, 'A sublime joy took possession of his bodily frame. The attraction of cognition of God cast its ray.' He cut off his hair, and gave gold to the poor. As this state continued, strange rumours of his mood and wonderful lies spread among the people, and hopeful insurrections began. But 'in a short space of time he, by God-given strength, turned his face to the outer world and attended to indispensable matters.'

His religious concern became intellectual. He saw that good, wise, and pious men disagreed as to the truth, so he built a House of Worship to find it by discussion. Being still an orthodox Mussulman, he invited at first only Moslems, sheikhs, sayyids, doctors of Islamic law, and certain nobles. There they discussed abstruse problems from after sunset of a Thursday until noon the next day, with the untired Akbar usually presiding over the liberal-minded and the bigots. Sheikh Mubharak asked why the emperor should not be arbiter of all spiritual disputes — pope as well as king? A heady thought. The orthodox mullahs signed a document giving spiritual leadership to Akbar, in 1579.

The debates in the House of Worship grew acid, and Akbar saw no freshness or truth. 'Although I am master of so vast a kingdom,' he said wearily, 'and all the appliances of government are at my hand, yet, since true greatness consists in doing the will of God, my mind is not at ease in this diversity of sects and creeds; and apart from the outward pomp of circumstances, with what satisfaction, in my despondency, can I undertake the sway of empire? I await the coming of some discreet man of principle who will solve the difficulties of my conscience.'

His attention recently had been caught by the Portuguese Jesuits of Goa. For there had been a conscientious Jesuit, unknown and thinking himself unheeded, who had refused to shrive parishioners who falsified their taxes. A religion which taught such detached honesty appealed. When Akbar met various Portuguese, he asked about the unknown Christian theology, but never of a sufficiently learned mind to satisfy his keen inquiry. Finally he asked the Viceroy of Goa to send Christian scholars to him.

So the good Jesuit fathers, Aquaviva and Montserrate, travelled from their dense green Goa, crowned by Vasco da Gama's castle, on inlets of iridescent bay. They bobbed in little boats over water like a peacock's tail, up to the port of Surat, then rode for about two months as part of a motley caravan of travellers under the ripe sun, sleeping in caravanserais, sometimes in beds beset by scorpions, or under the placid cooling stars. They left Goa in November, and not until the end of February did they reach Fathpur Sikri.

It would be a feather in the cap of the Jesuits, of Portugal, of all Christian sixteenth-century Europe, to convert the 'most mightie and invincible' Akbar.

When the fathers saw from a distance the walls of Fathpur Sikri, they gave thanks to God. 'They then began to gaze with the keenest delight upon the great size and magnificent appearance of the city. On entering the city, they became the cynosure of all eyes on account of their strange attire. Everyone stopped and stared in great surprise and perplexity, wondering who these strange-looking, unarmed men might be, with their long black robes, their curious caps, their shaven faces, and their tonsured heads.'

Akbar welcomed them — guardedly at first. When the fathers were refreshed, they gave him a Bible, written in four languages. He kissed it courteously and put it to his head. Then he led the priests to his private room, where he opened the books 'with reverence and joy,' and put them in beautiful cases. Perhaps these were the ministers of the soul whom he sought.

At night he held the first debate between the Christians and the Moslems — tonsured, black-robed Portuguese and white-turbaned Indians. All courtesy and careful precedent were observed, but there were knife thrusts for the favour, or the soul, of Akbar, who presided, fascinated and shrewd. The debate was, said Father Montserrate, on 'the accuracy and authority of the gospel versus the lies and vanities of the Koran.' At the end, the jewel-browed emperor said to the Jesuits, 'You have proved your case entirely to my satisfaction, and I am very well pleased with the religion contained in your law; but I should advise you to be cautious in speech and action, for your opponents are unscrupulous villains.' As a matter of fact, Akbar himself needed to be cautious at this time, for a rebellion was mounting like a low breaker. He spoke as politician, but continued as inquirer: 'Now I want more enlightenment on these points — how the Most High can be both three and one, and how can He have a son, a man born of a Virgin? For these ideas are entirely beyond my comprehension.' The fathers did not answer him squarely on these points. They told him to pray God for enlightenment.

At one point the Moslems saw themselves worsted, and suggested an ordeal by fire — a Moslem to walk through flames carrying the Koran, and a Christian carrying the Bible, the one who came through unscorched proved truthful. Akbar, weary of arguments for the night, urged this dramatic spectacle — as good as an elephant fight. But Father Aquaviva was shocked. Akbar should not be a miracle-hunter. Although the Jesuits would gladly die a thousand times, it was against their principles to ask God for a miracle. 'An evil and adulterous generation seeketh a sign,' he said.

Akbar had a point to gain. 'God forbid that I should have summoned you in order that you might suffer a calamity.' He wanted primarily to punish a certain insufferable Moslem. Still the Jesuits refused. 'I only want you to say you will undergo it,' argued Akbar. 'I myself will loudly announce it.' The priest, unarmed and untended in the powerful king's empire, said, with fine courage, 'We shall as publicly declare that we will do no such thing... if this man deserves punishment, what need is there of adopting this roundabout and disingenuous course in committing him to the flames?'

The first Jesuits were high-minded and transparently sincere. They worked and split hairs to uphold their tenets. They stood ready to die, and their sincerity held Akbar's respect. He allowed them to take him to task about his sins, the cruel gladiatorial combats where men fought to kill, the lewd degenerates on his streets, and finally, his harem. The priests actually told Akbar that he should keep only one wife. 'The rest are all courtesans and adulteresses, whom it is wickedness to retain.' Akbar listened, but did not diminish his harem. Such of his wives as heard of the fathers' bold stand undoubtedly used their connivance against the Christians.

The Fathers' bold vision — of persuading Akbar from his pomp and indulgence by the power of thought — was not impossible. Akbar approved — detachedly — their zeal for poverty and chastity, and was 'strongly attracted to a life of devotion and renunciation of worldly affairs.' With kindness and affection he said he wished Christians to live freely in his empire. But until 1602, he did not give Jesuits a written order, which they had long sought, to convert his subjects.

He experimented with a Christian education for his second son, Prince Murad, making Father Montserrate tutor to the docile, bright little boy, and frightening the child by telling Montserrate to punish him at need. Little Murad, of Persian and Mongolian and Turkish blood, accordingly spent his days learning Christian doctrine and writing a copy-book of pious Jesuit sentiments. He died a drunkard.

Akbar's flirtation with Christianity stirred the powerful resentment of the orthodox Moslems, fanatic always. In 1580, he faced a crisis of empire. The revolt and general discontent in India was focussed by a man named Shah Mansur, whom Akbar had raised from a clerk in the perfume department to be vizier. He was a strict and dogmatic Moslem and a strict and dogmatic accountant. His stern honesty in reforming the cavalry made him most unpopular, so that some of the stories of his treason may have been invented. But he was offended by Akbar's freedom, and led the clerical party of discontent, which could easily have flamed into a general revolt. He wrote to Akbar's half-brother in Kabul, 'Come avenge the insults being heaped upon Muhammad.'

Mirza Muhammad Hakim, viceroy of Kabul, was a bigot and a sot. He was glad to take advantage of the unrest in India to invade.

Akbar's power hung in the balance. The cat of India's loyalty might jump either way. He lifted the unwieldy mass of army into action and marched toward Kabul. He took Shah Mansur along with him as a precaution, but was deeply disturbed when, upon more seeming proof of treason, he had to execute him. And he also took, along with soldiers and harem and bazaars and jugglers, Father Montserrate.

Mounted scouts rode ahead to clear a wide swath of emptiness before the slow march of his army, armoured elephants with turrets on their backs, mounted archers and pikemen and cavalry. On the first of the slow-stepping elephants rode the trumpeters and drummers, all silent but one drummer, who sounded his deep note at slow intervals. Townspeople ran to the balconies and roofs to look. The emperor, alert and powerful and splendid of himself, was followed by cavalry reining to slow pace, and elephants. A strange group of five hundred old men, dignified and venerable as a Greek chorus, drove all comers from the road before the queens, hidden as mummies in brightly painted houdahs on elephants. Camels carried their ladies-in-waiting, each under a large umbrella. Pack-elephants bore the treasury, and endless creaking baggage-carts and mules filled the dusty distance.

Beyond his own frontiers, Akbar sent heralds ahead to say that no one who remained peaceful would be harmed. He bound many small kings into loyalty by bribes or promises. At sight of his huge army, almost anyone was ready to agree.

To feed the army he offered towns exemption from taxes and imposts if they would sell provisions cheaply. This seemed to rob one treasury chest to pay into another, but it made prices low in the camp bazaars. The king and each great noble had his own bazaar, managed by nomad tribes following camp.

At night Akbar's immense white pavilion was pitched in a pleasant spot, and the tents of princes and nobles, grouped in definite order. Peace and rest could settle on all, for the king posted three hundred scouts at a radius of eighteen miles, a guard of watchfulness.

The flower of Akbar's army was the cavalry, with officers from Kandahar and Baluchistan and the Kabul Valley as well as Mongols, Persians and Turks, and the Rajputs, whom he trusted. These officers maintained their own troops from their pay, or the province granted them; each unit had its own mess and was an independent entity. Each fighting man had three or four servants. Akbar kept iron control over all. Once, because an officer had stopped short of finding a certain ford, accepting hearsay instead of observing, he had the man flung into the wild river, bound on an inflated ox-skin. The whole army crowded to see the gasping officer tossed at the mercy of the current, weeping and begging pardon as he swept past the royal tent. Finally Akbar had him rescued, entered in the inventory, and sold as a slave. Later he pardoned him, but he had showed his hand of steel, and the army did not need much of such discipline.

He went on to Kabul, stopping at a saint's birthplace where naked yogis lived, and he himself did reverence with bare feet and loosened hair. He found time to talk again to Father Montserrate, and to ask why the Lord Jesus, who was so anxious to have the Jews believe in him, did not accept their challenge when they told him to come down from the cross. The answer was that mankind needed to learn to have faith, which Akbar heartily approved. But then he wanted to know why Christ let Saint Thomas, who lacked faith, put his fingers into the wounds. He also asked what Christians mean when they say that God the Father has no mortal body, and yet that Christ sat at the right hand of his Father.

Unbridged rivers were difficult things to get armies across. Akbar rested for fifty days before the flooded Indus, swollen by the melting of Himalayan snows — a river so mighty that sailors said it divided the sea for fifty miles with sweet water. His nights were spent in councils of war, his days in hunting, or holding games or shows, while he waited for the river to subside. The Indian custom was to make temporary bridges of boats tied together only by grass ropes, over which was laid a path of branches, bushes, and hay. Usually animals and men perished at each crossing. Akbar ordered each type of troops — cavalry, baggage, archers — to go separately and in single file, so that if a bridge parted, the river took no great toll. And elephants had to swim.

In every detail Akbar was practical, thorough, and prudent, except that he allowed soothsayers to decide by augury or astrology the moment for advance — a thing which Babur called pure foolishness. They told him to send young Prince Murad ahead with experienced generals to face Hakim.

Fortunately, with scarcely a show of battle, brother Mirza Hakim, who had retreated to Kabul, decided to make peace. In about ten months, with little fighting but a mighty threat, the insurrection at home and danger from Kabul was settled. Akbar was thereafter secure to do as he chose in government or religion.

But Father Montserrate might have spared himself the long march to Kabul. Akbar, as he had opportunity, asked why priests were celibate, since God commanded all men to have wives and continue the descent from Adam. He asked details about the last judgment — as an administrator himself; whether Christ would be the judge, and when it would occur — a very literal, practical mind asking for details as definite as pebbles.

Akbar did not wholly accept Christianity. He stumbled against its doctrines of Trinity and the incarnation, and various practical reasons forbade his becoming a Christian. The first Jesuits sadly asked permission to return to Goa. All their sincerity and high tower of arguments had not won great Akbar's soul.

He had been considering other religions. 'For the Gentiles regard their law as good, and so likewise do the Saracens and Christians. To which then should we give our adherence?' he asked.

Sometimes he was thought a Hindu, for he might appear with their sectarian marks on his forehead. He also invited a Jain guru to his court. The holy man walked all the way from Gujarat, according to the rules of his order. After much talk he persuaded the emperor to release prisoners and caged birds, abstain from animal food and hunting. Akbar revived the ancient Buddhist and Jain law that put a man to death for killing an animal. The old guru, conscious of work well done, starved himself to death, in approved Jain fashion.

The emperor had a high opinion of the Sikhs, and when Brahmins complained that they were diverting people from prescribed religious customs, he was pleased when a Sikh said: 'The Brahmins claim to be the equal of God. The guru maketh no such boast, for he knoweth he is God's slave.'

More spectacularly Akbar took Zoroastrian doctrines and ritual from the Parsees. Many said he wore the sacred girdle of the Parsees under his clothes. He accepted the sun as the symbol of divinity, and went through its ritual of worship. He had the sacred Parsee fire kindled in the palace, never to go out, and made his courtiers rise when candles and lamps were brought in at night. Four times a day he repeated the one thousand and fifty names of the sun, telling them on a rosary of jewels. By 1580, while the Christians were still trying to prove their case by logic, he had begun to prostrate himself in public before the sun and fire.

No man quite read his hidden mind. He may have done it all for diplomacy. But testimony agrees that he was sincerely religious. Perhaps each religion appealed to a different side of his nature — Christianity to his integrity, the Jain to his kindness, the Hindu and Parsee to his mystic need to worship, and to something showy and egoistic that was growing in his later years.

In time, in that all-worshipping India, he did not deny himself a share of the puja that his people were ready to give trees and stones and ghosts. When he told the names of the sun, he sat where he could be seen, and the crowd prostrated themselves and adored. Some made vows not to drink or rinse their mouths until they had seen him.

Easy is the descent of an autocrat — the dropsical enlargement of an ego. It would take an amazingly great person to have accomplished all that Akbar had done by mind and muscle, and then to lose himself, to give up the warm vanity, the large happiness of conceit; to subdue a hot, well-fed ego to the discipline of a searcher for truth. Unlikely — and yet, the supreme leap to make, the last test of greatness. Akbar could not quite take that hurdle.

Clearly observant and unbigoted, he saw sensible men, abstemious thinkers, and a supply of miracle-makers in all religions. Why should truth be confined to one? He decided to make an ultimate creed that would contain the best from each. It was partly an administrative idea to unite discordant peoples. 'For in empire,' he said, 'it is a bad thing to have the members divided among themselves and at variance. We ought, therefore, to bring them all in one... with the great advantage of not losing what is good in any one religion, while gaining what is better in another.' A mild and beneficent idea. But he made a magpie's nest of sticks and straws.

The preamble to the new creed, divine monotheism, said that all religions have much in common, and that God and man are one in a mystic sense. Then it continued that people will naturally look to their king — and expect him to be their spiritual leader — for a king possesses, independent of men, the ray of divine wisdom. The religion practically defied the emperor as vice-regent of God; and included the adoration of the sun, and veneration of fire and lights, and the partial prohibition of animal food.

Akbar set out to build a body of religious custom, which without roots soon withers. His ritual had about as much dignity as that of a fraternal lodge. In an initiation ceremony, the novice took his turban in his hands and put his head on the feet of the king. The king extended his hand, raised the suppliant, and put his turban back. The members of the lodge were to greet with the words 'Allahu Akbar' (God is great, or Akbar is God), and to reply 'Jalla Lalaluhu' (Glorious in his glory) — a hint of the radiant sun.

Many rules were ordained between 1583 and 1584 — fantastic and trivial details. If a disciple died, his relatives were to 'hang some uncooked grains and a burnt brick around the neck of the corpse, and burn it at a place where no water was.' Certain regulations were borrowed from Hinduism. Members should abstain from eating flesh; nor should they use the same dishes as butchers, fishers, and birdcatchers. The slaughter of cows had a death penalty. Garlic and onions and beef and beards were prohibited.

Akbar's real tolerance broke down somewhat when he turned against the religion of his childhood with rather pointed insults, slept with his head to the east — because good Mohammedans slept with heads toward the west — would not allow new mosques to be built, forbade the Mohammedan Feast of Ramazan, the prayers and the Mecca pilgrimage.

On the other hand, he was especially lenient to Hindus. A disgruntled courtier, Badaoni, wrote, 'The real object of those who became disciples was to get into office; and though His Majesty did everything to get this out of their heads, he acted very differently in the case of the Hindus, of whom he could not get enough; for the Hindus, of course, are indispensable; to them belongs half the army and half the land.'

In spite of the establishment of his own religion, Akbar twice again invited Jesuits to come to discuss Christianity. Jerome Xavier, the grand-nephew of Saint Francis, came on the third mission. Akbar was cordial. He embraced the images of Jesus and Mary which they brought, and went to the litany service on bended knees and with hands clasped in the Christian attitude. His son Salim, heir to the throne — in gratitude for whom he had moved to Fathpur Sikri — also seemed very devoted to the Christians. Salim had been prince too long.

But if the last Jesuits were encouraged, they soon saw how the land lay. Father Xavier wrote: 'The king has banished Mohammed from his thoughts, and is inclined toward Hinduism, worships God and the Sun, poses as a prophet, wishes it to be understood he works miracles through healing the sick by means of the water in which he washes his feet. Many women make vows to him for the restoration of health to their children, or for sons. The Hindus are in favour just now, and I do not know how the Mohammedans put up with it.'

The last Jesuit mission might well have been bewildered. Neither they nor Akbar had the fine sincerity of the first meeting; each had hidden political motives. Akbar wanted to be rid of Portugal, and the missions were a means of espionage. The fathers, especially of the third mission, were not without guile, and to some extent were acting as political agents for Portugal. They violently opposed an Englishman named John Mildenhall, who came in 1603 soon after the East India Company had got its charter from Queen Elizabeth, and who was trying to get as good terms to trade as the Portuguese. In spite of their machinations and possible attempts to poison, Mildenhall arranged to get his request granted.

Although Akbar finally gave the Jesuits a written order allowing them to convert his subjects, and although he took the fathers with him on his Deccan campaign, there was no hope that he would make his empire Christian, as Asoka had made it Buddhist. Yet this was the nearest that India came to having a layer of Christianity over its older practices.

The same Akbar, whose mind, intricate as a hickory nut, ordered all the absurd regulations and allowed himself to be worshipped, was capable of saying: 'There is no need to discuss the point that a vacuum in nature is impossible. God is omnipresent'; and, 'There exists a bond between the Creator and the creature which is not expressible in language.... Who can sever the attachment of the rational soul to the Supreme Being?'

A king may be the greatest on earth and not escape bitterness. A prudent Mogul emperor father should die suddenly and young. Otherwise disillusionment awaits him from his sons. Gentle Prince Murad, who had written copy-book maxims under kind Father Montserrate, turned insatiable drunkard; the third son, Daniyal, whom Akbar sent to conquer the Deccan, had his dose smuggled in the barrels of muskets, or under men's turbans, till he died. And Salim grew too old waiting. There is a story that he hated his father the more because, when Akbar saw lovely Anarkali of his harem smile at Salim in a mirror, he ordered her walled alive. And Salim lavished his love on her sculptured coffin. Salim was the chief cause of sorrow of great Akbar's latter years.

The campaign to conquer the Deccan was acid — too bad to have it the last taste in the mouth, after the masterly, straightforward conquests of middle age.

Akbar needed to take the impregnable fort of Asirgarh, before he could conquer the Deccan. This fort was on a high mountain guarded by three concentric lines of fortifications, and supplied with water from a living well, and all the wood and vegetables to maintain a garrison of seventy thousand. A king and seven princes guarded it with eight brave captains in command. There was no chink of weakness.

In such an ultimate test Akbar's ambition prevailed over his sense of fairness. Nothing had so thwarted him before. The great clement Akbar lost his perspective. He invited King Miran to come down to negotiate, under most strict pledge of freedom, then kept him prisoner. When the young son of the Abyssinian governor of the fort came as ambassador to protest, and proudly said that the fortress would not yield, Akbar, instead of generously admiring the boy's courage, had him killed. Finally he bombarded with the most potent weapon — money. Quantities of gold and silver went secretly to the defenders, who weakened and sagged, until the fortress, and with it the whole kingdom, fell in 1601. Ahmadnagar, Berar, and Kandesh now belonged to Akbar, but his last battle was no credit to his soldiery.

In 1601, fifty-nine-year-old Akbar returned to Agra. Prince Salim, the longed-for, was thirty-two. He had inherited enough fortune to finance an open rebellion. Salim marched, with thirty thousand cavalry, to within seventy-three miles of the capital. Akbar sent a threatening letter, but, as a sop to his ambition, gave him the government of Bengal and Orissa. Salim paid no attention to this legitimate rule, but called himself king at Allahabad and began to coin his own money. The emperor consulted his trusted Abul Fazl, who saw the need of a strong arm, and offered to bring the prince, bound, to court. Whereupon Salim hired a bandit chief to kill Abul Fazl, his father's dearest friend, and insulted the old man's head by throwing it into the refuse.

Akbar grieved sharply and doubly, both for his true friend and his treacherous son. For three days he did not show himself at his palace window — a dangerous omission.

Salim continued at Allahabad, his father's only surviving son and heir, a rebel, with plenty of opium and drink and indulging in cruel punishments and flayings alive.

In 1604, Akbar decided to march against his saint-given son. And here Hamida Banu Begam, the spirited little girl of the desert escapings, now seventy-seven years old, played her last rôle. She knew that Akbar, once roused, would totally destroy the son of his affection. She tried in every way to persuade him not to go, and when she could not succeed, fell ill. Akbar had to stay by her bedside and her death made him lose heart to march. Diplomats then persuaded Salim to come forward, as his father's only son, and be reconciled. It was prudent, for there was a question of making the grandson Khousru — a gracious and fine young man — his heir. So Salim came to court. As he prostrated himself reverently, Akbar suddenly led him to an inner room and slapped him violently several times. Then he reproached him bitterly, and withal taunted him because, with thirty thousand cavalry, he had not been man enough to fight openly. Akbar contemptuously treated him as a patient, had him shut in a bath with a doctor in attendance, and deprived of opium, until sympathetic ladies of the harem persuaded Akbar to let the prince live in state again.

The bitter rebellion lasted for nearly four years. For less than a year the father and son lived in ostensible peace. Then Akbar caught a fatal dysentery — or was he poisoned? No one knows.

Father Jerome, calling, found him gay and cheerful, surrounded by courtiers, in no mood for exhortation. Two days later he could not be admitted. And no one ever knew in what belief, if any, Great Akbar died. Salim at the last came to stand beside the strong man's bed. Akbar could not speak, but made a sign that unworthy Salim should put on the imperial turban and take the sword of Humayon, which hung at the foot of the bed. He died in October, 1605.

A gap was made in the wall and Salim and the grandson carried his body to the tomb at Sikandera, with few following in mourning, and little sign of grief that the great conqueror of India, and her most benevolent ruler, was dead. In the time of his great-grandson, wild Jat villagers desecrated his tomb, stole the bronze gates, the ornaments of gold and silver, and dragged out his bones and threw them angrily into the flames.

Allahu Akbar!

19. *Jahangir and Queen 'Light of the World'*

Ruled 1605–1627

THE beauty of high Kashmir is focussed in gardens laid out by the Great Moguls — and especially loved by one queen called Nurjahan, 'Light of the World.'

Prince Salim, the sulky son who defied Akbar, met his master in this Persian wife. Her taste, formal yet graceful, stamps the buildings which she left, especially the tomb near Agra of her father, Itimad-ud-Daula, the first of the precise white marble delicacies in India, and the terraced gardens of Kashmir.

Akbar had conquered Kashmir and built his fort on a hill. Nurjahan and her emperor enjoyed the place. The Vale of Kashmir is an oval plateau, mile high, ringed by mountains that go bare of snow in summer and are mere foothills for the Himalayan snow peaks behind them. In the spring Kashmir has warm soft air, clear as diamonds. Autumn is mild as a yellow apple, and the tall poplar avenues turn the colour of sunshine, and the enormous chenar trees are like old copper. The Jhelum River loops and winds its reflecting way through the Vale, and is fed by or feeds the placid lakes under hill walls.

At the foot of ample hills, Nurjahan and Jahangir built gardens of formal beauty, geometric in pattern as a rug, but varied by the deep friendliness of shade trees and little fruit orchards. The essence of their delight is a watercourse with falls and fountains, flowing from the mountain background to the lake foreground, bisecting the green with silver spray.

To be paddled today over a lake, hung between sky and peaks and their reflection, to Shalimar Bagh; to visit the mossy arches of the octagonal pool at Verinag; to drink tea in the flowered trifle of walled garden called Chashmi Shahi; or to see the rose-walled ruin at Manasbal Lake, poignant in decay, facing the most dramatic beauty of the mountains — is to feel a touch of Nurjahan, her clarity and discretion and certainty.

Her miniatures show a stylized, exotic little figure, with a mass of long black hair, great oval eyes, with fine jewelry on her wrists and hair and ankles, and transparent veilings over her silk trousers — as equestrienne or queen. Other women of rank in her period lived hidden lives, secret and mysterious, peering out through carved fretwork windows and curtains to broken glimpses of the bright movement outside, seeing the whole world patterned by lattice; creatures knowing only their husbands and swarming women and servants of the household, whose sole existence was to please the somewhat jaded lord or intrigue for place for a son. Yet suddenly, in this century or that, such a guarded woman was able to act with the boldness and strategy of a general. Nurjahan entered Jahangir's career when he was forty-two years old, and did what she pleased with it.

Prince Salim mounted the solid throne of Akbar in 1605, in his thirty-eighth year, as the Emperor Jahangir, 'World-Seizer.' Freed of restraint, he proved to be a 'merry creature of many moods,' very, very fond of his bottle. He swayed between tenderness and cruelty, sensitiveness and callousness, energy and sloth. He had ability, and began his reign with some firmness and liberality, but lapsed with the years as though his fibres slackened. Neither in conquests nor government did he greatly change Akbar's India, simply let it loosen a little, in everything but display. He inherited hordes of treasure, and enjoyed them.

Picture him in his gold brocade coat (or sheer white lawn), wearing a turban with a plume of heron feathers, set with a ruby as big as a walnut, with pearls and diamonds hanging from him. His sword-hilt was of gold, the scabbard set with jewels. Emeralds and diamonds were thick in his rings and armlets. He was no more luxurious than the period sanctioned, though the display was mounting from Akbar. Once, when he dined away from the palace, the whole mile underfoot was laid with precious silks and velvets, at a cost which would equal about seven hundred thousand dollars. But, as he sensibly remarked in his diary: 'Let it not produce a smile that I should have set my heart on the delusions of this world. Am I greater than Solomon, who placed his pillow in the wind?'

He did not let religious heart-searching furrow him deeply. He could coquette with the Jesuits and their Christianity, and hang pictures of the Virgin and saints in his rooms, and allow the Portuguese liberty to have their Masses and Catholic processions and a church in Lahore — until politics interfered. Though professedly a Mohammedan, he could imitate a few of Akbar's religious discussions. He was tolerant to Hindus, though he thought ordinary Hinduism 'a worthless religion.' But he was not the man to let it bother him, or to think seriously of renouncing the world. It was too pleasing a world.

'For forty days and nights,' he wrote in his self-conscious journal, 'I caused the state drum to strike up without ceasing.' This was on coming to the throne. 'The ground was spread with costly brocades and gold-embroidered carpets. Numbers of blooming youths, beautiful as young Joseph in the pavilions of Egypt, clad in dresses of the most costly materials, woven in silk and gold, with zones and armlets sparkling with the lustre of the diamond, the emerald, the sapphire, and the ruby, awaited my commands, rank after rank, in attitudes most respectful.' What could be pleasanter?

His court knew how to delight his whim. Jahangir stopped once with a loyal lady in winter when the trees were bare of blossoms. She set four hundred artisans at forced labour in her garden, to tie paper and wax flowers and fruit to the trees. Delighted Jahangir wrote: 'Every tree and shrub seemed as abundantly furnished as if in the very freshness and bloom of spring... orange, lemon, peach, pomegranate and apple... every species of rose and other garden flowers so perfect, that when I first entered the garden I forgot it was not spring, and unwittingly began to pluck at the fruits and the flowers.'

Feasts were spread under canopies of deepest green velvet for three days and nights; then the usual exchange of gifts began. 'The ladies of my harem, to the number of four hundred, were all presented with a tray of four pieces of cloth of gold of Khoras, and an ambertich, or perfume stone, worth no less than three hundred toumans.' His hostess gave the emperor lavish presents, and he gave her pearls and rubies worth eight lakhs of rupees, and added one thousand horse to her father's rank. It is hard to add and subtract properly, but the lady may have had a little the worse of the bargain in tangibles, if not in royal favour. Certainly the artisans did, who pasted up flowers like the Duchess's gardeners, with no reward but a few blows.

Jahangir was a taster of extremes — equally keen in tenderness or cruelty. His affections were strong. He had been madly in love with Anarkali, the pomegranate blossom of Akbar's harem, if the passionate inscription he had exquisitely carved on her marble coffin is sincere — 'Ah, if I could see the face of my beloved, to the day of judgment I would give thanks to my Creator.' He loved his first wife, daughter of the Rajah of Amber, writing of her: 'How can I describe her excellence and good nature? Her affection for me was such that she would have given a thousand sons as ransom for one hair of mine. She was my first bride... in my youth. Her death had such an effect that I did not care to live.' His final almost slavish devotion was to Nurjahan.

Yet he was equally a connoisseur of cruelty and could think of good ways to torture. Prince Khusru was his eldest son, born of the beloved Amber princess. The prince was 'the very love and delight' of the common people and a most appealing figure. 'A gentleman of very lovely presence and fine carriage,' wrote the English chaplain Terry, 'who contented himself with one wife, which with all love and care accompanied him in all his streights.' Such a prince, humane and tolerant, was the hope of the country. But unfortunately he rebelled and tried to take the throne from his opium-loving father six months after his coronation.

Jahangir, victorious, had the sharp stakes prepared, and Khusru's followers lined an avenue impaled on stakes or hanging from trees. Jahangir forced his son to ride through the lane of anguish, detailing General Mahabat Khan to point out to him the tortured faces of his friends. Khusru cried out that his father should have punished him rather than the men who did nothing but follow his commands. Jahangir with a lifted eyebrow offered to do it. Khusru begged the death, saying he found no joy in existence after his gallant friends perished. But his father allowed him to live, partially blinded. In time, perhaps in fondness, he let his guard relax vigilance. Khusru might have survived if it had not been for the black jealousy of his younger brother Prince Khurram, pushing up like a seed through stones to the throne.

As the supreme judge of the land, Jahangir invented unusual punishments and revived some which Akbar had discarded. Once he had a culprit's eyelids sewed up; he put victims in the fresh warm skins of animals; he had a man dragged by elephants till his bones were bare. He decided, after thought, that the punishment for matricide was to have the murderer stung to death by snakes; and a court lady who kissed a eunuch he buried alive up to the neck, leaving her head exposed to the deadly sun, having the eunuch cut to pieces before her.

The callousness of a child criminal was not incompatible with very delicate fancies. Marching once through the unbelievable wild flowers of Kashmir, in a particularly brilliant field he called his men to gather blossoms and set them in their turbans. As they went before him, a bobbing field of wild flowers on the march, he cried out with pleasure.

At evening he entertained convivially, sitting cross-legged on his little throne, 'all clad in diamonds and pearls and rubies, before him a table of gold, on it about fifty pieces of gold plate, all set with stones.' 'Froliquely' he commanded his noblemen to drink from the several wines standing by in great flagons. Sometimes the evenings grew very frolicsome, for Jahangir's average at its greatest rose to about twenty cups of spirit or four cups of opium a day.

Foreigners came into the picture in 1608. A figure of a different silhouette was introduced before the throne — cape, doublet, and hose among the turbans and Persian coats. Stout Captain William Hawkins presented letters from King James, asking trading privileges. The hearty English captain who could bring his sails from England had especial qualifications as trade ambassador. He could speak in Turki — and he could drink with Jahangir, bottle for bottle, till the emperor fell asleep.

But Hawkins, who seemed to be under full sail, was thwarted by the Portuguese, bitter, and fearful of losing their monopoly. The Jesuits, in Akbar's last days, had tried in every way to block an English John Mildenhall — according to his account not stopping short of attempted poison. So Jahangir made Hawkins, willy-nilly, marry an Armenian Christian girl to watch his food. Portugal was dying on its feet and her viceroys represented a waning power. Goa had fallen from prosperity with the destruction of Vijayanagar. But the Portuguese made a desperate struggle. They represented to Jahangir that the concessions to the English were an act of war, and got him to revoke them. Captain Hawkins left in 1611, stepping through webs of intrigue. A year later the Portuguese were high-handed enough to seize four imperial ships of the wobbly Mogul navy, and at that they fell into disgrace with the king, their churches were closed and their people banished. The stage was once more favourable to the English, whom Jahangir saw as a counterbalance of power.

In 1615, England sent the first formal embassy to the Mogul court. Sir Thomas Roe marched up-country to the emperor, to get a treaty for security of trade for the East India Company, now settled at Surat on the coast. Sir Thomas was a courtier and a trained diplomat, and maintained his sturdy dignity in the overwhelming splendour.

The story of his gifts to Jahangir — the inevitable gifts — is naïve and characteristic. The solid English presents did not measure up. Persia knew how to do the thing better. The Persian ambassador — and Persia was very haughty then — knocking his head against the ground, presented Jahangir with twenty-seven Arabian horses, nine large mules, seven camels laden with velvet, two chests of Persian hangings, one rich cabinet, forty muskets, five clocks, one camel laden with cloth of gold, eight silk carpets, two rubies, twenty-one camel-loads of wine, fourteen camel-loads of distilled sweet waters, seven of rosewater, seven daggers set with precious stones, five swords, and seven Venetian looking-glasses.

The list of presents from the English was very homespun in comparison, but they had rather prided themselves on their gift of a strong English coach drawn by four horses, with a skilled coachman to drive. The coach was lined with crimson Chinese velvet. Jahangir did not think much of the Chinese lining. He had the coach taken completely apart and a duplicate made of each part. Then the two coaches were set up, the old one relined with rich silver cloth brocaded in silk flowers and the new upholstered with cloth of gold. In each he put silver nails in place of brass. Then he was ready to ride in the English coach — and he never tipped the coachman less than ten pounds for a drive.

Jahangir made his three appearances to the people at dawn, noon, and night, on an eastern, southern, and western balcony. Between seven and nine at night he sat in a spacious room made bright as day by many lights. Here Sir Thomas Roe usually made his addresses to him, for the king was then affable and full of talk and drink. The courtiers smelled pleasantly to the English, in whose land one still cleaned house by piling one layer of rushes on top of another. The English chaplain observed: 'The people there often wash their bodies and keep their feet as clean and sweet as their heads. The better sort anoint themselves very much with sweet oils, which makes their company very savoury.'

It was a matter of pride with Jahangir, a part of dignity, to keep an ambassador dangling and never give a definite answer. Sir Thomas Roe never got a real treaty, but he left in 1619 with many trade concessions that laid a foundation for the East India Company's prosperity.

Sir Thomas Roe had glimpses of the queen whose favour it was well to court. Nurjahan, only a little too late to be contemporary of Queen Elizabeth, suggests a comparison and contrast. Elizabeth ruled openly in her own right, but Nurjahan was managing for the most part behind veilings and screens. Though she had freedom, boldness, and guile that rivalled Elizabeth's, she kept discreetly to the tradition of ruling only through her lover. An Indian queen who defied that tradition — Razziya — had failed. Nurjahan pulled the intricate puppet strings, and Jahangir and the generals danced.

Her life had begun in lowest misfortune and reached this height of power. She was born on a melancholy caravan in Persia. And if it had not been for a cobra, according to one legend generously lent her, she would have died at birth. Trailing over the desert, her dejected parents went with a group of merchants and stragglers who had joined for safety. The Persian mountains were bare and bright, the land a hot mirror of sky, and the wells long marches apart. Nurjahan's father had once been wazir to the Governor of Khorassan, but, displaced and unlucky, he set out as an emigrant for India, carrying all his remaining goods. The caravan was attacked by robbers, who left him in absolute beggary. In that situation his wife gave birth to a baby girl.

The father observed, quite reasonably, that she was an unlucky baby; better be rid of that little calamity-bringer. So her unhappy mother had to leave her on the glaring sand, while the caravan lagged on. The heat of the blank earth and the staring sun would kill her. Her mother could not help looking back. She saw a cobra gliding toward the baby. The brown snake did not strike, but reared and spread its hood to shade the child from the sun. So it stayed, sheltering the infant.

'A sign — a sign! She is lucky, after all!' cried the mother.

The father considered. Certainly such a cobra must be an omen. So they took back the child and named her Mihrunissa — 'Sun Among Women.' She proved to be quite the luckiest baby of her generation and the making of the family fortune.

A more prosaic tale says that a merchant of the caravan, seeing the child's beauty, picked her up, and, while searching for a wet-nurse, returned her to her own mother.

Safely in India, her father managed to reach the court of the Emperor Akbar, who quickly saw his qualities. For, according to chronicle, Mihrunissa's father was 'clever and skillful in writing and transacting business. He had studied the old poetry and had a nice appreciation of words. His generosity to the poor was such that none was turned away disappointed from his door.... In the taking of bribes he was most uncompromising and fearless.' That is to be noticed.

Little Mihrunissa grew up in Akbar's red sandstone capital. There is a popular story of her meeting with Prince Salim in childhood — at the fair where the wives of noblemen tended booths in shrewd and gay bargaining, trying to sell their fine tissues and embroideries to the royal family. The place was alive with vivid-coloured, laughing women. Mihrunissa, a twelve-year-old girl, rested for a moment by a stone well, when a bejewelled little boy saw her. He immediately thought of something that she could do to add to his comfort.

'Hold my pigeons,' he ordered, giving her his two pet tumbling birds, and running off. He came back to find her with only one bird.

'How did it get away?' stormed the spoiled boy, who was later to revive impalements.

Mihrunissa looked at him. Then she deliberately lifted up her henna-pointed hand, and sent the second bird free.

'Just like that,' she said coolly.

The boy knew his master. Whether he sensed a clarity and decision that could lead his devious weakness, or whether he fell in love with her pretty hands and bracelet-clinking arms, no record tells, and it probably never happened. But the story says that he remained so passionately devoted to her that when he grew old enough he planned actually to marry her. When such mesalliance threatened, Akbar had Mihrunissa married to Sherafgan, whom he sent to govern in distant Bengal. Jahangir was suitably married to the daughter of a great Rajput prince. That should have ended the affair, but the stars in their courses, or the cobra, fought for a brilliant destiny for Mihrunissa.

Jahangir became emperor. His important and loving Rajput wife died, and he did, for some reason, send envoys to arrest the Persian girl's husband. Sherafgan, resisting, killed the imperial messenger. Thereupon Mihrunissa was forwarded like an express package to the harem of Jahangir. But they reckoned without Mihrunissa. She would not go tamely into the harem of the king who had killed her husband. Not for all his wild elephants.

She would not even accept money from him. She lived for four years, necessarily at court, but in seclusion, supporting herself entirely by the rare needlework which she could do. In 1611, however, she went to a festival, where the emperor saw her, and 'a key was found for closed doors, a restorative for broken hearts, and on a certain New Year's festival, she attracted the love and affection of the king.'

This time she complied. When she finally married Jahangir, she captivated him completely. In a few days she was his favourite wife, and the emperor called her Nurmahal, 'Light of the Palace.'

Jahangir had a harem of four hundred women. He made Nurmahal superior to them all. The situation held extreme difficulties for one less gifted. There have been poisonings in the Orient for smaller offences. And in a collection of the most beautiful and graceful women in India, glittering like so many peris in flower-coloured veilings shot with gold, with ancient wiles in their minds, and intrigue as a part of their nursery lore, there was not too distant possibility that some other woman of strong will might gain ascendency over the emperor. Nurmahal forestalled that in the full tide of the emperor's early passion for her. She made no enemies by her methods. For those women of charm and force, whom she might dread, she had splendid marriages arranged, and then sent their husbands to govern distant provinces.

Soon 'Light of the Palace' was not expressive enough of the emperor's admiration, and he renamed her Nurjahan, 'Light of the World.' And the lady who had refused to accept any court money now set a high price upon herself. Jahangir writes that he assigned her a dowry amounting to about thirty-five million dollars, 'which sum she requested as indispensable for the purchase of jewels, and I granted it without a murmur.'

Jahangir, flaccid and affectionate, bringing his annoyances and perplexities to the fountained and cushioned room, found that the engaging creature in gauze and jewels had a way of clearing his doubts by one apt remark. He marvelled at her. He gave her the rank of commander over thirty thousand horsemen. And that was not enough. He had coins struck which bore her name, saying, 'By the order of King Jahangir, gold has a hundred splendours added to it by receiving the impression of the name of Nurjahan, the Queen.' He gave her the rights of sovereignty over all India.

(*a*) QUEEN NURJAHAN, LIGHT OF THE WORLD

(*b*) NISHAT BAGH, THE GARDEN OF GLADNESS, KASHMIR

The great cities on the plains of India spread in splendour and squalor — the mud-baked walls of unkempt alleys crowding the green spots of gardens that enclosed noblemen's houses. On the plains Nurjahan and Jahangir lived within fort walls, whether in crowded ancient Lahore or scattered Agra, by the pale, sand-spitted river Jumna.

The poor people they governed were living in low and mean houses of earth and straw, set close together in villages, very bare. The Mohammedans, according to Terry, were generally lazy, living off the Hindus, who were industrious in their many rigid castes, tilling and planting, or making rare handicrafts in wood or ivory, mother-of-pearl, and tortoise-shell, working with few tools, but with 'tooth and nail, ears and toes, as well as fingers.' Such people were timorous and gentle, very polite and faithful in service, but oppressed by the great lords who rode lolling at ease upon palanquins carried on men's shoulders. 'They make the shoulders and joints of those that feel their heavy weight to bow and buckle under their burdens.'

Jahangir, supreme over all these, was judge and jury and legislature and cabinet and commander-in-chief of the army. No wrangling parliament, no tottering cabinets, no critical press — just the emperor, sitting enthroned cross-legged in audience to his people. 'L'état, c'est moi.'

The time came when the state was not even Jahangir — the state was Nurjahan.

At dawn every day, according to tradition, the emperor must show himself to his people. A crowd waited silently and patiently under the bulging red sandstone walls, watching for the appearance of their jewelled and heron-feathered monarch in the carved niche of his window. Sometimes a poor man had a petition. A string was let down from the balcony and the humblest driver of a water buffalo, in a dingy loincloth, might have his plea drawn up to the king. One morning there was an unusual murmur in the crowd. Nurjahan showed herself at the window beside the emperor.

That was the tacit symbol of her rights of sovereignty, a demonstration more vivid to the people than her name on the golden coin. But she did more than that.

The chief business of the state was still transacted at two daily meetings, the emperor's public audience and his private audience. For the full public audience Jahangir's habit was to sit under a canopy out-of-doors in the Agra fort, all his nobles standing below him in their appointed places.

Soon Nurjahan the Persian appeared with the emperor to hold audience equally with him. Then she appeared alone before the nobles, making decisions herself and giving judgments in place of the emperor. To imagine the boldness and direct simplicity of

Nurjahan — a blend of Portia with Sheherazade — one must remember the other Mogul empresses, who were seen by no man but their husband, and all the other guarded great ladies of India. Jewels in a casket — jewels in excellent safe-deposit.

Nurjahan appeared coolly in place of the besotted king. The reins were in her hands. She had Jahangir appoint her father Itimad-ud-Daula as prime minister — an able, if greedy, adviser. Gradually she displaced most of the former officials of the realm and appointed men of her own blood or alliance to their posts. Her brother, Asaf Khan, commanded the army. This caused bitter murmurings, but was within her rights, since Jahangir gave her sovereignty over India.

'Of my unreserved confidence, indeed,' Jahangir wrote in his journal, 'this princess is in entire possession, and I may say without a fallacy that the whole fortune of my empire has been consigned to the disposal of this highly endowed family; the father being my diwan, the son my lieutenant general with unlimited powers, and the daughter the inseparable companion of my cares.'

Not everyone was disappointed to have the clear-headed queen taking the reins in place of an often befuddled king. She won 'golden opinions' for her beauty and intelligence, for her good sense and steadiness. Her mind cut through difficulties, and she solved problems that were an *impasse* to others. Her justice was renowned all over India, and her mercy to suppliants and charity to undowried or orphaned women. The lovely lady who had supported herself by the fineness of her embroidery in an age of exquisite workmanship was merely governing India. And the kingdom, according to the standards of the day, was in fair shape.

Jahangir meanwhile was flattening himself out of the way. He was very jolly about it saying that so long as he could hunt and drink, he had all he wanted. He put the kingdom in the most capable hands. Whether he was actually relieved to give up the boresome details of government, as an executive might turn things over to a capable woman secretary, whether he was so passionately in love that he saw it all through a glorious haze, or whether he realized his weakness and was saving his face, it is hard to judge. Wine and opium give forgetfulness of inferiority. But there is too much bravado in that and in the way he decorated a palace with his 'escutcheons' — the winecups and flagons, slender-necked, sketched in jade and carnelian in the marble niches. Make a jest of it. Nurjahan was the better man.

Nurjahan, generous and just, had her faults. She followed one Oriental custom rather too closely. She had a flair for costly gifts — almost an appetite one would call it, if her taste were not so rare. Her father, the prime minister, was bold in the matter of taking bribes, and Nurjahan succeeded in enriching herself at the expense of the people. She was unconcerned with the happiness of the mass of toilers under the Indian sun, and considered them mainly as a source of revenue for her buildings. She would have been exceptional in that age if she had imagined beyond that. But in spite of the golden bells at Agra, the peasants were oppressed. Villages unable to pay their full revenue might be made a prize, and women and children sold as slaves. Some peasants escaped from their lords and left the fields empty. As a background to the lavishness there were crumbling villages.

Each year when the great heat came to the plains, Jahangir's opium-heated blood burned, and whenever peace and policy allowed, he took the favoured of his court over the mountains to his little paradise of Kashmir.

They went regardless of hardships and dangers. 'At the foot of the mountains of Kashmir,' Jahangir wrote of one journey, 'snow fell without intermission for seven days and nights. There was no fuel.... The army was accompanied by fakirs in extraordinary numbers, and as they must have perished, I ordered a lak of camels to bring fuel, and provided each mendicant with a vest stuffed with cotton and a sheepskin coat.' A fairly magnificent gesture. At night the jackals wailed in the cold, and Jahangir, in the excess of his tenderness or tipsyness, ordered them to be supplied with coats also.

To reach Kashmir they climbed a pass eleven thousand feet high. The elephants' feet swayed ponderously up over the steep snow of the Pir Panjal Mountains. Golden howdahs on their backs hid the clutching Mogul women, squatted in silks and gauzes and obscurity. The ladies peered out at the vertical chasms below, at the sharp tips of firs and deodars beneath them. At the head of the harem elephants rode the focussing point of all the emperor's lavishness — Nurjahan, 'Light of the World.'

Her long dark eyes were not missing much, and her very slender wrists guided the caravan as definitely as if she held the reins. Nurjahan, with fine-spun, long black hair holding pearls or glowing rubies, with clear amber skin, and her black eyes lengthened and deepened by kohl, her small hands and bare feet reddened with henna, did not mind the lurching of the elephants and the danger, and was not frightened at the summit of the pass when an ascetic dared come out and warn the emperor's cavalcade not to make noise or they would startle down a snow avalanche.

The royal camp went over the land as it came, whether in levels or Himalayan folds. Forests were cleared and rivers bridged as they approached. Yet they did not stint themselves for that reason. Elephants, camels, mules, and men carried two complete and identical camps up and down gullies and over the jagged rooftops of mountains. On the plains the elephants carried the heavy tents, the great audience canopies, and council rooms, hung with velvets; camels took the lighter tents, mules carried baggage and cooking-pots, and men carried on their heads the fragile porcelain and gilt beds. In the difficult hills more and more burdens went to the coolie porters. Jahangir followed the plan of Akbar in having one camp sent ahead to be perfect by nightfall, so that he rode in to his orderly city of tents, often twenty miles in circuit, laid out symmetrically and by the same plan. One could come by dark and turn automatically down the right lanes to his own tent. The emperor rode past screens of strong red cloth with variegated stripes, or of rich painted chintz, and the figured satin that hid the women's tents. Banners hung down still in the yellow Indian twilight. Beyond the royal camp were the bazaars, the townful of merchants. There were tents even for the lead-horses, for choice elephants, and for hunting cheetahs; and tents to cover the fruits and sweets and Ganges water and the saltpetre with which it was cooled.

In the years when all this subtlety and splendour climbed the passes to Kashmir, the Pilgrims sailed for America and cut down a few trees for log cabins and made a few graves under corn-fields.

Jahangir and Nurjahan, safely over the rugged peaks, could forget the struggles of the snow passes, the shivering holy men, the slipping elephants, and sharp precipices. Kashmir lay before them in the spring, its hills terraced with flooded rice-fields, its soil succulent with giant trees — Kashmir of lakes and looping rivers.

Under the mountains and beside the lakes Nurjahan and Jahangir enjoyed these gardens, where the court, more gorgeous than all the tropic birds, could cool their foreheads in fountain spray. Sometimes they would live in Shalimar Bagh, which Jahangir had built. They were paddled across Dal Lake, under the camel-backed bridge, down a canal a mile long, over the images of mirrored chenar trees. Leaving the brightly painted barges they went up the broad grassed levels of terraces to the mountain base. The lowest terrace was the outer garden for retainers, the middle the emperor's garden, with his pavilion bridging the fountain course. Nurjahan's ladies were carried to the topmost terrace, above which the mountain rose sheerly, where dark trees shaded them from the pointed sun rays, and they were hidden from the court below. From this vantage-point the ladies could look down to see the fountains' waters running in their paved bed, spraying in sunlight between the trees and trellised walks. On either side of the feathery fountains lay the bright friendliness of differing flower-beds — the lilac thickets, the tulips, lilies, or narcissus.

The empress might take her ladies to her pet smaller garden, Chasma Shahi, backing to a mountain, with a fiercely bubbling spring that rose in a large stone vase in the upper pavilion, flowed down a terrace and through a wooden garden house, then amazingly dropped eighteen feet over a carved chute below.

Nurjahan's brother, bold Asaf Khan, built himself twelve-terraced Nishat Bagh, the 'Garden of Gladness.' All around the lakes the emperor and empress could go from one spot of shade and water and stately view to another. One of the empress's favourites was the garden at Verinag. Today only twenty-four arches surrounding the octagonal tank are left, with stairways to the vanished palace above. Mysteriously green water cooled the temperature several degrees in the alcoves around the tank at hot noonday. In the pool the sacred carp wore gold rings in their gills, with Nurjahan's inscriptions on them.

Jahangir liked this place, and left a polished black marble slab which said, 'The King raised this building to the skies: the angel Gabriel suggested its date — 1609.' And the builder carved this 'God be praised! What a canal and what a waterfall! Constructed by Haider by order of the King of the World, the Paramount Lord of his Age, this canal is a type of the canal in Paradise, this waterfall is the glory of Kashmir.'

But the peace of Kashmir was not for Nurjahan in the year 1626. The emperor's four sons had been four spear-points against him. Of these, the third son, Prince Khurram, called Shahjahan, was proving strongest. He had been given charge of his eldest brother, blind Khusru, 'the gentleman of very lovely presence.' This was done with the consent or connivance of Asaf Khan and Nurjahan, for the empress at first favoured Khurram. To put one rival prince in charge of another tacitly meant his death, and nobody investigated much when Khusru was strangled. The second son, Parwits, was a worthless sot. That left Shahryar, nicknamed 'Good for Nothing.' Nurjahan transferred her favour and plotting to him when she married him to her daughter by her first husband.

Shahjahan made a strong rebellion in 1622, when Jahangir, weak and ailing, ordered him to get Kandahar back from the Persians. Shahjahan had shown his strength in the Deccan and Rajputana, and now it took the force of the kingdom to subdue him. Jahangir wailed over his son: 'What shall I say of my own sufferings? In pain and weakness, in a warm atmosphere that is extremely unsuited to my health, I must still ride and be active, and in this state must proceed against such an undutiful son.' By 1625, some peace was arranged between the prince and his father, but Shahjahan remained an exile in either the Deccan or Rajputana, sending his two sons, Dara and Aurangzeb, to court as hostages — two slender boys, one of whom was later to murder the other.

In such rebellions some general is likely to develop his own strength. Mahabat Khan, master of eight thousand horse, was a noble and generous man, and fearless. Very ably he had helped to drive Shahjahan into exile in Rajputana, where the prince lived not too uncomfortably in a marble palace on a lake in Udaipur, looking at his father's escutcheons, the delicate wine flagons, on the walls, and comforted by the wife for whom he was to build the Taj Mahal.

Nurjahan soon realized that Mahabat Khan was too strong a trump card to leave in the hand of any princely son who might try to capture the emperor and put him in prison and take the throne himself, after the manner of princes. So she and her brother Asaf Khan, now prime minister, decided to put an end to the threat of the general's power.

Asaf Khan sent a messenger ordering the old warrior's recall. Mahabat Khan had lived too long at a Mogul court to be guileless. To be sure, he came back, but he came more swiftly than expected, and brought with him five thousand Rajput soldiers and a supply of battle elephants. Jahangir was camped by the Jhelum River on the way to Kabul, and a bridge had been built over the powerful stream. Asaf Khan with a mass of troops had crossed the river that day, leaving the emperor and the women and children weakly guarded. The city of tents with its lanes and banners lay open to him. Boldly yet quietly Mahabat Khan made his way with his dust-raising horsemen straight to the king's tent. The useless guard tried to stop him.

'This temerity and presumption exceed all bounds,' he cried weakly.

Jahangir, coming out surprised, saw that he was overpowered and yielded without a blow. The general respectfully persuaded him to control his fury, and pretend that they were starting out peaceably together on a hunting party, then took him to his own quarters and held him prisoner. It happened so simply that for a time no one realized that Jahangir had not gone hunting, and Nurjahan crossed the river to visit her brother. Mahabat Khan destroyed the connecting bridge between the empress and the weak emperor.

But until he had captured the queen in this game of chess, he had not really captured the king. On her wrong side of the river Nurjahan realized the crisis. She called together her chief nobles and spoke to them clearly. 'This has happened through your neglect and stupid arrangements. You must do your best to repair this evil.'

They decided to ford the river back to camp and give battle. But the river was swift and powerful. In a bad ford, with horses slipping and swimming and stumbling, or swirled downstream, the water became a tangle of noblemen and confusion. Many soldiers began to retreat to the safer bank.

Seeing the probability of panic, the empress sent her messenger: 'The Begam wants to know if this is the time for delay and irresolution. Strike boldly forward!'

Knowing their reliance on a leader, she mounted an elephant and rode toward the shore under the arrows of hostile Rajputs. One arrow hit the mahout prodding her elephant to the crossing. Nurjahan pulled it out of his neck herself, and tried to go onward. She was not afraid. Once she had shot a charging tiger. But the mahout was too badly wounded to manage the elephant, and the animal plunged back with them. Nurjahan was helpless, her brother was captured and forced to support Mahabat Khan as actual ruler of India.

Still her wit and spirit were undampened. Jahangir was now only the figurehead emperor, taking orders from Mahabat Khan. The easy man soon grew rather to like his captor and showed him marks of imperial favour, and privately warned him that Nurjahan was a designing creature. Whether he was a little tired of the certain control of Nurjahan and her brother and decided to play Mahabat Khan against them, or whether he was so easily affable that he really liked the old soldier, considered him a brave fellow, and hated to see him outwitted, is a guessing matter.

Nurjahan, having tried masculine boldness and decision, now tried feminine wiles. She was too meek for Mahabat Khan. She begged him to let her return to comfort the ailing emperor. Once back with Jahangir, the rest was easy. Since he was still nominal king, she persuaded him to order a review of his troops. And because Mahabat Khan, with the reality of power, need not fear this dumb show, she succeeded in making him absent himself in order not to precipitate a clash of rival factions. The sturdy general's guile failed him. He left the emperor surrounded by only a few guards and retired to a distance. Now Nurjahan, herself overlord of a district, could order up her own body of cavalry. During the manœuvres of the review, she told them to press close to the emperor's guard. With their threatening and wild dashes they overawed the men, who let the emperor go free. The tables were turned. Nurjahan now had her brother released, and she and Jahangir were once more in control of India. Could anyone act with a neater combination of male and female, Occidental and Oriental, qualities?

But her power was near its end. The emperor was sickening. At fifty-nine he was an old man, and in spite of her faithful nursing, he fell ill of asthma, asking to be buried in one of his favourite Kashmir gardens. Nurjahan's claim to power was entirely gone with his death. She made one last play, with the youngest prince, Shahryar, married to her daughter, as pawn. If she backed this prince against Shahjahan, and her daughter became empress, she might rule India still from behind the scenes. She failed. Shahjahan made himself emperor. His throne was secure until his own sons should grow up.

Nothing is more expressive of Nurjahan's clarity and sense than her instant relinquishment of all lavishness and glory when she knew that her hand was played. She was given an adequate income, but she went into strict retirement, dressed always in white as mourning for her husband, and gave herself up to piety and good deeds and gardens. Of course, she may have had a discreet word or two to say to the growing rival princes. It is hard for an expert to give up the game. But to all appearances she might never have left the obscurity of the harem where she had earned her living by needlework before 'a key was found for closed hearts.'

Today in India wherever one sees buildings that she has left — from her own enrichment at the expense of the people — they are none the less charming, expressive of clear taste, defining imagination in grace and precision, restraining splendour with lightness. Even the baked-clay simplicity of her own modest tomb near Lahore, arched under a quiet dome, a dim interior looking out through round arches to a garden where green parrots sit like blossoms on a mango tree — even here one feels her taste. There is charm in the faded painting on the wall of sprays and baskets of flowers, the flowers she had loved in Kashmir.

20. *Shahjahan, Who Lived in White Marble and Jewels*

Ruled 1628–1658

THE Emperor Shahjahan lives in memory as a romantic figure because he built, and fairly breathed, palaces of white marble and jewels, the adult type of the house of cake and frosting. His taste was pleased by screens of the thick white stuff pierced with frost patterns, cold, smooth walls inlaid with vines of lapis, turquoise, cornelian, and jade; water running through channels in marble floors, slipping into shell-shaped pools; a peacock throne of jewels — all too dreamlike for this grubby world. The man who conceived the pearl shapes inside the red sandstone fort walls in Delhi and Agra, and who built the Taj Mahal, cannot escape the rôle of romantic.

The truth that the most beautiful of the fantasies, the Taj Mahal, was built to eternalize a deep love, fits the perfection of its purity.

But there is little purity in the story of Shahjahan, whose career began in rebellion and murder and ended in sombre bitterness of captivity. His reign was the full tide of Mogul prosperity. He held the country for thirty years in comparative steadiness and peace. Save for his lavish building, he did not contribute. Save for that lavish spending, which was depleting his empire, he did not greatly detract. His building fixes for time the memory of the most chaste and elegant luxury.

Prince Khurram, who won the slight title Shahjahan, 'Lord of the World,' was the third son of Jahangir.

When his affable and befuddled father received the English ambassador, Sir Thomas Roe noticed this haughty prince standing apart. 'I never saw so settled a countenance,' he wrote, 'nor any man keep so constant a gravity, never smiling nor in face showing any respect or difference of men; but mingled with extreme pride and contempt of all.' He was already a conqueror at twenty-two. He had made the Rajputs of Mewar, the proudest of the Clan of the Sun, admit Mogul overlordship and give tribute of a thousand horsemen (though never a bride).

Possibly the prince was annoyed at the English, for he met them when they were travelling up-country to his father's court, and he was campaigning with a 'marvellous great retinue.' He stopped them forcibly, to see what sort of presents they had for his father. The English guessed that the young man would not let anything good escape him, so they regretted that the presents were sealed and they dared not open them, and pacified him with such gifts as a pair of rich embroidered gloves — which he could not wear in hot India — and an embroidered perfume bag, and such trifles from King James's England. After forcing them out of their way for three days, the prince saw nothing to gain, and let them go.

When he was twenty, already married and the father of two children, he was given dark-eyed and devoted Arjumand Bana Begam as wife, the niece of Nurjahan, and daughter of bold and predatory Asaf Khan (the great lord who treated himself as a king, with his twelve terraced gardens in Kashmir, his feasts of fifty dishes). Nineteen-year-old Arjumand was called Mumtaz Mahal, 'Ornament of the Palace.' She was silently, passionately devoted to Shahjahan, and he to her. The outer world did not know her. She never appeared as her aunt did, having neither the need, since her husband was no broken reed, nor possibly the taste or ability. But she had the family force and charm, and held lavish Shahjahan devoted to her alone until her death at thirty-nine. Since, according to one traveller, the Moguls ignored any wife after she was thirty, Nurjahan and Mumtaz Mahal were exceptional women.

The marriage was politically strong, since it won Shahjahan the support of Asaf Khan, and it was passionately satisfying to him. The Persian girl Arjumand needed to go to no holy man. One child after another was born — eight sons and six daughters in eighteen years; too many rival sons for the empire, and too much exhaustion for the devoted wife, who followed him, bearing children as they went, through campaign and exile.

After Shahjahan had rebelled and refused to help his father win back Kandahar, he lived in exile four years, from 1623 to 1627. The years of exile were not necessarily all bitter. There were certain pleasures in living in a white palace rising like a boat from the shining lake at Udaipur, with a stone maze in a water courtyard, in which swimmers could play hide-and-seek. Rather a paradise with a favourite, devoted wife. The sunny lolling by waters was ended when the news came, in October, 1627, of Jahangir's death. Shahjahan, then in the Deccan, rushed north, sending ahead efficient orders to kill all his male relatives.

Khusru had been already strangled, and was now mourned as a saint by the people. Prince Parwits had died from drink or poison — no one bothered to question much. Shahryar nicknamed 'Good for Nothing,' even though married to Nurjahan's daughter and supported by her cunning, had no chance against Shahjahan backed by Asaf Khan, and was caught and blinded. One way or another, all his male relatives, except one who escaped across the border, were killed. In February, 1628, Shahjahan without opposition mounted the throne of India. He made it a peacock throne.

He inherited this wealth: A yearly revenue from the country of about two hundred and twenty million rupees, and thirty million for his own privy purse from the crown lands — the rupee worth two shillings then and buying about seven times what it does today. He had two underground treasure-storerooms, each seventy feet square and thirty feet high, one holding gold, and one silver. The Mogul jewels were his to play with. Shahjahan hung on his head and neck and arms and waist jewels worth two million rupees, and, when he took them off, gave them to the women of the harem to keep. He could choose one of two identical rosaries, limp strings of a hundred and twenty-five large mild rubies, set with a topaz between each pair, and the middle ruby weighing a hundred and twenty-eight carats.

The rest of his jewels, valued at three million rupees, were kept by slaves in the outer apartments. Shahjahan decided that it was a pity not to have them seen. He ordered them set into a throne. The shifting masses of brilliance were brought before him, and he ran his fingers through and held them up and cannily chose the stones to use. The goldsmiths set to work in 1628 — while Myles Standish was cleaning his muskets in Plymouth — on a gold, bedlike throne, six feet long and four feet broad, studded with jewels, with twelve pillars green with emeralds holding up an enamelled roof — the workmanship and beauty of the enamel as rare as the stones. The throne was named from the two peacocks who stood with tails spread, made of jewels to give the colour of their feathers. It took seven years to make.

While the peacock throne was being built, a famine spread in the Deccan and Gujarat. Shahjahan had been responsible for some of the waste; he had gone to besiege Bijapur in 1630, and allowed his armies to destroy crops and kill people on whichever road they marched. Local supplies gave out. But the dread lack was widespread. The official historian Abdul Hamid wrote: 'Life was offered for a loaf, but none would buy; rank was to be sold for a cake, but none cared for it... the pounded bones of the dead were mixed with flour and sold... destitution at last reached such a pitch that men began to devour each other, and the flesh of a son was preferred to his love.' Pestilence came with the famine, deathly sickness that carried off seventeen of the twenty-one English traders settled at Surat. Naked dead were dragged out by the heels, and in some places stolid Peter Mundy, travelling up from Surat to Burhanpur, could hardly find room to pitch his tent, clear of corpses. Shahjahan did not adequately meet the spreading horror. To be sure, he reduced taxes by one eleventh — when the land was bone-bare of produce and could yield nothing. He started a few soup kitchens and gave away a hundred and fifty thousand rupees — not worth the ruby on his aigrette.

Mumtaz Mahal was with him at Burhanpur, and in the second year of the famine, her fourteenth child was to be born. For thirty hours she suffered, and the legend says that the child cried out from her womb, and she knew by that she must die. In June, 1631, she died, when she had been empress only four years. She did not live to see her husband sitting on his peacock throne or living in his marble masterpieces.

Shahjahan was overpowered with grief. For a week he did not show himself to his people — a desperate omission. He let the governing of India go by. He wanted to turn fakir. He gave up colours and scents and jewels and forbade music and song for a time. If he went to the harem, he came out weeping, saying, 'Nobody's face can delight me now.' He cried beside her body, 'Empire has no sweetness, life itself has no relish for me.' His dark beard turned rapidly white.

He ordered the tomb for his wife. He bought land on the Jumna River from Rajah Jai Singh, the grandson of Akbar's friend and brother-in-law, Man Singh. In 1632, the Taj Mahal was begun. All the master architects of India submitted plans, but no one is certain who the final architect was. When the emperor chose a design, a wooden model was made. He studied it and suggested details of beauty. For eleven years it was building, Shahjahan watching it rise by the river with delight in the perfect finish of each part. The man who made the dome was named Ismail Khan Rumi. The writer of Tughru inscriptions came from Kandahar, the master mason from Agra, the chief carpenter from Delhi. In the pure marble, the flowing pattern of vines was inlaid in twenty kinds of semi-precious stones sent from afar — cornelian from Kandahar, lapis from Ceylon, onyx from the 'upper world,' gold stone from Basrah, and jasper from Persia. When all was finished, and the garden with its reflecting pool and cypress laid out, Mumtaz Mahal's body was placed underground. Shahjahan planned that opposite her tomb, across the slow Jumna, his own should rise in black marble.

He decided it was his duty to continue as emperor, and went back to the routine of his government. Opinions differ as to his reign. Tavarnier said he ruled like a father of his country, and that the police were so strict in all things that the roads were safe and there were few robbers. He was not so tolerant as Akbar and Jahangir however. There was a period when he ordered many Hindu temples destroyed, and a few years when he was maddened by Portuguese action to persecute Christians. But his repressions did not have the effect of rousing strong rebellions, and he had no foreign aggressor to meet.

Building was his originality. The taste of the emperor or his period was the culmination of Islamic elegance — just before it lost the strength of its solid forbears. The lightness and grace were breath-taking, and the proportions just and secure. Whether or not the somewhat feminine Saracenic architecture satisfies, this was its final expression.

Shahjahan spent the equivalent of about three million pounds sterling on his buildings. From 1632 to 1637 he lived at Agra, making his fairy-tale palaces within the walls of the fort that Akbar and Jahangir had used. Then he decided that Agra was too hot in the summer to be a capital. For more than six months of the year people slept outdoors — commoners in the streets, and the better classes on their watered terraces or gardens. One could not bear to touch a hand then even to marble walls, although the palace had underground chambers for the heat of day, and plenty of water was raised to flow through channels and fountains in the rooms. Moreover Shahjahan probably wanted a memorial to himself, separate from associations with his father and grandfather. So from 1633 to about 1650 he was creating his new Delhi — Shahjahanabad — using up old Hindu temples in the process, and raising lovely white marble domes and pavilions set in gardens within red sandstone fortress walls. He built the great Friday Mosque at Delhi — a little too suggestive of striped candy, but magnificent. In Lahore he built a palace and the white Shalimar Gardens, and mosques and forts in Kabul and Kandahar and Ajmere. The buildings of Shahjahan are always beautiful. His contribution is the last breath of wonder to India.

Shahjahan was a steady ruler. His day of work was regular. Though he sat in marble elegances, he was not idle upon his cushion. It was his habit to wake at four and say a prayer with his face turned toward Mecca, and recite verses of the Koran, before he went for prayer in the royal mosque. Next he showed himself at his eastern window to the crowds for more than half an hour and listened to complaints, or possibly saw an elephant fight at dawn under the fort walls. At Agra his public audience was held on the spot where Akbar and Jahangir had sat under canvas. Here Shahjahan had built a red sandstone hall over two hundred feet long, painted with white lime and supported by forty pillars, open to the air on three sides. In the centre of the fourth wall, Shahjahan sat in a niche of pure white marble, inlaid by a Florentine artist with a pattern in *pietra dura.* At a grand darbar, his sons stood to right and left, and the chief officers of state faced the emperor rank upon rank in precise gradation, crowding within the silver fence. Beyond that precious railing in the courtyard, the lesser officials found place under a gold-embroidered canopy. Here governors and chiefs of departments brought reports and petitions, and needy scholars and pious men asked help. Here he watched his saffron-legged horses and black-stained elephants led past to show their condition. After about two hours he went to his hall of private audience, a delicate marble canopy with a frail inlay of gold and semiprecious stones. In Delhi this was a building like a jewel-case for the peacock throne. Through the coolness of white, shell-fluted arches he could look out to gardens glowing as enamel, and believe the Persian verse written on its walls, 'If there is a Paradise on earth, it is here — Ah, it is here, it is here.'

In such a building he drafted important letters or revised firmans and sent them to be sealed by the great seal, which Mumtaz Mahal used to keep. He fingered the trinkets his antlike artisans brought for inspection, or looked at architects' plans and sent messages for their guidance. Wednesday was the great day of court, with the qazis, judges of canon law, and the adils, judges of common law, grouped before him to receive his deciding judgment. Then, after secret consultations in the Shahburj, the impassive emperor went for his lunch and siesta to the harem, where rosewater flowed through the channel in the floor and 'in its passage made such a pretty murmur as helped to tie their senses with the bonds of sleep.' Fans moved the air; masseurs were at call gently to grip the arms and shoulders and stir the blood agreeably. These hours between twelve and four were not entirely carefree. When the empress lived, she had gathered the pleas of needy women, orphans, or genteel poor, or beggars, and this was the hour for women's petitions. The emperor considered, and gave lands or pensions or jewels.

When the heat was beginning to calm at four in the afternoon, he again held a public audience and prayer — rhythmic and athletic regimented Moslem prayer. At six-thirty he and his chosen gathered in the Paradise-on-Earth Hall, lit with perfumed candles in jewelled candelabra, and, after finishing more affairs, listened to music. By half-past eight he left the courtiers to go to the harem, where his women sang and amused him. When he went to bed, a reader sat behind a screen reading books of travel, or the lives of saints and prophets! His favourite books were the life of his ancestor Timur and Babur's autobiography, to whose syllables he went to sleep.

Very stately, and with good taste, he reigned for thirty years. During that time the affairs of foreigners in India were developing and changing. The Portuguese lost ground. At Hugli, near where Calcutta was to begin, the Portuguese traders under a firman from the emperor had built a port settlement and were very high-handed. They had their own customs house and imposed revenues on imports, especially on tobacco. They undertook a slave trade, and seized orphan children to bring them up as Christians, forcing themselves on Shahjahan's attention by stealing two slave girls whom Mumtaz Mahal claimed. He ordered the Portuguese exterminated — no less. The Governor of Bengal, who had to undertake it, was afraid of the business-like arms and ships of the foreigners, so he collected a huge force to attack the little settlement. About three hundred armed white men and seven hundred converted native soldiers — and thousands of non-combatants — resisted for three months, then with misery and pestilence died. Four thousand were taken prisoner to Agra and offered the choice of conversion to Islam or torture. Their fierce religious faith made them choose — as the Moslems put it — to 'go from prison to hell.' That ended the Portuguese — and Christian — influence in Mogul India.

Down on the coast where Madras now spreads, where huge surf then rolled in to a harbourless shore, a piece of land was granted in 1639 to an English trader, the first land owned by England in India.

The beloved Mumtaz Mahal had left six children who reached maturity. All had sharply defined characters, and they played among themselves and their father an amazing drama over the stage of India. The four brothers had two sisters. Each girl, forbidden to marry because a princess's husband was dangerous, focussed her talent of intrigue in the service of a beloved brother.

Dara Shikoh was the oldest son, and best beloved by Shahjahan. He, like Khusru, seems to have been attractive, thoughtful, and kind, loyal to his father and loving to his family. Like Akbar, he was fascinated by comparative religions, and read the Talmud and the New Testament, as well as the Hindu Vedanta and the works of Moslem sufis. The Persian translation which he had made of the Vedanta was that which reached Europe. He studied with yogis and fakirs. Although he was nominally a Mohammedan, this free-thinking spoiled him as a rallying-point for fanatics. The handsome prince stayed about his father's court until he was forty-two, living almost royally, his father's right hand. People who came to court knew they had to buy Dara's favour. The ease and subservience spoiled him. He had no shrewd campaign experience to test his toughness, no knowledge of how men act in desperation. Witty, polite, and a little disdainful, in the security of his father's court his judgment was not tried. The elder princess, Jahanara, gay and good-looking, her father's favourite, was Dara's partisan.

Shuja, the second son, was like Dara, more discreet and firmer, but lost himself in his pleasure. Wine, women, and song made him neglect everything else and disqualified him as a serious rival.

The youngest son was Murad Bakhsh, a bold swordsman and hearty eater, without brains, but with boundless courage.

It was the third son, Aurangzeb, long-fingered, thin-lipped, who threatened. Crafty and devious, with the excellent refuge of piety, Aurangzeb was like an animal with two holes. When his worldly schemes made a dangerous exit, he had piety as a way out. He could remark that he meant to give up ambition and turn fakir. The most zealous Mohammedan could not find a flaw in his religious regularity.

Aurangzeb's training-ground was chiefly the Deccan. The Moguls had not yet conquered all of those five proud kingdoms. Akbar had only begun, and Jahangir had not succeeded. Shahjahan campaigned there in 1635 and 1636, with ruthless wastage and sale of prisoners as slaves, and forced Golconda and Bijapur to accept his terms, pay a gift and do as he told them, although they still were theoretically independent states.

He left Aurangzeb, at eighteen, as his viceroy, and the boy had to govern four provinces — Kandesh, Berar, wild and hilly Telingana, and Daulatabad. The Deccan lands were in poor condition, their revenue sunk to one third. They were a drain on the empire. The boy was strict and able, and was making improvements, when chance and intrigue recalled him to other government and campaigns. When he was footloose again, the bitter hatred between him and Dara prevented his staying at court. He was sent back to the Deccan.

This time he went boldly forward with his schemes, treacherous or otherwise, to take rich Bijapur and Golconda. These were his methods: In Golconda there was a certain Persian adventurer named Mir Jumla, a no-one-at-all, who became a rich diamond merchant, then wazir, then conqueror, in the name of Golconda, of southern lands, and looter of temples. He grew insolent and dictatorial to the king, and when checked, wrote to Persia, to Aurangzeb, to Bijapur, any or all, to arrange the best terms for treachery. Finally, when his drunken son vomited on the royal carpet, the long-suffering king imprisoned him and his family. Aurangzeb persuaded Shahjahan to send an ultimatum demanding their release. Without giving the king time to receive and follow Shahjahan's orders, Aurangzeb sent cavalry against him, with these instructions: 'Qutb-ul-Mulk is a coward... surround his palace with your artillery, and also post a detachment to bar his flight... But before doing so, send a carefully chosen messenger to him saying, "I have been so long expecting that you would meet me and hospitably ask me to stay with you. But as you have not done so, I have myself come to you." Immediately on delivering this message, attack him impetuously, and if you can manage it, lighten his neck of the burden of his head.'

That was the manner in which Aurangzeb acted. Before he could capture Golconda by siege, however, Dara and his sister got the ear of Shahjahan, who learned the story of treachery and angrily called Aurangzeb away from the siege. Aurangzeb was like a dog on leash, bounding at each capital, and jerked back just as he was going to seize it. He took the three-moated, walled fort of Bidar, a sweet-palaced, university city, and was practically ready to defeat Bijapur, when Shahjahan stopped him and made peace. But he had won the great prize, Mir Jumla, with diamond bags and the even more precious artillery of trained European gunners.

While Aurangzeb was doing all this conniving and fighting, Dara had stayed at court acting as viceroy of the Punjab, but with only one campaign, the third futile and costly attempt on Kandahar, to his military experience.

In September, 1657, Shahjahan fell dangerously ill, when his four sons were men between thirty-three and forty-three years old. As if the starting-gun had sounded, the race for the throne began. Dara alone did not rebel. He nursed his father faithfully, and even though Shahjahan made a will leaving him the sovereignty of India, he did not assume it, but acted in his father's name and interest. In Bengal, Shuja proclaimed himself king, and one army had to be sent after him. From his south, cautious Aurangzeb seized the ferries so that no news of whatever he might do could get through to his father. He and Murad had corresponded and made alliance, but crafty Aurangzeb wanted to temporize, and send hollow letters of friendship to Dara. They had agreed to divide the empire, and by the terms of the agreement, Aurangzeb's brains were to be paid better than Murad's brawn.

Aurangzeb, while writing his father that his loving heart was distracted by the sad news of his health, and that like a loyal son he was hurrying to Agra, collected saltpetre and sulphur for making munitions, and was taking gunpowder and fuses from the forts. In February, he joined Murad who could not wait to declare himself emperor, and the combined armies marched north. Near Ujjain, they defeated the imperial army, divided by feuds between Rajput clans, and hampered because Shahjahan had given orders to spare his sons.

Dara, the last defence of the emperor, then led a great force out of Agra. With care he took all forts and fords along the Chambal River, thinking himself firmly entrenched against his lean brother. Aurangzeb simply learned of an obscure ford forty miles upstream and forced his men to it, though five thousand died of thirst in the terrible May heat. He got behind Dara and had a free road to Agra.

Dara was hindered also by orders of the emperor, who hoped naïvely that his sons would stop quarrelling. When Aurangzeb's smaller army came up, dog-weary, Dara rode out to see them, but failed to attack instantly with his fresh troops. That was his undoing. Aurangzeb rested his army all night, and in the morning, his seasoned men on seasoned horses, supported by crack European artillery, attacked. The Rajputs, loving Dara, fought wildly, in the yellow robes of finality. But Dara made tactical mistakes and the last charge of Aurangzeb came on like waves of the sea. The fight was already decided when Dara was persuaded to leave his elephant and mount a horse. His troops, half dead with heat, in armour that blistered their skins, saw his elephant howdah empty, and thinking him dead, fled in disordered dismay.

Dara, dazed, taken from the field, reached Agra at nine at night, and shut himself up in the palace, too broken-spirited to see his father. He begged to leave. With his wife and children he set out toward Delhi at three in the morning. Shahjahan sent him mules carrying gold coins. Faithful men trailed after or joined him, until by the time he reached Delhi he had five thousand followers.

Aurangzeb, after the battle, told Murad the victory was entirely due to his courage and that his reign would date from that day. He said he preferred a life of piety to the throne, anyhow. The brothers stayed ten days in a garden outside Agra, while many of the emperor's men and officers deserted to them. In June they began to besiege the Agra fort. It was too strong to take, so they cut off the water supply in midsummer.

Shahjahan sat in his white marble rooms; the watercourses were dried, the fountains and baths were stark stone. The heat baked without relief, and soon the drinking-water gave out. The courtiers, unused to suffering, slipped down over the fort walls. Shahjahan endured it for three days, then begged Aurangzeb not to kill him by thirst. Aurangzeb only wrote curtly, 'It is your own doing.'

Shahjahan surrendered. He stepped down from his peacock throne. Aurangzeb made him prisoner in the harem of the palace. Princess Jahanara tried to make peace, but failed.

Now Murad began to wonder. His officers advised him to get clear while he could. Aurangzeb soothed him, gave him money and horses, and asked him to a feast; and when he was quite drunk, seized him and sent him to Gwalior Fort, where three years later he was beheaded.

The story of Dara's flight is tragic. One kingdom could not hold the two brothers. He retreated from place to place. Though all the Punjab was devoted to him, his despair infected the courage of his men. Relentless Aurangzeb let nothing stop his pursuit. Even when Dara had fortified Ajmere, holding the pass between two hills, apparently impregnable, Aurangzeb while attacking the front sent mountaineers up the steep cliff, and had him surrounded. Everywhere Aurangzeb sent letters and bribes ahead, and Dara now found people turned against him. His beloved wife was ill, and they had to go on — with one horse, one bullock cart, five camels — on toward the Sind. It was like Humayon's exile, only sadder. The illness and death of his wife prevented his escape to Persia. Frantic with grief, the world grew dark, he cared for nothing. He sent his remaining seventy men to escort her body to be buried in a saint's graveyard in Lahore. Whereupon an Afghan chief, upon whose hospitality he had thrown himself, could not resist a bribe.

Dara was paraded through Delhi under the sun of August on a shabby elephant in a dirty dress, with a slave with drawn sword behind him. The people wept and lamented, but did nothing — and Dara was soon killed.

His handsome son was sucked into the vortex of his defeat. Sulaiman, who had been victorious in Bengal, but had turned back to save his father, was finally captured fleeing over the snows of high Ladak toward Tibet. The lovely youth, whom all the ladies admired and pitied, was given poison.

Now Shahjahan sat in the Agra palace. No friend could see him. Spies listened to all he said. He was guarded by an insulting eunuch, who treated him like a slave. And he had time to think of his three sons dead, and one holding him prisoner. His consolation was the beautiful Jahanara, so like her mother, who tended him devotedly, and his concubines and dancing-women.

Helpless, the old king wrote bitter letters to his son, and Aurangzeb smugly answered he was merely the chosen instrument of God. 'I was compelled,' he wrote, possibly sincerely, 'out of regard for the next world, to take up the perilous load of the crown.' Father and son quarrelled over the crown jewels that Shahjahan had so gloated over. Aurangzeb insisted upon keeping them, saying he was God's custodian.

Shahjahan warned him that his own sons might rebel, to which the present emperor confidently answered, 'Everyone gets from God according to his own intentions, and as my intentions are good, I believe that I shall not get anything but good [from my sons].' The gods were laughing.

Shahjahan gave up his futile protest. In his grief, he turned to prayer. For six years he lived in Agra Fort, thinking of the space where his own black marble tomb was to have been. He died in 1666, seventy-four years old. According to legend his last hours were in the octagonal Jasmine Tower, the pure carved trifle, from which he could see the Taj Mahal looking no bigger than one of his former pearls.

21. *Aurangzeb, Who Earned His Shroud*

1659–1707

FOUR dropsical minarets and a narrow and bigoted dome rise from Aurangzeb's imitation of the Taj Mahal, near Aurangabad in the Deccan. For months the ox-carts were carrying loads of marble to make a tomb for his proudest wife. But all the effort produced only a Taj Mahal like a reflection in a distorting mirror. Grace and a sense of proportion were left out of Aurangzeb's nature. The tomb is what one might expect.

And a strange little Hindu shrine hidden in Deccan wilds fixes the memory of the terror he left in the hearts of simple people. A long dark tunnel, tended by calm-eyed, nearly naked Brahmans, burrows into a hill. At the far end is a statue of Vishnu in his boar incarnation, scrambling for dear life into the earth, leaving only his rear exposed to the red paint of worshippers. The popular legend today which explains his curious position is that originally he was on the outside, but he heard that Aurangzeb, the idol-smasher, was coming. And although he was not afraid, he thought it prudent to burrow deeper and deeper. In fact, he is still digging farther from daylight each year, to escape Aurangzeb.

Aurangzeb left no buildings such as Shahjahan gave to India. He is recalled more often by the broken noses or heads of Hindu gods — a trail that does credit to his greatest virtue, industry. He devoted the forty-nine years of his reign, grimly and conscientiously, to ruining India.

He really was conscientious. He followed as exactly as he could all the rules of the Hanifa sect of Mohammedans, and wanted to impose the religious laws he approved on his millions of subjects. He was unsparing of himself. No coolie in the land worked longer than he. All his life, from his teens to his ninetieth year, he was fighting — with time out for prayers. His private life was self-denying (that is, if one excepts the murders). His choice of food and dress was austere in that time of display. He kept strictly to the Koranic four wives, taking only one concubine, his aunt's wanton slave girl, in a single outburst of 'shameless importunity.' He was learned, and could speak Arabic and Persian, Turki and Hindi. In pious humility he made copies of the Koran which he sold for the holy mendicants, and he sewed little caps that earned enough annas to buy a coarse shrift to wear in his grave.

He was hardened and trained from his eighteenth year in body-wasting campaigns, and he was a scrupulous administrator, a perfectionist, trying with clerical thoroughness to oversee each detail. He was shrewder than any enemy — except perhaps that Shivaji, reincarnation of Satan. Believing that trickery was a necessary weapon of kings, he outschemed them all. But his cunning overreached itself. Only a stringently ungenerous man could practise such guile and undervalue the human despair he caused.

With human beings he was penny-wise and pound-foolish. Either Babur's warmth or Akbar's tolerance, added to his own qualities, could have made him great. He might have then avoided the wastage of Sikh and Maratha uprisings, and the first toe-holds of the French and English in India. He might have held the Mogul dynasty steady. With half his talent and a better disposition, he would have been magnificent.

But Aurangzeb had hollows in his heart. He was bored with painting, he had no humour, and he was to banish music entirely from his court. Loyalty and affection were blanks to him. His crop in life and empire was briars and thistles. Aurangzeb went back to strictest Moslem piety — reversing the generosity of Akbar — piety such as Ala-ud-Din of the Khiljis had held, back to the theory that the emperor is the shadow of the one God, and the faithful are his soldiers, whose duty is unquestioning obedience; and that infidels — who should in strictness be killed or converted — may by utmost tolerance be allowed to live under handicaps.

Long-nosed Aurangzeb, who seems always to have had a white beard, always to have been old, who usually wore the sheer white unadorned cotton robe of the pious, is curiously like other self-righteous Puritans, certain of salvation, sure that they represent God — except that he added Oriental cunning and Timurid cruelty.

The story of his reign follows almost tragic lines, for the seeds of defeat were in his nature, and the retribution he suffered for his own choices was almost accurate. His reign rose to a climax when he had conquered more land in India than any other emperor, not excepting Asoka or Akbar, and was taking tribute from the unmolested south of Trichinopoly.

Then all the troubles grew hydra heads — if he cut one, two arose. With all his great enemies gone, a hundred little ones sprang up. He lost control over his wasted land and died bitterly, the cornerstone of chaos.

He began with all the splendour he had stolen from his father and brothers, all the treasure hidden in the white marble, exquisite cities, the horde that Akbar's conquests had brought and Shahjahan's thirty years of peace had held. This treasure did not mean a prosperous country and rich peasantry; it meant solid hard gold and jewels hidden in vaults. And he started with a magnificent coronation to bring exclamations of wonder from visitors hardened to the display of Versailles.

His promise to India was not entirely bad. His apprenticeship under Shahjahan, as general or governor of provinces, seemed encouraging. He was a cool fighter. In a fierce battle with the Uzbeks, he spread his carpet on the battlefield, and, unarmoured, calmly said his prayers. The enemy, open-mouthed at such nerve, generously waited for him to finish. As Governor of Gujarat he had checked robber bands and rebels, and had done the same in Multan and Sind. Governing the Deccan provinces, with sterile soil and the fields turned desert from rainless years, and farmers ruined by the caprice of extortioners, he extended Todar Mall's system as he could, and made treasury loans to poor peasants to buy cattle and seed. He appointed honest men, and an inspector of ordinance to see that imaginative graft was checked. All these things were to his credit to balance against his inhumanity in stealing the throne.

During his first twenty-four years of rule, when his capital was in the north at Agra and Delhi, the surface appearance of might in the Mogul dynasty was unscratched. He remitted, theoretically, the taxes which had cost merchants high tolls on road, ferry or provincial boundary. He put down the usual revolts that followed such a turmoil of uncertainty, the bandits that sprang up in a war-burdened land, and a crop of pretenders who rose like the ghosts of Dara and his son to haunt him. Though frequently moving about, fighting, he considered that a wise policy for a king. He added Assam and Ladak to his tributaries.

The appearance of public splendour was not lessened by his private simplicity. When he went out on his travelling throne, borne on the shoulders of eight men, or on his elephant, all his courtiers had to go along on horseback, swallowing the dust they raised or soaked by thunderstorms, while the king sat dry. These very splendid lords who sniffed the dust were dressed most elegantly in stuffs heavy with gold thread, and when on their own lesser occasions they went out, they travelled like little emperors attended by horsemen and men afoot, with servants waving peacock fans to keep the flies from their faces, or carrying the drinking-bottle and spittoon, developed in tobacco or betel-chewing countries.

This display cost money. So did war. Aurangzeb's arithmetic for India did not come out even.

The cavalry lords under the Mogul system did not inherit their office or wealth; at their death it went back to the emperor's control. The sons of Uzbeks, Persians, Arabs, and Turks, who chiefly made Aurangzeb's courtiers, were fresh adventurers with no backlog of inheritance. Since their fortunes fell with the emperor's, they depended entirely on him for living. From their salaries they might slice a little of each underling's pay. One lord of five thousand, whom the French physician Bernier served, actually supplying only five hundred horsemen, saved nearly five thousand crowns a month for himself. Yet, because of the upkeep of huge establishments, of wives and servants, camels and horses, all to maintain splendour, and from the costly presents they had to return ceremoniously to the emperor, most of the great lords were in debt. It would have been neater to pay them less, and demand fewer jewels in return — easier bookkeeping and planning — but not India.

Aurangzeb had to find the wherewithal to pay for his war of accession. Even in the first years of his reign he was embarrassed. The burden of battles he piled on the ultimate peasant accumulated. A number of his campaigns were needless, instigated by too literal piety and lack of imagination.

Early in his reign he undertook to manage the morals of the country, and appointed his mansabdars to the board of censors to enforce the laws of the Prophet, to forbid drinking of distilled spirits and beer and gambling and illicit sex relations, and to publish the omission of Moslem prayer and fast. The board of censors, rather overwhelmed by the task, began with violence, and soon let it all lapse.

But Aurangzeb's literal mind still wanted literal Moslem law enforced. In the twelfth year of his reign he revived the special tax on Hindus, the hated jizya, a graded tax which fell most heavily on the poor, taking six per cent of their gross produce, while their Moslem neighbours went free. He removed from Moslems irritating inland transport duties and left them in force for Hindus. With a Nazi-like stringency, he tried to remove the minor Hindu clerks and accountants from government office, unless they accepted Islam. This was not quite possible. He trampled harmless vanity by forbidding any Hindu except a Rajput to ride in a palki or on a blooded horse or elephant, or to carry arms. And to make himself thoroughly popular with the overwhelming majority of his subjects, he reverted to the practice of breaking up Hindu temples.

A crop of troubles followed each repressive measure. When he revived the poll tax, the Hindus felt so strongly that a mass of them blocked his path to the great mosque of a Friday, beseeching him to end it. His answer was to send elephants to trample the mob. When he destroyed the magnificent temple in Mathura, the Hindus around Krishna's holy city rebelled. The Jat peasants rose savagely against his repression, and were reckless enough to shame the emperor by desecrating the tomb of his ancestor Akbar. It was ironic that Akbar, who began the policy of tolerance, should have his bones insulted because his great-grandson reversed his ideas.

Aurangzeb also changed Akbar's policy toward Rajputs. That was particularly short-sighted, or obstinate, because the Rajput princes and their troops formed some of his strongest support. A closely linked chain of cause and effect ended in ruin. He alienated the Rajputs, his rebellious son joined them, and they in turn handed the prince to the Marathas, the persistent uprising Hindu enemies of the Moguls. A son joined to the strong Marathas was one cause of taking Aurangzeb to the Deccan, where the last half of his reign went in wastage.

The country had no breathing-space to recover between his campaigns. There were the Sikhs, the religious warriors, a unit of power whom he persecuted and provoked, and the Afghan border tribes whose entangling wars prevented him from using their shrewd mountain soldiery against his other hill foes. But his most severe campaigns were against three internal enemies — the Rajputs, the surviving Deccan sultanates of Bijapur and Golconda, and the Marathas.

At his accession the Rajput states were either quiet or loyally serving the Moguls. The Mohammedan people of Bijapur and Golconda, behind great walls, lived in tottering moral fibre and accumulated wealth, preferring not to provoke the remembered Aurangzeb. The only self-starting enemy — an aggressor with the energy of a persistent mosquito — was the free-lance Shivaji, who was organizing into a hard-hitting force the scattered Hindu race of Marathas.

Shivaji is turned god today by one sect of nationalists, who honour him as patron deity of uprising. He has a temple, and on the Dasahara Festival Day, men and boys in his country parade the roads shouting, 'Victory to Shivaji.' He was an amazing person, a religious bandit who developed a touch of greatness under responsibility. The race which he restored to power was the last triumphant force in crumbling India before the English.

These Marathas were a very ancient people. The Chinese traveller Yuan Chwang, who visited King Harsa, wrote that the country of Maharashtra was regularly cultivated and very productive. The people, he said, were honest and simple, of stern, vindictive character, grateful to friends, relentless to enemies. They had chivalry then, and gave warning to an enemy before attacking him — a chivalry which later disappeared. They kept several hundred mighty champions, who drank wine until one man, lance in hand, was courageous enough to challenge ten thousand comers. And they sent intoxicated elephants against the enemy. King Harsa could not conquer them.

In the course of time they had lost their national unity and many of their qualities of dignity and chivalry, and were a race or caste scattered through different states along the narrow western coastal strip and up on the plateau and hills which rise sheerly above the ocean — rugged, penurious land of difficult crops. As a modern race they had pioneer virtues, literal practical minds, brave but cunning. Sharper-witted than the Rajputs, they had neither their sloth nor their patrician standards of honour and dignity.

Shivaji was brought up by his pious mother, a high-caste Hindu lady, who turned to religion for solace when his father ignored them, leaving them on his grant of land near Poona. His father was a respectable chief who served as headman of two villages under Bijapur. Two strong influences on Shivaji were his mother's religion and the coastal hills. He grew agile as a monkey in the rocks and jungles, and his hardy boyhood playmates became the nucleus of his predatory forces, peasantry of the Maratha and Kunbi castes, swift-moving bands who struck and dodged.

His religious instructor, Ram Das, the Maratha poet, told him: 'Gods, cows, Brahmans, and the faith, these are to be protected.... In all the earth there is not another who can save the faith. Why live when religion has perished? Gather the Marathas together, make religion live again; our fathers laugh at us from Heaven.'

And as champion of a trampled, majority people, who had been treated as dirt because of their religion, Shivaji snowballed his power.

As a private person he did not tally badly. He was a devoted son, a loving father, and good husband. He was abstemious and controlled; he was tolerant of other religions and would not let mosques and Korans be treated with disrespect; he held captured women safe until their relatives came for them — and he kept his own army clear of the encumbrance of women followers. He had complete control of his troops, and could keep them from looting if he wished. He had the magnetism of a leader, swift ability to read character, and hard, practical sense. But as an enemy schemer there is little wonder that he was called the incarnation of Satan.

At nineteen he captured his first fort, and from that time on was a conqueror to fear. He took one state by sending an envoy to the Rajah to ask his daughter in marriage, instructing the envoy to murder the would-be father-in-law when he had gained the audience. With the Rajah dead, he struck instantly at the leaderless garrison. The kingdom fell to his hand like a ripe peach. In 1659, the dowager queen of Bijapur sent her envoy Afzal Khan to call the wild man to account for his raids. This story varies. The Marathas say the envoy had instructions to murder Shivaji.

Others deduce that he went in good faith. The two men met with due ceremony in a rich tent raised on the crest of the hill, below a fort and overlooking a wide valley. The Bijapur troops were kept out of the way. Shivaji seemed to have no army. Both men appeared unarmed. When they embraced sweetly, Shivaji opened his hand hiding a set of steel claws, and tore out Afzal Khan's bowels. Then he leaped for safety, calling his troops, who rose from all sides and destroyed the Moslems.

When Aurangzeb sent his uncle, viceroy of the Deccan, to capture Shivaji, the Mogul thought himself safely encamped in Poona, surrounded by his harem and guards and ten thousand soldiers. But Shivaji, with four hundred men went, at dark, into the city he knew so well, telling the sentry he brought troops to the viceroy. They hid till all the servants were thick with sleep after their heavy meal following the day's fast of Ramzan, then from a kitchen they unbricked a wall to the harem, and actually reached the viceroy and cut off his thumb and killed his son and several servants. The humiliated viceroy, after this disgrace, had to ask for his recall.

Aurangzeb then sent against him Jai Singh, the Rajah of Amber, the man who built the strange astrological observatories near Delhi and Jaipur that rise like the geometry of the moon. The Maratha forts threw down lighted naphtha flares, leather bags full of gunpowder, bombs, and big stones, and such miscellaneous welcome. Jai Singh, as a fellow Hindu, preferred to negotiate with Shivaji. He finally persuaded him to come to court at Agra.

That was a moment in which Akbar would have managed to win a loyalty, but which Aurangzeb in his meanness missed. Shivaji was a great man in his wilds, but a little man when he stood before the Emperor of India, sitting on the peacock throne before salaaming kings. A flattering attention might have turned his vanity to good account.

Aurangzeb, in his public audience, after calling graciously, 'Come up, Shivaji Rajah,' sent him back to stand among the third-class nobles. Precedence is most jealously loved in India. Shivaji saw in front of him a certain man's back which he had last seen running from him in battle. He fainted from shame. His indignation was indecorously expressed. And he soon found himself in a palace which became a prison, walled by guards of artillery. Almost anyone else would have lost his head — both ways.

But Shivaji escaped like a magician from his knots. First he dismissed his men to safety. Then he let it be known that he was ill, and to propitiate the gods of sickness he sent out large hampers of food daily, carried on poles over the shoulders of two men, as gifts to Brahmans. The guards at the gate poked swords through the baskets, but, as days passed, and only food went out, they grew lax. On the first day after the guards failed to poke, Shivaji, pretending severe illness, put his brother in his place in bed, flinging over the coverlet an arm which wore his bracelet. Then he and his son escaped in the baskets, and the brother later strolled out in his own person. Satan had flown off with Shivaji. He went home by most roundabout trails, and proceeded to organize the nation of Marathas which was to be the triumphant foe of the decaying Moguls.

For the years from 1667 to 1669 Shivaji was quiet, busying himself establishing a government based upon the Code of Manu. He appointed a peshwa, prime minister, as chief of a council of eight advisers, each theoretically in charge of a department, such as finance or foreign affairs. One adviser had the duty of expounding sacred Hindu law. A panchayat, or jury of neighbours, settled minor disputes. The clerical work was done by Brahmans, because the fighting Marathas scorned to read and write.

Much of the Maratha state revenue was simply robbery, or a sort of blackmail — the Maratha 'chauth,' one fourth the revenue of any land claiming immunity or protection from Shivaji. It was not entirely pleasant to live under his rule. An English traveller, Dr. Fryer, wrote in 1673, 'This is the accustomed sauce all India over... the great fish prey on the little.' People were racked and tortured to force them to confess where their money was hidden. Shivaji sat in his tent cutting off the heads and hands of those who concealed their wealth.

It is amazing how often robbery and religion went together in India — bandits in the name of the faith.

Shivaji gained fame and strength because he brought the Hindu religion into temporal power again.

Aurangzeb was not quite sensible enough to leave him quiet. He demanded some arrears of tribute which Shivaji had no idea of paying, whereupon the Hindu chief looted a matter of fifty-one villages and audaciously imposed blackmail on places in Kandesh subject to the emperor himself. The Maratha army depended on light cavalry—rough riders over broken country. Their simple war machine could run circles around the encumbered, harem-and-bazaar-bothered Mogul armies.

Twice Shivaji insulted the power of Aurangzeb by swooping down on the wealthy port of Surat, a city north of the present Bombay, nourishing two hundred thousand inhabitants, with infant colonies of English, Dutch, and French traders. He did what he pleased with all but the fighting foreigners. In the second raid, the French bought him off, but the English, amazingly, with fifty sailors, defended an unfortified open house against the looting of his fifteen thousand — which shows the low morale of

Aurangzeb's troops, since such a small nucleus of pluck could inspire respect in the bogey-man, Shivaji.

Although death ended his menace in 1680, and his son Sambhuji was a violent, capricious rake, who could not hold the nation together, yet the followers by this time had had enough spirit and skill injected into them to do damage in smaller groups as separate gadflies.

Such were the Marathas who were to keep the old man, Aurangzeb, wearily in his war tents.

Aurangzeb definitely provoked the Rajputs. He did not even spare temples in the city of Amber belonging to his ally Jai Singh whom he probably schemed to poison. He tried to steal the infant heir of Mawar. With a small cunning, he plotted to make a wedge of Moslem rule through Rajputana by conquering the State of Mawar (now Jodpur). But the Sun Rajputs of Mewar made single cause with their neighbours, and both took to the hills between their two states. From this strong centre they could fling themselves down on either side, before the Mogul reinforcements could make a long détour around the base. With the advantage of home and familiar mountains, and the urge of self-defence, the Rajputs put terror into the hearts of the Moguls.

Aurangzeb's son Akbar, neither too energetic nor too capable a general, nevertheless resented it when Aurangzeb criticized him sharply for his failure to conquer them. The censure fanned the rebel spark in every prince. Akbar deserted to the Rajputs, who promised to help him steal his father's throne if he would restore a more liberal policy. Aurangzeb now tasted his own bitter medicine. When he sent letters of parental moralizing to his son, the prince replied saucily: 'What good did you do to your father that you expect so much from your son? O thou that art teaching wisdom to mankind, administer to thine own self what thou art teaching others!'

Actually Aurangzeb was in sharp danger. He was at the city of Ajmere with only a few clerks and eunuchs and doddering soldiers, his faithful fighting divisions over a hundred miles away, while Akbar was backed by his Mogul command (none too willing, to be sure) and thirty thousand Rajputs. If Akbar had been the man his father was, Aurangzeb, too, would have ended his days as prisoner in some fortress. But the prince, with one hundred and twenty miles to march to strike his father, loitered and wasted fourteen days on the journey. Meanwhile Aurangzeb sent wild couriers who got reinforcements to him from practically the same distance in two days. When the Moguls discovered that the old man was fortified, they began to desert Akbar. But his Rajputs were a solid thirty thousand.

The imperial rat in the trap, threatened by his son, used his old cunning. He enticed Akbar's commanding general to his death by a threat to his family. And he wrote a letter, which he contrived to have intercepted by the Rajputs, praising Akbar for luring the Rajputs to their destruction between two Mogul forces. The Rajputs did not wait to waken and question the sleeping Akbar, who had given orders not to be disturbed. They galloped off in a body. To go to sleep master of thirty thousand, and to rub the eyes on waking and find only a few camp servants around, is appalling. Akbar himself ran as fast as he could. The chivalrous Rajputs, discovering their mistake, turned back to take the prince under their protection. With patience and skill they got him through enemy country, where every pass and ferry was guarded by Aurangzeb's men, until they deposited him with the Maratha troops under Shivaji's son. This rebellion diverted Aurangzeb from the Rajput war. Mewar was able to make terms and recover, but Mawar was so worn and torn that for thirty years the state was a pestilence-ridden desert.

In 1681, Aurangzeb, with his rebel son at large among the Marathas, decided it would be wise to go himself to the Deccan. His officers there had loitered and deceived and prolonged their campaigns, because it was their livelihood. The Deccan was called 'the bread of the soldiers of Hindustan.' Also, he wanted to fulfil the ambition of his youth, to get the rich morsels his father had pulled from his grasp, the Mohammedan States of Bijapur and Golconda.

Bijapur fell first, the splendid city, thirty miles around, with its battlemented grey fort walls bearing bell-metal cannon, called haughtily, 'Lord of the Plains'; with a king's tomb rearing a dome larger than Saint Paul's in London. Bijapur, mighty in walls, fell after fifteen months' hopeless suffering, the garrison apparently simply losing heart. The high-nosed emperor went to the Heavenly Palace, sitting under its magnificent arches, to receive submission from the descendants of the men who conceived such beauty. Bijapur's architectural grandeur was emptied of life in two years. A plague swept away the people, and the great grey walls remained, guarding nothing.

When Bijapur fell, Golconda was left exposed. Golconda's name has come down in sounding power as a synonym for fabulous riches. Sinbad the Sailor went there. He threw pieces of meat down the diamond mines, so deep that the stars showed by daylight to any unfortunate who fell in. Sinbad did not risk that. He dropped the meat onto the chunks of diamonds jutting out or lying loose, and big birds floating in the sky swooped down after the meat. Sinbad caught them and took the clinging diamonds away.

Since the time of Sinbad, Golconda's history had been brief.

It was one of the five states that split from the Bahmani kingdom. In 1507, its first king took the title of Kutb Shah. The fable of its wealth was not unfounded; it had fertile irrigated fields, and land touching the coast at ports including San Thomé, where Saint Thomas of the Bible miraculously lived. The Persian adventurer, Mir Jumla, who rose to be diamond merchant, prime minister, and a power in the state, a conqueror who went looting the old temples of the south, and who finally deserted to the Mogul side, used to measure his diamonds by the forty-pound sackful. He had twenty such.

The last Kutb Shah, named Abul Hasan, was a gentle and dissolute soul, who had spent about sixteen years in agreeable idleness as a saint's disciple before he was married to the princess, heiress to the throne of Golconda. His ministers were stronger than he, and he left the government largely to a Hindu named Madanna, while he spent his days in the harem with dancing-girls, according to the popular picture of Eastern monarchs. Haiderabad was his capital city on the plains, first named for a king's mistress, an Indian Babylon where twenty thousand prostitutes danced before the king every Friday, and where twelve hundred leather bottles of fermented palm juice emptied themselves daily. The city of Haiderabad lies open on the plain, and the fort called Golconda rises on a hill a few miles away.

Aurangzeb had several pretexts, if he needed them, to attack the Kutb Shah. 'The evil deeds of that man pass beyond bounds of writing,' he justified himself, 'but by mentioning one out of a hundred... some conception of them may be formed. Placing government in the hands of infidels, giving himself up to debauchery, drinking, and wickedness day and night.' Also, Kutb Shah had subsidized Shivaji and hung a wreath of jewels around his horse's neck.

The Golconda troops were cut by feuds, and the Moguls pursued them in confusion to Haiderabad. Instead of rallying to defend the city, nobles and commanders and the helpless king rushed as fast as they could up to the Golconda Fort, leaving first the rabble and then the incoming soldiers to loot their china and carpets and horses and money. Dishonoured women ran unveiled. Everyone began a mad race to the fort. Once in Golconda, they could feel safe.

Golconda's height is satisfying, a bird's height over the plains. The level land floats away dwarfed and misted and tilting to the horizon. The people who breathlessly climbed with what bundles they could to the fort felt utter security behind the walls of solid granite. The bastions were built of solid blocks, some weighing a ton. Rising fifty feet high these semi-circular towers bulk against the blue sky as the symbol of strength. The only approach to the city was through a walled lane, whose closed gates were spiked with spear-points against elephants, gate after gate topped and dominated by parapets hiding guns and soldiers. In the lowest part of the fort there was room for the whole population of Haiderabad, stone or stucco houses for the rich, temples and mosques, barracks and stables, armouries, caravanserais, offices, palaces, and harems. There were cultivated fields and wells large as houses, with arcades surrounding the steps leading down to their cool depths, giving an unfailing water supply. Above it all a flight of two hundred steps cut in stone led to the uppermost citadel of the citadel, built on solid granite.

Golconda's men kept up a discharge night and day, from towers and walls, of cannon-balls, bullets, rockets, and fiery missiles.

Aurangzeb, after first observing the rite of purification, sewed the seams of the first cotton bag to be filled with earth and thrown in to fill up the moat.

But though Aurangzeb's locust hordes were outside, Golconda need not fear. He pitched his tents about a mile and a half away on the fantastic rock-heap hills. The sixty-nine-year-old emperor had not lost any of his determination. He came in January, 1687, to besiege. A less grim man would have given up.

The Maratha cavalry, dashing about to help Golconda, cut off his food supplies. Famine came into his camp, and with it, pestilence. The heavy monsoon rains flooded rivers and spoiled the siege works and the Mogul tents rose like bubbles from a sea of water and mud. The old man had to cope with sickness and starvation of his army. Abul Hasan and his besieged people, living in dryness and comfort, looked out after the monsoons to a spreading whiteness on the plain below. It was like snow — but snow never falls below that Deccan sky. The spreading whiteness, growing imperceptibly from night to night, was from the bones of Aurangzeb's dead, washed by rains and bleached by sun.

Yet the emperor held steadily to his idea of starving the fort into submission.

Such action as the Moguls had attempted had failed. Golconda's men had made successful sorties and put spikes in the enemies' guns. Twice the Moguls had laid mines under Golconda's walls and stood ready to rush in through the breach, when the mines blew out against themselves. Once, in May, the chief of siege put scaling-ladders up one of the bastions and almost got two men up to the top, while the sentry slept. But a pariah dog, nosing about the wall for corpses, was startled by the stealthy crawlers and barked and yelped, rousing the sentry. Abul Hasan, with humour, gave the dog a golden chain and a collar set with jewels and a golden coat, and three titles to equal those of the siege commander — and the dog, unclean to Mohammedans, sat always on a cushion in the royal presence.

To weaken Mogul morale further, Aurangzeb's son, Prince Muazzim, who did not like to ruin a brother sovereign, tried to negotiate with Abul Hasan, and the emperor had to make him prisoner — his second traitor son. He cried out to his wife, 'Alas, alas, I have razed to the ground what I have been rearing the last forty years.'

Finally the morale of the Mogul camp, beside its hill of bones, was quite gone, and Aurangzeb tried his trump — bribery. His men paid a Golconda soldier to open a postern gate. Stealthy Moguls crept in and opened the main gate to a flood of their army.

A single Golconda rider, who deserves his immortality, Abdur Razzak Lari, without time to saddle or finish dressing, fell upon the incoming Moguls like a maniac, slashing wildly. He did not stop fighting until he had seventy wounds, an eye so badly wounded that he could not see, and his horse reeling from loss of blood. Only then did he give the horse rein, and fall fainting in a garden. He was captured, but so admired that the emperor gave orders to nurse him back to life, and took him later into high command.

Abul Hasan, meanwhile, knowing by the tumult that the end had come, sat upon his throne in the citadel and waited to receive the enemy with the dignity of a royal host. Some say that he told the dancing-girls and musicians to keep on — that every moment spent in such enjoyment was a gain. He bore his imprisonment philosophically, accepting it as part of the inequality of life.

This was apparently the utmost blow that a conqueror need strike to spread himself over all India. The tributary lands fell with the cities. Bijapur and Golconda had swallowed the southern territories of the Hindu State of Vijayanagar, and Aurangzeb could call himself master of all those lands.

Shivaji's son, Sambhuji, meanwhile was little more than a dissolute brigand looting with no plan or organization, so that the Maratha kingdom fell to decay under his rule; there was no safety on the roads, and no security for artisans, and the number of families of weavers in Bombay dropped from six hundred to fifty. In 1689, one of Aurangzeb's generals captured Sambhuji, abusive and insulting. Aurangzeb had him dressed in buffoon's costume with bells, and mounted on a camel and paraded through camp to the beating of drums. Then for his bitter insults he was tortured for two weeks, and his limbs hacked off one by one and thrown to the dogs. When he was at last dead, his head was stuffed with straw and exhibited to drumbeat and trumpet throughout the towns of the Deccan. What sights those sleepy villages have seen! Prince Akbar escaped to Persia and, although he tried, he did no further harm.

Aurangzeb, at seventy-one, was supreme. All his great enemies

AURANGZEB IN OLD AGE

were ended. He took tribute from the farthest south — Trichinopoly and Tanjore.

It was time for him to go home and consolidate his administration. An adviser suggested it, but Aurangzeb bitterly and conscientiously refused. The last twenty-six years of the old man's life were spent in army tents — often enduring floods and plague — futilely trying to capture one little fort after another, while new sets of trifling enemies arose on all sides, unchecked from the slackness of the administration and the corrupt fibre of his officers. He had sown the dragons' teeth and he stood up in his old age, helplessly hacking down each new crop, and plunging himself and his dynasty and country further in debt with the fall of each little fort.

His shrewd bribery began to cost too much. He had offered so many jagirs to renegade fort commanders that there was not even land enough in his empire to supply them. The generals who deserted found they got nothing but a problematical promise to pay.

The government in the north, far from his observation, grew slack and lawless in many parts, and corrupt men did more or less what they chose. Even inside his own army there were plots. Aurangzeb thought he was doing his duty. 'The ruler of a kingdom should not spare himself from moving about,' he wrote his son, 'and avoid staying in one place which outwardly gives him repose, but brings down a thousand calamities.'

He did not realize the calamity he had brought about. The peasants were the essential wealth-producers of India, and the country depended upon their industry. For although places like Bengal were easily fertile, other lands needed much labour to develop. When contractors who paid an annual rent to the emperor got what they could from the peasant, an oppressive man fairly drove the farmer from the land. Bernier wrote of the jagirdars: They 'have an authority almost absolute over the peasantry, and nearly as much over the artisans and merchants of the towns and villages within their district; and nothing can be imagined more cruel and oppressive than the manner in which it is exercised. There is no one before whom the injured peasant, artisan or tradesman can pour out his just complaints... the judges are not invested with sufficient power to redress the wrongs of these unhappy people.' The golden bells at Agra were not enough. Anyhow, the emperor was in the Deccan. Bernier continues:

> As the ground is seldom tilled otherwise than by compulsion, and as no person is found willing and able to repair the ditches and canals for the conveyance of water, it happens that the whole country is badly cultivated, and a great part rendered unproductive from the want of irrigation. The houses, too, are left in a dilapidated condition,

> there being few people who will either build new ones or repair those which are tumbling down. The peasant cannot help asking himself this question: 'Why should I toil for a tyrant who may come tomorrow and lay his rapacious hands upon all I possess and value?'

Even the artists and artisans, making things of delicate beauty under the patronage of emperor or courtier, protected and more highly paid, were not too happy in Bernier's estimation.

> It should not be inferred from the goodness of the manufactures that the workman is held in esteem, or arrives at a state of independence. Nothing but sheer necessity or blows from a cudgel keeps him employed ... he can never become rich... if money be gained, it does not in any measure go into his pocket, but only serves to increase the wealth of the merchant, who, in his turn, is not a little perplexed how to guard against some act of outrage and extortion on the part of his superiors.... A profound and universal ignorance is the natural consequence of such a state of society.

The old emperor in the Deccan, hammering wearily away at one little fort or cavalry band after another, did not consider the broad base upon which the prosperity of India must rest — his people.

It was not entirely Aurangzeb's fault that his dynasty was decaying and the country approaching political demoralization. The despotic system depended so entirely upon the particular despot. The races in India had perhaps grown weary. The climate had its sapping effect upon the last invaders. But certainly Aurangzeb could have helped instead of hindered.

But many forces brought about the eighteenth-century weariness and degeneration in India. The peasants had never, as a mass, tried to remedy their condition. It was inconceivable to people bred in submission to ancient tradition, and caste isolation. The idea of a constitution which gave power to themselves did not germinate under Indian heat. Hinduism was partly responsible for two barriers to progress — the rigid walls of little castes kept people from uniting as human beings; and the philosophy which undervalued this world turned the flood of thinking and energy away from this life, into dreams of the next life, or sequence of lives, or the desired extinction. The stream of mental power turned a mill of fantasy. Perhaps some great mind thereby perceived transcendent truth. But little men's effort and attention went to propitiating demons, to all sorts of imaginary ceremonies prescribed by the sacred books, and to endless piffling magic whose object was release from the present — escape, escape from the hounds of incarnation — at the same time worshipping fertility gods for more sons.

And the Moslems, though unified men who enjoyed the present, with the intolerance of such rulers as Aurangzeb for the majority of their subjects, with their despotism, uninquiring minds, did not, except in the case of an Akbar or Sher Shah, help India, whose poor were too often driven by cudgels and whose rich too often buried their gold.

Neither did the great harems foster strength of character, where jealous wives and eunuchs spoiled the little sweetmeat-fed princelings, petted and initiated into sensuality. They were not the sort of hothouses to grow altruistic rulers.

Into this India, held to an appearance of unity by old Aurangzeb's imperial boundaries, new races of northerners had intruded.

Europe came trading. Portuguese, then Dutch, French, and English.

During Aurangzeb's reign the Portuguese had faded from power, but the English and Dutch were great rivals for Oriental trade. The Dutch were paying most attention to the spice isles, the French were as yet staying in small port settlements, but the English were getting into the foreground. The traders at Hugli, in Bengal, under a fire-eating governor of the East India Company, got into a miniature war with Aurangzeb at Surat, and he ordered the infidels expelled from his realm. But in 1690, the Governor of Bengal invited Job Charnok back to Hugli, and the picturesque nabob, who saved a Hindu widow from a funeral pyre and married her, raised the English flag on the banks of the Hugli, where white, modern Calcutta has grown. At about the time of Aurangzeb's death, the two rival East India companies, which had been fighting like Kilkenny cats, were fused into one monopoly.

But the complicated story was not to be finished in the lifetime of Aurangzeb. With him the empire of India ended. Shadow kings were to follow as Mogul emperors, so weak that wild raiding Nadir Shah of Persia stole the very peacock throne from under them, and the Maratha Confederacy for a giddy moment held most of India under their noses, until a Mohammedan coalition only just prevented the Hindus from ruling the land again.

Dying Aurangzeb was the last political unity in India. After him — the centrifugal forces.

Aurangzeb knew that his end was coming. Toward his ninetieth year he was still trying to rule India himself, and had his faculties if not his judgment. Languor and weakness were chaining him, but his will would force him up and to work. Counting his long life of effort, he saw it totalled dust and ashes. His old friends were dead, and all his wives but the sensual Udaipuri. His rebel son had died in exile, and his most gifted daughter in the prison to which he sent her. His other sons were nothing to lean on. Kam Baksh had streaks of insane folly. But Aurangzeb wrote last letters to two of them, to Kam and to Azam. His mind went back to his youth; his old sense of guilt may have rankled — he had to justify himself to an audience who knew little and cared less about his murdered brother Dara.

To Kam he wrote: 'Worldly men are deceivers... work ought not to be done by hints and signs. Dara Shukoh made unsound arrangements, and hence he failed to reach his point.' At ninety the old man still had to defeat handsome, popular Dara. 'Never trust your sons,' he continued, pathetically and terribly, 'nor treat them in your lifetime in an intimate manner, because, if the Emperor Shahjahan had not treated Dara Shukoh in this manner, his affairs would not have come to such a sorry pass.'

To Azam he wrote farewell:

> Peace be on you!
>
> Old age has arrived and weakness has grown strong; strength has left my limbs. I came alone and am going away alone. I know not who I am, and what I have been doing. The days that have been spent except in austerities have left only regret behind them. I have not done any [true] government of the realm or cherishing of the peasantry.
>
> Life, so valuable, has gone away for nothing....
>
> All the soldiers are feeling helpless, perturbed like me... who, having chosen to leave my Master, am now in a state of trepidation like quicksilver.... Though I have strong hopes of his grace and kindness, yet, in view of my acts, anxiety does not leave me. When I am parting from my own self, who else would remain to me?
>
> Whatever the wind may be,
I am launching my boat on the water.

His will, that had worked so hard without wisdom, held him at the last to his best accomplishment, piety. The white, trembling old man forced himself to repeat the Islamic confession and keep his fingers moving on the rosary while he was gasping his dying breath. On Friday, February 20, 1707, he died — the last of the great Moguls.

End

INDIA with her past of pearls and poverty, savages and mystics, saints and tyrants, multitudes of inarticulate, custom-bound plodders, her artists, fighters, and degenerates, her criminal castes, her high-born priests, her tough Pathans, her hidden jewelled women, her women beasts of burden, her differing philosophic values, her gods — how should anyone enclose India in a book?

And how can anyone assume that it is simple to fit an India with that living past into strange Today. India must make an adaptation. Her multitude of anachronisms in their beauty and decay meet the shock of the present. Opposing values, of an extraverted civilization — observing sciences, machines, a democratic theory, and all the care of life, of women and children, a practical cleanliness as opposed to a poetic — these things, the genius of Today, crash against her introspective development.

India is like an artist who wakes to find a house to tidy; a poet with an undernourished family to provide for. Such an artist, such an unkempt house! Such a poet, and such a thin-boned family! The pangs of adaptation are slow and appear timeless, but if seen in swifter timing would be as dramatic as the throes of birth or the chance of dying.

A civilization, based on ancient cult, fantasy, and poetry, and philosophic disregard of outer fact, meets a civilization based on observation and disciplined regard for outer fact, on practical ability in this world, and rather a thinness of poetry. What should it keep of old and take of new — even if only one person could choose, not three hundred and fifty millions?

If this book has any plea, it is to those who assume that India's thousand difficulties are simple, or that she has only one Gordian knot, to be cut by any one sword.

CHRONOLOGY

Age	*Art and Architecture*	*Literature*
Indus Valley civilization 3500–2700 B.C. Age of Stone and Copper	Mohenjo-Daro and Harappa — city buildings Carved seals, figurines, games, jewelry, in museums at excavations	
Dravidian Supremacy	Undiscovered.	
Age of Vedic Aryans First invasions variously estimated from 2500 B.C. to 1500 B.C. End of period about 550 B.C.		Hymns of the Four Vedas — 1200–800 B.C. Rigveda Max Müller: Sacred Books of the East Griffiths, R. T. H.: Vedic Hymns: Wisdom of the East Series Brief selections Brahmanas — 800–600 B.C. Priestly literature Upanishads — 600 or 550 B.C. Max Müller — Sacred Books of the East
Gautama Buddha. 563–482 B.C. Mahavira, founder of Jain Religion — died 527 B.C.		
Invasion of Alexander the Great. 326 B.C.	Greek influence on later Gandhara school of sculpture — collections at Peshawar, Muttra, Lahore Museums Remains at Taxila	Observations of Alexander's soldiers, in J. W. M'Crindle: The Invasion of India by Alexander the Great
Mauryan Empire. 321–184 B.C. Chandragupta Bindusara Asoka — reigned 274–237 B.C. Built	Primitive Sculpture—three statues in round at Calcutta and Muttra museums Asokan architecture — Persian influence Remains of pillared hall near Patna Rock-cut shrines in Barabar Hills in Bihar Asokan pillars — Delhi, Allahabad, etc. Lion capital in Sarnath Museum Bull capital in Calcutta Museum Small rail at Sanchi and part of Stupa	Mahabharatta — about 400 B.C. until 400 A.D. Translated by M. N. Dutt. Abridged. R. C. Dutt. Ramayana: written by Vilmiki probably between 400 and 200 B.C. Condensed into English verse — R. C. Dutt. Abridged translation (free) R. T. H. Griffiths — Arthasastra: Rules of a Practical Statesman — Translated: R. Sama Sastri Megasthenes—ambassador. J. W. M'Crindle: Ancient India as described by Megasthenes and Arrian. Buddhist Pali Canon: written about 1st Century after Buddha and gathered in Asoka's reign into three Baskets (Pitakas) Selections: Dhammapada: (Words of Religion): Max Müller Psalms of the Brethren: Mrs. Rhys David Jataka: E. B. Cowell

Age	*Art and Architecture*	*Literature*
From fall of Mauryan Empire to Rise of Gupta 184 B.C. — 320 A.D. Sunga dynasty reigned 184 B.C. to 72 B.C. over Patalipatra, Ujjain, Bharhut and Mathura (Muttra) and built Andhras, powerful Dravidian kings, established 220 B.C. and held Deccan until 3rd century A.D. and built Kushan kings of Mongolian origin ruled Kabul and N.W. India from about 50 A.D.–320 A.D. and patronized	Bodghaya carvings Bharhut Stupa — carved railings, now in Calcutta Museum Amaravati Stupa — carvings in Madras Museum Cave temples at Karli Carved gateway to Stupa at Sanchi Gandhara Buddhist Art	Continued growth of epics and lawbooks Bhagavad Gita — Translation by Max Müller Sir Edwin Arnold: Song Celestial Sacred Kural of Tiruvalluwar — 100–300 A.D. Heritage of India Series. Code of Manu — Sacred Law of Hindus. Perhaps in 1st Century A.D. and before 3rd century Translation: Burnell and Hopkins Lalita Vistara: Sanskrit Life of Buddha — the Mahayana Buddha turning God
Gupta Period — Classic Age 320–647 A.D. Gupta Dynasty 320–480 A.D. King Harsa 606–647 A.D.	Best examples of sculpture: Standing Buddha—Muttra Museum Seated Buddha—Sarnath Museum Buddha at Anuradhapura, Ceylon Ajanta Caves — 16, 17 and 19 — carving and frescoes Bagh Caves, frescoes Sanchi — small temple and hall Three temples at Aihole, near Badami Ellora 'The Carpenter's Cave' Cliff carving of the Boar incarnation of Vishnu — Udayagiri, Bhopal	Mahabharatta — full grown by 400 A.D. Panchatantra — Translation by Arthur W. Ryder, probably arose between 300–500 A.D. Taught science and worldly wisdom in fables which migrated through Persia and Arabia to Europe — and Boccaccio, Chaucer, La Fontaine, Grimm. Puranas: Myth and Kingly Story Kalidasa, greatest Sanskrit poet and dramatist wrote Sakuntala and Birth of the War God: Translation — Monier Williams Cloud Messenger: Translation — Charles King The Little Clay Cart: Play translated by Arthur W. Ryder Bana: Khadambari: translated by C. M. Ridding. Harsacarita — the Life of Harsa. Translation by Covell and Thomas Fa-Hien's Travels to India: Buddhist Records of the Western World. Translated by Samuel Beal Yuan Chwang's Travels to India — translated by Thomas Waters

MEDIEVAL HINDU DYNASTIES — SEVENTH TO THE TWELFTH CENTURY

Age	*Art and Architecture*	*Literature*
Chalukyas — repulsed King Harsa with intoxicated champions and elephants, but fell to the Rastrakutas in 753. They built	Temples and caves at Badami, Pattadakal, Aurangabad Caves at Ajanta, Nos. 1–5, 21–26 Caves at Ellora Das Avatara — Ten Incarnations Ravan ka khai — Excavation of Ravanna Dhumar Lena — Ramesvara	Hymns of the Saivite Saints 7th century Bhavabhuti — dramatist 8th century Sankara — born about 788 A.D. Vedanta Sutra and commentaries — the foundation of Vedanta philosophy. Translation by George Thibaut: Sacred Books of the East
Rastrakutas — ruled in Western Deccan. They built	The Kailasa Temple at Ellora Elephanta Cave (with Trimurti)	Puranas continuing Vishnu-Parana — Translation by H. H. Wilson
Pallavas — in south east — 400–750 A.D. Once vassals of Andhras — became dominant on south-east coast, constantly at war with Chalukyas. They built	Monolithic temples and carved cliff at Mamallapuram (Seven Pagodas), near Madras	Alberuni's India — Observations of an Arabic scholar in 1030 A.D.
Cholas, overcoming Pallavas, ruled part of Orissa, most of Madras Presidency, Madura and part of Ceylon. The conqueror, Rajarajadeva built	Tanjore Temple — about 1000 A.D.	
Kesari, or Lion Dynasty of Orissa built	Groups of temples at Bhuvanesvara — from 8th to 11th century	
King Lalitaditya of Kashmir built	Temple of Martand, Kashmir 8th century	1063–81 — Kashmir revision of Ocean of the Streams of Story, derived from 6th century collections

Twelfth to Sixteenth Century

Hindu

Age	*Art and Architecture*	*Literature*
Hoysala kings of Mysore built	Temples at Belur — 12th century Temples at Halebid — 13th century Temples at Somathpur — 13th century	Ramanuja 1175–1250 'Glorious Commentary' 12th cent. Gita Govinda 'Cowherd in Song' — Tantras and late Puranas. A technical literature, partly religious in law, grammer, philosophy, medicine and magic, astronomy and astrology, the science of love, politics, mathematics, including algebra and trigonometry. Songs of Kabir — translated by Rabindranath Tagore
Kings of Orissa built	Temple of Sun at Konarak, near Puri — 13th century	
Jain sect — Rajputana	Temples at Mt. Abu Rajputana — 1032 and 1232	
Pandya Kings (Dravidian) 1100–1350 built	Great temple Trichinopoly	
Last Hoysala king founded	Vijayanagar — City of Victory — about 1328	Traveller's accounts of Vijayanagar in R. Sewall: A Forgotten Empire
Rajputs of the House of the Sun built	Chitor Fort — 7th to 16th century Tower of Victory — 1440–1448	Rajput chronicles included in Col. Tod's: Annals and Antiquities of Rajasthan

Moslem

Age	*Art and Architecture*	*Literature*
Delhi Sultanate Kutb-ud-din 1191 built Iltutmish built Ala-ud-din of Khiljis built Ghiyas-ud-din Tughlak 1321–25, built Feroz Shah, 1354–1490, built	Mosque of the Might of Islam at Kutb Minar Kutb Minar Alai Darwaza Siri Tughlakabad Tomb Ferozabad, college and tomb at Haus-i-khas	Amir Khusrav — poet Many Moslem historians. See Edward Thomas: the Chronicles of the Pathan Kings of Delhi; and Elliott and Dowson: History of India as told by her own historians. Ibn Batuta — at Court of Muhammad Tughlak (Translation: Samuel Lee)
Ahmed Shah dynasty of Gujarat, founded city of	Ahmedabad — 1411 — especially beautiful blending of Hindu and Mohammedan art of building, called Gujarati architecture, lasted until 1538	
Malwa Sultans built	Mandu — magnificent fortress city — in early 15th century	
Bahmani dynasty, in the Deccan, and its offshoots built	Fortress cities (walls, mosques, palaces, and tombs standing) in Gulbarga, Bidar, Golconda Bijapur (Tavernier visited in 1648)	

Period of the Great Moguls
1526–1707

Hindu

Age	*Art and Architecture*	*Literature*
	South Indian bronzes	Tulsi Das wrote 'Lake of the Deeds of Rama' in Hindi
	Rajput miniature painting from 16th–19th century	
Tirumala Nayyak 1623–1639, built	Great temple at Madura	Tukaram — Marathi poet Many minor religious poets

Mogul

Emperor	*Art and Architecture*	*Literature*
Babur — ruled 1526–1530		Babur's Journal: translated by Sir Lucas King
Humayon — ruled 1530–1540; 1555–1556	Mogul School of Miniature painting began from Humayon's visit to Persia	History of Humayon by Gulbadan Begum (Princess Rosebody). Trans. Annette S. Beverage
Akbar — ruled 1556–1605	Tomb of Humayon — Dehli Parts of Agra fort Forts at Allahabad, Ajmere and Srinagar City of Fathpur Sikri	Abul Fazl: Akbarnama, and Ain i Akbari Montserratte's Commentary. Trans. S. S. Hoyland Du Jarric: Akbar and the Jesuits: C. H. Payne Ralph Fitch, Wm. Finch } Foster: Early Travels in India Badaoni — Moslem Historian
Jahangir — ruled 1605–1627 (Nurjahan empress)	Tomb of Itimad ud Daula, Nurjahan's father, near Agra Tomb of Jahangir, Shahdara, near Lahore Part of Lahore Palace Kashmir Gardens: — Verinag, Shalimar, Chasma Shahi, Achibal, Nishat Bagh Shalimar Garden — Lahore	Jahangir's Memoirs. Trans. Alex. Rogers, Henry Burrage, Ed. Capt. Wm. Hawkins: in Purchas his Pilgrims Sir Thos. Roe — Journal. Ed. Wm. Foster Edward Terry (Chaplain): reprinted from 1655 ed. Jahangir's India. Francis Pelsaert's observations. W. H. Moreland
Shahjahan — ruled 1627–1658	Agra fort — Pearl mosque, palaces, gardens Delhi fort and palaces Friday mosque Taj Mahal — Agra	Tavernier — Travels
Aurangzeb — ruled 1658–1707	Mosque at Lahore (accursed) Tomb of wife at Aurangabad	Bernier: Travels in the Mogul Empire

Index